MW01257176

Rousseau's Reader

Rousseau's Reader

Strategies of Persuasion and Education

John T. Scott

———

The University of Chicago Press

CHICAGO AND LONDON

The University of Chicago Press, Chicago 60637
The University of Chicago Press, Ltd., London
© 2020 by The University of Chicago
Published 2020
Printed in the United States of America

29 28 27 26 25 24 23 22 21 20   1 2 3 4 5

ISBN-13: 978-0-226-68914-2 (cloth)
ISBN-13: 978-0-226-68928-9 (e-book)
DOI: https://doi.org/10.7208/chicago/9780226689289.001.0001

Library of Congress Cataloging-in-Publication Data

Names: Scott, John T., 1963– author.
Title: Rousseau's reader : strategies of persuasion and education /
    John T. Scott.
Description: Chicago : University of Chicago Press, 2020. | Includes
    bibliographical references and index.
Identifiers: LCCN 2019037187 | ISBN 9780226689142 (cloth) |
    ISBN 9780226689289 (ebook)
Subjects: LCSH: Rousseau, Jean-Jacques, 1712–1778—Political and
    social views. | Philosophy, French—18th century.
Classification: LCC B2137 .B36 2020 | DDC 848/.509—dc23
LC record available at https://lccn.loc.gov/2019037187

♾ This paper meets the requirements of ANSI/NISO Z39.48-1992
(Permanence of Paper).

For my parents, Ann and Jarrett Scott,
who encouraged me to be a reader

Contents

Abbreviations

I refer to Rousseau's works by abbreviated titles. For the writings on which I focus, I use the abbreviated titles and do so parenthetically within the text. For other writings by Rousseau, I use an abbreviated title and identify the edition from which the work is drawn. All translations from primary and secondary sources are my own unless otherwise noted. I sometimes alter translations without so noting.

Emile *Emile, or On Education*. Translated by Allan Bloom. New York: Basic Books, 1979.

Inequality *Discourse on the Origin and Foundations of Inequality among Men*. In *The Major Political Writings of Jean-Jacques Rousseau*, ed. and trans. John T. Scott. Chicago: University of Chicago Press, 2012.

Sciences *Discourse on the Sciences and the Arts*. In *The Major Political Writings of Jean-Jacques Rousseau*, ed. and trans. John T. Scott. Chicago: University of Chicago Press, 2012.

Social Contract *On the Social Contract, or Principles of Political Right*. In *The Major Political Writings of Jean-Jacques Rousseau*, ed. and trans. John T. Scott. Chicago: University of Chicago Press, 2012.

CC *Correspondence complète*. Edited by Ralph A. Leigh. 50 vols. Oxford: Voltaire Foundation. 1965–91.

CW *The Collected Writings of Rousseau*. Edited by Roger D. Masters and Christopher Kelly. 13 vols. Hanover, NH: University Press of New England, 1990–2010.

OC *Oeuvres complètes*. 5 vols. Paris: Gallimard, Bibliothèque de la Pléiade, 1959–95.

Introduction

Writing some dozen years after the event that forever changed his life and would soon make him the most famous writer of his time, Rousseau described the effect on him of reading the prize essay question proposed by the Academy of Dijon: "Oh Sir, if I had ever been able to write a quarter of what I saw and felt under that tree, how clearly I would have made all the contradictions of the social system seen, with what strength I would have exposed all the abuses of our institutions, with what simplicity I would have demonstrated that man is naturally good and that it is from these institutions alone that he becomes wicked" (*Letters to Malesherbes*, *CW*, 5:575). Similarly, in a later account of the "illumination of Vincennes," Rousseau would appeal to the language of conversion in his own version of Saul on the road to Damascus: "At the moment of that reading I saw another universe and I became another man" (*Confessions*, *CW*, 5:294). A change in visual perspective is how Rousseau describes the discovery of the "system" of the natural goodness of man and his corruption in society that would animate and unify all of his works. He "saw" something he had hitherto not seen, and he makes it his mission as an author to make his readers see what he saw.

The paradox of Rousseau's thought and his writing is that he must persuade his readers that they are deceived by that which they see before their own eyes and they must learn to see anew. The process of changing the reader's perspective is exemplified by how he opens and closes the *Discourse on Inequality*. At the outset he writes of the difficulty of the precept inscribed on the Temple of Delphi: "And how will man ever manage to see himself as nature formed him, through all the changes that the sequence of time and things must have produced in his original constitution. . . . Like the statue of Glaucus, which time, sea, and storms has so disfigured that it resembled less a god than a ferocious beast, the human soul, altered in the bosom of society by a thousand continually renewed causes . . . has, so to speak, changed in appearance to the point of being almost unrecognizable" (*Inequality*, 51). In turn, by the end of the work, if he has been successful in persuading the reader of his account of human nature and development, "every attentive reader" will perceive the world differently: "Society no longer offers to the eyes of the wise man anything except an assemblage of artificial men and factitious passions which . . . have no true foundation in nature" (*Inequality*, 115–16). The attentive reader will learn to see with new eyes.

In this book I investigate how Rousseau persuades and educates the reader of his major philosophical works, the works that, he explained, together made up a complete system unified by the "system" of the natural goodness of man and his corruption in society (*Letters to Malesherbes*, *CW*, 5:575; *Letter to Beaumont*, *CW*, 9:28–29; *Dialogues*, *CW*, 1:22–23, 209–13): the *Discourse on the Sciences and the Arts*, the *Discourse on Inequality*, *Emile*, and the *Social Contract*.[1] I devote one chapter to each of these works, with the exception of *Emile*, to which I dedicate four chapters. I give more attention to *Emile* for several reasons. First, because Rousseau himself considered it to be his "greatest and best book" (*Dialogues*, *CW*, 1:23, 209–13). Second, because the work's textual complexity, not to mention its length, deserves extended treatment. Third, because, *Emile* has been strangely underappreciated by scholars despite Rousseau's claims about its importance.

Rousseau's philosophical project is essentially pedagogical in substance and form: to instruct his reader in the vision he saw with blinding force in the "illumination of Vincennes." Yet he cannot limit himself to reason alone because, as he himself emphasizes, what he has seen contradicts how we ordinarily view ourselves, our nature, and our social and political world. He therefore turns to a wide array of rhetorical and literary devices to persuade his reader: from choice of genre, complex textual structures, frontispieces and illustrations, shifting authorial and narrative voices, addresses to readers that alternately invite and challenge, apostrophes and metaphors as well as other literary devices, and, of course, paradox. My focus in this book is to analyze how the "form" of his writing relates to the "content" of his thought, and vice versa. It is through this interplay of form and content Rousseau that engages in a dialogue with his reader.

Rousseau's employment of rhetoric and persuasion is dictated not only by the central paradox of his thought, but also by his understanding of human nature. In the description of the "illumination of Vincennes" just quoted, Rousseau tells Malesherbes that he wishes he had "been able to write a quarter of what I saw and felt under that tree," suggesting that his *writing* is meant to convey what he *felt* as well as *saw*. Similarly, in the *Dialogues* he describes himself as "the author of the only writings in this era that bring into the soul of their readers the *persuasion* that dictated them, and about which one *feels* in reading them that love of virtue and zeal for truth are what cause their inimitable *eloquence*," and of his writings he says: "I found in them ways of *feeling* and *seeing* that distinguish him easily from all the writers of his time" (*Dialogues*, *CW*, 1:74, 212; emphasis added). In his discussions of rhetoric Rousseau consistently complains that the art of persuasion has been lost, in politics no less than in philosophy. "One of the errors of our age is to use reason in too unadorned a form, as if men were all mind," he explains: "In neglecting the language of signs that speak to the imagination, the most energetic of languages has been lost" (*Emile*, 321). Similarly, in the *Essay on the Origin of Languages*, he writes: "Open ancient history; you will find it full of those ways of presenting arguments to the eyes. . . . The object, presented before speaking, stirs the imagination, arouses curiosity, holds the mind in suspense and anticipation of what is going to be said." The speeches of the ancient lawgivers were filled with the "energetic language" of imagery. Unadorned discourse is woefully inadequate for "moving the heart and enflaming the passions" (*CW*, 7:290–91), and writing is an even less effective means of persuasion.

Since Rousseau is condemned to be a writer, he had to discover ways to communicate the feelings stirred by sight, and since he was trying to communicate a philosophical vision that contradicted the reader's ordinary ways of seeing, he had to find means for correcting that perspective. Let me sketch a few strategies he adopted to persuade and instruct his reader. First, although he begins the *Essay on the Origin of Languages* by lamenting the decline of persuasion, later in the work he waxes eloquent about the power of communicating the passions through music. Drawing on his profession as a musician and a musical theorist, then, Rousseau self-consciously fashioned his prose to elicit an emotional response. Indeed, he complained to his publisher for having corrected his prose, explaining, "Harmony appears to me of such great importance in matters of style that I put it immediately after clarity, even before correct grammar."[2] I wish I were qualified to analyze or assess his prose in this respect, but I am not. So let me turn from sound to sight.

Second, in his writing Rousseau employs rhetorical and literary devices that are often visual in nature. He asks his reader to "see" something: whether a picture of natural man sitting beneath a tree, his imaginary pupil, or simply "Behold!" He brings forward witnesses to testify to what they see, as in the famous prosopopoeia of Fabricius in the *Discourse on the Sciences and the Arts*, which he later claimed was all he was able to scribble down in his delirium on the road to Vincennes (*Letters to Malesherbes, CW*, 5:575). Through this visual imagery, he teaches his reader to distinguish appearance and reality, to see the truth of the natural goodness of man along with him despite appearances to the contrary. Relating his discovery of the natural goodness of man, he writes: "As soon as I was capable of observing men, I watched them act and listened to them speak. Then, seeing that their actions bore little resemblance to their speeches, I sought the reason for this dissimilarity, and found that since being and appearing were two things as different for them as acting and speaking, this second difference was the cause of the first, and itself had a cause that remained for me to seek" (*Letter to Beaumont, CW*, 9:52). He leads the reader through the same course of education.

Third, and with the same pedagogical aim, he frequently asks his reader to compare the images he evokes—for example, "natural man" versus "civil man," "my pupil" versus "your pupil"—in order to correct the reader's perspective. What he writes in *Emile* concerning how to train sight and the other senses is applicable to how he corrects the reader's vision. There he notes how the sense of sight can lead one to mistaken judgments because of the limitations and illusions caused by perspective. In addition to recommending that we verify by other senses what sight tells us, he suggests looking at the same object from different vantage points: "What is more, the very illusions of perspective are necessary for us to come to a knowledge of extension and to compare its parts. Without false appearances we would see nothing in perspective" (*Emile*, 140). While it is tempting to evoke Nietzsche and describe Rousseau as a perspectival philosopher, though of a very different sort, the more appropriate comparison is, I think, the Platonic Socrates. Socrates explains to his interlocutors that the world they see is actually a realm of images and shadows that they take to be real or true, and only the philosopher whose soul is "turned" will be able to see the light of the truth and to see the shadows for what they are. So too with Rousseau's mission as a philosophic writer of persuading and educating his reader. As Richard Velkley states, "Rousseau is one of the most dialectical of writers. To uncover the dialectic of his thought we must acquire the skill to follow Rousseau's complex rhetoric."[3]

Finally, all of the strategies for persuading and educating the reader I have just sketched suggest the importance of rhetoric for Rousseau. In the next section, I will discuss the relationship between philosophy and rhetoric in Rousseau's works, and in the protreptic tradition in philosophy more generally, in order to outline and defend the methodological approach I employ. For now I limit myself to a few remarks about the pervasive visual images Rousseau uses to persuade and educate his reader.

In encouraging his reader to adopt a new perspective Rousseau follows a distinguished tradition in classical rhetoric. One exemplar of this tradition is Thucydides, about whom Plutarch explained that the power of his work lie in his ability "to make the reader a spectator, as it were, and to produce vividly in the minds of those who peruse his narrative the emotions of amazement and consternation which were experienced by those who beheld them."[4] Rousseau himself alludes to Plutarch's characterization of the historian when he writes in *Emile*: "Thucydides is to my taste the true model of historians. . . . He puts all he recounts before the reader's eyes. Far from putting himself between the events and his readers, he hides himself. The reader no longer believes he reads; he believes he sees" (*Emile*, 239). The visual strategy in rhetoric was later codified in Quintilian's classic treatment: "There are certain experiences which the Greeks call *fantasia*, and the Romans *visions*, whereby things absent are presented to our imagination with such extreme vividness that they seem actually to be before our very eyes. . . . From such impressions arises that *energeia* which Cicero calls *illumination* and *actuality*, which makes us seem not so much to narrate as to exhibit the actual scene, while our emotions will be no less actively stirred than if we were present at the actual occurrence."[5] In drawing on this rhetorical tradition, Rousseau faces the extra hurdle of conjuring visions that lie beyond and even belie the reader's experience.

A Methodological Manifesto

That Rousseau would employ rhetorical or literary techniques in his novel, *Julie*, and other literary works or in his autobiographical writings is unsurprising and uncontroversial, and scholars of these works quite naturally have analyzed these rhetorical strategies and literary devices.[6] More surprising and controversial, perhaps, is the fact that Rousseau uses similar rhetorical and literary strategies in his more strictly philosophical works. After all, one might object, the purpose of philosophy is to convey the unadorned truth. The task of philosophy on this view is to employ reason, proceeding logically from premises to conclusions and adding soundness to validity through adducing evidence. Style might adorn the substance, but style is not the essence of the matter. Indeed, perhaps philosophy, like revenge, is a dish best served cold.

Rousseau's status as a philosopher has in fact been questioned owing precisely to the warmth of his rhetoric and his seductive style. His use of emotionally charged prose and evocative imagery, his appeals to the heart against the head, have even brought against him the charge of sophistry. Among his contemporaries, for example, his former friend turned implacable enemy, Friedrich Melchior Grimm, attempted to turn the nearly universal admiration for Rousseau's eloquence against him: "M. Rousseau was born with all the talents of a sophist. Specious arguments, a crowd of captious reasoning, of art and artifice, joined to a masculine, simple, and touching eloquence make him into a very formidable adversary for everything he might attack; but in the midst of the enchantment and magic of his richly colored prose, he will never persuade you, for only it is only the truth that persuades. One is always tempted to say: that is very beautiful and very false."[7] More recently, Bertrand Russell wrote: "Jean-Jacques Rousseau, though a *philosophe* in the eighteenth-century French sense, was not what we would call a 'philosopher.' Nevertheless he had a powerful influence on philosophy, as on literature and taste and manners and politics. Whatever may be our opinion of his merits as a thinker, we must recognize his importance as a social force."[8] And quite a force he exerted, for if Russell does not level the charge of sophistry, at least yet, he makes Rousseau responsible for Hitler. However that may be, within academic philosophy Rousseau has not garnered much attention, at least until a recent upsurge of interest.[9]

Even those more open to Rousseau as a philosopher often feel they owe something of an apology. For example, Judith Shklar begins her book: "Jean-Jacques Rousseau was not a professional philosopher. He never pretended that he was. His claim was that he alone had been 'the painter of nature and the historian of the human heart.' It was an art that did not demand great logical rigor or systematic exposition of abstract ideas. Rousseau did not even aspire to these accomplishments. He did not think that perfect consistency was really very important. What did matter was always to be truthful. By truthfulness he meant what we generally tend to call sincerity, and in his case it involved an overriding will to denounce the social world around him." Shklar seems to hesitate to accord Rousseau the title of philosopher and characterizes him as offering a "social theory," as the subtitle of her book suggests.[10] Even Arthur Melzer, whose book is dedicated to showing that Rousseau is a consistent and systematic thinker, nonetheless writes: "It is difficult to deny that Rousseau's style of writing is unsystematic. Believing that if one speaks to men's hearts, their minds will follow, he tends to paint rather than to argue. His works are as much novels as treatises."[11] Finally, John Rawls felt compelled to warn his students: "Style can be a danger, attracting attention to itself, as it does in Rousseau. We may be dazzled and distracted and so fail to note the intricacies of reasoning that call for our full concentration."[12]

The indictment of sophistry in the court of philosophy is at least as old as Plato's *Gorgias*, a work that also has the aim of exculpating philosophy from the charge of sophistry. There Socrates describes the rhetorician as akin to a cook pandering to the sweet tooth of a diner without knowledge of or concern for his health.[13] Of course, this characterization comes within a philosophic dialogue, a dialogue that by its very form, not to mention its content, is rhetorical. Could Plato have united the philosophy and rhetoric that Socrates draws asunder, rendering philosophy persuasive in part through adopting the dialogue form? Such a possibility is suggested in another Platonic dialogue concerned with rhetoric: the *Phaedrus*. Within a discussion of the utility of writing, Socrates objects that whereas speech or rhetoric can be adapted to the character and capacity of its audience, the written word is indiscriminately available both to appropriate and inappropriate audiences, and it can neither answer the reader nor defend itself.[14] Since the speech is found in a written work, we must assume that Plato thought he had answered Socrates' objection by writing dialogues. As we shall see, one of the main themes of my analysis of Rousseau's works is how he too responds to Socrates' concerns with writing. While once controversial in some quarters, scholars of Plato now widely accept that the dialogic form of his works is central to his conception of philosophy and philosophical writing. They therefore attend to the narrative structure of the dialogues (e.g., narrated versus performed), the dramatic setting, the characters of the interlocutors, and other features in analyzing Plato's works.[15] Attention to the rhetorical and literary features can be profitably extended to many writings in the history of philosophy.

Perhaps to the dismay of the coauthor of the *Principia Mathematica*, the history of philosophy is replete with works that are protreptic in nature, in other words designed to persuade and instruct, and that therefore employ rhetorical and literary strategies to that end.[16] Of course, by the very fact that all philosophical writings are just that, writings, their authors are engaged in rhetoric, whether trivially or interestingly so. As for the more interesting cases, restricting myself to more obviously "philosophical" works, in addition to Plato's dialogues, I might cite Cicero's dialogic writings, Seneca's *Moral Letters* and essays (or *dialogi*), Bacon's *New Atlantis* and *Essays*, Descartes's *Discourse on the Method*, Hume's *Dialogues concerning Natural Religion*, and perhaps the entirety of both Kierkegaard's and Nietzsche's output. Many of these writings can be characterized as essentially protreptic in intention and form, and to this list less manifestly "literary" works might be added: Aristotle's *Nicomachean Ethics*, Hobbes's *Leviathan*, Smith's *Theory of Moral Sentiments*, Kant's *Religion within the Boundaries of Mere Reason* and even the *Groundwork for the Metaphysics of Morals*, among others.[17] Indeed, in a recent exploration of the differing "densities" of texts of how authors engage their readers, Judith Schlanger rejects the characterization, and usually contemporary self-characterization, of philosophy as requiring a "plain, logical, explicit, developed exposition of the order of reasoning" with the goal of being informative and didactic. To prove the contrary, she lists many classic works of philosophy, most notably discussing a work where one might least expect to find an abundant deployment of rhetorical and literary devices: Kant's *Critique of Pure Reason*.[18] In short, Rousseau is in good company.

That said, most of Rousseau's writings are nonetheless unusually rhetorical and literary in form in comparison to those of most philosophers, even the majority of those to whom I just appealed. Assuming we accept that Rousseau is a philosopher—that is, that his works are intended to seek and elaborate the truth—the way in which he presents himself and his writings not only invites us to analyze their rhetorical and literary elements, but even demands that we do so. As for his self-presentation, Rousseau characterizes himself as engaging in philosophical questions, for example stating at the outset of the *Discourse on Inequality* that the subject of his work is "one of the most interesting questions philosophy might propose" (*Inequality*, 51). Yet his works are also filled with denunciations of philosophy. The philosophers, he says, "go everywhere, armed with their deadly paradoxes, undermining the foundations of faith and annihilating virtue" (*Sciences*, 25). Or: "A philosopher loves the Tartars so as to be spared having to love his neighbor" (*Emile*, 39). However, these denunciations are not indictments of philosophy per se, as Rousseau understands it, but criticisms of what he sees as the prideful, dogmatic, and irresponsible manner in which philosophy has been practiced, especially in his own time.[19] As for how he presents his writings, therefore, Rousseau's philosophy is fundamentally educational in intention, as already noted, and he therefore employs rhetoric and other devices to persuade and instruct the reader. These protreptic strategies are the primary vehicles, along with plain old-fashioned reasoning of course, by which this educational project is conducted.

Let me now speak to my interpretive approach to the interplay between the form and content of Rousseau's philosophical works. First, as to the content, my approach is a close textual analysis of Rousseau's works that presumes him to be a careful writer and assumes that he has a consistent philosophical "system" across these works, based in part on his own testimony to that effect. Of course, as my choice of language indicates, these interpretive assumptions are starting points subject to disconfirmation if we encounter careless writing and inconsistent ideas on Rousseau's part. With this caveat in mind, I will nonetheless confess that my analysis of the rhetorical and literary devices he employs to persuade and educate the reader puts unusual stress on the presumption of his being a careful writer, even a remarkably careful writer. For example, where other readers have seen unintentional slips on Rousseau's part, for instance in *Emile* when he seems to remind his imaginary pupil about running races that in fact involved a different child, I will argue that they are intentional, in this case included as a test of the reader's attentiveness and educational progress. Since I will have repeated occasion to discuss how Rousseau responds to the critique of writing advanced by Socrates in Plato's *Phaedrus*, I will say here that I subscribe to a rather strong version of the standard of "logographic necessity" Socrates puts forward for proper writing, that is, that every word is necessarily where it must be in the text with respect to the design of the work as a whole.[20] I prefer to run the risk of overinterpretation while keeping in mind Jonathan Swift's warning:

> As learned Commentators view
> In Homer more than Homer knew.[21]

Not expecting from my own readers the generosity I am granting Rousseau, I leave it to them to assess whether my analyses are persuasive.

The interpretive strategy of close textual analysis will be familiar to many scholars of political thought and philosophy, but in order to attend to the more rhetorical and literary elements of Rousseau's texts I also draw on literary criticism. As Paul de Man writes when beginning his interpretation of Rousseau, academic specialization "has often prevented the correct understanding of the relations between the literary and the political aspects of Rousseau's thought."[22] I hope my application of literary criticism will offer a corrective in analyzing the undeniably literary features of Rousseau's philosophic writings. Since I am particularly interested in the author-reader dialogue Rousseau creates through his texts, I have found literary theorists who focus on the author-reader relationship especially useful.

As for the author, I have found helpful Wayne C. Booth's *The Rhetoric of Fiction* (1961; 1983) and *The Rhetoric of Irony* (1974) for his concept of the "implied author," and also E. D. Hirsch's *Validity in Interpretation* (1967) for his defense of authorial intent and interpretive validity. The "implied author," a term coined by Booth, is not identical to the biographical author of a work, which is more how authorial intent is typically understood in political thought and philosophy, but instead the author as constructed in the text, for example through authorial and narrative voice, an author whom the reader infers from the text. Hirsch even more strenuously seeks to save the author and intentionality. While acknowledging that a reader can never know the author's intention with certainty, he nonetheless argues that we can validate a highly probable interpretation of a text through a process that takes place within the "hermeneutic circle," that is, where the parts necessarily being understood in terms of the whole and vice versa, through updating our interpretation as we read.[23] Booth similarly acknowledges the necessarily "closed" nature of interpretation.[24]

As for the reader, I draw on the school of literary criticism known as "reader-response theory," especially as found in Wolfgang Iser's *The Implied Reader* (1974) and *The Act of Reading* (1978) and as represented perhaps best by Stanley Fish's landmark study *Surprised by Sin: The Reader in "Paradise Lost"* (1967). As the term suggests, reader-response criticism focuses on the experience of the reader and how the "meaning" of the text is created through the activity of reading. In the versions of the approach I find most useful, the emphasis is less on the subjective or individual response of reader than on the intentional creation of an interpretive community by an author with the reader, or on the relationship between the "implied author" and the "implied reader." There are tensions between the approaches on which I draw, but my aim is not to reconcile them by engaging in literary theory myself and is instead avowedly piratical.

Contemporary students of literary criticism may blush at my arguably old-fashioned choices, but I would respond that the approaches on which I am drawing are a good match for the strategy I employ of close textual analysis based on strong assumptions about authorial intention. Both Booth and the theorists in the reader-response school wrote in reaction to the literary-theory movement known as the New Criticism and popular in the middle decades of the twentieth century. The New Critics adopted a formalist approach that focused on the literary text itself as a self-contained and self-referential aesthetic object, and they explicitly rejected questions of authorial intention (the "intentional fallacy"), on the one hand, and the reader's response (the "affective fallacy"), on the other. Different threats to the author and the reader arose later from the pronouncements of "The Death of the Author" by Roland Barthes (1967), the question posed by Michel Foucault in "What Is an Author?" (1969), and the deconstructionism of Jacques Derrida in *Of Grammatology* (1967), which of course focused on Rousseau, and from other scholars who have argued for the self-deconstructing nature of language and therefore of texts. For interpreters of Rousseau and other philosophers invested in authorial intention and interested in how authors interact with readers, then, the literary theorists I have looked to make for good allies.

Let me briefly expand on how these literary theorists approach texts, both in order to illustrate how they are useful for interpreting Rousseau and also in order to indicate their limitations for doing so. Booth's focus on the implied author is useful for my purposes in large part because of what he says about how authors relate to readers: "The author creates, in short, an image of himself and another image of his reader; he makes his reader, as he makes his second self, and the most successful reading is one in which the created selves, author and reader, can find complete agreement."[25] This dialogue requires "active collaboration" on the part of the reader. Rousseau provides a version of just this relationship between author and reader in the *Confessions* when, after stating that he has provided all the details about his actions, thoughts, and feelings, he writes: "It is up to [the reader] to assemble these elements and to define the being made up of them; the result ought to be his work" (*Confessions*, *CW*, 5:146–47).[26] A particularly interesting case of the necessary participation of the reader for my purposes is his discussion of authorial silence and other forms of challenges to the reader, which requires the reader to engage in the risky process of discriminating intentional tactics from simple carelessness on the author's part. As I noted above, a potential example of such a challenge to the reader on Rousseau's part is when he reminds Emile of running races with cakes for a prize when the earlier example of doing so involves not Emile but another child. Among other familiar narrative techniques that pose such a challenge, Booth discusses unreliable narrators and irony,[27] both of which are found throughout Rousseau. Finally, given my focus on how Rousseau educates his reader, Booth's closing remarks in *The Rhetoric of Fiction* are interesting: "The author makes his readers. If he makes them badly—that is, if he simply waits, in all purity, for the occasional reader whose perceptions and norms happen to match his own, then his conception must be lofty indeed if we are to forgive him for his bad craftsmanship. But if he makes them well—that is, makes them to see what they have never seen before, moves them into a new order of perception and experience altogether—he finds his reward in the peers he has created."[28]

A particular case of author-reader relations, and a particularly revealing case for the question of determining authorial intention, is the question of irony, which Booth takes up in *The Rhetoric of Irony*. Recognizing intentional or "stable" irony on an author's part is one of the challenges—and delights—of reading. Booth frankly acknowledges the hierarchical process of irony, for the author makes one statement only to subvert it by giving it another, higher meaning. The challenge to the reader is to recognize the irony and thereby join the author at the higher level. For the author, Booth remarks, the test can be "aggressive" or "competitive"; as for the reader, in addition to the possibility of humiliation for not recognizing the irony, the process can inspire feelings of cleverness and pride as well as the pleasures of a meeting of minds with the author.[29] All these motives are at play in reading Rousseau, at least as my own experience attests. As we shall see, Rousseau continually challenges his reader, often directly and aggressively, and just as often indirectly through irony and paradox. "Shall I speak now of writing?" he writes in *Emile*: "No. I am ashamed of playing with this kind of foolishness in an educational treatise" (*Emile*, 117). In any case, for Booth, irony is a revealing example of the self-enclosed process within a textual reading of how the reader must, so to speak, "make himself into that implied reader, and in some sense find the implied author."[30]

The reader-response approach offers similar benefits for examining the author-reader relationship in Rousseau. Iser develops his own conception of the implied reader through analyzing the novel form, and especially the eighteenth-century English novel, a genre that directly influenced Rousseau's own novel, *Julie*, and, I would suggest, *Emile*. Iser argues that a central purpose of the novel is to challenge the reader to examine his or her own world in light of alternative world presented in the novel, which is at once similar to the reader's world—and hence "realistic"—and yet different. "What was presented in the novel," he explains, "led to a specific effect: namely, to involve the reader in the world of the novel and so help him to understand it—and ultimately his own world—more clearly." Readers are therefore "forced to take an active part in the composition of the novel's meaning, which revolves around a basic divergence from the familiar."[31] Rousseau repeatedly uses such devices in his works, including in *Julie* and, more to my purposes, in *Emile*, where persuading the reader of the "reality" of his imaginary pupil is his primary pedagogical strategy in the work. But an explicit example can be found in the very beginning of his *Dialogues*: "Picture an ideal world similar to ours, yet altogether different. Nature is the same there as on our earth, but its economy is more easily felt, its order more marked, its aspect more admirable," and so on (*Dialogues*, *CW*, 1:9). Rousseau's aim in his philosophical works might be said to be precisely to get his reader to picture a different world that is somehow truer.

Fish's seminal study of Milton's *Paradise Lost* is likewise useful for reading Rousseau's works, including with regard to his central philosophical tenet of the natural goodness of man: "Milton's purpose is to educate the reader to an awareness of his position and responsibilities as a fallen man, and to a sense of the distance which separates him from the innocence once his."[32] Fish's examination of how Milton achieves this effect through poetic techniques on what he terms the "fit reader" (his version of the "implied reader") is analogous to how Rousseau educates what he terms the "attentive reader" through visual images and other techniques. Whereas Milton, in Fish's hands, teaches his reader to recognize his own participation in the story of the Fall both as a reader and as a human being, Rousseau intends precisely the opposite lesson. Although he agrees with Milton's, or Scripture's, sense of the distance that separates us from our erstwhile innocence, his aim is persuade his reader of the fundamental principle of his system of thought: that despite the evil the reader sees around him and feels within himself, man is "naturally good." In both Milton as Fish interprets him and Rousseau as I read him, then, the substance of the work is conveyed in part through its form.

So far I have stressed how these literary critical approaches can enrich a reading of Rousseau's philosophical works with regard to the author-reader dialogue and to how the form and content of these works are related. There is nonetheless at least one important limitation to applying these approaches wholesale to Rousseau: they are almost entirely meant to be applied to literary or fictional works and not to philosophical writings. (I use the terms "literary" and "fictional" loosely here.) The reader-response theorists in particular are primarily interested in the *aesthetic* response to a literary work and to these works as expressly literary or artistic. In the case of a novel as discussed by Iser, for example, the test of a successful meeting of the minds between author and reader would be something like verisimilitude: is the world depicting in the text recognizable as potentially real? This standard may have to be adapted somewhat when applied beyond the "realist" novel and its kin, for instance to fantasy or science fiction, but the fact that aliens tend to have heads, hands, and feet suggests that the test of verisimilitude still largely holds. In his discussion of the implied reader Iser reveals the assumption underlying his approach that it is appropriate for specifically literary or artistic works. He distinguishes between the ideal reader, who "would have to have an identical code to that of the author," and the implied reader, who is always at something of a distance to the text and its code as an aesthetic object, and who is Iser's focus. An ideal reader might be appropriate in reading certain kinds of genres, and we might conjecture it would be so for philosophic works *qua* philosophic works, but Iser argues such a reader response would be "ruinous for literature" because it would result in the "total consumption of the text."[33] Booth takes up the question of the appropriateness of his critical approach to different genres in a particularly helpful manner for my purposes. Booth discusses the "psychic" or "aesthetic distance" between the reader and the text, and therewith the author. A successful literary text is neither overdistanced, in which case it seems improbable, artificial, or absurd, nor underdistanced, in which case the literary object would be perceived as too personal and not enjoyable as art. In this context, then, Booth remarks about the limitations of applying the standard of aesthetic response to nonartistic works: "Different general values would be dictated if I were trying to deal with works as reflections of reality, in which case truth would probably be my over-all term; or as expressions of the author's mind or soul, in which case some general term like sincerity or expressiveness might be central."[34]

Of course, Rousseau's philosophical and other writings have been seen as both overdistanced and underdistanced, and as asking to be judged in terms of sincerity. Nonetheless, if we are going to read his philosophical works as philosophy, then *truth* would be the appropriate standard. Whatever the rhetorical and literary strategies Rousseau employs in his philosophical works, in the end they are intended to persuade the reader of the truth. Perhaps the best way to understand the admixture in Rousseau's works of philosophic intent and content, on the one hand, and rhetoric or literary form or elements, on the other, is to see him as manipulating the distance between the reader and the text, and therewith with him as author. For example, Rousseau often begins with what Booth terms *overdistanced* concepts and images that initially appear improbable or even false—for example, his portrait of natural man in the pure state of nature, or his imaginary pupil, Emile. But he then closes the distance, so to speak, moving beyond what would be a "proper" distance for a literary or artistic text that preserves its status as an aesthetic object toward what would be underdistanced for a literary text but appropriate for a philosophic work. In this light, to borrow Iser's terminology, Rousseau's reader would be transformed through the course of reading from an implied reader to something more like an ideal reader who is able to join Rousseau in seeing what he saw on the road to Vincennes.[35]

Reading Rousseau

Let me turn now to how previous interpreters have read Rousseau's writings in terms of the author-reader relationship and the interplay between content and form in his works. I do so in order to suggest both how my interpretive strategy is related to those of other scholars and especially how what I am offering that is novel and fruitful.

Interestingly, many interpreters who tend to disregard or downplay the author-reader relationship and other literary features of Rousseau's works occupy the opposite extremes of an interpretive spectrum with those scholars who, so to speak, privilege the head over the heart on the one end, and interpreters who privilege the heart over the head on the other. On the one end are scholars who employ textual analysis of his works in order to understand his philosophical system and to assess its truth. Such an interpretive strategy includes a number of methodological approaches, among others, traditional textual exegesis and analytic philosophy.[36] On the other end are what might be termed autobiographical interpretations, whether through a psychoanalytic lens or otherwise, that interpret Rousseau as principally attempting to convey his sentiments or psychic state. The most influential interpretation in this regard is Jean Starobinski, who famously argues that Rousseau seeks a "transparent" relationship both with himself and with his readers, a transparency that has been disrupted by various "obstructions" or "obstacles" arising from self-consciousness for oneself and social relations in relation to others. Starobinski gives pride of place in his analysis to Rousseau's autobiographical writings, where Rousseau presents himself in a self-revelatory stance: "I wish to show my fellows a man in all the truth of nature; and this man will be myself" (*Confessions*, *CW*, 5:5). Starobinski then reads Rousseau's other works, especially his literary writings and to a lesser degree his philosophical works, as expressions of his autobiographical impulses.[37] In this light, then, Rousseau's intention is to reveal his inner psychic state or the "truth of the heart," and his aim is therefore not truth in the sense of correspondence to external reality, but something like sincerity or authenticity. Above I quoted Shklar, who avows her debt to Starobinski: "What did matter [for Rousseau] was always to be truthful. By truthfulness he meant what we generally tend to call sincerity."[38] It is not my purpose here to examine, much less resolve, the relationship in Rousseau's thought between sincerity and truth;[39] perhaps it is best to agree with Starobinski, who (later) argued that Rousseau attempted to use a language that recaptures a union between truth and persuasion.[40] Instead, what I want to draw attention to is the feature fairly common to both of these opposite approaches: that of assuming that the authorial "I" in Rousseau's writings is the same as Rousseau himself. More generally, both approaches tend to neglect the rhetorical and literary features of his philosophical works such as authorial personae and narrative voices.[41]

The most extended study of Rousseau that focuses on the author-reader relationship across his works is Richard Ellrich's *Rousseau and His Reader* (1969). The decisive influence of Starobinski on Ellrich's interpretation is evident in his summary of his argument: "Rousseau's hyperawareness of the relationship with his reader is a literary manifestation of his obsession with the distinction between Self and Other, and with the concomitant problems of identity, self-definition, and conflict of minds and wills. His essential problem in conceiving of and dealing with his reader may be stated quite simply: a deep longing for perfect union between himself and his reader finds itself countered by the painful recognition, and eventual adaptation, of the reader's failure to enter into this perfect union." According to Ellrich, Rousseau turned to writing because of his frustration with and failure in actual conversation and communion with others. In addition, he argues that Rousseau's failure in his early works to establish perfect union with "real readers" led him in his later writings to construct an "ideal reader."[42] Ellrich takes up Rousseau's writings from the *Discourse on the Sciences and the Arts* to the *Reveries* to sketch a growing disillusionment on his part with his project of establishing this union with the reader. A pivotal work for his interpretation is *Emile*, which he argues exhibits the culmination of Rousseau's turn away from the real reader of his books to the ideal reader of his imagination. Indeed, according to Ellrich this turn occurs within *Emile* itself, with the early part addressing the real reader with growing frustration and then later parts speaking to the ideal reader: "The *Emile* shows Rousseau awakening from his dream of the perfect relationship with the ideal reader, or at least returning from the illusion of an exact correspondence between ideal and real reader."[43]

Ellrich's attention to the author-reader relationship in Rousseau's works is welcome, but his claims that Rousseau's aim was to establish perfect union with his reader and that he became increasingly pessimistic about doing so face substantial obstacles posed by the very texts he analyzes, as well as those he does not. For example, Rousseau begins the very first text under analysis, the *Discourse on the Sciences and the Arts*, by announcing that he knows he will not be understood by his readers: "I foresee that I will not easily be forgiven for the side I have dared to take. Clashing head on with everything that nowadays attracts men's admiration, I can expect only universal blame. . . . One must not write for such readers when one wants to live beyond one's age" (*Sciences*, 7). The polemical exchanges over the prize *Discourse* in which Rousseau engaged, which Ellrich does not analyze, reveal an author bent less on establishing perfect union with his readers than on challenging them. As for *Emile*, Ellrich's argument that the tone of Rousseau's interactions with the reader changes across the work is plausible, but if so it is explicable by other means. When he introduces his imaginary pupil, Rousseau explains: "In proportion as I advance, my pupil, differently conducted than yours, is no longer an ordinary child" (*Emile*, 51). As "my pupil" increasingly diverges from "your pupil," then, Rousseau will more frequently and more aggressively accuse his implied reader of not seeing properly, and so we should expect a change in his tone. Ellrich's interpretation is perhaps most convincing with respect to Rousseau's autobiographical writings, especially the *Dialogues* and *Reveries*. At any rate, like other autobiographical readings, as I have termed them, Ellrich assumes the authorial (or narrative) "I" in Rousseau writings is identical to Rousseau himself and does not consider the possibility that shifts in his authorial voice or author-reader relationships within and across his works are intentional rhetorical strategies.

Other scholars who have attended to the author-reader relationship in Rousseau range from those who share Ellrich's view that Rousseau seeks an unmediated relationship with the reader to those who claim that he is keen on exerting authority over the reader. Tracy B. Strong offers a highly egalitarian reading of Rousseau that shares some traits with the autobiographical approach, especially Starobinski's, but with more appreciation for the reader side of the author-reader relationship. Strong argues that Rousseau "wrote so as to require response of his readers," but he aims ultimately to elicit "a direct and unmediated response" through what Strong terms "self-deauthorization": "The authority of the book comes from the fact that it makes its own author unnecessary, indeed that it succeeds in deauthorizing Rousseau and replacing him with a human like any other human." For Strong, then, Rousseau as author disappears and cedes interpretive authority to the reader, and when he does speak with an authorial voice, rather than "a human one," he has succumbed to temptation and betrayed his intentions.[44] A less extreme egalitarian view is taken by Michel Launay, who sees in Rousseau a "contractual" relationship between author and reader on the model of the *Social Contract*. What distinguishes Rousseau's writing from literature or rhetoric, which retains an inegalitarian relationship between the writer or speaker and the audience, is "its contractual structure, implicating the reader in a relationship of one equal to another, which supposes a certain type of reciprocity, of mutual respect." After exploring the dialogic and dialectical features of Rousseau's texts, Launay relaxes his egalitarianism somewhat in a later formulation when he states that Rousseau's texts are structured in a way that the reader can "become" an equal, suggesting something more like the educational purpose of the texts of his that I have emphasized.[45] Ronald Grimsley presents Rousseau as attempting to involve his reader in his own vision of the truth of things, an approach more similar to my own here: "Rousseau's problem . . . is to make his reader aware of the immediate situation [of the world] and yet persuade him to go beyond it to a new possibility of existence." Grimsley focuses on *Emile* and, contrary to Ellrich's argument, suggests that Rousseau in fact makes less frequent use of direct addresses to the reader as the work advances "because he may reasonably assume to have secured (or lost!) effective contact with the reader by overcoming his prejudices and by awakening him to the possibility of a new experience."[46] Although Grimsley does not put it this way, he seems to assume that Rousseau retains his authority as an author with regard to the reader, with the question being whether the reader accepts the truth of his teaching. Finally, at the other end of the spectrum is Dena Goodman, who argues that Rousseau as an author is concerned with exercising strong authority, to the point of incapacitating the reader. With respect to the *Discourse on Inequality*, she argues that by using a narrative form and method he renders the reader a passive observer, and in doing so he "immobilize[s] the reader still further, to make of the actively critical reader a passive spectator of the narrative of human history set before him."[47] A similar stance is taken by Joan DeJean, who sees Rousseau as exerting the same obsessive authority over the reader as he does over his characters in *Julie* and *Emile*.[48]

There is something to perhaps each of these characterizations of the author-reader relationship in Rousseau's works. This should not be surprising for an author who worked in such varied genres and with different aims across various works. Melzer captures something of Rousseau's career as a writer when, seeking to explain the apparently unsystematic nature of his writings (but not his thought), he observes: "No other philosopher ever wrote so many of his major works, on questions or topics that arose, accidentally or that were not of his own devise," and that required such literary forms as academic discourses, encyclopedia articles, letters, treatises, and so on.[49] I suggest that this is precisely the place to start. We can understand the various author-reader relationships we see within and across Rousseau's works if we view them as being among the rhetorical strategies he employs to persuade and educate the reader. In this light, then, my approach is somewhere the middle of the range of interpretations of the author-reader relationship I have sketched, inviting the reader as pupil to share his vision while at the same time maintaining his authority as an educator.

I stated at the outset that Rousseau's philosophical project is essentially pedagogical in substance and form, and so if we see him as belonging to the protreptic tradition of philosophy with Plato and the Platonic Socrates at its head, then many of his rhetorical and literary strategies as an author are comprehensible. As Irene Harvey writes: "He insists the philosophical enterprise itself is essentially pedagogical. Insofar as it is a written challenge, philosophy produces itself necessarily in the form of a pedagogy, thereby entailing an essentially rhetorical dimension."[50] In his study of the protreptic tradition in ancient philosophy, James Collins identifies a number of typical features of protreptic discourse: (1) it is *dialogic*, even if it does not necessarily adopt the dialogue form; (2) it is *agonistic*, putting different views into competition; (3) it is *situational*, molded to the character of the participants, rhetorical situation, and audience; and (4) it is *rhetorical*, intended to persuade using appropriate means given the subject and particular intended audience.[51] Each of these elements can be found throughout Rousseau's writings. Restricting myself to the author-reader relationship by way of illustration, I suggest Rousseau's writings are (1) *dialogic*, especially insofar as he enters into a dialogue with his reader; (2) *agonistic*, for example when he challenges the reader, often expressly and even aggressively so; (3) *situational*, as suggested above with regard to the different genres he adopted for his writings and their intended audiences; and (4) *rhetorical*, as I hope I have already persuaded my reader.

Other scholars have noted these elements of protreptic philosophy in Rousseau's writings, though not generally in those terms or in a systematic manner. As for Rousseau as a situational and rhetorical writer, to use the terms above, a number of scholars have commented on the fact that Rousseau addresses multiple audiences, often simultaneously, in his works. For example, Matthew Maguire observes that there are "sometimes harsh distinctions between different kinds of readers in different texts," especially "the wise" and "others" among his readers. "Rousseau's readers receive drastically different but nonetheless 'authorized' impressions and lessons from his texts, from the so-called 'ordinary readers' to his so-called philosophical 'judges,'" Maguire explains, adding that "Rousseau believes himself to have considerable control over these lessons."[52] Other scholars have also noted Rousseau's multiple audiences and argued that he writes esoterically. For example, both Leo Strauss and Roger Masters have argued that Rousseau writes esoterically—for instance, speaking in the *Discourse on the Sciences and the Arts* to his true philosophers or "the wise" as a fellow philosopher and to "commen men" as a compatriot (see *Sciences*, 35) and drawing different lessons for each audience.[53] To this extent, then, these scholars have attended to the author-reader relationship in Rousseau's texts and his pedagogical purpose.

Especially attentive to the author-reader relationship and its dialogic character is Launay. Chronicling Rousseau's authorial stance in his texts, Launay comments on the "critical" or "polemical" mode he inscribes within his texts, their "dialogic" and "dialectical" nature of his writing, and the way in which he communicates with his reader with what I would term "pedagogical" intent.[54] Similarly, taking on the task of explaining Starobinski's continued fascination with Rousseau, Wilda Anderson argues that what he "saw or responded to was the very particular *reader* called for—or, better—produced by this conceptual dynamic" at play in Rousseau's works. In this light, then, she comments on Rousseau's inventiveness "to surprise his reader into a new perception of the world." Finally, she suggests that the supposedly transparent relationship Rousseau seeks to establish with the reader is a purposeful strategy on his part: "The opacity which the text is to dissolve is not really a state or state of mind from which to be released, but an illusion produced by the text in the mind of the readers to lure them into an attitude toward the authorial figure, toward in this case Rousseau."[55] In other words, and in terms stronger than those used by Anderson, Starobinski has become the reader Rousseau intended to create through his text.

A number of interpreters have focused on the agonistic character of the dialogue Rousseau conducts with his reader. For example, Starobinski argues that Rousseau's rhetorical effect on the reader is due in part to the way in which he alternates between "a movement of accusation" and "seduction." In reading *Emile* in particular, Starobinski shows how Rousseau passes from the accusatory to the seductive mode "often between successive paragraphs, or sometimes even within the interior of a paragraph": "Between the accusation that makes the reader culpable, and the tender words that aim to gain his heart and his faith, the tempo is often rapid."[56] In turn, Felicity Baker analyzes Rousseau's use of paradox as a pedagogical tool to persuade the reader in an "agonistic" manner. "Rousseau never wanted his writings to shock reason; it is not for this that he embraced the paradoxical expression: 'I prefer to be a paradoxical man than a prejudiced one' [*Emile*, 93]," she explains: "The 'land of chimeras' he preferred to frequent is opposed, he explains to us, to the 'land of prejudices' as truth is to falsity: paradox in Rousseau is therefore a veritable weapon, similar to that of Socratic irony; even if it seems to approach the absurd, for Rousseau it is situated at the other extreme of discourse from that of ridicule, as a corrupted rhetoric employed to vanquish true morality in the service of prejudice. The primary function of paradox in Rousseau is to astonish, but not to mystify the mind; what he aims at is astonishment on the part of someone who finally sees a veiled aspect of reality, and most of all the reality of language: paradox is didactic."[57] Schlanger makes a similar argument concerning writers' use of what she terms less "dense" literary techniques such as allusion, ellipses, and the like that "implicate" the reader and elicit the reader's active participation, explaining: "They excite interest precisely because they give an incomplete and suggestive message that leaves to the reader the task of completing it himself."[58] Although she does not illustrate the authorial strategies with reference to Rousseau, he certainly avails himself of such techniques with regularity.

As can be seen, then, a number of scholars have attended to the various aspects of Rousseau's protreptic philosophy, and other examples could be adduced. My aim in this book is to conduct a more systematic investigation of how Rousseau persuades and educates the reader in his major philosophical works. The few interpreters whose approach is most similar to my own have focused on *Emile*, which is perhaps not surprising given that it is, after all, an educational work. Approaching the work from the perspective of literary criticism, Laurence Mall investigates the rhetorical and literary aspects of *Emile*, including its hybrid genre as a treatise-novel, authorial voices, and other features.[59] In turn, Denise Schaeffer examines *Emile* as a philosophic work with pedagogical intent, namely as a training of the pupil's judgment, with the intended pupil being foremost the reader of the work.[60] I blend and build on their approaches in my analysis of *Emile* and extend them to Rousseau's other major philosophical works.

Rousseau's Readers and Rousseau's Reader

Before proceeding, I owe an explanation with regard to my choice of title given that, as noted above, Rousseau typically addresses more than one type of reader or audience in his works. Instead of *Rousseau's Reader*, singular, I might very well have titled this study *Rousseau's Readers*, plural. If I had gone with the plural I would have been able to speak consistently of "readers" in my analysis, and thereby avoided the gendered language when speaking of Rousseau's "reader," as in: "the reader has to do his part to understand the text." I apologize for the gendered language, making the inadequate pleas of the dictates of grammar and the fact that Rousseau usually, if not necessarily or always, assumes a male audience for his philosophical works.

I nonetheless have two substantive reasons for my choice of the singular *Rousseau's Reader*. First, and most important, even if Rousseau anticipates different readers or audiences, as he manifestly does, in terms of the text itself (as opposed to the actual reading of the text), these readers are all constructions of the author. To use the terminology of literary criticism discussed above, they are implied readers created by an implied author. Put differently, even if Rousseau as author anticipates a variety of readers, each of these readers is *a* reader constructed through the text. By using the singular *reader*, therefore, I am not claiming to identify *the* reader. If there is a single proper reader, singular, of Rousseau's works, it is the reader who recognizes that Rousseau anticipates and even constructs a variety of readers through his text and therefore adopts a variety of authorial postures and strategies. This, in fact, is my intention in this book.

Second, the plural title may have suggested a study of how actual readers reacted to and understood his writings, which is not my focus. Studies of this sort are valuable as a matter of intellectual history, and I would refer anyone to Raymond Trousson's magisterial account of how Rousseau's contemporaries throughout Europe responded to his writings.[61] Such studies throw light on how readers actually read and understood his works, or, as Trousson's study attests, how they frequently misunderstood them. I have occasionally referred to these actual readings of Rousseau to illustrate various points. Nonetheless, such studies are also necessarily limited in their utility for my purposes for at least two reasons. First, how readers understood Rousseau's writings is not the same thing as how he intended them to be understood. Indeed, Rousseau incessantly complained that his writings were *not* properly understood by his contemporaries, for example stating that the *Discourse on Inequality* "found only a few readers who understood it in all of Europe, and none of these wanted to talk about it" (*Confessions, CW*, 5:326). More important, within his own texts Rousseau anticipates being misunderstood by readers, and one of the rhetorical and literary strategies I examine in this book is his dialogue with skeptical and careless readers. Second, in part because he recognized that his thought would not be understood or accepted by his contemporaries given that he challenged the opinions of the age, Rousseau from the very outset of his philosophical career proclaimed: "One must not write for such readers if one wants to live beyond one's age" (*Sciences*, 7). Rousseau therefore both worked within the constraints of the writing and reading practices of his time and sought to break free of them, and the only way we can ascertain his intentions in this respect is to examine the author-reader relationship he crafts and employs within his works.

Outline of the Chapters

As I noted near the beginning, I devote a chapter each to Rousseau's *Discourse on the Sciences and the Arts* and *Discourse on Inequality*, then four chapters to *Emile*, and, finally, a chapter to the *Social Contract*. Although my argument does build across this book, the chapters are meant to be capable of being read on their own for those readers interested in specific subjects I take up. I have therefore permitted myself some minimal repetitions across chapters where necessary.

I begin in chapter 1 by analyzing the prize essay inspired by the "illumination of Vincennes": the *Discourse on the Sciences and the Arts*. As with the other works I examine, I frame my analysis by attending to the form and structure of the work. In the case of the *Discourse*, I emphasize its dual identity as a discourse for an academic-prize competition designed to be read aloud and as a published *Discourse* meant to be read. By attending to the differences between the spoken discourse and the written *Discourse* I inaugurate a theme that will be carried throughout this book: namely, how Rousseau addresses the challenge posed by Socrates' critique of writing as found in Plato's *Phaedrus*. Rousseau signals his concern with Socrates' challenge through his choice of the frontispiece for the published *Discourse*, the allegory of Prometheus bringing the arts to mankind, and with a note in the text that explains the allegory by associating it with the myth of Thoth related in *Phaedrus*. In order to see how Rousseau addresses the relationship between speech and writing raised by Socrates, therefore, I examine the paratextual elements he added to the published *Discourse*—including the title page, frontispiece, preface, and notes—in order to see how the form and content of the spoken discourse differ from the published *Discourse*. My aim in doing so is to examine the interplay between the form and content of the work, and I focus in particular on the education of the reader in distinguishing appearance and reality, for example to distinguish between the splendid appearance of the advancement of the sciences and the arts and the reality of moral corruption. Finally, this education culminates with a challenge to the reader with regard to the argument of the *Discourse* itself: to distinguish between the "apparent" and the "true" causal arguments of the work.

In chapter 2 I turn to the *Discourse on Inequality* and examine the form and structure of the work, once again beginning with its complex paratextual apparatus, in order to see how they condition the reading experience. For example, the *Discourse* includes extensive notes that make up about a third of the length of the work as a whole, but in the Notice on the Notes Rousseau suggests that the reader not read the notes along with the text and then challenges the reader who possesses the requisite "courage" to examine the notes on a second reading. Through this strange proceeding, then, Rousseau both makes available very different readings of the *Discourse*, for reading the work without the notes and reading it with them makes for two very different experiences in terms of both form and content and anticipates different types of readers. As for the body of the *Discourse*, I focus on Rousseau's account of natural man in the pure state of nature as presented in the first part. Rousseau's primary pedagogical aim here is to persuade the reader of the plausibility of his account of natural man as an asocial and undeveloped animal despite appearances to the contrary with regard to human nature. I therefore examine the rhetorical and literary strategies he uses to persuade the reader, including repeated comparisons between the "natural man" he asks his reader to envision along with him and the "civil man" before the reader's eyes.

Chapter 3 is the first of four chapters devoted to *Emile*. In this chapter I examine Rousseau's choice of the hybrid genre of a treatise-novel. When he announces that he will give himself an imaginary pupil in order to "avoid getting lost in visions" and appoints himself as tutor (*Emile*, 51), Rousseau confronts the reader with a paradox: how is this figment of his imagination the embodiment of reality instead of another "vision"? As with his portrayal in the *Discourse on Inequality* of natural man, then, he must persuade the reader of the truth of his imaginary pupil as an exemplar of the natural goodness of man and, simultaneously, of the artificiality of the children the reader has before his eyes. In addition to exploring his choice of hybrid genre, I analyze a number of the narrative devices Rousseau employs to test the reader's progress in his pedagogical project. These include persistent comparisons between "my pupil" and "your pupil" and the dialogues between author and reader of which they a part, stories of "true" and "false" Emiles that test the reader's ability to identify the proper pupil, and stories with intentionally inapt lessons or apologues. The purpose of these narrative devices is to engage the reader in the process of his education.

One common feature of all the works I am interpreting is the use of frontispieces, and they are one of the textual elements I analyzed in the chapters devoted to the two *Discourses* and will analyze in the chapter on the *Social Contract*. Chapter 4 is devoted in its entirety to an analysis of the five illustrations in *Emile*. These illustrations educate and test the reader of the work by their allegorical character and especially by the complex dialogue Rousseau establishes between the illustrations and the text. To take the frontispiece to book I and to *Emile* as a whole as an example, Rousseau proclaims that the allegory of Thetis dipping her son into the river Styx portrayed on the frontispiece is "clear" (*Emile*, 47), but analysis of the text reveals that it is far from clear, and is in fact is misleading. Unlike Achilles, but for his heel, Emile is not rendered invulnerable to loss and mortality and the passions such as anger and pride generated by a corrupt desire for domination and immortality. The other engravings Rousseau commissioned for *Emile* are similarly complex, and they constitute a test of the reader's progress.

In chapter 5 I explore one of the three explicitly separate sections Rousseau includes within *Emile*, namely the "Profession of Faith of the Savoyard Vicar." Rather than analyzing the substance of the theological and religious discussion in the Vicar's speech, however, I restrict myself to examining the structural elements of the "Profession" in order to understand Rousseau's intentions in including it and to discern its proper audience. I analyze the context in which the "Profession" is included, Rousseau's introduction to the "paper" supposedly written by someone else, the dramatic introduction to the "Profession," including the characters of the dramatis personae, and the dramatic setting of the speech. Two themes are particularly important in my analysis. The first is the question of interpretive authority, and I argue that Rousseau's disavowal of his authorship of the "Profession" is another instance of his doubling himself, for example as both author of *Emile* and the tutor within the narrative, and that he does so in order to shift interpretive authority from himself to the reader. Unlike the rest of *Emile*, where he maintains his authority to persuade the reader, he leaves it to the reader to judge the contents of the "Profession." Second, I examine the role of rhetoric in the "Profession" in light of Rousseau's discussions of rhetoric elsewhere in *Emile*. In particular, I focus on the now-familiar issue inspired by Plato's *Phaedrus* of how rhetoric should be adapted to the character and capacity of the audience. Among other things, this throws light on Rousseau's decision to put the Vicar's speech in a separate section of the work and have it delivered not to Emile, for whom the speech would not be appropriate or effective, but to another youth, who has a very different character and is thus in need of a different lesson.

If Rousseau's aim in *Emile* is to educate the reader, then the instances in the text of characters' reading should be illuminating. In chapter 6 I explore two examples: Emile's reading of Defoe's *Robinson Crusoe* and the role of the reading of Fénelon's *Adventures of Telemachus* within the story of Emile's courtship of his beloved. After proclaiming "I hate books" and alluding to the problem of writing posed by Plato's *Phaedrus*, Rousseau gives Emile the sole book that will compose his library: *Robinson Crusoe*. But not the whole of the novel, for he suggests that it must be stripped of "all its rigmarole" to make it appropriate for his pupil (*Emile*, 184–85). Nonetheless, he does not identify everything that should be excised: another test of the reader. I argue that what must be cut from Defoe's novel is its religious element, a concern chief on the mind of the self-proclaimed prodigal son marooned on a desert island, but an issue far from Emile's ken or concern. As for *Telemachus*, I analyze the roles the work plays in the romance of Emile and Sophie in book V, including in the second separate section of *Emile*, "Sophie, or the Woman."

The question once again deriving from Plato's *Phaedrus* of how individuals will react differently depending on their characters and capacities is central to Rousseau's employment of *Telemachus*, including his creation of two Sophies, "false" and "true" versions who have different reactions to the book owing to their different temperaments. Emile, in turn, is the only person in the story who has not yet read *Telemachus*, and therefore the actions and reactions of all the characters—and the reader of *Emile*—are conditioned by whether or how they have read the novel. Finally, when Emile does come to read *Telemachus*, the work serves as a democratized mirror of princes as he sets out, in the third and final separate section of *Emile*, "Of Travel," to learn about politics.

In chapter 7 I turn to the *Social Contract*. Rousseau's political treatise poses a challenge for my approach because, unlike the works I have examined so far, there is only the barest indication of the intended reader of the work, much less any dialogue between author and reader. What I examine, then, are what I suggest are the two principal readings of the treatise Rousseau makes available to any reader. The first reading is effectively signaled in the subtitle, *Principles of Political Right*, for the principles of political right are always and everywhere the same. The second reading is a work that also attends to the conditions for the creation and maintenance of a legitimate political association. In order to show how these two principal readings are made available by Rousseau in the text of the *Social Contract*, I first examine the précis of his political treatise contained in *Emile*, arguing that he provides only the first of these readings there of a treatise on political right. I then briefly analyze the structure of the earlier version of the work, the so-called Geneva Manuscript, in comparison to the structure of the final version of the *Social Contract*, and then the structure of the *Social Contract* itself, with the same intention. With these various structural analyses in place, I briefly outline the two principal readings themselves.

Finally, in the conclusion I return to the methodological issues of interpreting the rhetorical or literary aspects of philosophical works that I have discussed in this introduction and then tackled in my reading of Rousseau. While I of course hope that my interpretation of Rousseau's philosophical writings will add something new and important to the scholarship on his thought, I would also be pleased to see my interpretive approach applied where appropriate to other texts and thinkers. By way of illustration of how my approach might be extended, I conclude with a brief examination of the author-reader relationship in Hobbes's *Leviathan*.

Chapter 1

Appearance and Reality in the *Discourse on the Sciences and the Arts*

The story of the road to Vincennes and the "illumination" occasioned by reading the question proposed by the Academy of Dijon has been told many times, including at the outset of this book. Today we read the *Discourse on the Sciences and the Arts* with Rousseau's fame firmly in mind, and it is difficult to read it without thinking of his later works. Indeed, the relationship between the first *Discourse* and Rousseau's later writing is the principal subject of scholarship on the first *Discourse*. Rousseau himself later claimed that the *Discourse* was based on the "system" of the natural goodness of man and his corruption in society that unified all of his works (see esp. *Letters to Malesherbes*, *CW*, 5:575; *Dialogues*, *CW*, 1:9, 22–23, 212–14). While some scholars have accepted the author's testimony, others have argued that his prize essay at best contains elements of his later thought in inchoate form and is more of a rhetorical display piece than a philosophic work.[1] I will argue that the *Discourse* is substantively consistent with his other major works in most important respects, but I want to begin with a more naïve question meant to enable us to approach the work with fresh eyes. How do we put ourselves in a position to see the work as though we were readers encountering the prize discourse by the then-unknown author?

Several of the terms I have used in formulating this question already suggest the difficulties in answering it. First, the *Discourse* in its original form was not initially encountered by "readers" in the usual sense of the term, that is, as a published or circulated work, but rather by the judges in the Academy of Dijon, who listened as the submitted essay was read aloud; thus, its original audience consisted of auditors rather than readers.[2] Second, unlike the judges who awarded the prize to this essay, readers of the published version of the *Discourse* were already reading it through the lens of the fact that it had been awarded a prize. Third, the published *Discourse* differs in significant ways from the version heard by the judges in Dijon, as we shall see. Finally, all of these issues might be signaled in a summary way by observing that the titles by which we commonly refer to the work—the *Discourse on the Sciences and the Arts* and, alternatively, the first *Discourse*—are not in fact its title. Rather, the full original title is: *Discourse which took the prize of the Academy of Dijon in the year 1750, on this question proposed by that Academy: Whether the restoration of the sciences and the arts has contributed to purifying morals.* This cumbersome title (though not cumbersome by eighteenth-century standards) was attributed to "A Citizen of Geneva," and thus Rousseau's first major work was initially published anonymously. In order to access the work that made Rousseau famous, we need to approach it as his two initial audiences—the judges at the Academy of Dijon and the first readers of the anonymous published version—encountered it. We do so while acknowledging that this goal can only be attained by approximation, corrupted as we are by both foreknowledge and hindsight. I suggest that one way of undertaking this task is to attend to the form and structure of the work.

In this chapter I examine the *Discourse on the Sciences and the Arts* with the twofold audiences Rousseau indicates for the work, auditors and readers, in mind, and I attend to the different issues and lessons these two audiences receive. In doing so, I follow Rousseau's lead by focusing on how he confronts the very problems of speaking and writing for different audiences raised by Socrates' critique of writing in Plato's *Phaedrus*. Rousseau indicates that he has the Socratic critique in mind through his choice of frontispiece, the myth of Prometheus, and especially by the note related to the frontispiece in which he alludes to the *Phaedrus*.

The "Discourse" and the *Discourse*

When Rousseau read the question proposed by the Academy of Dijon for its prize in moral philosophy in the *Mercure de France* in October 1749, he was one among the many ambitious young men who had come to the capital of the Enlightenment to seek fame and fortune. He had found little of either since his arrival in Paris in the winter of 1741–42 with a new system of musical notation and two operas in hand. Rousseau's first experience with an academy, the Academy of Sciences, was not a success. While the academicians politely praised the *Project concerning New Signs for Music* read to them on August 22, 1742, they declined to endorse or financially support it. Rousseau's *Project* was not a submission for a prize essay competition, such as the "discourse" for the Academy of Dijon, but rather a "project" or proposal seeking approval and support. Likewise, the published version of his project, the *Dissertation on Modern Music* (1743), was a "dissertation," a literary form in which an author examined or discussed a subject ("dissertation" in both French and English coming from the Latin *disserere*, meaning to examine or discuss). In this case, Rousseau was explaining his new musical notation system and arguing that it was superior to the one currently in use. The prize competitions sponsored by academies across Europe on subjects of natural and moral philosophy, literary questions, or other topics required a different genre.

The *concours académique* was an important way for unknowns such as Rousseau to become knowns, or for already-knowns to acquire more reputation and authority. France was particularly heavily populated with academies, with about forty by Rousseau's time. Many of these academies were founded during the reign of Louis XIV, including some by the Sun King himself, as Rousseau himself notes in the *Discourse* when he applauds "that great monarch" and "his august successor" (Louis XV) for having established academies (*Sciences*, 32).[3] Naturally, the most important academies were established in Paris, but other such institutions were scattered across the country, including the Academy of Dijon, established in 1725. Other important academies were established in Berlin and elsewhere, often in emulation of the French model, as Rousseau also remarks in the *Discourse* (32). At the time Rousseau entered the lists, there were about two hundred prize competitions per year across a wide variety of subjects.[4] Among those who owed their reputation in part to winning an academic-prize competition were Fontenelle, more than one member of the Bernoulli family, Euler, Marat, Lavoisier, Necker, and Robespierre. Famous also-rans included Voltaire, who failed to win a competition on the nature and propagation of fire in 1738, and Napoléon Bonaparte, who wrote on happiness in 1791.[5]

The advertisement Rousseau read for the Academy of Dijon's prize competition in morality (*morale*) for 1750 included not only the question—"Whether the restoration of the science and the arts has contributed to purifying morals"—but also the amount of the prize (a gold medal worth thirty *pistoles*) and instructions to the entrants. As was the procedure for most such competitions, the submission had to be anonymous, accompanied by a sealed letter with the required epigraph to the discourse repeated on the envelope and the identity of the contestant inside; it could be written in either French or Latin; it had to be legible; and it had to be capable of being read aloud within thirty minutes.[6] For the 1750 prize competition, thirteen entries met the basic qualifications and were read across a number of weeks in the spring and summer of 1750. A few finalists were selected and reread, and then a winner was unanimously decided upon by July 9: Number Seven, identified by the epigraph, *Decipimur specie recti*. Rousseau was soon notified of his victory, and a surrogate collected the prize money. The Academy announced the winner in the November 1750 issue of the *Mercure de France*, along with a disclaimer stating that its decision did not necessarily mean that its members shared the author's views.

The *Discourse* was published anonymously in January 1751 by a Parisian who listed the place of publication as Geneva and two deceased Genevans as the publishers, with "tacit permission" for publication from the French authorities, thus playing the game of hide-and-seek, wink-wink nudge-nudge, that was a staple of eighteenth-century publishing in France.[7] An actual Genevan publisher soon pirated the original edition—another routine practice of the time—and published it shortly thereafter under Rousseau's name and presumably without his participation or approval. Finally, Rousseau's future publisher Marc-Michel Rey issued another version from his Amsterdam press in May 1751, once again revealing Rousseau's authorship.[8] The work made its author an overnight celebrity.

In order to understand Rousseau's *Discourse* in terms of its audiences, we should begin by discriminating between the "discourse" he submitted to the Academy of Dijon and the published *Discourse*. Rousseau himself states in the preface to the published *Discourse* that, not expecting to be honored with the prize, he initially "reworked and expanded this discourse to the point of turning it, as it were, into a different work." We do not possess this manuscript. Rousseau further explains in the preface that, having won the prize, he restored his work to its original version for publication. Or almost so: "I now consider myself obligated to restore it to the state in which it was awarded the prize. I have merely thrown in some notes and let stand two passages that are easily recognized and that the Academy would perhaps not have approved of" (7). Another misfortune, for the archives of the Academy of Dijon include only nine of the thirteen original entries, and Rousseau's is among the missing, making it impossible to compare the version read as part of the prize competition to the published version of the work. Lacking the original manuscript, we have to take his word for it. In any case, Rousseau himself draws our attention to the differences between the prize essay and the published version.

What, then, are the differences between the "discourse" and the *Discourse*? The notes Rousseau added are, of course, readily identifiable. By contrast, despite his claim that the two passages he added to the published version are "easily recognized," scholars have offered various conjectures about which passages were added.[9] Rather than play the scholarly sleuth with regard to the mysterious, I believe it would be more fruitful to begin with what is obvious but usually overlooked. Namely, all of the material in the published version that precedes the opening of the "discourse" proper—that is, the exordium, with the required epigraph at its head, the frontispiece, the title page, and the preface—was added for the published version.[10] Along with the notes, these parts of the *Discourse* are, in Gérard Gennette's terminology, the "paratexts" of the work.[11] The term *paratext* translates Gennette's *seuil* (threshold), and so we might characterize the frontispiece, title page, and preface as entryways into the main text that prepare and condition the experience of the reader of the "discourse" itself. In turn, the notes surround the main text, so to speak both bordering and breaching the bounds of the text. Our task, then, is to try to approach the original "discourse" without these additions and then to see how it is informed, altered, and so on, by the paratextual apparatus of the printed *Discourse*.

Perhaps it would be useful to diagram the structure of the published *Discourse*:

Table 1.1 Structure of the *Discourse on the Sciences and the Arts*

Frontispiece and title page	2 pp. in the Pléiade edition
Preface	1 p.
Exordium	1 p.
First part	10½ pp. including notes; approx. 9½ pp. without notes
Second part	14 pp. including notes; approx. 11½ pp. without notes

With the diagram in table 1.1 before us, we can discriminate between the "discourse" and the *Discourse*. Recall that the instructions for the prize competition required that the submission be capable of being read aloud within the space of thirty minutes. Rousseau's submission would have included the exordium, first part, and second part, without the notes (and without the mysterious two passages he added), meaning that his submission was about twenty pages (in the Pléiade edition), or approximately the maximum allowable length. The issue of length will be important when I turn in the next chapter to the *Discourse on Inequality*, which the academicians ceased reading when they realized the submission far exceeded the limit.[12]

An important consideration for understanding the first *Discourse* is the difference between a "discourse" designed to be read aloud and a published *Discourse* meant (primarily) to be read. A "discourse" (*discours*) at the time either denoted or, by extension, connoted a *spoken* form of argumentation.

The discourse form has its roots in classical rhetoric, which distinguished three forms of discourse: deliberative, judicial, and epideictic.[13] An academic discourse such as Rousseau's is a form of deliberative discourse, in which the speaker attempts to persuade an audience to take or to not take a certain action. For example, in a political context, the speaker persuades the audience to adopt (or not to adopt) a policy by discussing its worthiness (or unworthiness) or its advantageousness (or disadvantageousness). While originally a primarily spoken form, the term *discourse* was often used in the title of works, especially philosophical or similar works. A few such works with which we know Rousseau was familiar include Machiavelli's *Discourses on Livy*, Algernon Sydney's *Discourses on Government*, Bossuet's *Discourse on Universal History*, and, most famously, Descartes's *Discourse on Method*. Interestingly, none of these works play on the original spoken meaning or connotation of a "discourse," and so the term seems to have become relatively generic. This is not to deny that an author's decision to title a work a "discourse," rather than an "essay," an "inquiry," a "treatise," and the like, might be important for understanding the author's intention with regard to the work and its audience.

As for Rousseau, he does maintain and play upon the spoken character of the discourse form in the *Discourse on the Sciences and the Arts*, and he does so in the *Discourse on Inequality* as well, though to a lesser degree. In this regard, the contrast to Descartes's *Discourse on Method* is instructive. Despite its title, Descartes presents his work as an emphatically *written* work. For example, in the Notice (*Advertissement*) with which he opens the work, he begins by explaining: "If this discourse seems too long to be *read* in its entirety in one time," he has divided it into six parts. Similarly, he ends the Notice by speaking of the reasons he has "written" the work. Likewise, although Descartes refers to his work as a "discourse," in the first part of the work he problematizes the genre by also referring to it as a "writing" (*écrit*), which again suggests a written work, as well as a "story" (*histoire*) and even a "fable."[14] By contrast, Rousseau's *Discourse on the Sciences and the Arts* retains elements of the spoken character of a "discourse," which may not be surprising given that the work was originally designed to be a spoken discourse. However, his decision to carry this spoken character into the published version, and to draw attention to the fact in the preface, is significant.

The "discourse" read at the Academy of Dijon begins with the exordium, and Rousseau preserves the "spoken" character of the exordium in the published version. After the epigraph, to which I will return, the exordium begins as follows: "Has the restoration of the sciences and the arts contributed to purifying or to corrupting morals? This is what is to be examined. Which side should I take in this question? That,

Gentlemen, which suits a decent man who knows nothing and who does not think any the less of himself for it" (9). Rousseau addresses his audience, the members of the Academy of Dijon: "Gentlemen" (*Messieurs*). In the second paragraph he refers to the "tribunal before which I appear," maintaining the fiction that he is actually reading his "discourse" before the judges at the Academy of Dijon. In the same paragraph he also states that he dares to blame the sciences before "one of Europe's most learned societies" and "a famous academy"; he says he will defend virtue "before virtuous men"; and he claims that he fears doing so given "the enlightenment of the assembly listening to me" (9). In short, he emphasizes the fact that the "discourse" was designed to be read aloud.[15]

If the exordium is the part of the "discourse" (and then *Discourse*) where the spoken character of the work is most evident, there are also traces of it within the body of the work. In the exordium Rousseau addresses his judges as "Gentlemen" (*Messieurs*), and he recalls this address twice in the course of the "discourse." First, and logically enough, he does so in the first part when he finally explicitly answers the Academy's question concerning the relationship between the advancement of the sciences and the arts and moral corruption: "Where there is no effect, there is no cause to seek: but here the effect is certain, the depravity real, and our souls have been corrupted in proportion as our sciences and our arts have advanced toward perfection. Shall it be said that this is a misfortune particular to our age? No, Gentlemen, the evils caused by our vain curiosity are as old as the world" (14–15). His second direct address to those listening to him occurs in the second part. Having argued that splendid states where the sciences and the arts reign have been defeated by nations who preserve their simple mores, he asks: "What, then, precisely is at issue in this question of luxury?" In reply he argues that in states sated with luxuries an artist will seek the praise of his contemporaries, and then addresses his judges: "What will he do, Gentlemen? He will lower his genius to the level of his age and he will prefer to compose ordinary works that are admired during his lifetime rather than marvels that would be admired only long after his death." Having stated as much, Rousseau switches to the first-person plural, inviting his judges to join him as though someone else were now on trial: "Tell *us*, famous Arouet, how much you have sacrificed manly and strong beauties to *our* false delicacy, and how much the spirit of gallantry, so fertile in petty things, has cost you great ones?" (27; emphasis added). The seemingly gratuitous swipe at Voltaire has, of course, attracted notice. Less noticed is how Rousseau, as a *speaker* of the "discourse," invites his audience to join him ("us") in condemning as ordinary the productions of the most famous *writer* of the time. Indeed, in the preface Rousseau suggests a contrast between Voltaire and others who write only for their contemporaries in order to gain their praise and himself, who combats the opinions of his age: "One must not *write* for such readers when one wants to live beyond one's age" (7; emphasis added). Once again, this time in a subtle manner, Rousseau points to the differences between a spoken and a written work.

Finally, before turning to the published *Discourse* with an eye to reading the work with the spoken "discourse" embedded within it, I should address an obvious question: if a "discourse" is a rhetorical form whose primary purpose is persuasion, of what is Rousseau attempting to persuade his judges? Two answers immediately present themselves. First, he is trying to persuade them to award him the prize. Here he succeeded. Second, he is trying to persuade them of his thesis concerning the relationship between the advancement of the sciences and the arts and moral corruption. Here it is doubtful that he succeeded, especially given the Academy's published pronouncements that they did not necessarily agree with his argument despite having awarded him the prize. But persuading his judges to award him the prize did not necessarily entail convincing them of his argument, for such competitions were in many cases more about style than substance.[16] Rousseau's oratorical success within the genre of the "discourse" may well have moved the judges in his favor without their being convinced by his reasoning. As he himself stated in a defense of the work: "Besides, although I knew that academicians do not adopt the sentiments of the Author to whom they give prizes, and that the first prize is awarded not to the person they believe has upheld the best cause, but to the one who has expressed himself best" (*Letter . . . about a New Refutation*, *CW*, 2:175). Nonetheless, Rousseau himself claims in the exordium that his own reward, quite apart from the outcome of the competition, is to have "upheld the side of truth" (10). In short, whatever its rhetorical showmanship, Rousseau puts forward his "discourse" as a philosophical work. As we shall see, the philosophical character of the work is more apparent when Rousseau transforms the "discourse" into the published *Discourse*.

Reading the *Discourse on the Sciences and the Arts*

Upon opening the published *Discourse* we are presented with a frontispiece and title page. Along with the preface that follows, these are the prefatory paratextual elements that serve as the entrance into the main text. These paratextual elements are primarily concerned with the differences between a spoken work, such as the "discourse" read at the Academy, and a written work, such as the published *Discourse*. These differences raise the issue of the intended audience, or rather audiences, of the work.

Title Page

Let us begin with a brief consideration of the title page, brief because other interpreters have covered this ground, although I hope that my focus on the differences between the spoken and written aspects of Rousseau's prize essay will add something important.[17] The reader learns from the full title (see above) that the ensuing discourse won the Academy's prize and that it answered a certain question. The reader does not learn what the answer was. Further, as other interpreters have noted, by taking the persona of "A Citizen of Geneva" in answering a question posed by an academy in France, Rousseau suggests that he is a foreigner, literally and perhaps also metaphorically.

Rousseau's metaphorical foreignness is immediately emphasized by his choice of epigraph: "Here I am the barbarian, understood by nobody" (Barbarus hic ego sum quia non intelligor illis).[18] Rousseau could expect many readers (then, if not now) to recognize that the verse is drawn from Ovid's *Tristia*, in which the poet laments his exile in barbaric Tronis on the Black Sea by writing to those he left back in Rome. In the line quoted, Ovid turns the term *barbarian* on its head: surrounded by barbarians, he now finds himself the barbarian, for his speech meets with incomprehension. Nonetheless, Ovid is far from embracing the inversion or completing it, for example by implying that the "civilized" Romans are the true barbarians: he freely calls those hostile peoples who surround him "barbarians" and longs to return to civilized Rome. Rousseau could expect that many readers would know all this. Yet Ovid's fleeting identification as a barbarian opens the door for the Citizen of Geneva, already identified as an outsider, to take the part of the barbarian among the civilized and thus invert the civilized/barbarian dichotomy where Ovid does not.[19]

One final remark on the epigraph relating to the distinction between a spoken and a written work. Ovid calls himself the barbarian because those with whom he lives cannot understand his *speech*. But Ovid makes this complaint in *writing*, in a Latin poem addressed to an audience back home. Revealingly, the poem is characterized by Ovid from its very first line as a *book*: "Little book, I do not begrudge you, go without me to the city."[20] Rousseau imitates the poet by including Ovid's written verse about his failure to make his speech understood, for he presents the verse in the written paratext of the *Discourse* that introduces the reader to the initially spoken "discourse." Rousseau may be indicating that his speech will also fail to be understood and, additionally, that his written text may find readers who comprehend it.

To summarize with regard to the title page, Rousseau presents himself as an outsider, a foreigner, a barbarian through both his self-presentation as "A Citizen of Geneva" and his choice of epigraph. He also subtly raises the issue of the difference between speech and writing, but let me postpone that matter until after discussing the frontispiece. Does his perspective as a foreigner make him more prone to be taken in by appearances in the strange land he visits? Or does it make him more capable of seeing through those appearances? Perhaps both. Think, for example, about Montesquieu's *Persian Letters*, wherein the visitors from Persia write about what they see in France with a combination of wondering incomprehension and keen penetration. In this light, Rousseau's choice of the epigraph at the head of the "discourse" is significant: "We are deceived by the appearance of rectitude" (Decipimur specie recti; 9).[21] Perhaps the Citizen of Geneva is initially among the "we" who are so deceived at first, but is able eventually to see through appearances. As we shall see, through the text of the *Discourse* Rousseau will teach the reader to make the same progress.

Frontispiece

The reader's education commences with the frontispiece, displayed across from the title page. The frontispiece has also received useful analysis by previous scholars, who have shown how the illustration embeds the different audiences Rousseau addresses and the differing lessons he offers them.[22] My interpretation builds on these analyses but adds a new dimension through my focus on the spoken versus written aspects of the work. Because in due course I will examine a number of the frontispieces and illustrations adorning Rousseau's works, a few general remarks about these engravings are in order here.

Rousseau is not alone as an author in using engravings to illustrate his works, and his use of them should be interpreted in light of that tradition. Restricting ourselves to political thought, broadly understood, think of the frontispiece to Bacon's *Great Instauration* depicting a ship passing through the Pillars of Hercules, representing Bacon's call to go beyond traditional philosophy with his new scientific method. Perhaps the most famous frontispiece is the striking image that Hobbes commissioned for *Leviathan*. Hobbes's reconstruction of the traditional metaphor of the sovereign being the head of the body politic has received attention from a number of scholars,[23] and his less well-known frontispiece for *De Cive* has also attracted notice.[24] Another example is Vico, whose *New Science* is illustrated with an elaborate frontispiece elaborately described to introduce the idea of the work. As Quentin Skinner explains, the use of these frontispieces stemmed from a tradition of "emblem books" or *emblemata* popular among Renaissance humanists.[25] These emblem books included collections of illustrations, typically with accompanying texts such as poems or allegorical subjects that challenged readers to interpret or even decode the meaning of the illustration.

Rousseau's use of illustrations is unusually pervasive, and also interpretively more complex than perhaps any other political writer. Having formerly been apprenticed to an engraver, he was familiar with the art, and he commissioned frontispieces and illustrations for most of his major works. Producing the engravings was not an inexpensive endeavor,[26] and he strenuously negotiated with his publishers to ensure their inclusion and the quality of their execution. Rousseau explained the task he set his engravers in a letter: "It is not what the illustrator must depict, but what he must know in order to conform his work to it as much as possible. Everything that I have described must be in his head in order to put it in his engraving everything that can be placed there, and not to put anything there that conflicts."[27] His aim in including these illustrations can be further seen in the "Subjects of the Engravings" that accompanies *Julie*.

> Most of these subjects are detailed so as to make them understood, much more so than they can be in the execution: for in order to realize a drawing felicitously, the artist must see it not as it will be on his paper, but as it is in nature. . . . The artist's skill consists in making the viewer imagine many things that do not appear on the plate; and that depends on a felicitous choice of circumstances, of which the ones he renders lead us to presuppose those he does not. Therefore, one can never enter into too much detail when one wants to present subjects for engraving, and is absolutely ignorant of the art. Moreover, it is easy to see that this had not been written for the public; but in putting out the engravings separately, it seemed that this explanation [*explication*] ought to accompany them. (*CW*, 6:621)

As the editors of the English edition of *Julie* note, the term *explication* refers to a section included in many books of the period that decoded the allegories or clarified the subjects of illustrations (*CW*, 6:723 n.12). These illustrations are therefore first and foremost allegorical in nature. Rousseau's explanations of the engravings for *Julie* are quite detailed, with a lengthy paragraph or more describing each of the twelve engravings. Given what he states in the general remarks to the "Subjects of the Engravings," these descriptions must have resembled his instructions to Gravelot, who designed them. As for the frontispiece to the *Discourse on the Sciences and the Arts*, which Rousseau states was executed by Jean-Baptiste-Marie Pierre, one of the artists characterized in the text of the *Discourse* as destined to debase his talents to suit the taste of the times (28), Rousseau must have given him similarly detailed instructions. While we know that he was not pleased with the result,[28] given the habitual care he took with his engravings, we can be confident that the frontispiece of the *Discourse*, and the other illustrations I will analyze in this book, can be interpreted with similar care.

As noted above, the frontispiece to the *Discourse on the Sciences and the Arts* has received some attention from scholars, but the only sustained attempts to interpret the illustrations in relation to the text in Rousseau's corpus have been for *Julie, or The New Heloise*. Rousseau's best-selling novel contains twelve engravings, two for each of the six books into which the work is divided. The novel does not, however, have a frontispiece. In addition, the engravings illustrate the action of the narrative and therefore do not serve the same purpose as the frontispiece for the *Discourse on the Sciences and the Arts*, or his other works that include a frontispiece. Nonetheless, one common feature of the illustrations for *Julie* and the frontispiece of the *Discourse on the Sciences and the Arts*, as well as the *Discourse on Inequality*, is that they all refer to specific points in the text. As scholars who have examined *Julie* have shown, then, there is a dialogic relationship between illustration and text, meaning that they have to be interpreted in light of each other. As Philip Stewart suggests: "The illustration itself must be decoded and assimilated by the reader; and whether it is read before or after, it cannot be read simultaneously with or even independently of the passage to which it corresponds."[29] Interpreting these engravings requires oscillating between illustration and text, not as between portrait and original, but as self-referential texts that contain tensions both within themselves and in relation to one another.

The frontispiece to the *Discourse on the Sciences and the Arts* portrays three figures (fig. 1.1). In the center there is a nude young man standing on a pedestal, as if he were a statue, with his hands in an open gesture as though ready to receive something. To the man's right (the viewer's left) is Prometheus, holding a torch in his right hand and lowering it toward the man. On the other side of the central figure is a satyr, raising his left ("sinister") hand as though trying to touch the torch. The legend below the illustration reads, "Satyr, you do not know [*connois*] it," and

1.1 Frontispiece of the *Discourse on the Sciences and the Arts*

then, in what might be characterized as a note to the legend, the reader is urged: "See the note, p. 23."

If frontispieces are meant to be allegorical, the allegory seems at first glance to be clear. Given that Rousseau's prize essay is described on the facing page as concerning the restoration of the sciences and the arts, we readily surmise that Prometheus is bringing the sciences and the arts to man, represented by the torch he bears. In turn, the man seems ready to receive the gift. Finally, the satyr, which typically represents the baser passions such as lust, seems to desire the gift of fire. Without the legend, it is difficult to interpret the meaning of the satyr. The speech inscribed in the legend is addressed to the satyr as a warning, presumably by Prometheus, or by the author of the *Discourse*, or by both. If the satyr typically represents lust and similar passions, he is warned that he also does not "know," that he is ignorant, presumably of the effects of the fire he desires. The word being translated here as "know" (*connois*) might also be rendered as "be familiar with" or even "recognize," in which case we might say the satyr is deceived by the appearance of the fire. At any rate, the man is given no such warning. Given the subject of the essay announced on the title page, the frontispiece seems susceptible of at least two interpretations. First, that the restoration of the sciences and the arts represented by Prometheus's gift of fire is a benefit to some (man) and a curse to others (the satyr). Second, that while the sciences and the arts initially appear to be beneficial, they turn out to be dangerous, with the question being whether they are dangerous in themselves or only for some of those who desire to embrace them.

Let us now obey Rousseau's imperative in the annotation to the legend—"See the note, p. 23"—to learn how doing so affects our first impressions. Doing so, we find ourselves at the beginning of the second part of the *Discourse*. The note in question is added to the very first sentence of the second part, but let us obediently begin with the note itself, at the bottom of the page:

> The allegory of the fable of Prometheus is easily grasped, and it does not appear that the Greeks, who nailed him to the Caucasus, scarcely thought more favorably of him than the Egyptians did of their god Thoth. "The satyr," an ancient fable goes, "wanted to kiss and embrace the fire the first time he saw it, but Prometheus cried out to him: Satyr, you will mourn the beard on your chin, for it burns when it is touched." This is the subject of the frontispiece. (23 n.)

This confirms two impressions generated by the frontispiece: first, that it is allegorical, and second, that Prometheus is warning the desirous and ignorant satyr not to touch the fire because it burns. Curiously absent from Rousseau's explanation of the allegory is the man. Or perhaps the man is glossed in the note as the Greeks who supposedly punished Prometheus. There was no indication in the frontispiece of the god's punishment. Anyone even remotely familiar with the Prometheus myth would be aware that, far from being hostile to humans, Prometheus took pity upon the naked, shivering creatures and brought them fire; further, that it was not these men who punished the gods, but rather the Olympians, who were fearful of the rebellious creatures.[30] Rousseau alters the familiar myth by having mankind ("the Greeks") punish the god. If his hindsighted brother Epimetheus neglected to provide for man's needs, perhaps the foresighted Prometheus did not see far enough regarding the effects of his gift. If man initially welcomed Prometheus's gift, as portrayed in the frontispiece, the initial appearances of its beneficial effects were proven wrong by experience, and men then punished their false benefactor. To be fair to the god, however, the legend on the frontispiece and its amplified version in the note explain that it does in fact contain a warning, although it is addressed to the satyr.

The note explains the role of Prometheus in the frontispiece, but it also mentions his Egyptian analogue, the god Thoth or Theuth, and this less familiar reference leads us to the heart of the distinction between a spoken and a written work at play in Rousseau's *Discourse*. The story comes from Plato's *Phaedrus*, and Rousseau later remarked that this work was the inspiration for his frontispiece (*Letter to Grimm*, *CW*, 2:87–88). Appropriately for our consideration of Rousseau's rhetoric in the *Discourse*, *Phaedrus* is a dialogue devoted to rhetoric and how proper rhetoric must be molded to suit the person who is to be persuaded. Although this can be done at least in principle in speech, for example in the dialogue between Socrates and Phaedrus, it does not seem possible in writing. When discussing this issue, Socrates appeals to the myth of Thoth. The god Thoth came to Egypt with the arts, including numbers and calculation, geometry, astronomy, and especially writing, and presented them to the king, Thamos. Thamos asked him what was the use of each of the arts. When Thoth came to writing, extolling its virtue as an art to improve memory, Thamos objected: "For this will provide forgetfulness in the souls of those who have learned it, through neglect of memory, seeing that, through trust in writing, they recollect from outside with alien markings, not reminding themselves from inside, by themselves. You have therefore found a drug not for memory, but for reminding. You are supplying the opinion of wisdom to the students, not truth."[31] Having related this myth, Socrates goes on with his own argument concerning the defects of writing, which are not quite the same ones as those identified in the myth he relates. He complains that the written word is available both to appropriate and inappropriate audiences and that it cannot answer the reader and defend itself. Hence Plato's answer to Socrates' critique of writing is to compose dialogues: written works containing speeches.

Rousseau follows Plato's lead.[32] He imbeds a spoken work, the "discourse" addressed to the Academy of Dijon, within a written work, the *Discourse*. If the "discourse" is directed to a specific audience with a particular persuasive goal in mind, the *Discourse* will reach many unknown readers. The paratextual elements are all part of the explicitly written work, and throughout Rousseau draws attention to their written character. Along with the *Discourse* as a whole, these paratextual elements are directed at readers, and different types of readers, as compared to the "discourse" read aloud before the judges. By combining written and spoken forms of communication in the *Discourse*, Rousseau in his own way addresses the problems of rhetoric and persuasion raised by the Platonic Socrates.

Let us assume that, having obeyed Rousseau's injunction on the frontispiece to consult the note, the reader turns back to the frontispiece, perhaps to reexamine it in light of the explanation in the note. If so, the reader now has some idea of what Rousseau's answer—and perhaps also the complexity of his answer—to the question posed by the Academy of Dijon and included on the title page. The suspicion will be confirmed when we turn to the preface.

Preface

The preface to the *Discourse* is concerned with the author, the work, and their audiences. The tone is highly self-conscious, and indeed the first-person pronoun appears with striking frequency. Rousseau draws attention to his role as an author presenting his work to readers. The preface opens by pointing to the question of the Academy of Dijon included on the title page: "Here is one of the greatest and noblest questions ever debated." Rousseau then turns from their question to his answer: "This discourse is not concerned with those metaphysical subtleties that have spread to all fields of literature and from which the announcements of academies are not always exempt. Rather, it is concerned with one of those truths that pertain to the happiness of the human race" (7). Rousseau's purpose and his audience are broader than what would be required to answer the question posed: nothing less than the human race and its happiness.

The issue of the potential audiences or readers of the *Discourse* is

Rousseau's focus in the second paragraph of the preface. His first stab at the issue is to divide readers based on how they will react to his response to the Academy's question. Signaling his response, he states: "I foresee that I will not easily be forgiven for the side I have dared to take." Clashing with "everything that nowadays attracts men's admiration," presumably the sciences and the arts, he expects "universal blame." If he has been honored by the approbation of "a few wise men," he cannot count on the approval of "the public" (7). We now have two types of readers. The "few wise men" would initially appear to refer to the academicians who awarded him the prize, although we might come to doubt that attribution. As for "the public," Rousseau explains their predicted reaction by stating that that he is not concerned with "pleasing either the witty or the fashionable," those who are themselves eager to please or to flatter what "nowadays attracts men's admiration." The "witty" and "fashionable" are perhaps not "the public" itself, but are what we nowadays might term public opinion leaders. Or, given Rousseau's scathing remark later in the *Discourse* about "famed Arouet" prostituting his talent for public acclaim (27), perhaps they are actually opinion followers. At any rate, they are subject to the opinions that reign supreme at the time. If Rousseau expects only "universal blame" for his argument, it would seem that nearly all readers must be counted among "the public," readers who embrace "everything that nowadays attracts men's admiration." The word *ad-miration* has the root sense of "to look at" or "to regard," so what "attracts men's admiration" is what they are drawn to look at or esteem. Perhaps Rousseau's claim that he expects "only universal blame" is meant as a provocation designed to initiate at least some readers in the *Discourse*'s education in distinguishing appearance from reality.

Since Rousseau is concerned with the happiness of the human race, he must expand his inquiry beyond his own time. Just as he will enlarge the scope of his inquiry into the moral effects of the advancement of the sciences and the arts to "all times and places" (15), therefore, so he now enlarges his potential audience. The allegiance of "the public" he is presently addressing to the opinions of their time and place is an instance of a universal phenomenon: "In all times there will be men destined to be subjugated by the opinions of their age, their country, their society." Rousseau will write for a different audience: "One must not write for such readers when one wants to live beyond one's age" (7). Wishing to live beyond his own age and to write for "the human race" as a whole, he seeks readers who are not blinded by reigning opinions, who are capable of approaching the question—and Rousseau's answer—with a broader perspective. Finally, in the last paragraph of the preface

Rousseau reveals that, having won the prize and decided to publish his essay, he has restored his work to the original form with the additions to the published version, as I have already discussed.

A number of previous scholars have come to similar conclusions about the dual audiences of the *Discourse*. They have further generally suggested that Rousseau addresses "the public" with an exoteric argument (that the advancement of the sciences and the arts corrupts morals) and the few truly "wise" with an esoteric argument (that they, the few wise, can pursue the sciences and the arts without such corruption).[33] My own analysis of the *Discourse* generally parallels this interpretation, without any assumptions regarding esoteric writing, but my focus on the education of the reader leads me to approach the text from a different angle. The distinction between the "discourse" read at the Academy of Dijon and the published *Discourse* to which Rousseau himself draws our attention in the preface suggests another division of readers: those who heard the "discourse" without the paratextual material, including the preface, and those who read the *Discourse*. How does the presence and absence of this paratextual material affect the experience of these different audiences? Let us focus on the fact that Rousseau calls attention in the preface to the fact that he is addressing "readers," that is of a written work, both by saying that he is writing for "readers" as an author who appeals beyond his own time and by explaining the differences between the original "discourse" and the published version.

Publishing a work makes it available "beyond one's age" in a way that a speech cannot. For example, Socrates' discourse with Phaedrus, if it ever actually occurred, would not have lived beyond that moment except in their memory if Plato had not overcome his teacher's objections to written works. As an initially spoken work, the "discourse" pronounced at the Academy of Dijon cannot be made public and live beyond its time for various readers in the way that the published *Discourse* can. However, the longevity of the written word also poses difficulties for the author. To recur to an example Rousseau gives within the work itself: whereas the "impious writings" of Leucippus, Diagoras, and other ancient philosophic sectarians perished along with them, the invention of typography will render immortal the "dangerous reveries" of Hobbes, Spinoza, and other modern philosophers (33). Curiously, he does not mention the writings of the ancient philosophers that did not vanish—notably, for our purposes, Plato's dialogues. Rousseau himself would not have been able to allude to Socrates' speech about the problems that beset writing if Plato's *Phaedrus* had not survived, nor would he have been able to quote at length within the *Discourse* itself from Socrates' defense speech if Plato's *Apology of Socrates* had disappeared from print. Perhaps Rousseau's selective examples from among the ancient and modern philosophers concern not so much whether or not they wrote down their dangerous teachings, but instead whether or not they considered the problems of writing itself as raised by Socrates in the *Phaedrus*, especially the fact that writings are available to any reader without discrimination.

In sum, the reader of the published *Discourse* enters the text through the portal of the paratextual elements Rousseau places before the "discourse" proper, whereas the auditors of the "discourse" at the Academy of Dijon commenced their hearing at the point to which we are about to turn, the exordium, without any of these paratextual elements. Both the auditors of the "discourse" and the readers of the *Discourse* will have at least one experience in common: they will both learn from the outset of the texts with which they begin, whether the preface or the exordium, that Rousseau will answer in the negative, for the exordium begins with Rousseau stating that he will "dare blame the sciences before one of Europe's most learned societies" (9). What about the differences in their experiences? There are at least two related differences. First, without the benefit of the paratextual material available to the reader of the *Discourse*, the judges of the "discourse" would not have any hint that Rousseau's argument concerning the effects of the sciences and the arts will be more complex than simply arguing that they corrupt morals. Second, the judges would have no inkling that Rousseau is addressing different types of readers, in part in response to the issues regarding written works raised by Plato's *Phaedrus*.

Exordium

If the reader of the *Discourse* reaches the exordium by way of the prefatory paratextual material, along with the later note relating to the frontispiece, the judges at the Academy of Dijon began their reading of—or listening to—the "discourse" here. They knew nothing of the Citizen of Geneva, foreigners or barbarians, Prometheus, different types of readers and writers, and the like. While the preface is concerned with the author of a published work and his readers, the exordium regards a speaker and his audience, and above I pointed to traces of the originally spoken character of the "discourse" Rousseau elected to retain in the published version.

The very first thing the judges heard was the epigraph at the head of the exordium: "We are deceived by the appearance of rectitude" (Decipimur specie recti; 9).[34] As noted earlier, this epigraph was required in order to identify the author of the entry. Given the Academy's question, at least two things seem significant about the epigraph. First, the assertion that we are deceived by appearances. Second, that these appearances concern morals, specifically rectitude or, alternatively, uprightness or right (*recti*). Rousseau seems to imply that the appearance of purified morals is deceptive, thereby preparing the judges for his response to their question. More important for my focus on how Rousseau educates his readers, with the epigraph he commences an important mode by which he will conduct this education, namely of describing phenomena (such as the state of morals) that seem real at first glance but are revealed to be appearances that hide a different reality.

The readers of the *Discourse* are treated to the same course of education as the judges in discriminating between appearance and reality, but they are better prepared by the paratextual elements of the published work. Rousseau must intend for his reader to compare the epigraph to the *Discourse* to the epigraph to the "discourse."[35] Doing so underscores the theme of appearance versus reality, for the epigraph to the *Discourse* concerns what is held to be or appears to be barbarous as opposed to civilized, with the potential for inverting the terms. Similarly, the frontispiece and especially the note related to it reveal that the torch of the sciences and the arts brought by Prometheus initially appears to be beneficial but turns out to be injurious, or at least injurious to some people. Finally, unlike the judges, the reader has encountered the preface before turning to the exordium and therefore already knows what Rousseau's response to the Academy's question will be, whereas the judges at best have a hint from the epigraph. The reader of the preface also knows that Rousseau claims there that "the public" is always and everywhere subjected to the opinions of their time, place, and milieu, which are a kind of appearance, and as such cannot see the truth. In short, the readers of the *Discourse* are more thoroughly prepared for the education they will receive in seeing through appearances.

The exordium is the paratext to the "discourse" proper. The purpose of an exordium in classical rhetoric is to announce the subject to be discussed and to establish the speaker's authority, including his character or *ethos*.[36] Rousseau executes both tasks in the exordium. First, he announces the subject: "Has the restoration of the sciences and the arts contributed to purifying or to corrupting morals?" He alters the Academy's question by making the potential negative answer to their question more explicitly available, although in a defense of the *Discourse* he would express respectful surprise that the Academy even posed their theme in the form of a question (*Letter . . . about a New Refutation*, CW 2:176). He indicates that he will give just this response in the following paragraph. The judges hearing the "discourse" therefore learn from the outset what Rousseau's response will be. As for the readers of the *Discourse*, they already know this from reading the preface, if they haven't gleaned as much from the frontispiece and the passage in the text to which he there refers the viewer, so the effect of the exordium in this respect is to underscore the negative response.

Second, as for his qualifications to speak and his *ethos*, Rousseau explains that he will take the side in the question asked that befits a "decent man who knows nothing and who does not think any the less of himself for it." He thus establishes his moral character as a "decent man" (*honnête homme*) who will "defend virtue" (9). As for his self-characterization as a man "who knows nothing," he foreshadows his appeal to Socrates "speaking in praise of ignorance" before the tribunal that would condemn him for the side he took in his trial, saying to his own judges: "But *listen to* the verdict that the foremost and most unfortunate among them [*sc.* the wise] passed on the learned men and artists of his time" (18; emphasis added). In this regard, by maintaining the fiction that he is actually reading before the Academy of Dijon— "the tribunal before which I appear"—Rousseau effects a kind of auto-prosopopoeia that allows him to associate himself with the two figures he will later conjure up as though they were speaking to the tribunal: Socrates and Fabricius. Finally, Rousseau concludes the exordium by stating that having "upheld the side of truth" and claiming that, whatever the competition's outcome, the true prize will be found "in the depths of my heart" (10). Just as Socrates so to speak passes his own "verdict" on the Athenians, so too does Rousseau's initial submission to the authority of the judges before whom he speaks turn to his own assertion of authority.[37]

What about the reader of the *Discourse*? The reader has seen the author present himself as "A Citizen of Geneva," and therefore someone presumably concerned with republican virtue. The self-identification on the title page, unavailable to the judges, therefore adds a political twist to his self-characterization in the exordium. More important, as we have seen, the epigraph to the *Discourse* underscores the Citizen of Geneva's presentation of himself as an outsider, for "here"—in civilized France—he is the "barbarian." Turning to the exordium, then, the reader would read his self-characterization there as "a decent man who knows nothing" and defends virtue as much more of an outsider looking in, a barbarian among the civilized, than the judges would ascertain. The judges would certainly see Rousseau as, so to speak, the odd man out since he dares to "blame the sciences before one of Europe's most learned societies, praise ignorance in a famous academy." But it is likely that they would view him less as a barbarian invader than as one of their own, given that in addressing them he is adhering to the modes and orders of an academic-prize essay. For the readers of the *Discourse* the author is an outsider examining the reality and appearance of civilization who has declared that "the public" is in thrall to the opinions of their time, whereas for the auditors of the "discourse" the speaker is a politely dissenting insider who chooses virtue over enlightenment. Put differently, Rousseau's challenge to reigning opinion and appearances is much more aggressive in the *Discourse* than the "discourse."

The Terms of the Question: Appearance and Reality

The first several pages of the first part of the *Discourse*, those that precede Rousseau's direct answer to the question he is addressing, establish the apparent reality of the two terms of the question: first, the advancement of the sciences and the arts, and second, the state of morals. Yet these appearances will turn out to be deceptive in important regards, and so these first several pages constitute Rousseau's initial education of the reader in distinguishing appearance and reality.

Given his indication of the side he will take in the question, it may come as a surprise that the body of the discourse proper begins with a praise of enlightenment.

> It is a grand and beautiful spectacle to see man emerging, as it were, out of nothingness through his own efforts; dissipating by the light of his reason the shadows in which nature has enveloped him; rising above himself; soaring by his mind to the celestial regions; traversing with the steps of a giant, like the sun, the vast expanse of the universe; and, what is grander and even more difficult, returning into himself in order there to study man and to know his nature, his duties, and his end. All these marvels have been revived in the past few generations. (11)

Several critics suggested that the opening praise of enlightenment contradicted the argument of the work.[38] Yet in response Rousseau never gainsaid the progress of the sciences and the arts and in fact was at pains to deny he had. Instead, the question involves their effect on morals.

Rather than being a contradiction, the encomium is part of the education of the reader in distinguishing appearance and reality. To initiate his lesson, Rousseau must begin with how the matter appears to his audience, with the reigning opinions concerning the sciences and the arts, or what he calls in the preface "the opinions of their age, their country, their society" (7).[39] If he must begin with appearances, the opening paragraph appropriately centers on visual imagery. We are initially impressed by the "grand and beautiful spectacle" he conjures for us, with a "spectacle" being something we behold. Closer inspection reveals that Rousseau actually paints two movements of this Promethean image: man soaring through his reason into the physical universe and then an "even grander and more difficult" task of man returning to himself "to know his nature, his duties, and his end." These two movements capture the two parts of the Academy's question: the restoration of the sciences and the arts, on the one hand, and the state of morals, on the other. In terms of his reply to the Academy's question, the opening praise of enlightenment establishes the reality of first part of the question. The education of the reader consists in gradually questioning the initial impression of the apparent harmony between the two movements contained in this opening image. The man Kant called the "Newton of the moral world" will reveal himself to be less than sanguine about the harmony between the starry heavens above us and the moral law within us.

Rousseau sets up a reversal of appearance and reality in the second paragraph, where he recounts the revival of the sciences and the arts. Europe had fallen back into "the barbarism of the first ages," and the "peoples of that part of the world today so enlightened" fell into a condition worse than ignorance until a "revolution" brought them back to common sense as the sciences and the arts came back "among us." With this revolution, he concludes, "people began to feel the principal advantage of communing with the Muses, that of making men more sociable by inspiring in them the desire to please one another with works worthy of their mutual approbation" (11–12). The "sociability" of people and the "softness" (*douceur*) of their morals and manners are touted by many of Rousseau's contemporaries, such as Hume, Montesquieu, and the Encyclopedists, among others, as one of the principal benefits of the advancement of the sciences and the arts. More generally, these proponents of enlightenment championed the development of "commerce" (*commerce*), meaning interactions among human beings in general as well as economic interactions in particular, in what is known as the *doux commerce* school.[40] Rousseau alludes to such arguments here by the phrase translated above as "communing with the Muses," with "communing" translating *commerce*. What is meant as praise by these theorists—and more important, what initially seems to be praise coming from Rousseau—will soon turn out to be blame. He sets up this reversal in the passage quoted with the terms *sociable*, *desire to please*, and *mutual approbation*. These very traits of civility will turn out to be signs of moral corruption.[41]

The reader experiences the reversal of Rousseau's apparent praise of the civilizing effects of the advancement of the sciences and the arts over the next several pages, where the author establishes the reality of the second term of his question: the current state of morals. The reversal begins in the paragraph immediately following the first two paragraphs praising and recounting the restoration of the sciences and the arts. "The mind has its needs, as does the body. The latter make up the foundations of society, the former make it pleasant," he begins, innocuously enough. The next sentence begins to raise the reader's eyebrows: "While government and laws provide for the security and well-being of assembled men," and thus serve the needs of the body, "the sciences, the letters, and the arts—less despotic and perhaps more powerful—spread garlands of flowers over the iron chains with which men are burdened, stifle in them the feeling of that original freedom for which they seemed to have been born, make them love their slavery and fashion them into what are called civilized peoples." The needs of the mind, which seemed at first to make society "pleasant," like "garlands of flowers," turn out to conceal a harsher reality of servitude masquerading as civility. The reversal here is particularly signaled by Rousseau's concluding phrase, "what are called civilized peoples," inviting us to ironize the term "civilized" with scare quotes. The passage continues on a more political note, with Rousseau urging "earthly powers" to love and protect talents among those who cultivate the sciences, letters, and arts and counseling "civilized peoples" to cultivate them: "Happy slaves: you owe to them that delicate and refined taste on which you like to pride yourselves; that softness [*douceur*] of character and urbanity of morals that make relations [*commerce*] among you so affable and so easy; in a word, the appearance of all the virtues without having any of them" (12). What we initially take to be benefits are revealed to be the "appearance" of virtue masking its absence, "civilized peoples" in truth being "happy slaves." The distinction between appearance and reality has now become thematic.

If the main passage alone is politically pointed, the note Rousseau adds to the published *Discourse*, the very first note he joins to it, sharpens it considerably. To the sentence urging "earthly powers" to protect and encourage those who practice the sciences, letters, and arts, he adds a note that begins: "Princes always view with pleasure the taste for the agreeable arts and for superfluities that do not result in the exportation of money spread among their subjects. For aside from thereby nurturing in them that pettiness of soul so appropriate to servitude, they well know that all the needs which the people gives itself are so many chains with which they burden themselves" (12 n.).[42] The reader of the *Discourse* by "A Citizen of Geneva" learns that the apparent benefits of cultivating the sciences, letters, and arts are a cynical ploy by their rulers to further their servitude.

The judges of the "discourse" would not of course have read this note, and indeed they may not have read the passage in the main text to which it was attached either, for this paragraph is one that scholars have nominated as a primary candidate for one of the two mysterious passages he announced in the preface that he added to the text of the published *Discourse*.[43] Aside from suggesting that the bold political thrust of the passage, even without the note, may have offended the judges, scholars have also suggested that removing the paragraph does not interrupt the presentation of the "discourse." The previous paragraph ends with the passage concerning how the advancement of the sciences and the arts has made men more "sociable" and eager to please one another and seek "mutual approbation." If we take out the paragraph in question, the judges would have next heard: "This is the sort of civility, the more amiable as it affects to display itself less, that formerly distinguished Athens and Rome in the much-lauded days of their magnificence and their splendor. It is through it, no doubt, that our age and our nation will surpass all times and all peoples" (12). Without the intervening paragraph, the judges of the "discourse" would not receive the rough lesson in appearance versus reality that enables the readers of the *Discourse* to appreciate Rousseau's irony and anticipate the coming reversal. Further, the readers of the *Discourse* know with certainty from the preface that Rousseau added the note in question to the published version, whatever suspicions the reader might entertain about the main text. The very presence of the note therefore raises the issue of different audiences for the *Discourse* raised in the preface. In turn, the judges listening to the "discourse" would have neither the preface nor the note about "princes" to signal either the general issue of different audiences or the political division between princes and peoples.

The education in distinguishing appearance and reality with regard to morals continues over the next few pages and culminates in Rousseau's proposition that, on the basis of appearances alone, a stranger "would guess our morals to be precisely the opposite of what they are" (14). Immediately after the political paragraph just discussed, he discusses the "civility" that once distinguished Athens and Rome "in the days of their magnificence and their splendor" and that now characterizes "our age and nation." As noted, the readers of the *Discourse* would be in a better position than the judges of the "discourse" to perceive his irony. The education of the reader of the *Discourse* continues, and perhaps commences for the auditors of the "discourse," with an explicit contrast between appearance and reality in the following paragraph: "How sweet it would be to live among us if outward appearances were always the image of the dispositions of the heart, if propriety were virtue, if our maxims served us as rules, if genuine philosophy were inseparable from the title of philosophy!" (13). The mention of propriety recalls the epigraph to the "discourse"—"We are deceived by the appearance of rectitude [*recti*]"—thus fulfilling its prophecy.[44]

The qualities Rousseau mentions are all qualities of the soul, but he illustrates his lesson with a series of bodily images that are more readily visualized. "Richness of attire" announces an opulent man, but the "healthy and robust man is recognized by other signs." Stripping him of his clothes will reveal "strength and vigor of body" not be seen beneath the "gilt" of a courtier. The strength of the body becomes a metaphor for strength of soul: "Finery is no less foreign to virtue, which is strength and vigor of soul." Finally, the "good man" likes to compete in the nude, with no appearances to hide the truth, and he is said to spurn all those ornaments that "have been invented solely to hide some deformity." The training to see through bodily appearances prepares the reader to see through the outward manifestations of the qualities of the soul exhibited by his fellows in society: "Today, when more subtle study and more refined taste have reduced the art of pleasing to a set of principles, a vile and deceitful uniformity reigns in our morals, and all minds seem to have been cast from the same mold. Incessantly civility requires, propriety demands. . . . One no longer dares to appear to be what one is; and under this perpetual constraint, the men who make up that herd called society," everyone behaves alike. The breech between appearance and reality affects our relationships. "No more sincere friendships, no more real esteem, no more well-founded confidence," for everything is hidden "behind that uniform and deceitful veil of civility, behind that much-lauded urbanity we owe to the enlightenment of our age" (13).

The reader is now prepared for the culminating evocation of an untutored stranger. "Such is the purity our morals have acquired," Rousseau begins his peroration, and then adds a final thought:

> If an inhabitant of some far-off land sought to form an idea of European morals based on the state of the sciences among us, on the perfection of our arts, on the propriety of our theater, on the civility of our manners, on the affability of our discourse, on our perpetual professions of goodwill, and on the tumultuous competition of men of all ages and of all social conditions who seem anxious to oblige one another from the dawn of morn to the setting of the sun; that this stranger, I say, would guess our morals to be precisely the opposite of what they are. (14)

The structure of this lengthy sentence itself repeats and reinforces the point of the lesson. The reader is first lulled by the drumbeat of a list of apparent goods—the perfection of the sciences and the arts, propriety, civility, affability, professions of goodwill, obligingness—only to have Rousseau resume his authorial voice: "that this stranger, I say. . . ." That is, this stranger would be duped by these appearances, just as the reader had been before Rousseau began his course of education.[45] We might think of this "stranger" as being "A Citizen of Geneva," the outsider or "barbarian" who is at once too unschooled to see through the appearances of civilization and yet in a position once his eyes are opened to pierce the veil of civility in a way those formed by civility, propriety, and custom cannot.

The Apparent and True Causal Arguments of the *Discourse*

Having trained his reader to see through appearances concerning the two terms of the Academy's question, the advancement of the sciences and the arts and the state of morals, Rousseau is ready to answer the question. His response begins: "When there is no effect, there is no cause to seek: but here the effect is certain, the depravity real, and our souls have been corrupted in proportion as our sciences and our arts have advanced toward perfection" (14). At first glance, his argument seems altogether clear: the advancement of the sciences and the arts has caused moral corruption. This is certainly how almost all readers, including his critics, have construed the argument, and we should assume that it was Rousseau's intention that they do so. Moreover, these first impressions here are consistent with the indications in the preface and exordium of which side he will take in the question. We have already had indications that there is more to his argument. Further indications of complexity will come later in the *Discourse*, notably what he says concerning the "preceptors of the human race," who have pursued enlightenment without moral corruption and who should be encouraged in their pursuits (34–35). In sum, without denying the most obvious and undoubtedly intended interpretation of Rousseau's argument, as his students in distinguishing appearance from reality we should scrutinize his apparently clear response. We shall see that the initial or apparent causal argument of the work obscures the ultimate or true causal argument, which is, in fact, the obverse of the initial argument. In terming these the "apparent" and "true" arguments, I do not mean to claim that the apparent argument is not true in some sense, but that it is subsumed within the ultimate or true argument. Broadly speaking, Rousseau presents the apparent causal argument in the first part of the *Discourse*, along with hints of its inadequacy or incompleteness, and presents the true causal argument in the second part. By incorporating two causal arguments into his *Discourse*, Rousseau poses a test of the reader's progress.[46]

First Part: The Apparent Causal Argument

Let us begin with Rousseau's statement of his argument, which he frames in causal terms and which will turn out to be more complicated than at first appears:

> When there is no effect, there is no cause to seek: but here the effect is certain, the depravity real, and our souls have been corrupted in proportion as our sciences and our arts have advanced toward perfection. Shall it be said that this is a misfortune particular to our age? No, Gentlemen: the evils caused by our vain curiosity are as old as the world. (14–15)

In his statement of the thesis Rousseau treats the two terms of the argument in terms of cause and effect. Rather than the deductive argument we might expect, however, his procedure is inductive: an effect deemed "certain" leads him to infer a cause. Further, he alleges only a proportional relationship: wherever the sciences and the arts advance, there is a proportional corruption in morals.[47] He does not allege any direct causal connection between these two phenomena. Finally, while he is explicit and emphatic in identifying the "certain" effect—moral depravity and the corruption of our souls—he is less precise in naming the cause. Is it the sciences and the arts themselves? Or their "advancement"? Or "our vain curiosity"? Although he transforms the Academy's question into a scientific investigation of a cause-and-effect relationship that "has been observed in all times and in all places," the precise relationship is unclear.

In order to illustrate his cause-and-effect argument, Rousseau employs a metaphor that upon close inspection reveals his awareness that the apparent argument he initially puts forward is misleading and insufficient, and he also hints at the ultimate or true argument.

> The daily rise and fall of the ocean's waters have not been more regularly subjected to the course of the star that gives us light during the night than has the fate of morals and integrity to the progress of the sciences and the arts. Virtue has been seen to flee in proportion as their light dawned on our horizon, and the same phenomenon has been observed in all times and all places. (15)

Previous readers of this passage have concentrated on the paradox that Rousseau's critique of the sciences is modeled upon a scientific inquiry, but they have not analyzed the metaphor itself.[48] The metaphor of the causal relationship between the moon and the tides points to a remote cause to which he alludes but which he does not name, suggesting that his argument concerning the alleged influence of the sciences and the arts on morals also depends upon a more remote cause. The moon is reasonably identified as the cause of the tides, and here Rousseau follows Newton, one of the "preceptors of the human race" praised later in the work. Yet the relationship is actually more complex, since the earth's gravity causes the revolution of the moon, which in turn causes the motion of the tides on earth. There is therefore something more like a proportional influence between the moon and the earth, analogous to the proportional relationship posited between the advancement of the sciences and the arts and moral corruption.

More important, there is a more remote cause of both the terrestrial and lunar phenomena to which Rousseau alludes in his metaphor: the sun. He seems to indicate that the moon is not the ultimate causal force of interest when he writes that the diurnal fluctuations of the ocean's waters are subject "to the course of that star [*l'Astre*] which gives us light during the night." Since *astre* can refer to any supraterrestrial body that moves and does not necessarily indicate a star, Rousseau does not necessarily misidentify the cause in this analogy; but his suggestion that the moon "gives us light" is at best an incomplete characterization of the phenomenon. He hints at the true source of light when he continues his metaphor—and mixes it—in the next sentence: "Virtue has fled as their light dawned on our horizon." The rising sun replaces the waning moon as the cause. (The metaphor is prepared in the previous paragraph, when he imagines the stranger witnessing "our" obliging behavior from "the dawn of morn to the setting of the sun.") Rousseau suggests the remote influence of the sun when he attributes nocturnal light to the moon ("that star") and when he gives the sun a place in his analogical system by mixing his metaphor. In both cases, he points to a remote cause of these phenomena: the sun. What, then, is the equivalent of the sun in his argument concerning the advancement of the sciences and the arts and moral corruption? What is the actual source of light, of enlightenment?

Rousseau has already suggested the direction to look for the cause that lies behind both the advancement of the sciences and the arts and the corruption of morals. Answering his own question about how far his claim about the relationship between moral corruption and the advancement of the sciences and the arts might be generalized, he writes that "the evils caused by our vain curiosity are as old as the world." This reformulation of his argument could simply be a restatement, with "vain curiosity" replacing moral corruption as the effect. Alternatively, he may be indicating a different argument. At any rate, this statement concerning "our vain curiosity" is Rousseau's only explicit identification in this context of the cause of the moral corruption. We nonetheless have to wait until the second part of the work for him to identify curiosity and other human passions as the cause of corruption; the remainder of the first part is taken up with inductive evidence for his thesis, in keeping with the form of the thesis itself. Let us briefly follow him through the remainder of the first part.

With his thesis established, Rousseau immediately embarks on adducing evidence for it. This evidence takes the form of "historical inductions," as he terms them at the end of the first part (21). The historical tableau he paints employs visual imagery, either explicitly or implicitly, as though to persuade his reader to *see* along with him how the advancement of the sciences and the arts is always accompanied by moral corruption. "Behold Egypt," he begins, with "Behold" translating *Voilà*, with the root sense of "to see." Egypt, the "mother of philosophy and the fine arts," soon became the object of conquest by more virtuous peoples. Then: "Behold Greece." In his next example, Rome, Rousseau switches from the past tense he used for Egypt and Greece to the present tense, as though he and his audience find themselves in the Empire among a "crowd of obscene authors" looking back nostalgically at the virtuous Republic (15–16). His use of the present tense has precedent among the Roman authors themselves, perhaps most memorably in Livy's account of Lucretia's death. In any case, in his hands this switch of tenses where the present looks back at the past prepares the coming prosopopoeia of Fabricius at the end of the first part. Returning to his catalog of corruption, after adducing the Eastern Empire, the fall of whose capital was the occasion for the revival of the sciences and the arts that he seemed to praise at the outset of the "discourse," Rousseau moves to his last example and the only contemporary one: "But why seek in remote times proofs of a truth for which we have enduring evidence *before our eyes?*" (15–16; emphasis added).

With these examples of moral corruption coming in the train of the flourishing of the sciences and the arts before the reader's eyes, Rousseau provides a parallel set of examples of peoples who, "protected from the contagion of vain knowledge," had healthier morals and were therefore able to conquer the more civilized nations. Their virtue was not fortuitous, he claims, for they were "not unaware" of the frivolous activities of their more civilized neighbors, who "lumped together other peoples under the contemptuous name of barbarians" (16–17). Recall that the "Citizen of Geneva" identifies himself on the title page as a "barbarian." At this point in the text, then, Rousseau completes the inversion of terms "civilized" and "barbarian." This inversion is underscored by a paratextual element of the published version, namely a note he adds to the previous paragraph in which he lists examples of barbarians who conquered civilized peoples in which he remarks on the "happy nations" found in the Americas. He appeals there to the authority of Montaigne and his admiration for these "savages," ending the note with a quotation from the conclusion to the essay "Of Cannibals": "'But just think!' he says, 'they don't wear breeches!'" (16–17 and n.). In this regard, it is notable that Montaigne begins "Of Cannibals" with a story illustrating our mistaken propensity to judge what is foreign as barbarian and then proceeds in the essay to invert the civilized/barbarian dichotomy, and Rousseau follows him in doing so.

Rousseau returns to his visual imagery as he completes the inductive enterprise of the first part by contrasting Sparta and Athens: "Could I forget that it was in the very bosom of Greece that a city *was seen* to arise which was as happy for its happy ignorance as for the wisdom of its laws. . . . ! O Sparta!" By contrast, Athens was distinguished by "politeness and good taste," appearances of the "civility" that the reader has already learned to depreciate and is therefore prepared to see through the "elegance" of the display Rousseau conjures: marble and canvas "seen all over," astonishing works that endure as models to admire for "every corrupted age." However, "the *picture* [*tableau*] of Lacadaemon is less brilliant," and only the memory of its virtue remains to us (17–18). Rousseau turns at this point to the example of Socrates as a wise man who escaped the general corruption of his time, and then to Fabricius, whom he calls back to life to witness the corruption of his city. I will return to these instructive examples, but first permit me to finish pursuing the thread of the causal argument of the work.

The shift from the initial or "apparent" causal argument of the *Discourse* to the ultimate or "true" argument comes with the transition from the first part to the second part, where Rousseau turns from treating the sciences and the arts as an inferred cause to considering them as an effect whose cause must be sought. He signals the inadequacy of this mode of argumentation at the end of the first part when he says that he will turn in the remainder of the essay to "consider the sciences and the arts in themselves" and thereby to discover where "our reasoning" coincides with the "historical inductions" he has thus far provided. He will accept these inductions only insofar as they agree with our "reasoning" (21). This reasoning is found in the second part of the work.

Second Part: The True Causal Argument

"It was an ancient tradition passed down from Egypt to Greece that a god who was hostile to men's tranquility was the inventor of the sciences," Rousseau begins the second part, and adds the note explaining the allegory of Prometheus pictured in the frontispiece. The phrasing with which he begins the second part—"It was . . ." (*C'étoit*)—echoes the beginning of the first part—"It is [*C'est*] a grand and beautiful spectacle . . ." (11). The reader is primed to reevaluate the opening praise of Enlightenment.

After recounting this tradition concerning the birth of the sciences, Rousseau offers a new causal argument that locates the source of corruption in the human psyche:

> Indeed, whether one leafs through the annals of the world, whether one supplements uncertain chronicles with philosophical research, human knowledge will not be found to have an origin that corresponds to the idea one would like to have of it. Astronomy was born from superstition; eloquence from ambition, hatred, flattery, lying; geometry from avarice; physics from vain curiosity; *all of them*, even moral philosophy, *from human pride*. The sciences and the arts therefore owe their birth to our vices. (23; emphasis added)

Human pride is the source of "all" human learning and also the cause of its corruption. The moral corruption that Rousseau appears to argue is caused by the advancement of the sciences and the arts is in actuality the cause of their birth, progress, and corrupting effects.

Just as Rousseau illustrates his statement of the apparent causal argument in the first part with a metaphor of the moon and tides, so too does he employ a literary device at the outset of the second part to capture his statement concerning the "sources" of the sciences and the arts: the allegory of Prometheus. I discussed this allegory when examining the frontispiece, so let us see how education in appearance and reality will affect our interpretation of this portion of the text now that we have reached it in our reading. First, the judges listening to the "discourse" get only a hint of the allegory from the opening sentence of the second part, quoted near the beginning of this section. If the judges of the "discourse" think here of Prometheus, they would perhaps infer the lesson that the gift of fire initially appears to be a benefit but turns out to harm, but the lesson is not emphatic. As for the readers of the *Discourse*, however, they have seen the frontispiece and read the note. Now the allusion to Prometheus is explicitly confirmed, and the reader learns from the note that the subject of the frontispiece is the god's warning to the satyr who wanted to embrace fire. The lesson of an apparent blessing's being in reality injurious is firmly underscored.

As we have also already seen, the myths of Prometheus and Thoth to which Rousseau refers in the note recalls Plato's *Phaedrus* and Socrates' discussion there of the problems of writing given the various characters and capacities of different readers. This issue is raised by the continuation of the passage Rousseau quotes in the note without providing a source reference, in contrast to the epigraph from Ovid on the title page. The "fable" concerning Prometheus comes from Plutarch's "How to Profit from One's Enemies."[49] As a number of interpreters have noted, the continuation of the original subverts or at least complicates the warning to the satyr that fire burns, for Prometheus goes on to reveal that the fire "gives light and warmth, and is an implement serving all the arts providing one knows how to use it well."[50] As these interpreters also argue, based in part on this note, Rousseau simultaneously addresses his *Discourse* to two audiences, which we can restate in terms of the apparent and true causal arguments of the work. He directs the apparent argument toward "the people," who are corrupted by the sciences and the arts because of the passions, above all human pride, that Rousseau reveals in the main text as the source of the sciences and the arts and that are represented in the frontispiece by the amorous satyr. The second lesson of the true causal argument is directed toward those who can pursue the science and the arts without such corruption, the "preceptors of the human race" to whom Rousseau will later turn. Without the note, the judges would have no inkling of this double readership and double lesson.

When one of his critics declared himself confused by the allegory of Prometheus, Rousseau himself deciphered the allegory:

> I would have believed I was insulting my readers and treating them like children by interpreting such a clear allegory for them—by telling them that Prometheus's torch is that of the sciences, created to inspire great geniuses; that the Satyr who, seeing fire for the first time, runs to it and wants to embrace it, represents common men, seduced by the brilliance of letters, who surrender indiscreetly to study; that Prometheus who cries out and warns them of the danger is the Citizen of Geneva. (*Letter to Lecat*, *CW*, 2:179)

We learn here that Rousseau identifies himself with Prometheus as the bearer of light, thus confirming our suspicion that the warning to the satyr found in the legend to the illustration comes from both the god and the author of the work. Interestingly, given my focus on the differences between a spoken and written work, the caution is presented in the form of a spoken warning from Prometheus and a written warning from the Citizen of Geneva.

Before continuing to pursue the true causal argument of the *Discourse* through the remainder of the second part, it would be useful to pause briefly to review the other notes Rousseau added to the *Discourse* and especially how they relate to the note concerning Prometheus.

As the three notes I have thus far examined may suggest, there is no obvious pattern to the ten notes as a whole. One hypothesis that might be entertained based on the first note I discussed, concerning how princes encourage the sciences and the arts to keep their subjects enchained, is that the notes contain material that would not have been politic to include in the submitted "discourse." Nonetheless, there is only one other note that potentially fits this mold, namely the one that cites the source for the passage in the main text as *Philosophical Thoughts* (30 and n.). This anonymous work by Diderot was published five years earlier, condemned by the Parlement of Paris, and publicly burned, so it was too controversial for Rousseau to cite openly in the "discourse." The other notes are innocuous enough.

Several notes are, however, interesting with respect to the distinction between spoken and written works signaled by the reference to Plato's *Phaedrus* in the note concerning Prometheus. The first of these is the second note, added to a paragraph near the beginning of the *Discourse* devoted to the dangers of the vices hidden beneath the "uniform and deceitful veil of civility" (13–14). In the note, Rousseau cites Montaigne's "Of the Art of Discussion": "*I like, states Montaigne, to argue and discuss, but only with a few men and for my own sake. For to serve as a spectacle for the great and vie with others by parading one's own chatter is, I find, a most unbecoming occupation for a man of honor.* This is the occupation of all our wits, save one" (14 n.). The theme of this note is speaking, implicitly as opposed to writing, and the question of audience. Montaigne wants only to confer with "a few men," whereas his *Essays* are available to any reader, which is an issue he raises at the end of the essay with the concluding discussion of his reading of Tacitus. Rousseau has also indicated in the preface that he has different readers in mind, including those who will blame his work because they are subjected to opinion and thus blinded by the "uniform and deceitful veil of civility" he describes as characterizing the times. Among the few to whom he wants to speak is the one person who is not occupied with chattering in order to serve as a spectacle to others, presumably Diderot; what Rousseau is willing to say to his friend in private is different from what he will write publicly. The second note concerned with speaking and writing is the note concerning Prometheus. The third note is attached to the passage in which Rousseau voices his concern that the invention of typography will allow "the dangerous reveries of the likes of Hobbes and Spinoza" to endure (33). In the note he predicts that European sovereigns will emulate Sultan Ahmed, who had the printing press destroyed, and he adds a further story concerning Caliph Omar's being asked what should be done with the library at Alexandria, to which the caliph replied that all books not in accord with the Koran should be burned and that all books in agreement with the Koran were redundant and should therefore also be burned (33–34 n.). The story is reminiscent of the myth of Thoth being presented with various arts, including writing. At any rate, this is the last note added to the text, and, interestingly, it circles back thematically to the very first note in which he explains why princes encourage the sciences and the arts. In sum, at least some of the paratextual material found in the notes Rousseau added to the published *Discourse* echo the concern with spoken versus written discourse that he first raises in the preface.

Let us return to the true causal argument of the *Discourse*.

After his opening statement concerning the source of the sciences and the arts in the human passions, Rousseau turns his focus to the connection of the arts with luxury: "The defectiveness of their origin is only too clearly brought back to mind for us in their objects. What would we do with the arts without the luxury that nourishes them?" (23). Rousseau associates the arts with luxury, whereas he associates the sciences with idleness (or, less pejoratively, leisure), and so the ensuing analysis of the sciences and the arts proceeds along related but somewhat separate lines.[51] Luxury is both the object of the arts and the condition for pursuing them (it "nourishes" them). The desire for luxury is born, like the sciences and the arts themselves, from corrupt human passions: "The misuse of time is a great evil. Other evils still worse accompany them. One of them is luxury, born like them from men's idleness and vanity. Luxury rarely proceeds without the sciences and the arts, and never do they proceed without it" (25). Although his phraseology of luxury and the sciences and the arts "proceeding" together is in keeping with his earlier statement of the causal argument of the work concerning the "proportional" relationship between the advancement of the sciences and the arts and moral corruption, Rousseau indicates the priority—temporal and by implication logical—of luxury in the causal chain. While luxury itself can be considered as the product of the sciences and the arts and their goal, the desire for luxury is the cause of their advancement.[52]

The focus on luxury enables Rousseau to join his causal inquiry to the education of the reader in distinguishing appearance and reality because, considered as an object of our desires, luxury is a manifestation of our desire to display our superiority, taste, and similar attributes through appearances. Immediately following the passage clarifying the causal relationship between luxury and the sciences and arts, he writes: "I know that our philosophy, ever fertile in singular maxims, claims— against the experience of every age—that luxury makes for the splendor of states" (25). Rousseau asserts that luxury and good morals or virtue are incompatible. Echoing his list in the first part of the barbarians who conquered civilized peoples, he provides similar examples for his thesis, culminating in his call to politicians (*politiques*) to reflect on these examples, "and . . . learn for once that with money one has everything, save morals and citizens" (26–27). At this point he frames his question: "What, then, precisely is at issue in this question of luxury? To know what is more important for empires: to be brilliant and transitory or virtuous and lasting. I say brilliant, but with what luster? The taste for splendor is hardly ever combined in the same souls with the taste for the honorable" (27). Rousseau's language of "splendor" and the like recalls his seeming praise of enlightenment early in the work for making men "sociable" and for the "civility" that characterized Athens and Rome "in the much-lauded days of their magnificence and splendor," which will make "our age and our nation" surpass all others (11–12). In case we are initially attracted by the appearances of splendor, he once again reveals to the reader what lies beneath: "brilliance," "luster," and "splendor" turn out to be false, frivolous, and noxious. Having torn away the veil of splendor, Rousseau does the same for the motives of artists who pander to the corrupt taste of their times, addressing his judges ("Gentlemen") and putting a question to Voltaire: "Tell us, famous Arouet, how much you have sacrificed manly and strong beauties to our false delicacy, and how much the spirit of gallantry, so fertile in petty things, has cost you great ones?" (27).

Rousseau completes the visual education concerning the arts and luxury with another image that inverts the initial precedence of splendor over simplicity: "One cannot reflect on morals without taking delight in recalling *the image* of the simplicity of the earliest times. It is a lovely shore, fashioned by the hand of nature alone, toward which one continually *turns one's eyes* and from which one reluctantly feels oneself moving away." He then traces the departure from this lovely shore with further visual imagery: "When innocent and virtuous men enjoyed having the gods as *witnesses* of their actions, they lived together in the same huts." But then they grew weary of "these inconvenient *spectators*" and relegated the gods to temples, then took up residence there themselves and built entrances that displayed their vices in stone, "when they could be *seen*, so to speak, set up on marble columns and engraved on Corinthian columns" (28; emphasis added).

The concern with luxury is engendered by corrupted passions and morals, but Rousseau is particularly concerned with the correlate of luxury and idleness: inequality. The "necessary consequence of luxury," he asserts, is "the dissolution of morals." As luxury spreads, the arts are "perfected"; taste is therefore corrupted, and virtue deteriorates (27–28). Anticipating the *Discourse on Inequality*, Rousseau completes the argument by adducing the social source of corruption: inequality: "From where do all these abuses arise, if not from the fatal inequality introduced among men by the distinction of talents and by the degradation of virtues?" The "fatal inequality" Rousseau identifies here pertains immediately to inequality of "talents," of a society where reputation and reward are accorded to the artistically talented regardless of their moral virtue: "It is no longer asked of a man whether he has integrity but whether he has talents, or of a book whether it is useful but whether it is well-written. Rewards are bestowed on the witty, and virtue remains without honors" (31). What makes this inequality so "fatal," however, is the political authority and inequality that underlie and accompany the inequality of talents. Rousseau does not develop the political dimension implied by his argument, doubtless because doing so would have been impolitic, at least in his essay submission. He does signal this dimension, however, especially in the printed version of the *Discourse*, by identifying himself as "A Citizen of Geneva" and especially with the very first note he added (and perhaps the passage to which it is attached) concerning how "Princes" promote the spread of the sciences and the arts in order to increase the chains binding their peoples. For now, however, we see that Rousseau has identified the cause—moral corruption stemming from pride and actuated by social and political inequality—that lies behind the effect—the advancement of the sciences and the arts and their corrupting effects.[53]

Rousseau turns from his causal inquiry into the relationship between the arts and luxury to an examination of the sciences. As noted above, his arguments concerning the arts and luxury, on the one hand, and the sciences and idleness, on the other, proceed along somewhat different lines, they are nonetheless related insofar as luxury and idleness relate to inequality.[54] His analysis of the advancement of the sciences also parallels his discussion of the arts because, like the arts, the sciences as he encounters them in his century have been popularized and therefore suffer from the "inequality of talents" and moral corruption.

For this reason, he always speaks of the "advancement" of the sciences and the arts. Yet he also distinguishes the taste for learning from learning itself, the sciences as a "fashionable" pursuit from the sciences in themselves. He hinted at this distinction when in the beginning of the "discourse" proper he began to reverse the appearances of enlightenment and civility: "How sweet it would be to live among us if outward appearances were always the image of the disposition of the heart . . . if genuine philosophy were inseparable from the title of philosophy!" (13). This distinction enables him to treat the sciences in themselves separately from their advancement as a social phenomenon and therefore acknowledge a legitimate form of inequality in the sciences.

As in his argument concerning the arts, when considering the sciences as a social phenomenon Rousseau focuses upon the corrupt motives and social conditions that lead to their advancement. He argues that moral corruption stems not so much from learning itself as from the importance placed on a reputation for learning. When the desire for a reputation for learning displaces true learning, the sciences become fashionable, and their pursuit is corrupting (31). In other words, he indicts the advancement of the sciences as a "fashionable" pursuit of the century of Enlightenment. In order to earn a reputation for learning, vulgar scientists prostitute their talents by popularizing the sciences and nourishing a taste for letters in the populace. He argues against the popularization of the sciences, asking what must be thought of "that throng of rudimentary authors who have removed from the temple of the Muses the difficulties that guarded access to it" and "those compilers of works who have indiscreetly broken down the door of the sciences and let into their sanctuary a populace unworthy of approaching it" (34).

His analysis of the corrupt motives and effects of the sciences as social phenomena is balanced by a separate argument about the potential benefits of the sciences when in the hands of those not infected by vanity. Only those who are worthy by virtue of their genius should pursue the sciences: "If some men must be allowed to give themselves over to the study of the sciences and the arts, it is only those who feel they have the strength to walk alone" in the footsteps of individuals such as Verulam, Descartes, and Newton "and go beyond them" (35). I will return to these exemplary geniuses and the conclusion of the *Discourse*, but having completed the analysis of the apparent and true causal arguments of the work, I want to return to the three exemplary figures Rousseau names near the end of the first part, to whom I promised to return and, as we shall see, parallel the three exemplary geniuses named at the end of the second part.

Socrates, Cato, and Fabricius

When following the apparent causal argument in the first part of the *Discourse*, I noted how Rousseau appeals to the examples of Socrates, Cato, and Fabricius to illustrate his supposed argument that civic virtue and philosophy are incompatible, but I postponed my discussion of these exemplars in order to continue to pursue the causal argument of the work. I did so in part because I believe the foregoing analysis of the apparent and true causal arguments of the *Discourse* will help us better understand the role of the figures of Socrates, Cato, and Fabricius in the education of the reader.

Recall that his appeals to the authority of the archetypes of the philosopher and the citizen come toward the end of the first part. He raises the figure of Socrates immediately after comparing the fleeting splendor of Athens to the solid virtues of Sparta with an admission: "Some wise men, it is true, resisted the general torrent and protected themselves against vice while in the abode of the Muses" (18). This is the first clear indication in the work of the coming argument that the few wise can pursue the sciences and the arts without moral corruption. Socrates is his exemplar here, and he presents Socrates' testimony in the form of a speech before the court: "But listen to the verdict that the foremost and most unfortunate among them passed on the learned men and artists of his time" (18). And appropriately so, for Socrates' speech is drawn from his defense as portrayed in Plato's *Apology of Socrates*. Yet, much like his predecessor himself, Rousseau turns the tables to put the Athenians on trial.

The passage from Plato's *Apology of Socrates* that Rousseau quotes (with some alterations, as we shall see) is the famous examination of those reputed to be wise. In Rousseau's version, Socrates examines the poets, then the artists, and then the sophists and orators. Rousseau's Socrates then summarizes what he has learned: that his interlocutors believe they know something even though they know nothing, "'whereas I, if I know nothing, am at least not in doubt about it. . . . I am ignorant of what I do not know.'" Note that Socrates in Rousseau's presentation states, "I know nothing." After finishing the lengthy quotation of Socrates' speech, Rousseau returns to his authorial voice to explain what the reader is to have learned: "Here, then, is the wisest of men in the judgment of the gods and the wisest of the Athenians according to the view of all Greece, Socrates, speaking in praise of ignorance!" (18).

What is the lesson? Within the context of the apparent causal argument claiming that everywhere the sciences and the arts are pursued virtue is corrupted, the case of Socrates appears at first glance to support the argument. Socrates prefers ignorance to knowledge, with the assumption being that ignorance is somehow consistent with virtue. Yet the reader might be disconcerted by how the Socrates who is alleged to speak in praise of ignorance is characterized both before and after the quoted speech. Rousseau introduces Socrates as the "foremost" among the "wise men" who dwelled in the abode of the Muses without catching the contagion of vice. In turn, after the speech he states that Socrates was "the wisest of men" in the judgment of the gods and the Athenians and all of Greece. In other words, Socrates is emphatically characterized as being wise. The apparent lesson to be learned from the example of Socrates about the praise of ignorance veils a different lesson concerning the relationship between wisdom and ignorance, and their relationship to virtue.

A more learned reader might at this point recall or consult the Platonic original, which will reveal how Rousseau has changed both the content of Socrates' speech and, more important, the lesson to be learned from it. As Trousson has shown, the passage comes from a translation by Rousseau's then-friend Diderot, done while Diderot was in prison at Vincennes and therefore exactly contemporaneous with Rousseau's discovery of his "system" that resulted in the *Discourse*.[55] As a number of scholars have noted, Rousseau makes several changes in the passage (both from the Platonic original and from Diderot's translation) that are significant.[56] First, rather than having Socrates examine the politicians, poets, and artisans, as in the Platonic original, Rousseau has him examine the poets and artists, as well as the sophists and orators (18). The swap of artists for artisans makes sense given that Rousseau is examining the effects of the sciences and the arts, primarily what we would call the "fine arts," which are more clearly associated with luxury and inequality. The change of sophists and orators for the original politicians has a similar effect, for sophists and orators are more associated with claims to superiority (purported wisdom and the capacity to persuade crowds), whereas in the Platonic original Socrates' questioning of the Athenian politicians, those held wisest by the *demos*, has an antidemocratic flavor. In short, these changes make the Socratic testimony more appropriate for Rousseau's immediate purposes.

More important for the reader of the *Discourse*, however, is how Rousseau changes the lesson of Socrates' speech.[57] Rousseau has Socrates summarize what he has learned from his inquiry: that his interlocutors believe they know something even though they know nothing, "'whereas I, if I know nothing, am at least not in doubt about it. . . . I am ignorant of what I do not know'" (18). In the Platonic original, in turn, Socrates summarizes the result in this way: "So I asked myself on behalf of the oracle whether I would prefer to be as I am, being in no way wise in their wisdom or ignorant in their ignorance, or I have both things that they have. I answered myself and the oracle that it profits me to be just as I am."[58] Note that Plato's Socrates does not deny that he knows *something*, whereas Rousseau's Socrates comes close to saying he is simply ignorant: "I know nothing." This change prepares Rousseau's own summary of the lesson to be learned from his quotation of this version of Socrates' defense speech: "Here, then, is the wisest of men in the judgment of the gods and the wisest of the Athenians according to the view of all Greece, Socrates, speaking in praise of ignorance!" (18). Rousseau has Socrates praise ignorance, which is a stronger claim than Socrates' testimony that ignorance is preferable to false knowledge. Rousseau too will acknowledge in the *Discourse* (and in defenses of the work) that he agrees with Socrates on this point, but for now he places Socrates in the camp of the happily ignorant.

One more aspect of Rousseau's use of Socrates is worth noting, for it is related to my focus on the difference between spoken and written discourse, which is of course also drawn from a Platonic original. As noted, Rousseau quotes Socrates's speech, and before doing so he emphasizes that it is a speech: "But listen to the verdict," he writes in the imperative, as if speaking before the judges at the Academy of Dijon. But the reader of the *Discourse* experiences his introduction to Socrates' speech as writing. In turn, after quoting Socrates' speech, Rousseau writes: "Here, then, is the wisest of men." As it did earlier in the *Discourse*, "Here" translates *Voilà*, ("to see"). Rousseau therefore evokes Socrates as though he were also speaking before the judges, or in the mind's eye of the reader. All this may seem rather subtle, but Rousseau himself draws attention to the issue of spoken and written discourse after claiming that Socrates has praised ignorance. He imagines bringing Socrates back to life "among us," and in addition to claiming he would not change his opinion about "our learned and our artists," he states that Socrates would not write books but instead leave behind "the example and memory of his virtue" (18–19). This example and memory would come in the form of speeches, as in the Platonic dialogues and as in the one Rousseau has just quoted.

Rousseau's evocation and quotation of Socrates is a form of prosopopoeia, and it is followed by the prosopopoeia of Fabricius that he later said was the germ of the *Discourse* he composed while delirious from the sudden illumination on the way to Vincennes (*Letters to Malesherbes*, *CW*, 5:575). But not so soon. In between Socrates and Fabricius is the figure of Cato. Rousseau characterizes Cato as continuing in Rome what Socrates began in Athens by loosing his fury on the Greek sophists who were corrupting his countrymen (19). But are Socrates and Cato actually engaged in the same pursuit? Insofar as they attack sophists and orators—the two categories of interlocutors Rousseau adds to Socrates' list of those he examined—they may be said to pursue the same enterprise. However, Socrates does so in the name of wisdom, whereas with Cato it is in defense of civic virtue. Even if Plato portrays Socrates as caring for the virtue of his fellow citizens, the grounds of his own virtue, nature and knowledge, are very different from those of Cato, custom and belief. Until the philosophic sects succeeded in infiltrating and corrupting Cato's fatherland, Rousseau writes, "the Romans had been content to practice virtue; all was lost when they began to study it" (19). But Socrates did study virtue. Cato would seem to be a halfway figure between Socrates the philosopher and Fabricius the citizen, for he is a citizen aware of the threat of philosophy or, more generally, the advancement of the sciences and the arts.[59]

The different grounds of virtue between Socrates and Cato are illustrated in a footnote later in the *Discourse* attached to Rousseau's lamentation concerning how the cultivation of the sciences is harmful to "moral qualities." Youth will be taught "everything, except their duties," he writes, and then asks: "What must they learn? This is certainly a fine question! Let them learn what they must do as men, and not what they ought to forget" (30). To the word *men* Rousseau refers the reader to a note that begins: "Such was the education of the Spartans." He then quotes a lengthy passage from Montaigne's "Of Pedantry" concerning the education of the ancient Persians that is itself a quotation from Xenophon's *Education of Cyrus*. In this passage Xenophon relates how the young future king was given the task of acting as a judge in a dispute between two of his classmates. A larger boy had taken a large tunic from a smaller boy and given the boy his own smaller tunic. When Cyrus judged that the exchange was just based on "suitability," he was struck in the face by his teacher for not having judged based on justice understood as (legal) ownership (30–31 n., quoting *Education of Cyrus* 3.16–17). The two bases of justice in the story might be characterized as being founded on nature (*physis*) as opposed to law (*nomos*), which is a foundational conceptual distinction in the history of political philosophy. Returning to Socrates, then, one might characterize his defense speech as given in Plato's *Apology of Socrates*, which of course Rousseau has quoted at length, as a conflict between Socrates' search for justice and virtue in the name of *physis*, on the one hand, and the Athenian *nomoi*, on the other. In this light, again, Socrates and Cato are engaged in different pursuits and defending different concepts of virtue, and Rousseau's revisions to the Platonic Socrates and his elision of Socrates and Cato obscure the difference. The footnote added to the published *Discourse* draws attention to this difference in a way that the main text does not.

To return to the three exemplars: "O Fabricius!" Rousseau interjects to begin his prosopopoeia. Unlike Cato, Fabricius lived before the introduction of philosophy in Rome, nearly a century before the Censor: "What would your great soul have thought if—to your own misfortune, called back to life—you had seen the pompous appearance of that Rome saved by your might and made more illustrious by your respectable name than by all its conquests?" Note the visual imagery of "pompous appearance," appearances beneath which Rousseau's imagined foreigner visiting Europe would be unable to see but that Rousseau's reader has learned to do. Fabricius is not deceived by appearances: "'Gods!' you would have said, 'what has become of those thatched huts and those rustic hearths where moderation and virtue once dwelled? What fatal splendor has replaced Roman simplicity? What is this strange language? What are these effeminate morals? What is the meaning of these statues, these paintings, these buildings?'" And so on. Rousseau even has Fabricius underscore his own ability to see through the appearance of "splendor" and the like by bringing forth his own witness, Cineas (a Greek emissary), who "was dazzled neither by vain pomp nor by an overly refined elegance" when speaking to the Roman Senate: "What, then, did Cineas *see* that was so majestic? O citizens! He *saw a spectacle* that neither your wealth nor all your arts will ever produce, the noblest *spectacle* that has ever appeared beneath heaven: the assembly of two hundred thousand virtuous men . . ." (19–20; emphasis added).

If Rousseau has succeeded in his educational program, the reader should be able to see with Fabricius's eyes, to see through the appearance of splendor that veils vice. The first lessons in distinguishing appearance and reality culminated early in the first part with his imagined "inhabitant of some far-off land" who, based on civility and other false appearances, would "guess our morals to be precisely the opposite of what they are" (14). The reader would be in the same position as the stranger without Rousseau's instruction. Now nearly at the end of the first part he imagines Fabricius as a stranger in his own land, a stranger with whom the reader can sympathize in a different way than before. Having raised the shade of Fabricius, Rousseau then concludes the first part by carrying his reader to the present: "But let us leap over the interval of space and time and see what has happened in our lands and *before our eyes*" (20; emphasis added). If Rousseau has succeeded, the reader is now a stranger in his own time and place: "This is how luxury, licentiousness, and slavery have in all ages been the punishment for the prideful efforts we have made to leave that happy ignorance in which eternal wisdom has placed us. The thick veil with which it has covered all its operations seemed to warn us clearly enough that it did not destine us for vain studies. . . . Peoples: know once and for all, then, that nature wanted to keep you from science" (20). The warning on the frontispiece uttered by Prometheus and written by the Citizen of Geneva is now addressed by Rousseau to "Peoples." Let us now turn in conclusion to see how he addresses a different audience at the end of the second part.

The "Preceptors of the Human Race"

The exemplary figures of Socrates, Cato, and Fabricius toward the end of the first part of the *Discourse* have their counterparts toward the end of second part: Bacon, Descartes, and Newton. Let me pick up the thread where I left my analysis of the true causal argument of the work in the second part to go back to Socrates, Cato, and Fabricius.

At the end of the paragraph following his discussion of the "fatal inequality" that is the source of the abuses he has chronicled, Rousseau alludes to the prize for which he is competing, asking whether the "glory" attained by the winner matches the virtuous action of having founded the prize in the first place. This is an interesting self-referential moment that calls attention to the original character of the *Discourse* as a "discourse" spoken before the Academy of Dijon. The succeeding paragraph begins: "The wise man does not run after fortune, but he is not insensitive to glory" (31). Unlike those scientists and artists who chase fortune and esteem, the "wise man" can legitimately be motivated by glory, true glory. Rousseau's remark on the wise man here recalls his earlier evocation of Socrates. In this way, then, he picks up the trail he began with Socrates by distinguishing between those individuals who can pursue the sciences and the arts without moral corruption and those who cannot. He does so here in terms of distributive justice, remarking that the truly wise, who are worthy of the greatest rewards, are discouraged by the fact that such rewards are given instead to those with "agreeable talents" (31–32). When he discussed Socrates earlier he drew attention to the fact that Socrates engaged in speech, speech such as that which Rousseau quotes, and not in writing. Now, turning to the issue of writing, he raises the question of different sorts of readers that he first mentioned in the preface.

The way Rousseau approaches this subject picks up on both his reference to the prize competition of the Academy of Dijon and his remark about the "wise man," which recalls Socrates. First he discusses academies, characterizing them as a partial remedy for the corrupting effects of the advancement of the sciences and the arts found within the poison itself. Such academies supposedly contain the noxious effects of enlightenment by restricting access only to the worthy, "dedicated to disseminating not only agreeable enlightenment, but also salutary teachings throughout the human race" (32). These remarks have been taken by some interpreters to be ironic. Others, whether or not they take them as ironic, have suggested that this is one of the passages Rousseau added to the published *Discourse*, because the Academy might not have approved of them.[60] When writing in defense of the *Discourse*, Rousseau insisted that his praise of academies was sincere, and that such institutions were necessary and even beneficial in times of corruption—though only in such times (see *Observations*, *CW*, 2:52–53). At any rate, how one interprets this passage depends on what kind of learning and what kind of scholars Rousseau believes these academies are promoting. If they are applauding "agreeable talents," as suggested by his statement that they disseminate "agreeable enlightenment," then Rousseau would be condemning them. On the other hand, insofar as they are actually restricting their attention to the truly "wise," then Rousseau would be approving them. Rousseau has prepared the reader to ask this question, whichever interpretation prevails. He forces this question in this context when he writes: "I will simply ask: what is philosophy? What do the writings of the best known philosophers contain?" He portrays them as charlatans hocking their wares on the public square: "'Come to me, it is I who alone do not deceive'" (32–33). Note that Rousseau emphasizes that these philosophers produce *writings*, and he underscores the fact by giving them a *speech*. Their speech is far indeed from a profession of Socratic ignorance. These philosophers are dangerous dogmatists, not the truly wise.

The issue of the dangers of writing becomes thematic when Rousseau next turns to the printing press, an issue I discussed briefly when introducing Rousseau's concern with writing indicated by his allusions to the myths of Prometheus and Thoth. Whereas the impious writings of the likes of Leucippus and Diagoras perished with them, typography will enable the "dangerous reveries" of Hobbes, Spinoza, and their ilk to last forever. "Go, famed writings of which the ignorance and rusticity of our forefathers would not have been capable," Rousseau says, apostrophizing these written works; "escort to our descendants those even more dangerous works that reek of the corruption of our own age's morals." He then imagines these unlucky descendants exclaiming, "'Almighty God . . . deliver us from the enlightenment and fatal arts of our fathers and give us back ignorance, innocence, and poverty, the sole goods that might create our happiness and which are precious in thy sight'" (33–34). Rousseau thereby recalls his prosopopoeia of Fabricius, who also began by calling on the divinities. As with Fabricius—as well as with Cato, who represents the virtuous citizen aware of the dangers of philosophy— the condemnation of the writings of the philosophers is made in the name of virtue. Returning to the present, Rousseau complains about "rudimentary authors" who have removed the salutary barriers to the temple of the Muses and those "compilers of works" who have made these writings available to "a populace unworthy of approaching them" (34). Again, his emphasis is on the dangers of *written* works.

With the central defect of written works made indiscriminately available to readers of different capacities and characters now firmly stated, Rousseau addresses his *Discourse* to two different audiences. First, he addresses those he terms the "preceptors of the human race.... Those whom nature destined to make its disciples." Second, and in conclusion, he addresses "common men" men like himself, or so he claims, "to whom heaven has not imparted such great talents and has not destined for so much glory" (34–35).

The three "preceptors of the human race" Rousseau names at the end of the second part of the *Discourse*—Bacon, Descartes, and Newton (34)—balance the three exemplary figures he named near the end of the first part—Socrates, Cato, and Fabricius. As we saw, unlike Cato and Fabricius, who are clearly examples of virtuous citizens, Socrates is a more ambiguous figure, a "wise man" who resisted the torrent of vice and who is said to "praise" ignorance. Socrates is a different kind of citizen, one who combines the life devoted to philosophy with a concern for the virtue of his compatriots. In this light, then, it is interesting that Rousseau calls Francis Bacon by his title, Baron Verulam, and draws attention to the fact that "perhaps the greatest of philosophers" served as the chancellor of England (34–35). Like Socrates, then, Bacon combines philosophical and political pursuits, if in a very different way.

When discussing the praise of Enlightenment with which the "discourse" proper begins, I noted that it seems surprising that Rousseau would begin his argument in this way, and it may seem equally surprising that he would end the work by praising the same three exemplary geniuses singled out by d'Alembert in the preliminary discourse to the *Encyclopedia*, which appeared shortly after the *Discourse* was published and contains a brief response to Rousseau's prize essay.[61] Nonetheless, the capacity for some exemplary geniuses to pursue the sciences without being morally corrupted suggests that the opening praise of Enlightenment is sincere on one level, as we have seen Rousseau himself insisted in defense of the work. By characterizing these individuals as those who "feel the strength to walk alone," Rousseau suggests that it is less their genius than their independence from popular trends and opinion that enables them to pursue the sciences without corruption. While "not insensitive to glory," they are not actuated by mere vanity to develop "agreeable talents" (31). The future author of the *Reveries of the Solitary Walker* who has entered the lists at the Academy of Dijon in part for the sake of glory must number himself among these philosophers, but one who warns both philosophers and citizens of the corrupting effects of the advancement of the sciences and the arts as a popular pursuit. As the Promethean allegory from the frontispiece intimates, the sciences themselves may bring light when properly handled, but they burn when their advancement becomes fashionable due to corrupted passions, and above all pride. The analysis of the sciences in themselves therefore leads to a different conclusion concerning the relationship between the sciences and inequality than the treatment of the sciences as a social phenomenon. Unlike the social and political inequalities associated with vanity and luxury, the natural inequalities of the mind are not in themselves corrupting—or illegitimate. In addressing such individuals, Rousseau encourages them to pursue the sciences "to raise monuments to the glory of the human mind" (35).

Rousseau concludes the *Discourse* by addressing a different audience: "As for us, common men, to whom heaven has not imparted such great talents and has not destined us for so much glory, let us remain in our obscurity" (35). The philosopher Rousseau here resumes his identity as the Citizen of Geneva concerned with virtue. In this light, he might be said to embrace and represent both the exemplars of civic virtue and of exemplary geniuses, and most especially Socrates.[62] As for "us" common men, Rousseau prescribes the pursuit of virtue: "O virtue! Sublime science of simple souls, are there so many efforts and preparations needed to know you? Are not your principles engraved in all hearts, and is it not enough to learn your laws to return into oneself and to listen to the voice of one's conscience in the silence of the passions?" (36). Recall that in the opening praise of enlightenment Rousseau concluded the paragraph by writing that "what is grander and even more difficult" than soaring with the human mind in the celestial realm is "returning into himself in order there to study man and to know his nature, his duties, and his end" (11). For the likes of Socrates, or of Bacon, Descartes, or Newton, a philosophic basis for morality is possible, but for "us" common men Rousseau suggests a similar, and surer, basis in the voice of the conscience.

Finally, Rousseau concludes the *Discourse* with a reference to Athens and Sparta and a self-referential allusion to the spoken "discourse" he has just delivered. In the first part, within his historical testimony of the conjunction between the appearance of the sciences and the arts and the moral corruption that followed, Rousseau drew a comparison between Athens and Sparta, stating that the splendor of Athens to which the uninitiated reader would be attracted is surpassed by a "less brilliant" Lacadaemon, where virtue reigned (17–18). Now, at the conclusion of the *Discourse*, he recurs to the comparison. The "common men" who pursue virtue, like the Spartans, should be kept apart from the famous men who are "immortalized in the republic of letters," like the Athenians. He concludes: "Let us try to establish that glorious distinction between them and us long ago noted between two great peoples: that the one knew how to speak well, and the other to act well" (36). Having carried the prize, Rousseau has of course spoken well as a citizen of the republic of letters and gained glory, but as the Citizen of Geneva he writes of civic virtue.

Chapter 2

Picturing Natural Man in
the *Discourse on Inequality*

The *Discourse on the Origin and the Foundations of Inequality among Men* is the writing in which Rousseau later stated he more "openly" displayed the principles of his philosophical system of the natural goodness of man (*Confessions*, *CW*, 5:326). Within the *Discourse* he claims that he has "demonstrated" in the work that "man is naturally good"—oddly enough, in a note, a point to which I will return (*Inequality*, n. IX, 127).[1] This note is attached to an important passage in the main text in which he argues that "the faculty of self-perfection," or "perfectibility," is the distinguishing attribute of human beings, with the supposed proof by observation that man alone is capable of deterioration, his unique faculty making him "in the long run the tyrant of himself and of nature" (73). More broadly and less rhetorically, Rousseau's claim is that human beings are uniquely malleable. This malleability enables Rousseau to stage comparisons between the human being before the reader's eyes, "civil man," and the being Rousseau conjures in the text for the reader to visualize, "natural man." One such comparison comes in the note in question, where he prepares his claim about having demonstrated the natural goodness of man with a contrast between "natural man" and "civil man." Whatever one might think of his supposed demonstration, I suggest that his primary method of persuading his reader of the natural goodness of man and his corruption in society is through a series of such comparisons. Rousseau must persuade his reader of the possible reality of natural man, which means educating the reader to see civil man, whom he initially sees as real, as artificial, and then to compare the beings before his eyes and the being Rousseau portrays for the mind's eye.

What is Rousseau's ultimate purpose in thus persuading the reader? In the preface to the *Discourse on Inequality* he addresses his readers:

Let my readers not imagine, then, that I dare flatter myself with having seen what appears to me so difficult to see. I have begun some lines of reasoning, I have hazarded some conjectures, less in the hope of resolving the question than with the intention of clarifying it and reducing it to its genuine state. Others will easily be able to go farther along the same path, without it being easy for anyone to reach the end. For it is no light undertaking to disentangle what is original from what is artificial in the present nature of man, and to know correctly a state which no longer exists, which perhaps never did exist, which probably never will exist, and about which it is nevertheless necessary to have correct notions in order to judge our present state properly. (52)

As we saw with the *Discourse on the Sciences and the Arts*, Rousseau employs visual imagery: he does not want his readers to think he has "seen what appears to me so difficult to see." Likewise, as in the earlier work, he instructs the reader to distinguish between appearance and reality: to disentangle what is "original" from what is "artificial" in the "present nature of man," a present condition that we initially take to be natural but that he will reveal as artificial. Doing so will enable us "to judge our present state properly." This is the overriding purpose of the *Discourse on Inequality*: to correct our judgments of our present state.

But what about his portrait of natural man in the pure state of nature? Rousseau admits his account is conjectural. Is it conjectural in the sense of a scientific hypothesis, the sort of "hypothetical and conditional reasoning" similar to the reasoning physicists employ with regard to the formation of the world, as he will later characterize his endeavor (62)? Some interpreters have argued as much, taking Rousseau's account of human origins and development as a hypothesis in principle amenable to testing by evidence.[2] Most interpreters have nonetheless viewed his account as strictly conjectural, or a kind of thought experiment. If so, why does Rousseau go to such lengths to persuade the reader of the plausibility of his portrait of natural man? My own view is that his account of natural man in the pure state of nature is a kind of limit case of human nature, a condition that almost certainly never actually existed as a matter of historical fact, but one that can, so to speak, be approached asymptotically through reasoning or meditating on the human psyche and that can be "seen" through an act of imagination.[3] To give but one reason for my view, careful scrutiny of his account of natural man in the pure state of nature reveals that perfectibility, the distinctive faculty that enables human beings to develop, is already in play in natural man. This indicates that Rousseau's portrait of the pure state of nature as a condition where perfectibility is not yet activated is a kind of fiction or, better, an ideal type.[4] The challenge to the reader of the *Discourse on Inequality* includes not only discriminating "natural man" from "civil man," but also interrogating Rousseau's portrait of natural man. Meeting both of these challenges persuades and educates the reader to "see" natural man in order to judge his present condition properly. In this light, then, I suggest that my investigation is largely compatible with any number of interpretations of the status of his account of natural man.

In this chapter I explore how Rousseau persuades and educates the reader to accept his portrait of natural man and thereby to exercise proper judgment concerning human nature and the human condition. I do so by first examining the paratextual apparatus of the *Discourse on Inequality*, including the title page and frontispiece, the dedication, the preface, the exordium, and the notes, in order to see how the structure or form of the work conditions the experience and evolving education of the reader concerning its substance, namely the doctrine of the natural goodness of man. I then analyze the first part of the work, where Rousseau presents his portrait of natural man, to see how he persuades the reader to accept his own vision of human nature. Because my focus is on his portrait of natural man, I give only passing attention to the second part of the work and the account there of human development.

The "Discourse" and the *Discourse*

Like the *Discourse on the Sciences and the Arts*, the *Discourse on Inequality* was prompted by a prize competition announced by the Academy of Dijon, in this case for its 1754 prize. The *Discourse* therefore takes the form of an academic discourse. Or at least nominally so. Rousseau later claimed that he knew that he would not be awarded the prize in this second attempt of his because the work was too bold.[5] It was also too long. Even the body of the "discourse" itself, without the extensive paratextual materials added for the published version, far exceeded the limit prescribed by the Academy for being read aloud, indeed, by about as much as threefold. The judges ceased reading the submission when they realized as much.[6]

Rousseau both adopts and flouts the traditions for an academic discourse in the *Discourse on Inequality*. Like his prizewinning essay, the "discourse" portion of the *Discourse* contains an exordium addressed to his judges in the form of a speech, and the "discourse" itself is divided into two parts.[7] Although Rousseau occasionally points to the spoken character of the "discourse" form within the work and very occasionally addresses his judges, his second *Discourse* contains only the barest indications of an embedded spoken "discourse." For example, he never addresses his judges at the outset or within the text with the form of "Gentlemen" that he used in the *Discourse on the Sciences and the Arts*. At one point he does refer to his "judges" and begs them to suspend their "reading" in order to consider a question, perhaps for another academic-prize competition, concerning whether society had to be already formed for language to originate, or vice versa (79–80). The "reading" here seems to mean reading aloud a spoken discourse. He also refers to his "judges" at the end of the first part (90), although, as we shall see, it is not clear whether he has in mind the members of the Academy of Dijon or the judges he himself indicates are qualified to assess his work. By contrast, when he moves to conclude the second part and the work as a whole, he appeals to "every attentive reader" (115), suggesting a written rather than a spoken work. In short, and in keeping with Rousseau's own testimony on the matter, it seems that he projected the *Discourse* as a published work, perhaps even from the outset.

The published version does nonetheless maintain at least the appearance of a "discourse" imbedded within the *Discourse* with an elaborate paratextual apparatus that calls attention to the differences between the academic "discourse" and the published *Discourse*. Like the *Discourse on the Sciences and the Arts*, these paratextual elements include a title page, frontispiece, preface, and notes. Rousseau explicitly separates the notes from the body of the *Discourse* by placing at the end of the work, rather than at the foot of the page as in the *Discourse on the Sciences and the Arts*. They are also far lengthier. In addition, the *Discourse* includes a Dedicatory Letter, as well as a "Notice on the Notes" and a page presenting the question by the Academy of Dijon, the latter two elements immediately before the "discourse" proper, which begins with the exordium. The different functions and audiences of the main "discourse" and the paratextual elements will once again be an important part of my analysis of the work in terms of the education of the reader.

Perhaps it would once again be useful to diagram the structure of the published *Discourse*:

Table 2.1 Structure of the *Discourse on Inequality*

Frontispiece and title page	2 pp. in the Pléiade edition
Dedicatory letter	10 pp.
Preface	6 pp.
Notice on the notes	1 p.
Question posed by the Academy of Dijon	1 p.
Exordium	3 pp.
First part	29 pp.
Second part	29 pp.
Notes	Approx. 32 pp. after resizing font

Looking at table 2.1, we can see how remarkable the structure of the work is. Out of about 120 pages of text total, just half is the "discourse" proper, with the other half being the paratextual material. Indeed, the reader of the *Discourse on Inequality* has to make his way through nearly as many pages before reaching the "discourse" proper as the reader of the *Discourse on the Sciences and the Arts* read in toto. Also notable is the fact that the first part, second part, and notes are approximately equal to one another in length. Finally, as we shall see, in the Notice on the Notes Rousseau suggests that the reader—of the published *Discourse*, that is—not read the notes along with the text, at least the first time through. The experience of the reader, just based on length alone, would be entirely different depending on whether or not the notes are read. I will attend to some of these issues as I progress.

Entering the Labyrinth of the *Discourse on Inequality*

The paratextual apparatus with which the *Discourse on Inequality* begins conditions the experience of the reader, as we saw previously with the *Discourse on the Sciences and the Arts*. Also as in his prize essay, Rousseau utilizes this apparatus to present himself as the author of the work, and to do so by adopting different roles or personae, which he achieves by addressing himself to different types of readers. Unlike the earlier *Discourse*, however, in this work he does not provide any explicit indication of the issues concerning writing and reading raised by Plato's *Phaedrus*. Nonetheless, we will see that he still has these issues in mind.

Title Page

The reader of the *Discourse on Inequality* first encounters the title page, which includes the title of the work, the author's name, an epigraph, and also a small illustration of its own. The title Rousseau gives his work is *Discourse on the Origin and the Foundations of Inequality among Men*. Unlike the *Discourse on the Sciences and the Arts*, he does not include the Academy of Dijon's question on the title page (as part of the title itself in the case of his prizewinning essay), nor is there any mention that the work was occasioned by an academic-prize competition. The reader has to wait until the end of the initial paratextual elements of the published *Discourse*, and just before the opening of the "discourse" proper, before Rousseau reveals the academy's question. In short, the title page suggests that the *Discourse on Inequality* stands on its own as a published work.

The title page announces that the work is by "Jean-Jacques Rous-

seau, Citizen of Geneva." By proclaiming his authorship, Rousseau takes
responsibility for the work, as he would for all of his major writings
after the (initially) anonymous *Discourse on the Sciences and the Arts*.
His proclamation of his authorship was unusual in a century populated
almost entirely by works published anonymously or pseudonymously.[8]
By presenting himself as the Citizen of Geneva, Rousseau adopts the
persona of a citizen and indicates his republican sentiments. As with
the *Discourse on the Sciences and the Arts*, he thereby presents himself as
something of an outsider, especially if we consider his primary audience
to be monarchical France. His self-presentation as the Citizen of Geneva
is particularly important given the subject of the work announced in
the title: inequality. The reader may well already expect that he will criticize the reigning political, social, and economic inequalities of France
and beyond.

The anticipation of Rousseau's critical stance is underscored by the
small illustration he includes on the title page. Unlike the frontispiece,
this picture (fig. 2.1) has received no attention from scholars. It portrays
a seated woman in Roman garb: Liberty. She holds a staff with a cap
atop it, which we can deduce from other elements in the illustration is a
Phrygian cap, a hat thought to be worn by manumitted slaves in ancient
Rome and therefore a symbol of emancipation. The other symbols in
the illustration are also concerned with liberty and servitude, including the broken shackles at the woman's foot, an open cage behind her
with the bird flying out, and a cat at her feet. Cats appear to have been
associated with liberty in the period, the feline being called "the enemy
of all constraint" in an allegorical dictionary of the period.[9] (At any rate,
Rousseau himself did so, as a bizarre episode with James Boswell illustrates. Asked by Rousseau whether he preferred cats or dogs, Boswell
opted for the canine. Rousseau immediately pounced on the poor Scots-
man's choice by saying that dogs are slavish creatures who will obey
their masters' commands, whereas felines choose whether or not to
obey.[10]) The illustration thus contains a series of symbols of freedom,
which again suggests to the reader something of the argument of the
work. Interestingly, Rousseau would later include a somewhat different
version of the same illustration on the title page of the *Social Contract*,
thereby connecting the two works.

Finally, the title page includes an epigraph, identified as being drawn
from book I of Aristotle's *Politics*: "What is natural has to be considered
not in beings that are corrupted, but in those that truly act in accordance
with their nature" (Non in depravitis, sed in his quae bene secundum
naturam se habent, considerandum est quid sit naturale).[11] A reader
familiar with the *Politics* would recall that Aristotle begins the work with

DISCOURS

SUR L'ORIGINE ET LES FONDEMENS
DE L'INEGALITE' PARMI LES HOMMES.

Par JEAN JAQUES ROUSSEAU

CITOYEN DE GENÈVE.

Non in depravatis , fed in his quæ bene fecundum
naturam fe habent , confiderandum eft quid fit naturale. A RISTOT. Politic. L. 2.

A AMSTERDAM,

Chez MARC MICHEL REY.

MDCCLV.

2.1 Illustration on the title page of the *Discourse on Inequality*

a general discussion of understanding the nature of beings in terms of their "end" or "completion" (*telos*). In the case of human beings, according to Aristotle they are naturally "political animals" because it is in the city (*polis*) that they attain their end (*telos*), which is the full development of their specific excellence or virtue (*aretê*) as human beings, including the exercise of speech or reason (*logos*). The reader might also recognize the specific passage Rousseau quotes concerning the need to investigate the nature of beings in their fully developed (as opposed to corrupted) form as coming from the very beginning of Aristotle's treatment of natural slavery. The natural slave is properly a slave, according to Aristotle, if he is by his own nature incapable of attaining the end of a human being, and especially the full exercise of reason. In terms of the passage Rousseau quotes, then, the natural slave is "corrupted" in relation to those who "truly act in accordance with their nature." Scholars who have discussed this epigraph have explained how Rousseau turns Aristotle on his head: first, he rejects the teleological approach of the philosopher by orienting his own investigation by the "beginnings" of human beings (the "state of nature") rather than the "ends" (the city, or civilization); second, he posits that human beings by nature are not the rational, speaking, moral, political animals Aristotle thought them to be; third, he argues that these prosocial and prerational human beings are in fact by nature "good," and not the undeveloped or "corrupted" beings Aristotle would assume.[12] This is all correct, I think, but I suggest that the first-time reader of the *Discourse on Inequality* would at best realize this only after reading the work.

What would strike this first-time reader about the epigraph? First, any reader would glean that Rousseau will investigate the subject announced in the title—the origin and foundations of inequality—by looking at what is in accordance with nature, whatever that turns out to mean. Second, if this reader recognizes the epigraph is drawn from Aristotle's discussion of natural slavery, especially given the other references and symbols on the title page concerning servitude and freedom, he would likely anticipate that Rousseau will argue against the naturalness of slavery and other inequalities. In short, to this extent the epigraph would reinforce the impressions given by the other elements included on the title page.

Let me raise one more point suggested by the epigraph that will turn out to be particularly significant for understanding Rousseau's stance as an author. Namely, although he identifies himself as a Citizen of Geneva, by his choice of epigraph he also associates himself with Aristotle, a philosopher. In short, Rousseau identifies himself with both the citizen and the philosopher. To anticipate, he will carry both of these identities through the work. For example, in the Dedicatory Letter, which comes immediately after the title page and frontispiece, he dedicates the work to his fatherland, "The Republic of Geneva," as a fellow citizen. In turn, in the preface and exordium he presents himself as a philosopher addressing his fellow philosophers with the entire human race as his audience. He adumbrates his dual citizenship, so to speak, on the title page.

Frontispiece

Across from the title page is the frontispiece Rousseau commissioned for the work (fig. 2.2). The frontispiece depicts a partially clothed man, a "savage," to judge by his garment, who is also wearing a necklace and a sword. Before him is a bundle of clothing, and the gesture of his right hand suggests that he has just thrown it down. In addition, he appears to be speaking. He stands between two groups of men. To his right (the viewer's left) is a group of European men. One man is seated and looking pensive as he considers what the savage is saying, and the others are standing behind him, looking either at the bundle of clothing or the savage himself as though listening to his explanation for having thrown it down. Behind these men are European-style fortifications. The savage man points with his left hand toward his left (the viewer's right) to a group of primitive huts along the seashore with barely visible people seated before them. Behind this group is the sea dotted with European ships. Beneath the illustration is a legend, "He goes back to his equals," and a reference below: "See Note XIII, p. 259."[13]

The frontispiece lends itself to a ready interpretation. The man stands between civilization and primitive society: he casts off the clothes that symbolize civilization, and he points toward the primitive society as if to indicate the direction he will now take, going back to his equals. In other words, it portrays a rejection of civilization and an embrace of the primitive or natural. However, the partially dressed savage man seems to be somehow between civilization and barbarism, or perhaps simultaneously civilized and barbaric. This dual identity mirrors the dual identity Rousseau himself adopts on the facing title page as a citizen and philosopher. Perhaps Rousseau wants us to identify him with this half-savage, as he does with Prometheus on the title page to the *Discourse on the Sciences and the Arts*. What if we add the information provided by the illustration's legend? It states that the savage "goes back to his equals," suggesting that he departs from the inequalities of civilization and returns to the equality of savage society (although his possession of a sword and other accoutrements or attributes of civilization

2.2 Frontispiece of the *Discourse on Inequality*

may complicate the matter of whether he is equal to those to whom he returns). In terms of the subject announced in the title, Rousseau raises the question of inequality through the legend and further suggests that the *Discourse* will somehow contain a critique of the inequalities that reign in civilized societies by an appeal to what is "natural," apparently including natural equality.

As with the *Discourse on the Sciences and the Arts*, Rousseau sends the viewer of the frontispiece to a note. He makes it easy for the reader to locate the note by including the page number where it may be found, a procedure he does not follow with his references to the notes within the text itself. As we shall see, these notes are explicitly separated from the main text by being placed after it, a decision Rousseau himself discusses in the Notice on the Notes when he states that that the notes "are not good to read with the text" (57). Apparently, the note on the frontispiece to which he refers the reader, who has not yet been so advised, is good to read with the illustration.

If the curious reader turns to note XVI, he will find a discussion of how Europeans have failed to win over the savages they have encountered to their own way of living, even with the aid of Christianity. When they do convert, they do not adopt European morals. When they are brought to Europe they view the luxuries and arts with wonder but without desire; here Rousseau tells a brief story about a North American chief who refused all the gifts with which he was presented as useless, accepting only a woolen blanket, which the chief describes as almost as good as an animal skin (an opinion of which Rousseau says he would be disabused if it were to rain).[14] Admitting that habit attaches us to what is familiar and therefore that these savages may not appreciate the supposed benefits of European goods and morals, Rousseau presents a story of an individual who was in a position to judge of both. This is the subject depicted on the frontispiece. He introduces the story as follows: "I will limit myself to citing a single well-attested example and which I offer to be examined by the admirers of European civilization." He thus specifies his audience: admirers of civilized Europe. He then quotes an account of a Hottentot on the Cape of Good Hope who was raised by the governor of the region in the European fashion and in the Christian religion. Returning to the cape after being trained in the business of the Dutch East India Company, and visiting his relatives upon his return, the Hottentot arrives at the fort dressed only in a sheepskin and carrying a bundle of his former European finery and presents himself to the governor. Having done so, Rousseau continues, "he delivered this discourse to him," and to this phrase Rousseau adds a callout to a footnote that reads: "See the frontispiece." Returning to the text of the note, Rousseau then quotes this "discourse," in which the Hottentot renounces the Christian religion and announces his intention to live in the customs of his ancestors. He asks of the governor only the favor of keeping the necklace and sword he is wearing for love of him. With that, the Hottentot runs off without waiting for a response and is never seen again (n. XVI, 148–49).

To begin, the note identifies the figures and the action portrayed in the frontispiece. The would-be "savage" at the center of the illustration is the young Hottentot raised in the European fashion, the pensive man seated to his right is the governor, and the huts and peoples toward whom he points to his left are his Hottentot relatives. The forts behind the civilized men and the ships at sea behind the primitive huts are representatives of colonialism, here the Dutch East India Company, as well as of Christianity, which we learn only from the note. Finally, the Hottentot has just thrown down the bundle of clothing and is in the midst of his "discourse" explaining his resolution to quit civilization and return to barbarism. We also learn what he has to say about retaining the necklace and sword. So far the reader is essentially confirmed in the initial impression gained from the frontispiece itself, albeit with more detail.

Let me now turn to some more interesting features of the interplay between the frontispiece and note XVI. First, Rousseau describes the speech delivered by the Hottentot to the governor as a "discourse."[15] This description recalls the title of the work. The Hottentot and Rousseau both deliver a "discourse," thus confirming the author's identification with the main subject of the frontispiece. Furthermore, the footnote added right at the point where Rousseau states that the Hottentot is about to deliver a "discourse" directs the reader back the frontispiece, and the reader would see that the Hottentot has just begun the "discourse" he is about to read in note XVI. The very beginning of Rousseau's *Discourse* with the "discourse" portrayed in the frontispiece places the reader in media res of the speech and action of the Hottentot.

Finally, and more speculatively, there is an interesting relationship between the substance of Rousseau's argument and the experience of reading these interrelated textual elements: that is, the frontispiece, note XVI, the footnote to note XVI sending the reader back to the frontispiece, and, finally, the main text of the "discourse" to which note XVI relates. Namely, it puts the reader into an endless circuit, a kind of timeless condition without progress, which is precisely the point Rousseau makes at the relevant point in the main text. First of all, if the reader slavishly followed the text, he would bounce back and forth between the note to the epigraph referring him to note XVI ("See note XVI, p. 147") and note XVI, with its footnote returning him to the frontispiece ("See the frontispiece"), without ever reading either the Hottentot's "discourse," much less Rousseau's *Discourse*. Compare this proceeding with the *Discourse on the Sciences and the Arts*, where the footnote to the text to which Rousseau sends the viewer of the frontispiece states, "This is the subject of the frontispiece" (*Sciences*, 23 n.), without initiating a cyclical reading.

This interpretation following the course of the slavish reader may seem forced. More interestingly, then, we find the same cycle if we add the passage of the main text of the *Discourse* that contains the reference to note XVI. If the reader were to locate the place in the main text he would find himself at the point where Rousseau is describing "nascent" or "savage" societies, such as the Hottentots described in note XVI, which he describes as having attained "a golden mean between the indolence of the primitive state and the petulant activity of our pride" (97). This stage of development, he states:

> must have been the happiest and most durable epoch. The more one reflects on it, the more one finds that this state was the least subject to revolutions, the best for man (XVI), and that he must have left it only by some fatal accident which for the sake of the common utility ought never to have happened. The example of savages, almost all of whom are found at this point, seems to confirm that the human race was made to remain in it forever, that this state is the veritable youth of the world, and that all subsequent progress has been in appearance so many steps toward the perfection of the individual, and in fact toward the decrepitude of the species. (97)

Substantively, one can hardly imagine a better summary of the *Discourse on Inequality* with which to begin the education of the reader who has followed this trail of internal textual references. Further, we see now that the Hottentot is indeed half-civilized and half-natural, as suggested by his clothing as displayed in the frontispiece and by the story of his education in note XVI, for the stage of development being portrayed is "a golden mean" between primitivism and civilization. As to the endless cycle of reading, if the reader has found his way here he would read this passage, then go to note XVI, then be sent back to the frontispiece, then back to note XVI, then back to the main text, and so on, round and round. In short, he would find himself permanently at the stage Rousseau identifies as "the happiest and most durable epoch" of human development, the "best for man," and one in which it seems "the human race was made to remain in it forever." In sum, the process of reading mirrors the substance of Rousseau's argument, thus educating the reader through both form and substance.

The Dedicatory Letter

On the title page Rousseau identifies himself both as a citizen and a philosopher, but in the Dedicatory Letter he restricts himself to the persona of a citizen. One lens through which the work is meant to be read, then, is the perspective of citizenship. Citizens are always citizens of a particular city or state. The "Citizen of Geneva" immediately embraces the particularity of his citizenship in addressing the Republic of Geneva: "Convinced that it is fitting only for the virtuous citizen to pay to his fatherland such tribute as it may acknowledge, for thirty years I have worked to deserve to offer you public homage." This homage is animated by his "zeal" rather than by the "right that ought to authorize me," he explains, and goes on to speak of his "good fortune" to have "been born within your walls" (41–42). In short, Rousseau's having been born a citizen of Geneva is a matter of fortune or accident, not nature. By admitting that he does not have the "right" that would authorize him to address his fellow citizens, he alludes to his loss of citizenship owing to his having run away from the city at age fifteen. In fact, when he wrote this Dedicatory Letter, he was returning to Geneva to reclaim his citizenship. He alludes to this journey when he closes the Dedicatory Letter by dating it from Chambéry (50), that is, outside of Geneva itself.[16] If the "Citizen of Geneva" of the title page of the *Discourse* presents himself as an outsider to the primary audience of monarchical France, Rousseau also positions himself as both an insider and an outsider in relation to his fatherland: he simultaneously is and is not a Citizen of Geneva.

Rousseau's position as a half-outsider among his fellow Genevans gives him a critical perspective on his native city, and to this extent he transcends the perspective of a citizen and approaches that of a philosopher. He initiates this critical gaze when he alludes at the outset to the subject of the work he is dedicating to the Republic: "Having had the good fortune to be born among you, how could I meditate on the equality nature has placed among men and on the inequality they have instituted without thinking of the profound wisdom with which both, happily combined in this state." (41). As the reader already knows from the title, the subject of the *Discourse* is inequality, and Rousseau here first remarks on natural equality and instituted inequalities.

From his perspective as a half-outsider, he states that he finds himself unable to restrain himself from "offering this picture [*tableau*]of human society to that people which, of all others, appears to me to possess its greatest advantages and to have best prevented its abuses" (42). Curiously, the picture he paints for the next several pages is not one of Geneva. The entire picture is presented in the conditional, beginning: "If I had had to choose my birthplace, I would have chosen a society of a size limited by the extent of human faculties," and continues: "I would therefore have wished," "I would not have wished," "I would have sought," "Rather, I would have chosen [a] republic where," and so on (42–45). Rousseau in fact did not get to choose his birthplace; he is a citizen of Geneva by fortune of birth (and "The Citizen of Geneva" by choice). Although Rousseau seems to encourage us to assume he is describing Geneva, where all these wished-for qualities are found, he is instead describing an idealized version of his fatherland. In fact, within this picture, Rousseau proclaims that Rome, not Geneva, is "the model for all free peoples" (43). His apparent praise of Geneva in the Dedicatory Letter contains veiled criticism of the affairs of his native city, particularly the effective usurpation of sovereign power by the elites, contrary to the (quasi-) democratic constitution of the city and also contrary to the principles of political right he will later present in the *Social Contract*, which the Genevan elites correctly took to be an attack on them. One indication of the critical thrust of the Dedicatory Letter is that whereas he addresses his fellow citizens as "MAGNIFICENT, MOST HONORED, AND SOVEREIGN LORDS," at the beginning and elsewhere (41, 45, 50), when he turns to the magistrates in particular he addresses them as "MAGNIFICENT AND MOST HONORED LORDS" (47, 48).[17] The details of his implied criticism of Geneva do not concern us here, except insofar as we see how Rousseau's posture as a half-outsider is an enactment of an educational technique he will employ throughout the *Discourse*.

Rousseau's adoption of the perspective of a half-outsider when presenting his picture of the political society he would choose if he were able to do so is underscored by another paratextual element, namely a note that he adds. In the paragraph to which the note is attached, Rousseau writes that his hypothetical society would not have anyone "inside the state" that was above the law and no one "outside of it" who could impose any laws on it. This phrasing parallels Rousseau's own status as someone both inside and outside Geneva: "For regardless of what the constitution of a government may be, if there is a single man who is not subject to the law, all the others are necessarily at his discretion" (42–43). To this sentence he adds a callout to the very first note: note I. Having viewed the frontispiece and having been referred there to note XVI, the reader already knows that the *Discourse* includes quite a number of notes following the main text. As with the frontispiece, however, the reader has not yet read Rousseau's advice in the Notice on the Notes not to read the notes with the text. If the heedless reader turns to note I, he finds a story from Herodotus. The story relates how after the death of the false Smerdis, a magis who impersonated the heir to the throne, the seven liberators of Persia met to decide what form of government to give the empire. Otanes was strongly in favor of a republic, but seeing that the others were in favor of a monarchy, he withdrew his claim to the throne and asked that he and his posterity be "free and independent." Rousseau adds that even if Herodotus had not informed us of the restriction on that grant, it would have to be assumed, for otherwise Otanes would have been "all-powerful in the state and more powerful than the king himself" (n. I, 119). He coyly does not tell us what that restriction was.

How does the story in the note relate to the text of the Dedicatory Letter? First, it is an example of what Rousseau is immediately discussing there, namely, that no one inside the state should be above the law and nobody outside of it should be able to dictate the law. Otanes has to withdraw from the state, for otherwise he would be above the law, and promise that he and his descendants will not transgress the law of Persia, because then he would be able to dictate the law from without. Second, and more interesting, is the parallel between Otanes and Rousseau. Otanes is a republican who leaves a monarchy, whereas Rousseau is a republican returning from a monarchy to Geneva, a republic. Both Otanes and Rousseau are liminal figures, simultaneously inside and outside their states.

After painting his picture of the political society he would join were he able to do so, Rousseau turns to his fellow citizens and once again alludes to the events of his "imprudent youth" that cost him his citizenship, reminding us thereby of his status as a half-outsider. In this role, then, he explains that were he to address his fellow citizens directly, he would do so with "something like the following discourse" (45). We already saw that the Hottentot pictured on the frontispiece delivers a "discourse," and so by once again using this term to describe his imagined speech to his fellow Genevans, he calls to mind the title of the work as a whole as a "discourse." How does the "discourse" in the Dedicatory Letter relate to the *Discourse on Inequality*? First, and once again, Rousseau immediately embraces the particularity of being a citizen of a certain city: "My dear fellow citizens, or rather my brothers, since the ties of blood as well as the laws unite almost all of us. . . ." Second, and also once again, having done so he calls attention to his status as a half-outsider: it gives him great pleasure to ponder the good things enjoyed by his fellows, "[of] which none of you perhaps senses the value better than I, who has lost them" (45). Third, he then turns to reflect on their current "political and civil situation," which he does for the remainder of the Dedicatory Letter, and once again he laces the seeming praise for the magistrates' conduct with criticism (45–50).

Two details of his "discourse" regarding the substance and pedagogical strategy of the Dedicatory Letter in relation to the *Discourse* as a whole will suffice. First, the issue of equality and inequality arises when he addresses the magistrates after a highly romanticized portrait of his own father, saying that artisans such as Isaac Rousseau would be derisively called "workers" and "the people" in other countries, but are recognized by the magistrates of Geneva as "your equals by education as well as by the rights of nature and of birth, your inferiors by their will" (48). Needless to say, the magistrates of Geneva, through their effective assumption of sovereign power and their behavior toward their fellow citizens, did not display such solicitude for equality, so this is a good example of the critical thrust of the Dedicatory Letter in relation to the central subject of the *Discourse*.

Second, as for his rhetorical and pedagogical tactics, in the previous chapter on the *Discourse on the Sciences and the Arts* I drew attention to one technique Rousseau uses there: the education in distinguishing between appearance and reality. Rousseau employs this technique throughout the Dedicatory Letter by first presenting his picture of the political society he would join if he could and then addressing his "discourse" to his fellow Genevans. In both cases he holds up a mirror to them that reveals the distance between appearance and reality, for example their true constitutional order as an oligarchy masquerading as a democracy. He also utilizes a specific instance of the technique at the end of the "discourse" addressed to the Genevans, perhaps in order to underscore the lesson. Summing up his hopes for his fellow citizens due to the advantages they enjoy (or could enjoy), he writes of the city:

> It will not shine with that brilliance by which most eyes are dazzled and the puerile and fatal taste which is the most mortal enemy of happiness and freedom.... Let supposed men of taste elsewhere admire the grandeur of palaces, the beauty of carriages, superb furnishings, the pomp of spectacles, and all the refinements of softness and luxury. In Geneva only men will be found; yet such a spectacle also has its value, and those who seek it out will be worth just as much as the admirers of the rest. (50)

As in his prizewinning essay, where Rousseau teaches the reader to appreciate the spectacle of the sciences and the arts and the luxury that nourishes them as false appearances, and to revalue the plain face of

virtue and citizenship, here Rousseau instructs his fellow citizens—
and the reader of the Dedicatory Letter—to see through the deceptive
brilliance "by which most eyes are dazzled." His concluding remarks
about witnessing the "spectacle" of men in Geneva calls to mind the
prosopopoeia of Fabricius in his prize essay, who recalls the "spectacle"
of the Roman citizens in assembly (*Sciences*, 19–20). Perhaps revealingly, and as indicated by his Dedicatory Letter's characterization of
the Romans—not the Genevans—as the "model for all free peoples"
(43), Rousseau terms the "spectacle" found in Geneva as one of "men,"
not of "citizens." Once again, his perspective as a half-outsider with
respect to the Republic of Geneva gives him a critical perspective that
transcends his simple persona as a citizen.

Preface

Rousseau adopts the persona of a citizen in the Dedicatory Letter, but
in the preface he presents himself as a philosopher, and there is no
mention of citizens. Among the most important rhetorical and pedagogical techniques he employs in the preface is, once again, to teach
the reader to distinguish between appearance and reality. The education of the reader begins at the very outset of the preface with his image
of the statue of Glaucus representing the human soul, which, like the
statue, is unrecognizable because of the changes it has undergone (51–
52). And he concludes the preface by casting "a calm and disinterested
eye" at human society and the foundations on which it is built (55–56).
In between these visual images is his discussion of the proper method
for investigating his subject and an exercise in conceptual clarification
with regard to natural law. The discussion of methods and concepts
serves to alter the reader's perspective from the initial visual image of
the statue of Glaucus to the concluding ocular inspection of the foundations of society.

The preface opens with Rousseau associating himself with a philosopher and speaking to the difficulty of his subject: "The most useful
and the least advanced of all human knowledge appears to me to be
that of man (II), and I dare say that the inscription on the Temple of
Delphi along contained a more important and more difficult precept
than all the hefty books of the moralists" (51). If we think of the *Discourse*
in architectural terms as a temple, like the Temple of Delphi, then the
reader finds an inscription above the entrance to Rousseau's temple.[18]
The inscription on Apollo's temple, "Know thyself," is particularly associated with Socrates. As in the *Discourse on the Sciences and the Arts*,
where he began by proclaiming his "ignorance" and where he cited

Socrates' defense speech at length, Rousseau identifies himself with the philosopher. Rousseau's announced subject is "man." He explains: "As such I consider the subject of this discourse to be one of the most interesting questions philosophy might propose, and unfortunately for us one of the thorniest philosophers might resolve" (51). Since the reader of the preface is reading a portion of the work contained only in the published version, the reference to "this discourse" seems to refer to the book itself, a written work. Rousseau has already said that the precept inscribed on the Temple of Delphi associated with Socrates is more important and more difficult than "all the hefty books of the moralists." He thereby subtly distinguishes between written works and spoken discourse, such as practiced by Socrates as he pursues the dictum to know thyself. Later in the preface, he will set aside "all scientific books that teach us only to *see* men as they have made themselves," and will instead "meditate" on the human soul (54; emphasis added). Rousseau thereby rejects the visual evidence concerning human nature ("see men as they have made themselves") purveyed by these books as false or misleading appearances and instead practices "meditation," a kind of inner eye of discursive introspection, in order to see man properly.

Returning to the beginning of the preface, the very first sentence sends the reader to a note that also points to the need for introspection to attain self-knowledge and that likewise rejects books as the source of such knowledge. Once again, the reader has not yet been warned not to read the notes with the text. The callout to the note comes midway through the sentence, after the word "man" as the subject of the human knowledge we are to seek and before his reference to the precept inscribed on the Temple of Delphi. (The callouts to the notes often come midway through sentences, an odd procedure that is perhaps worthy of note.) The note (n. II) begins with Rousseau saying that he will confidently rely on an "authority" for philosophers because "they alone"— philosophers, that is—know how to discover and appreciate the "solid and sublime reasoning" found in these sources. He then quotes a passage from Buffon that begins: "'Whatever interest we may have in knowing ourselves, I wonder whether we do not know better everything that is not ourselves.'" Buffon goes on to say that we are provided with external senses to promote our self-preservation, but we rarely make use of an "interior sense" we must use if we are to "know ourselves"—it has dried up for lack of exercise (note II, 119–20).

What are we to make of this note? For one thing, it indicates again that Rousseau is presenting himself in the Preface as a philosopher, first in the text proper and now in this note. For another, he will consult authoritative sources in his inquiry, such as Buffon's book. But let me remark on two important shifts in this consultation. First, Rousseau as a philosopher asserts his own authority to "discover and appreciate" what Buffon or any other potential source has written, whether or not the author himself appreciates it. Second, the source Buffon explains we must consult is not a book or even external evidence;[19] rather, it is the "interior sense." What this "interior sense" may be neither Buffon nor Rousseau explains, but at any rate the authoritative method of inquiry of which Rousseau apparently approves involves a form of introspection or meditation. If the reader now returns to the main text of the preface and continues to read the sentence to which the note is attached midway through, the need for self-knowledge and the difficulty of attaining it expressed in the passage from Buffon quoted by Rousseau is reaffirmed by his reference to the inscription on the Temple of Delphi. Like Buffon's (written) text, the inscription "Know Thyself" is written or engraved, but also like Buffon's text it calls for its reader to engage in introspection, or a kind of dialogue with oneself. The written work calls for a kind of spoken response, and we can assume this is Rousseau's intention in presenting the reader with his *Discourse*. Rousseau's educational program in the *Discourse* is based, in part, on the rejection of what we appear to learn from our external senses, what we see with our eyes, in favor of what we learn from introspection. The note serves as a kind of advertisement for this education.

Returning to the main text, after raising the difficulties as to how man will "ever manage to see himself as nature formed him" given the changes that time and things must have produced in his original constitution, Rousseau illustrates both the method for properly seeing the human soul and the difficulties in doing so with an image drawn from Plato's *Republic*: "Like the statue of Glaucus, which time, sea, and storms had so disfigured that it resembled less a god than a ferocious beast, the human soul, altered in the bosom of society . . . has, so to speak, changed in appearance to the point of being almost unrecognizable" (51). As Masters argues, Rousseau inverts the Platonic image. For Socrates, the metaphor of the statue of Glaucus represents the true, unified, godlike human soul hidden beneath the deformed appearance of the passions, whereas for Rousseau, beneath the alterations of time, society, and the passions we also find the true and unified soul, "a being always acting according to certain and invariable principles" (51)—but it is the soul of an animal, not of a god.[20] Once again, this is all correct, but it is also a rather sophisticated reading not available to most readers. What I would like to point out is more obvious: that both Socrates and Rousseau use the metaphor to illustrate how outward appearances are misleading, and how reality is hidden beneath these experiences.

Like Plato (and Socrates), Rousseau must teach his readers how to distinguish between appearance and reality, if for different metaphysical and epistemological reasons.[21] In this respect Rousseau once again models himself on his predecessor(s).

The image of the statue of Glaucus illustrating the difficulty in "seeing" the human soul, given all the changes that must have altered its appearance, contains a premise Rousseau does not state or defend: that human nature has undergone change. This is the first hint we have of what Rousseau, in the body of the discourse, will argue is the defining characteristic of human nature: perfectibility. The statue of Glaucus representing the soul as formed by nature before these changes occur therefore stands as an initial visual reference point, an artful image the reality of which Rousseau must persuade the reader. Curiously, the metaphor employs something artificial, a statue, to stand for something natural, the human soul.[22] A number of interpretations of this surprising turn in his trope are possible. He may be signaling that the supposedly original or natural form of the human soul beneath all the changes it has undergone is actually artificial in some sense—for example, an artifact of the imaginative meditation he employs and therefore a kind of regulative idea rather than an empirical claim. This interpretation would perhaps align with his claim that perfectibility is the defining feature of human nature, for if human nature is essentially malleable, then the image of changelessness and timelessness captured by the statue of Glaucus is at some level an imaginative construct.[23] Or Rousseau may be drawing attention to his own role as an artist constructing the image and metaphor, which, whatever its empirical status, is part of his educational program for the reader.

After remarking on the difficulty of his inquiry, especially owing to the changes he asserts have occurred in human nature, Rousseau makes his first address to the reader: "Let my readers not imagine, then, that I dare flatter myself with having *seen* what appears to me so difficult to *see*" (52; emphasis added). As I noted in the beginning of this chapter, the ensuing passage concerns the "conjectures" Rousseau explains he has made concerning what explains the differences between what is "original" and "artificial" in the "present nature of man" (52). The status of these conjectures has caused scholars to occupy themselves with trying to determine whether his account of the state of nature and then human development is strictly conjectural or hypothetical, as most presume, or has the status of a scientific hypothesis that is subject to confirmation, at least in principle, as some argue. What I once again wish to draw attention to, however, is Rousseau's use of visual imagery. His reader should not imagine he has seen what seems to him difficult to see. But his very use of visual imagery suggests that he has indeed seen something and that he is going to try to persuade his readers to accept his vision, whatever its scientific or historical status. Let us say that at least the initial role and value of the image of the statue of Glaucus is meant to motivate the inquiry into separating what is natural from what is added or artificial in the human soul, an inquiry that might not even occur to us to undertake if the image did not raise the question in the first place. In this light, the image is a propaedeutic. The image may also later turn out to reveal the truth about human nature, which has been obscured by the appearances we are taught to see and remove—but only after first undertaking the analytic exercise. Let us therefore focus on the propaedeutic strategy.

My conjecture about the initial role and status of the image of the statue of Glaucus as a pedagogical tool helps explain how Rousseau now proceeds in the preface. "This research, so difficult to carry out, and to which so little thought has been given until now," he explains, "is, however, the sole means left to us for removing a multitude of difficulties that conceal from us the knowledge of the real foundations of human society" (53). Note the language of concealment. The analytic investigation ("removing") is meant to reveal what is concealed ("the real foundations of human society"). Because we have a false understanding of human nature due to our taking appearances for reality (the present appearance of the statue of Glaucus, the present appearance of human nature), we misunderstand the core concepts of natural right and natural law required for understanding and judging "the real foundations of society." "It is this ignorance of man's nature that throws so much uncertainty and obscurity on the true definition of natural right" (53), he continues, again using visual imagery, here of obscurity. Rousseau then launches into a highly compressed critical survey of the use of the concept of natural law. The main conclusion he reaches is that human beings do not naturally have the reason needed to grasp the natural law supposedly required to found human institutions: "All that we can see very clearly on the subject of this law is that not only must the person's will it obligates be able to submit to it knowingly for it to be law, but also it must speak directly through the voice of nature for it to be natural" (54). In short, we must find another basis for understanding and judging the foundations of human society.

Rousseau is now ready to sweep aside confounding appearances and to begin anew, and he casts his inquiry once again in visual terms: "Setting aside, therefore, all scientific books that teach us only to *see* men as they have made themselves, and meditating on the first and simplest operations of the human soul, I believe I *perceive* in it two prin-

ciples preceding reason" (54; emphasis added). "Perceive" here translates *appercevoir*, which can mean "to perceive" in the sense of "to see"
or "to glimpse," but which has a connotation of intellectual "seeing," or
"intellection," especially in a philosophical context (e.g., Kant's "tran-
scendental apperception"). The process of meditation and apperception is analogous to sight, where we perceive something not visible to
the observing eye. These two principles turn out to be self-preservation
and pity, although Rousseau does not name them here. He argues not
only that these principles are prior to reason, but also that they can be
understood without recourse to "sociability," thus upending the previous natural law tradition and almost the entire philosophical tradition before him. He also argues that all of the rules of natural right
appear to him to flow from these principles (54–55). Reestablishing the
study of the foundation of human society on natural right has a number
of advantages, according to Rousseau, for doing so can "dispel those
crowds of difficulties that present themselves regarding the origin of
moral inequality, the true foundations of the body politic, the reciprocal rights of its members, and a thousand other similar questions, as
important as they are poorly elucidated" (55).

The ocular education of the reader in seeing through appearances
culminates in the concluding paragraph of the preface, where Rousseau
turns to considering the foundations of human society "with a calm and
disinterested eye." The results of the inspection are difficult to gauge,
and the ambiguities are captured by his use of the term *foundations*. Of
course, Rousseau has already used this term in the work's title. However,
the title of the work answering the question of the Academy of Dijon
differs from the question itself in a key respect. The reader has to wait
two pages after the preface to learn what the question was, but we can
anticipate. The question asked concerns, first, the origin of inequality
among men and, second, whether this inequality is "authorized by natural law" (59). Having demolished natural law in the preface, Rousseau
quite naturally excludes that portion of the question and substitutes
his own: "foundations." As if to underscore this substitution, Rousseau
repeats the title of the *Discourse* immediately following the page where
he reproduces the question asked by the Academy of Dijon, namely at
the head of the exordium. Indeed, a small detail in his repetition of
the title seems to emphasize this substitution, for this version of the
title reads: "Discourse on the Origin, and the Foundations of Inequality among Men" (61). The effect of the comma inserted here, assuming
the insertion was intentional, is disjunctive: the origin of inequality is
a separate issue from its foundations. If the concept of natural law is
freighted with moral meaning, Rousseau's substitute of *foundations*

is remarkably neutral. Are foundations meant to be grounds for claims concerning inequality or human society generally, that is, a moral basis? Or are they empirical claims about the actuality of things, regardless of, or perhaps in spite of, their morality? With this question in mind, let us return to the conclusion of the preface.

When viewed with "a calm and disinterested eye," Rousseau writes, human society "seems at first to exhibit only the violence of powerful men and the oppression of the weak," and "human establishments appear at first glance to be founded on piles of quicksand" (55). The language of vision is rife here: "at first seems," "exhibit," "appear at first glance." In short, the inequities of existing political societies are obvious. Yet Rousseau continues by seeming to overturn these first appearances: "It is only by examining them closely, it is only after having swept away the dust and sand that surround the edifice, that one perceives the unshakable base upon which it is built and one learns to respect its foundations" (55–56). Again, the language of sight: "examining," "perceives." But does Rousseau actually deny the first appearances of inequity? He does not. He does deny that human establishments are erected on quicksand, as they first appear to be, and instead claims that we perceive upon closer inspection that they are built on an "unshakable base." So far, this seems to be an empirical claim, not a judgment on whether this "base" or "foundation" is just or unjust. But Rousseau also states that we learn to "respect" these foundations. What does this entail? The etymology of the word *respect* has the visual sense of "look back at," so perhaps when we "look back at" these human establishments, we will "respect" them in the sense of "honoring" them in a qualified manner; perhaps they are better than the alternative.

Finally, Rousseau concludes the preface with a quotation possessing an explicitly pedagogical imperative:

> Learn what the god has ordained for you,
> And what is your place in human affairs.
>
> ————————
>
> [quem te deus esse
> Jussit et humana qua parte locatus es in re
> Disce.][24]

In short, the reader is admonished to learn.

Notice on the Notes

The final prefatory paratextual elements to the *Discourse on Inequality* to consider before turning to the "discourse" proper are the Notice on the Notes as well as the page that reproduces the question posed by the Academy of Dijon.

The Notice on the Notes calls attention to the fact that we are reading a written text, and it also points to the distinction between the "discourse" proper and the published version by focusing on a paratextual element added to the published version, namely the notes themselves. The Notice is curious in several respects. First, its placement is odd.[25] As we have already seen, Rousseau has already referred the reader to three notes: on the frontispiece, in the Dedicatory Letter, and in the preface. So the reader already knows that there are a number of notes following the main text before reading the Notice. Second, while notifying his reader that he has "added some notes to this work," Rousseau suggests that the reader should in fact not read them: "These notes sometimes stray far enough from the subject that they are not good to read with the text." The Notice (*Advertissement*) is therefore something of a warning (*advertissement*). For this reason, he explains, he has "relegated [the notes] to the end of this discourse, in which I have tried my best to follow the straightest path." He then tempts at least some readers by saying that those who have the "courage" to start over can amuse themselves by perusing the notes, a process that he likens to beating the bushes with a stick to flush out small birds and game: "There will be little harm in others' not reading them at all" (57). In writing this, Rousseau thereby divides his readers into two types: the "courageous" ones, who will reread the work along with the notes, and the timid or obedient ones, who will not read the notes at all. Perhaps there is a third type: readers like me, who take Rousseau to be playing the Satanic role of the tempter—that is, those who have the temerity to ignore his advice and read the notes along with the text in the first place. As mentioned earlier, the reader would have an entirely different reading experience depending on how he proceeds. If we recall the discussion of the problem of writing that is available to different types of readers in Plato's *Phaedrus* and his allusion to the work in the *Discourse on the Sciences and the Arts*, Rousseau's Notice on the Note has the effect of sorting his readers into different lots suited to their capacities and temperament.

Several details of the Notice on the Notes raise the issue of the relationship between the written *Discourse* of which it is a part and the putatively spoken "discourse" that follows it. He explains that he has added some notes to "this work," that they are not good to read with "the text," and that he has placed them at the end of "this discourse." If the notes are obviously part of the written work, the "discourse" to which Rousseau here refers would seem to be the spoken "discourse," the part of the work in which he has stated he taken "the straightest path."

The spoken "discourse" is embedded in a written "work," prefaced and succeeded by an elaborate paratextual apparatus that is characterized as being read, not heard. In any case, the Notice on the Notes and the instructions it contains for *reading* the work are manifestly part of the paratextual elements of the published *Discourse*, like the notes themselves. Later I will discuss the notes themselves and how they affect the reading experience.

Immediately following the Notice on the Notes is a page that reproduces the question proposed by the Academy of Dijon, identifying it as such: "What is the origin of inequality among men, and whether it is authorized by natural law" (59).[26] Because I have already discussed several issues related to this page, I will summarize them quickly. First, at this point the reader has not yet been informed that Rousseau is even addressing a question posed by an academy, unless he presupposes that the title itself indicates the work is an academic-prize discourse. In this sense, the placement of this page seems to draw attention to the fact that what follows, the "discourse" proper, is an answer to the Academy's question. If so, then is it possible that the prefatory paratextual elements, or even the paratextual apparatus as a whole, are somehow not addressed to the Academy's question? At any rate, the placement of this page once again draws attention to the distinction between the "discourse" and the *Discourse*. Second, the reader of the *Discourse* knows from the title and the preface that Rousseau's subject is the origin and foundations of inequality among men, but he does not know the precise question to which the author is responding until now. Third, by reproducing the Academy of Dijon's question on this page and then repeating the title of the *Discourse* (with the slight variation of the added comma) at the head of the exordium on the very next page, Rousseau invites the reader to compare the two and discover that he has eliminated any mention of natural law, substituting instead the issue of "foundations." Given his dismissal of natural law during his exercise in conceptual clarification in the preface, we should not be surprised. Let us now turn to the "discourse" proper.

The "Discourse" on Inequality: The Exordium

The essay Rousseau submitted to the Academy of Dijon is not extant, so although we can readily identify the paratextual materials he added for the printed version of the *Discourse*, including the notes, we do not know how the text of the "discourse" may differ, if at all, from what he submitted. (He did make some corrections and small additions that were incorporated in later editions, but those are readily identifiable.)

Nonetheless, one alteration is apparent. As already noted, Rousseau repeats the title of the *Discourse* (with the added comma) at the head of the exordium, but the version submitted to the Academy of Dijon would have been headed with a required epigraph to identify the author of the anonymous entry by matching it to the sealed envelope with the same quotation on the outside and the entrant's name on the inside. The epigraph to the submitted "discourse" was the one Rousseau elected to use on the title page of the published *Discourse*: *Non in depravitis, sed in his quae bene secundum naturam se habent, considerandum est quid sit naturale.*[27] Given common practice, and given how he presents the epigraph at the head of the exordium in the *Discourse on the Sciences and the Arts*, it is highly unlikely that Rousseau would have identified the source of the quotation, as he does on the title page of the published version. The epigraph to the submitted "discourse" is therefore more opaque in meaning than on the title page of the published version. More important, as noted above, whereas the placement of this epigraph on the title page along with its attribution to the "Citizen of Geneva" adumbrates Rousseau's dual citizenship as a citizen and a philosopher, the placement of the same epigraph at the head of the exordium, not to mention the absence of the dedication to the Republic of Geneva, indicates only Rousseau's philosophic persona.

As already discussed with regard to the *Discourse on the Sciences and the Arts*, an exordium is the part of a spoken or putatively spoken discourse addressed to an audience in which the speaker announces the subject and his qualifications for addressing it. In the preface to the *Discourse on Inequality*, Rousseau adopts the spoken character of a discourse and addresses his judges: "It is of man that I am to speak, and the question I am examining tells me that I am going to speak to men, for such questions are not proposed by those who are afraid to honor the truth. I will therefore confidently defend the cause of humanity before the wise men who invite me to do so, and I will not be dissatisfied with myself if I prove myself worthy of my subject and my judges" (61). The immediate judges of the "discourse" are the members of the Academy of Dijon. Without the prefatory paratextual materials found in the published version, however, these judges would not know that Rousseau has altered their question. In fact, despite his initial praise for the question the academicians proposed, in the next paragraph Rousseau calls into question their motives. Distinguishing there between "physical" (or "natural") inequality and "moral" inequality, he states that asking whether there is an essential connection between natural and moral inequalities (of status, wealth, power, etc.) would "be asking, in other terms, whether those who command are necessarily better than those who obey, and whether strength of body or of mind, wisdom or virtue, are always found in the same individuals in proportion to their power or riches—a question perhaps good for slaves to debate within earshot of their masters, but not befitting rational and free men who seek the truth" (61). In short, his judges at the Academy of Dijon have asked a potentially dishonest question. The reader of the *Discourse* will already be aware of Rousseau's concern with slavery and freedom from the illustration on the title page and perhaps also the epigraph there drawn from Aristotle's discussion of natural slavery.

An exordium is classically used by speakers to establish their qualifications; but Rousseau uses his exordium to call into question the qualifications of his judges. Nowhere here does he directly speak to his own qualifications or character, as he did in the *Discourse on the Sciences and the Arts* when he characterized himself as a "decent man" defending virtue. Yet he asserts his qualifications at the end of the exordium by dismissing the members of the tribunal and identifying more proper judges: "As my subject concerns man in general, I will try to adopt a language that suits all nations—or, rather, forgetting times and places, considering only the men to whom I speak, I will imagine myself in the Lyceum of Athens, rehearsing the lessons of my masters, with the likes of Plato and of Xenocrates as my judges, and the human race as my audience" (63).[28] Although he adopts the persona of a citizen in his Dedicatory Letter, underscoring the particularity of place and time as a Citizen of Geneva, in the preface and especially in the exordium he presents himself as a philosopher whose discourse reaches beyond all times and places, addressing the entire human race.

The other main purpose of an exordium is to define the subject of the discourse, and Rousseau does do this in his exordium, again by altering the subject proposed by the Academy of Dijon. Asked to discuss inequality, he begins by distinguishing between two sorts of inequality: "physical" inequalities of body or mind established by nature and "moral or political" inequalities established by some sort of convention. His inquiry will therefore involve understanding the relationship between the two forms of inequality:

> What, then, precisely is at issue in this discourse? To indicate in the progress of things the moment when, right replacing violence, nature was subjected to law; to explain by what chain of marvelous circumstances the strong could have resolved to serve the weak, and the people to purchase fanciful tranquility at the expense of real felicity. (61–62)

Rousseau's articulation of what is "at issue" in his discourse is highly ambiguous and unstable. This ambiguity and instability are produced in this passage by a literary technique of which the author is quite fond, namely a version of chiasmus (from the Greek *chi* [χ]), where the order of pairs of words, grammatical constructions, and so on is reversed in such a way as to disrupt expectations. The entire passage is filled with binary terms—right versus violence, nature versus law, strong versus weak, fanciful tranquility versus real felicity—which Rousseau presents in a nonparallel manner. Let me focus just on the first two pairs: "To indicate in the progress of things the moment when, *right* replacing *violence*, *nature* was subjected to *law*." We might expect *right* to parallel *law* and *nature* to parallel *violence*, but Rousseau presents them in reverse order. The first words in each pair, *right* and *nature*, seem to go together, as in "natural right," but then the second words in each pair, *violence* and *law*, seem antithetical. Does law do violence to nature and right instead of solving the violence that occurs in nature? Is law in fact based on the law of the stronger, for example, rather than a defense of the weak against this violence? Does the institution of law produce fanciful tranquility rather than real felicity? Rousseau invites the reader to reconsider his subject: How are natural and moral or political inequalities related? Are existing inequalities justified?

In the exordium Rousseau presented the image of the statue of Glaucus to represent the human soul as having undergone so many changes that it is almost no longer recognizable, thus commencing the education of the reader in distinguishing between appearance and reality. He now uses this lesson in the preface to criticize his philosophical predecessors: "The philosophers who have examined the foundations of society have all felt the necessity of going back to the state of nature, but none of them has reached it." Of course, not all philosophers have employed the concept of the "state of nature." To take a notable example, the philosopher Rousseau cites in the epigraph to the *Discourse on Inequality* did not. In saying this, then, Rousseau aligns himself with Hobbes, Locke, and other philosophers who do use the concept, and in doing so rejected Aristotle and others, while at the same time criticizing them for not going far enough. In essence, the philosophers of the state of nature have mistaken appearance for reality: "In short, all of them, speaking continually of need, greed, oppression, desires, and pride, have carried into the state of nature ideas they have taken from society: they spoke of savage man and they were depicting civil man" (62). Let me call attention to the visual element of the verb *depict* (*peindre*). Rousseau will begin the first part of the *Discourse* with his own portrait of natural man, which replaces the depiction of his predecessors. He must persuade his reader of the truth of this image.

In Rousseau's closing of the exordium, he calls attention to the fact that he is presenting a "discourse" and specifies his proper judges and audience. Having criticized Hobbes and the others for not going back "far enough," he repeats what he had said in the exordium about the hypothetical character of his depiction of the state of nature and then human development, here in relation to scriptural account of the Garden of Eden, and argues that religion does not forbid us from forming conjectures about "what the human race might have become if it had been left to its own devices." This, he claims, is "what is asked of me, and what I propose to examine in this discourse" (62–63). Given the location of this statement at the end of the exordium, by "discourse" he means primarily the spoken "discourse." As such, then, he makes its spoken character explicit. He imagines himself appearing before his true judges, the ancient (pagan) philosophers, with the human race as his audience. I have already discussed this substitution of judges and audience.

The exordium concludes with an address to the human race, beginning with an apostrophe: "O man, whatever land you may be from, whatever your opinions may be, listen: here is your history such as I have found it reads, not in the books of your fellow men, who are liars, but in nature, which never lies" (63). Rousseau's "discourse" takes the form of a speech, and he exhorts his audience to listen. He will teach his audience that their views about human nature, appearances taken from experience and books, are not true, are even lies. Instead, they will read the truth in nature. (One might have expected him to write that they will read it in "the book of nature," but he does not.) Finally, he foretells the reaction of his audience: "There is, I feel, an age at which the individual man would want to halt. You [*Tu*] will seek the age at which you would wish your species had halted" (63). In the remainder of this concluding passage, Rousseau continues to address the audience by the familiar *tu*, not the formal *vous* one would expect if he were addressing his judges at the Academy of Dijon. The teacher forms an intimate acquaintance with the pupil.

Portraying Natural Man in the Pure State of Nature

The very first paragraph of the first part presents a visual image of natural man, and one might characterize the entire first part, and especially the initial description of "physical man" over the next ten pages or so, as Rousseau's attempt to persuade the reader of the plausibility of that image. Before presenting this image, however, he begins somewhat oddly by stating what he will not argue or entertain in his account of natural man. Specifically, however important it may be to judge the natural state of man correctly, he explains, "I will not follow his physical organization through its successive developments." He will not investigate whether his nails were once claws, whether he originally walked on all fours, and so on. He will not do so, he states, because he can form "only vague and almost imaginary conjectures," given that comparative anatomy has "as yet" made too little progress in such studies and that observations by naturalists are "as yet" too uncertain (65). As Masters notes, Rousseau thereby effectively approves of the sort of investigation he will not himself undertake and opens the door for those who might pursue the subject of such changes in man's physical constitution provided they have more adequate evidence. Masters also argues that many of the notes Rousseau adds to his discussion of "physical man"—beginning with note III, attached to his remark that man may have originally walked on all fours—contain potential evidence for considering such physical changes.[29] I believe Masters is correct that Rousseau approves of such investigations if they are based on the solid evidence that he himself admits he lacks, and it may also be the case that many of Rousseau's notes do provide tentative evidence for these physical changes.

I will postpone a discussion of the notes for now. Let me instead remark that by taking man as he is presently physically constituted, Rousseau makes his initial portrait of natural man more potentially persuasive: he invites the reader to recognize natural man as a fellow human being, or even to recognize himself in natural man, in a way that would not be possible if he were a hairy, clawed quadruped hanging from a tree. Put differently, Rousseau allows the reader to recognize natural man as a fellow human being, a *semblable*, to use his terminology. The term suggests similarity—or, more precisely, the appearance of similarity. Rousseau presents us with ourselves, so to speak: "I will suppose him formed from all time as I see him today: walking on two feet, using his hands as we do ours, directing his gaze toward the whole of nature, and surveying with his eyes the vast expanse of heaven" (65).

The visual nature of Rousseau's initial portrait of natural man as something he can "see," even giving natural man the erect posture that will enable him not only supposedly to "gaze" at nature but to look us in the eye, is reinforced by another portrait in the next paragraph. Picking up on the image from the preface of the statue of Glaucus, Rousseau states that he will "strip this being" of all endowments or faculties he could have acquired in order to consider him as he comes from the hands of nature. He then presents the statue restored to its original condition: "I see an animal less strong than some, less agile than others, but, all things considered, the most advantageously physically organized of all. I see him satisfying his hunger beneath an oak, quenching his thirst at the first stream, finding his bed at the foot of the same tree that had furnished his meal, and with that his needs satisfied" (66). His task is now to persuade his reader to "see" natural man along with him.[30]

Over the next several pages, Rousseau considers what he will term "physical man" (71), namely his physical constitution as initially portrayed in the image of man sitting beneath an oak. He makes a number of arguments meant to persuade us that this solitary animal could survive. First, he argues that the earth is naturally fertile, in absolute terms but also, and more important, in relative terms, given that man's apparent lack of instinct with regard to diet would enable him to subsist on nearly anything. Second, he argues that constant physical exertion would render natural man robust. Third, he argues against Hobbes that man is not naturally aggressive. However, rather than speaking to natural man's relations with his fellow humans, and thus Hobbes's state of war of all against all, he initially confines himself to discussing his relations with other animals, arguing that natural man can survive among the animals. Fourth, he argues that childhood, old age, and illnesses are not a threat to the species. Fifth, he suggests that other physical needs, for example for clothing and shelter, are not needs for natural man. Finally, recalling his initial portrait of natural man slumbering beneath the tree that furnished his meal, Rousseau concludes his consideration of physical man by writing: "Alone, idle, and always near danger, savage man must like to sleep and be a light sleeper like the other animals, which, since they think little, so to speak sleep the entire time they are not thinking" (71). The requirements of survival render savage man an animal with keen senses when he leaves the shade of his oak.

Having summarized Rousseau's various arguments in his portrayal of physical man, let us see how he makes them persuasive beyond the conviction the arguments themselves might carry. The main technique he uses in this regard is to invite the reader to join him in imaginatively comparing the natural man he has portrayed to examples of civilized man he could actually witness.

The first instance of this technique comes after his argument concerning how natural man is rendered robust through physical exertion. In order to illustrate how the exercise of his body gives natural man "a robust and almost unalterable temperament" from childhood onward, Rousseau compares this training to a civilized example: "Nature makes use of them precisely as the law of Sparta did with the children of its citizens: it renders strong and robust those who are well constituted and causes all the others to perish" (66). Nature is a rigorous schoolmistress. Rousseau invites the reader to entertain an analogy to make the unfamiliar (natural man) imaginable by analogy to the more familiar (Spartan), but in this case the "familiar" is what is only just barely imaginable for his readers, namely the virtuous citizen made robust by the laws. In other words, if the Spartan is almost unimaginably robust, savage man by analogy must be even more so. Rousseau pushes the reader to the edge of what he can imagine. He then introduces a comparison to the human beings the reader actually has before his eyes by staging a fight with "civilized man," a mere shade of the Spartan citizen: "Give civilized man time to gather all his machines around him, and there can be no doubt that he will easily overcome savage man. But if you want to *see* an even more unequal fight, put them face to face, naked and disarmed, and you will soon *recognize* the advantage of constantly having all one's strength at one's disposal, of always being ready for any eventuality, and of always carrying oneself, so to speak, wholly with oneself" (66–67; emphasis added). By asking the reader to visualize this uneven fight, Rousseau puts the image into motion and thereby makes it seem more real and thus potentially persuasive. Indeed, we might find ourselves cheering for natural man.

Having had the reader compare savage man and civil man, Rousseau continues with the theme of comparison by addressing Hobbes's claim that man is aggressive. According to Rousseau, natural man compares himself to the animals among which he lives in order to assess the physical risk they may pose. He must "measure himself against them" (67). The reader has imaginatively measured natural man against civil man in the fight Rousseau stages, and now he can, so to speak, see through natural man's eyes to measure himself against the beasts. Rousseau then adduces examples of savages who, as voyagers have witnessed, show no fear of ferocious beasts (68), once again using examples that the reader can in principle experience, even if only through travel accounts, better to visualize the image he presents.

Through the rest of his account of "physical man" Rousseau continues to employ the technique of comparison by moving back and forth between descriptions of natural man and comparisons to civil man. For example, after claiming that the risks of childhood, old age, and illness are common to man and beast and thus pose no particular threat to natural man, Rousseau fortifies his case by arguing that it is civil man who runs these risks: "The extreme inequality in our way of life—excess of idleness among some, excess of labor among others," and so on, are "fatal proofs that most of our ills are own work, and that we would have avoided almost all of them by preserving the simple, uniform, and solitary way of life that was prescribed to us by nature" (69). Rousseau's logic here is of course terrible, for even if "our way of life" carries with it the physical and other maladies he chronicles, this hardly proves that the life "prescribed to us by nature" is healthy. Indeed, the evidence he adduces of hunters coming across animals whose wounds have healed without medical attention elicits the question of what happened to those injured animals that the hunter does not encounter. I will return to these indications that the natural condition is not as hospitable as at first appears later in this chapter. Only insofar as his portrait of natural man is persuasive does the contrast between natural man and civil man become persuasive: "Let us therefore beware of confusing [*confondre*] savage man with the men we have before our eyes" (70). If Rousseau has been successful, the reader will no longer mistake natural man for civil man, the image in his mind's eye for the ones "before our eyes."

Rousseau turns at this point in his account from considering "physical man" and asks the reader to join him in looking at this being from another perspective: "Let us try to look at him now from the metaphysical and moral side" (71). The consideration of "physical man" can be a visual inquiry, even if only through the imagination, and we have seen Rousseau employ visual devices to persuade the reader. The "metaphysical and moral side" he now asks us to "look at" is not visible in the same way. "I see in every animal only an ingenious machine to which nature has given sense to revitalize itself and protect itself, up to a certain point, from everything that tends to destroy or disturb it," he begins; "I perceive precisely the same things in the human machine, with this difference: that nature alone does everything in the operations of the beast whereas man contributes to his own operations in his capacity as a free agent" (71). What is the relationship between what he sees (*voir*) in observing the behavior of animals and what he perceives (*appercevoir*) about human beings? As noted above with regard to the passage in the preface where Rousseau states what he has "perceived" in the human soul through meditation, the verb *appercevoir* has a primarily intellectual rather than visual connotation. We can only "perceive" the "operations" of our soul through introspection. Of course, we could be wrong both about the mechanical operations of the beast and about the free operations of ourselves, and in fact Rousseau will immediately put aside his claim about freedom's being the distinguishing attribute of human nature for the "faculty of self-perfection" or "perfectibility" (71–72).

My task here is not to enter into an interpretation of what Rousseau means by "perfectibility," so let me restrict myself to suggesting how he makes his assertion plausible. The faculty of self-perfection or perfectibility is essentially the uniquely human capacity to develop, on the level of both the individual and the species. Rousseau's first proof (if that is what it is) is a comparison to animals, which are the same at the end of a thousand years as they are their first year. Unlike the beasts, he also argues, man alone is capable of retrogression: "Man alone is liable to becoming imbecile." This claim sets the stage for the main "proof," which is a claim less about natural man than about civil man:

> It would be sad for us to be forced to agree that this distinctive and al-most unlimited faculty is the source of all man's misfortunes, that it is this faculty which, by dint of time, draws him out of that original con-dition in which he would pass tranquil and innocent days, that it is this faculty which, over the centuries, by causing his enlightenment and his errors, his vices and his virtues, to bloom, makes him in the long run the tyrant of himself and of nature (IX). It would be horrible to be obliged to praise as a beneficent being the person who first suggested to the inhabitants of the banks of the Orinoco the use of those boards he binds to his children's temples, and which assure them at least a por-tion of their imbecility and of their original happiness. (72–73)

The "proof" of natural man's "original condition" before he developed is that this development has brought civil man, the "man" of today, to the point of being "the tyrant of himself and of nature." Between natu-ral man and civil man is the intermediary figure of the savage peoples living on the banks of Orinoco. As earlier he introduced his first com-parison of natural man and civil man engaged in a fight with the distant but imaginable figure of the Spartans, so now he concludes the compar-ison with the also distant but more readily imaginable figure of these savage peoples. With his framing of these examples in temporal terms ("over the centuries"), Rousseau makes the contemporary reader look backward, so to speak, from the present to the less civilized peoples and then to natural man in his "original condition." Note also his use of chiasmus in describing the effects of perfectibility: "by causing his enlightenment and his errors, his vices and his virtues." If we initially take enlightenment to be a virtue, the reversal makes us associate it instead with vice. This reversal is in keeping with Rousseau's overall reversal of the connotation of *perfection* in identifying the "faculty of self-perfection" or perfectibility as the distinctive human faculty.

In the passage just quoted, Rousseau sends the reader to a long note: note IX. It effectively expands on the main passage, including through a series of comparisons of natural man to civil man. The note begins with such a comparison:

> A famous author, calculating the goods and evils of human life and comparing the two sums, has found that the latter greatly surpassed the former and that all things considered life was a rather poor present

for man. I am not at all surprised by his conclusion; he drew his arguments from the constitution of civil man. If he had gone back to natural man, it can be concluded that he would have found very different
results, that he would have perceived that man has hardly any other
evils than those he has given himself, and that nature would have been
justified. (n. IX, 127)

As with the main passage, then, the "goods" enjoyed by natural man—
and shortly the "natural goodness" of man himself—is presumed by
subtraction of the "evils" experienced by civil man. If we view things
properly, Rousseau continues, "one cannot but be struck by" the dispro-
portion between how little all of the goods of civilization have done for
human happiness and therefore to "deplore man's blindness" (ibid.). If
Rousseau has succeeded in his educative project, in part through these
comparative images of natural man and civil man, the reader should no
longer blindly admire the apparent goods of civilization.

The rhetorical strategy of note IX continues in the same way, with
Rousseau moving between depictions of the evils experienced by civil
man and the supposed goods experienced by natural man, and he
does so by using the visual imagery of seeing through appearances.
For example, the second paragraph begins: "Men are wicked; sad and
continual experience spares the need for proof. Yet man is naturally
good—I do believe I have demonstrated it." Once again, the supposed
demonstration of the natural goodness of man, as seen in natural man,
is presumed by subtraction of the wickedness of the men we have before
our eyes. In the remainder of the paragraph Rousseau depicts the prideful and even sinister motives of civil man, demanding: "Let us therefore
see through our frivolous displays of good will to what goes on in the
depths of our hearts." The next paragraph presents a parallel depiction of savage man, who is not actuated by pride. Then the following
paragraph invites a comparison, beginning: "Compare without prejudices the condition of civil man with that of savage man" (n. IX, 127–28;
emphasis added). The remainder of note IX chronicles the evils that
come from the sciences and the arts, luxury, and the like, in a manner
strongly reminiscent of the *Discourse on the Sciences and the Arts*. Finally,
Rousseau concludes the note by asking: "What, then? Must we destroy
societies, annihilate thine and mine, and return to live in the forests
with bears?" Of course not, he answers; but the lesson to be drawn is
to see that in civil society, "more real calamities than apparent advantages always arise" (n. IX, 133). Note once again the language of appearance and reality.

To return to the main text: having illustrated his claim that perfectibility distinguishes human beings by pointing to the evils of civilized man, not surprisingly, now that we have noticed his proceeding, Rousseau returns in the next paragraph to savage man: "Savage man, left by nature to instinct alone . . . will therefore begin with purely animal functions (X)" (73). And after fewer than ten lines of text, back goes the reader to another long note.

The theme of note X might be said to be how to properly observe what is before our eyes; it is a continuation of Rousseau's visual education of the reader. He begins: "Among the men we know [or recognize—*connoissons*]—whether for our own part, or from historians, or from travelers—some are black, others white, others red," and so on. The great variety among human beings, well beyond the superficial appearances, he claims, "can surprise only those who are accustomed to look solely at the objects that surround them" (n. X, 134). Most of the note is given to accounts of primates that Rousseau conjectures may be primitive human beings. He criticizes the observations that have been made of these primates because they have been based on false assumptions about the distinction between human beings and the other animals, and he therefore points to his own argument in the main text concerning perfectibility to correct "how poorly these animals have been observed and with what prejudices they have been seen." He also admits that he himself made similar mistakes in observing monkeys, "since my ideas were not at that time turned in this direction" (n. X, 136–37). (We will see him admit similar failures of observation in *Emile*, and I will suggest that these admissions are part intended to make readers more amenable to recognizing similar failures in themselves.) Finally, toward the end of the note he calls for philosophers to travel as "observers" with "eyes made to see" (n. X, 139–41). Note X therefore continues the education of the reader in seeing properly.

Returning to the main text, Rousseau presents what is perhaps the most philosophic argument of the *Discourse on Inequality* through a compressed account of the dynamics of human psychology. "Human understanding owes much to the passions" because reason is used to satisfy the passions. The passions, in turn, derive their origin from our needs, and these needs are either natural or acquired. The psychological dynamic outlined here is the foundation for the analytic procedure in the first part of the work, where he strips down human nature to its bare essentials, as well as for the synthetic procedure in the second part, where he argues that new needs lead to new passions and thus to the development of reason and other faculties. For now, however, he restricts himself to natural man. "Savage man, deprived of every kind of enlightenment, experiences only the passions of this type," meaning those from the "simple impulsion of nature": "His desires do not exceed his physical needs (XI). The only goods he knows in the universe are food, a female, and rest; the only evils he fears are pain and hunger. I say pain and not death, for an animal will never know what it is to die, and the knowledge of death and its terrors is one of the first acquisitions man has made in moving away from the animal condition" (73).

If Rousseau has succeeded in making his portrait of natural man persuasive, the reader should be disposed to agree with the great distance between natural man in the "animal condition" and civil man, with his needs, passions, faculties, and fear of death. In the passage just quoted, he sends us to yet another note—the third on a single page (of the edition I am using). To the relief of the reader who has the temerity to turn to the note, this time it is very brief. "This appears perfectly evident to me," he begins, referring to his statement in the main text that natural man's desires do not exceed his physical needs," and continues: "And I cannot conceive from our philosophers where would have arisen all the passions they attribute to natural man" (n. XI, 141). This remark recalls his criticism in the exordium of the philosophers of the state of nature who have mistaken natural man for civil man. Given what he writes in the main text just after the callout to note XI about the fear of death not being natural, he would seem to have Hobbes in mind. Be that as it may, once again, if the reader has been persuaded by the comparisons of natural man and civil man, he should now agree with Rousseau that his claim is "perfectly evident," another ocular term.

Returning to the main text again, in the next two paragraphs Rousseau concludes this portion of his account before turning to a digression concerning the origin of language. In the first of the paragraphs, he claims that he can support the psychological dynamic he has sketched concerning the relationship between human needs, passions, and reason is correct by showing how the extent of progress of the human mind made by more or less civilized nations across time and space is proportioned to the needs they received from nature or those that circumstances have given them, and so it is a synthetic application of his theory (73). This would be the kind of evidence that a reader could in principle have before his eyes, at least through historical and ethnographic accounts. Rousseau's argument concerning human nature would then enable the reader to correctly observe and understand such evidence, much as the observers of primates in note X would be able to make proper observations. The second of these paragraphs is a description of natural man that, as we have seen elsewhere, effectively proceeds by negation and is an analytic application of the theory: What if we take away all the needs, passions, and faculties we have acquired?

His imagination portrays nothing to him; is heart asks nothing of him. . . . The spectacle of nature becomes indifferent for him by dint of becoming familiar to him. There is always the same order, there are always the same revolutions. He does not have the mind to wonder at the greatest marvels, and it is not in him that one must seek the philosophy man needs in order to know how to observe once what he has seen every day. His soul, which nothing agitates, gives itself over to the sole feeling of its present existence, without any idea of the future. . . . Such is, even today, the degree of the foresight of the Carib: in the morning he sells his bed of cotton, and in the evening he comes weeping to buy it back for not having foreseen that he would need it for the coming night. (74).

We see a familiar pattern. First, Rousseau presents his portrait of natural man after having discussed examples of civilized peoples by way of counterpoint. Second, he includes an intermediary figure, here the Carib, as he did earlier with the Spartans and the inhabitants on the banks of the Orinoco, to help bridge the gap of imagination in visualizing natural man.

The description of natural man given over the "sole feeling of his present existence" recalls the initial portraits Rousseau gave of him at the outset of the first part: first, constituted the same as we see humans "today," including "directing his gaze toward the whole of nature, and surveying with his eyes the vast expanse of heaven," and, second, sitting beneath an oak, his needs satisfied (65–66). But now we learn that natural man is no stargazer. This depiction of natural man thus circles back to the initial portrait and, if Rousseau has succeeded in persuading his reader, effectively completes it. Having done so, Rousseau launches into a digression concerning the difficulties in accounting for the origin of languages. I will return to this digression, but perhaps, given the profusion of notes we have just encountered, this is an opportune moment to discuss the notes added to the published *Discourse* and how they affect the reading experience.

Notes on the Notes

How do the notes affect the reader's experience and education? Or, rather, the different experiences of various readers, for as we learned from the Notice on the Notes, Rousseau counsels most readers not to read the notes along with the text, challenges "courageous" readers to read them when going through the work a second time, and perhaps also invites yet other readers to ignore his advice and to read the notes the first time through.

Before discussing how the notes affect the reading experience, I need to address a bibliographic matter concerning different editions of the *Discourse on Inequality*. The English and French editions I have been using are based on the version contained in the *Oeuvres complètes* of 1792, as edited by Pierre-Alexandre DuPeyrou from a copy of the work that included Rousseau's corrections and additions.[31] The notes in this edition are numbered consecutively with roman numerals, and this is how I have referred to them here. However, as first noted by Heinrich Meier, in the original 1755 edition of the work Rousseau used a different system for the notes that employed a combination of numbers and letters,[32] namely, I = (*), II = (*2), III = (*3), IV = (*a), V = 4, VI = 5, VII = (*d), VIII = 6, IX = 7, X = 8, XI = 9, XII = 10, XIII = (*b), XIV = 11, XV = 12, XVI = 13, XVII = (*c), XVIII = 14, XIX = 15. Rousseau's reasons for using this mixed system are unclear, and I will not attempt to account for it. Let me restrict myself to remarking that the original system makes the reader's task of reading the notes along with the text even more difficult than in the edition employing consecutive numerals. Apart from the reference on the frontispiece sending the reader to the specific page for note XVI (originally n. XIII), the other callouts to the notes within the text do not provide a page number, meaning that the reader must make an effort to find them, a search made more difficult if there are both numbers and letters for the notes and, indeed, still more difficult by the fact that the letters are not even in order (a, d, b, c). If the reader does persevere, Rousseau provides the page number of the main text at the head of each note, making it easier for the reader to return to the main text. In short, the original system Rousseau used for the notes seems designed to dissuade the reader from reading the notes with the text and makes the reading experience even more disruptive for those who do have the courage to read them, whether on a second reading, as Rousseau advises, or otherwise. Let me now turn to a discussion of how the reading experience is affected by the notes.

Let me begin with some perhaps obvious, but unappreciated, features of the reading experience with regard to the notes. As I detailed when discussing the structure of the *Discourse on Inequality* and its elaborate paratextual apparatus, the notes placed after the end of the text of the "discourse" are almost exactly the same length as either the first part or the second part (approximately thirty pages in the Pléiade edition). These notes are nonetheless very unevenly distributed between the two parts. Whereas the first part has thirteen notes (nn. III–XV) totaling about twenty-six pages, the second part has four notes (nn. XVI–XIX) totaling about four pages, with the majority of that text being note XVI. What is the effect of this distribution of notes?

As our encounter with three notes on a single page (nn. IX, X, and XI) might already have suggested, the overall effect of reading the notes in the first part is to interrupt and prolong the reading experience. The reader who reads the notes will spend twice as much time reading the first part as the second part. The reader is, so to speak, trapped in the pure state of nature with natural man before his eyes. And I suggest that this is exactly what Rousseau intends. The reader makes no progress, especially at the dense pack of notes IX, X, and XI, and this is precisely Rousseau's argument at this point in the text: without the aid of circumstances, natural man does not progress. By contrast, the second part takes the reader from the point where natural man exits the pure state of nature all the way to the present day in half the time, covering "multitudes of centuries in a flash" (93–94), as Rousseau characterizes his account. Indeed, if readers have already read note XVI by heeding the imperative on the frontispiece to do so, their reading experience of the second part would be virtually uninterrupted. The experience of reading each part of the work therefore corresponds to a central feature of his argument in each half and accords with the different challenges Rousseau faces in each part in persuading the reader.[33]

Let us now consider the experience of the obedient reader, the reader who follows Rousseau's advice not to read the notes. Perhaps this reader has consulted the three notes that come before the author counsels the reader not to read the notes: note XVI, to which the frontispiece refers, and which relates the story of the Hottentot returning to his equals; note I, attached to the Dedicatory Letter and telling the story of Otanes; and note II, from the beginning of the preface, which quotes Buffon about consulting the "interior sense." I submit that reading these notes does not strongly affect the reader's experience of the main text, up to this point and perhaps as a whole, one way or another. What would the reader lack, then, if he did not read the other notes we have encountered so far (nn. IV–XI), or the remainder of the notes?

Arguably the most important note this reader would skip is note IX, where Rousseau proclaims that he has demonstrated that man is naturally good. This seems like a major omission given that the natural goodness of man is the central doctrine of Rousseau's entire system. True, in the main text there is a paragraph (81) that raises the question of whether natural man can be said to be good or evil and does so in part by drawing a comparison to civil man's evils, as Rousseau does in note IX. However, the general impression of this paragraph is that natural man is neither good nor evil, and it lacks the emphatic claim found in the note about having demonstrated man's natural goodness. Note IX ends with Rousseau stating that it would be a misinterpretation of his work such as offered by his "adversaries" to think he is arguing that we should go back and live in the forest like bears (n. IX, 133), and so the obedient reader would likewise miss this warning. Insofar as the reader is persuaded by the plausibility of the account of natural man in the main text, and especially by the comparisons of natural man to civil man to the latter's detriment, then the effect of not reading this note would seem to be a fairly primitivist interpretation of the *Discourse on Inequality*.[34] Perhaps Voltaire, who wrote that Rousseau's book made him want to walk on all fours again, did not read the notes. This is certainly the experience of many of my students who choose to obey Rousseau rather than follow my instructions.

What about the other notes? As mentioned above, many of them contain discussions of the physical attributes of natural man, often with analogies drawn to other animals. For example, note IV entertains the possibility that humans were originally quadrupeds, note V suggests that humans may originally have been frugivorous, note X raises the possibility that orangutans are primitive humans, and the like. Without reading these notes, the obedient reader would be left with the initial portraits of natural man as we see him today—upright and walking on two feet or as sitting beneath an oak—unchallenged. In other words, the strategy of inviting the reader to imagine natural man at the outset as a possible *semblable* and then gradually persuading the reader of the plausibility of this image would be reinforced.

What if the reader consults these notes, either in rereading the work or from the outset? Scholars have offered various interpretations of how these notes should be read. At one end of the spectrum is Masters, who argues that many of the notes provide potential scientific evidence for the account of natural man as described in the main text. The evidence is relegated to notes, according to Masters, in part because it is not conclusive since we do not "as yet" have sufficient observations on the matter—as Rousseau states in the main text before sending the reader to note III about the possibility that humans were originally quadrupeds. For example, the suggestion in note V that humans might be naturally frugivorous ends with Rousseau opining that "if the human species was of this latter genus, it is clear that it would have had a much easier time subsisting in the state of nature and much less need and fewer occasions for leaving it" (n. V, 124). Likewise, the conjecture in note X that anthropoid animals such as orangutans may be undeveloped humans would underscore natural man's primitive animal condition. Under Masters's interpretation, then, the notes lead us to contemplate the possibility that humans are naturally even more animalistic than he assumes in the main text.[35]

At the other end of the spectrum is Velkley, who argues that the notes intentionally undermine the argument of the main text, revealing the "impossibility" of Rousseau's image of natural man. To take the same notes, Velkley points out that the evidence drawn from the configuration of human teeth in note V suggests that humans are naturally carnivorous or omnivorous, with all the issues of fights among animals for food, pack behavior, and so on, that would make the state of nature less peaceful and less solitary than Rousseau would lead us to believe. Likewise, he points out that the anthropoid animals in note X seem to exhibit foresight, knowledge of death, and other characteristics that Rousseau denies to natural man. According to Velkley's interpretation, then, the notes are among the features of Rousseau's text that should make us realize that humans were never the unchanging, simple animal he portrays for us.[36]

Although I have arrayed these two interpretations as endpoints on a spectrum, they both have in common that the result of each is to undermine the initial portraits of natural man. As for Masters's interpretation, if the notes invite us to consider possible changes in natural man's physical makeup, the effect would be to shatter the image of the initial portrait of natural man as our *semblable* and therefore make it more difficult for the reader to imagine or identify with such a being. As for Velkley's interpretation, the attentive reader of the notes will already have had this image disrupted. What is also common to these two interpretations is that they both so to speak introduce time into Rousseau's portrait of natural man. Masters's reading introduces time in the form of history—that is, changes in human nature over time—while Velkley's interpretation introduces time in the form of self-consciousness, foresight, and the like into human beings, individually and collectively. Consider in this light now the portraits of natural man Rousseau has painted for us. First: "I see him satisfying his hunger beneath an oak, quenching his thirst at the first stream, finding his bed at the foot of the bed of the same tree that had furnished his meal, and with that his needs satisfied" (66). Second: "His soul, which nothing agitates, gives itself over to the sole feeling of its present existence, without any idea of the future" (74). The second example in particular suggests a timeless condition, both in the sense of a lack of any change or progress and in the sense of a lack of consciousness of the self through time. Rousseau's account in the main text invites us to picture natural man in the pure state of nature as though he were an insect encased in amber, frozen in time. Reading the notes creates a wrinkle in time that problematizes this portrait and leads the "courageous" reader to reconsider what, precisely, Rousseau would have him learn.[37] In other words, the notes pose challenges to the reader. As I return to the main text, then, I will attend more carefully than I have thus far to the ways in which Rousseau undermines or complicates the apparent portrait of natural man.

The Aporetic Digression on the Origin of Languages

To return to the main text, after completing his initial portrait of natural man by having the reader imagine him given over to "the sole feeling of his present existence," a condition where time exists neither for the individual natural man nor for the species, Rousseau works to keep him there, so to speak, with a lengthy digression on the difficulties in understanding the origin of language. The digression comprises nearly a quarter of the length of the first part as a whole (plus a lengthy n. XII). The aporetic character of the digression is evident at the outset: "The more one meditates on this subject, the more the distance from pure sensations to the simplest knowledge increases *in our eyes*; and it is impossible to conceive how a man, by his strength alone, without the aid of communication, and without the spur of necessity, could have bridged so great an interval" (74; emphasis added). "Our eyes" are visualizing the intellectual challenge posed by our "meditation" on the subject, and this is set against the impossibility of conceiving how "a man" could bridge the gap, that is, the solitary natural man we have just visualized. And this aporetic character is explicit at the end of the digression, where Rousseau begs his judges to stop to consider the central difficulty in this inquiry, leaving to someone else to examine "this difficult problem: Which was more necessary, an already formed society for the institution of languages or already invented languages for the establishment of society?" (79–80). The overall effect of the digression, then, is to prevent the reader from being able to imagine how natural man could possibly leave the pure state of nature, and thus to lend further support to the initial image of a solitary natural man sitting alone beneath an oak.

The argument of the digression is largely philosophic in character, with Rousseau considering how general ideas could be formed, languages regulated, and so on, all in the service of emphasizing the difficulty of comprehending how language could have developed. There are two interesting passages in the digression related to my emphasis on the visual education of the reader. To begin with the second, in his discussion of the difficulties in forming general ideas, Rousseau suggests that a monkey eats a certain nut because "the sight" of it recalls the sensations he experienced from it on a previous occasion, and that this sensory experience falls short of a general idea. "Every general idea is purely intellectual," he explains; "if imagination becomes the least bit involved, the idea immediately becomes particular. Try to draw for yourself the image of a tree in general: you will never succeed in doing so. In spite of yourself, it will have to be seen as small or large, bare or leafy, light or dark" (79). What, I ask, is Rousseau doing with his portrait of natural man if not inviting the reader to imagine a particular being rather than "man in general"?

The second example of visual imagery in this digression works both to support his portrait of natural man and to undermine it. Turning to the specific question of accounting for the origin of languages, Rousseau cites his friend Condillac on the subject: "But since the way this philosopher resolves the difficulties he himself raises concerning the origin of instituted signs shows that he assumed what I question— namely, some sort of society already established among the inventors of language . . ." (75–76). To make such an assumption, he argues, "would be committing the error of those who, in reasoning about the state of nature carry into it ideas taken from society, always *see* the family" in existence (76; emphasis added). We need to distrust the testimony of our eyes and learn, along with Rousseau, to see differently. In rebuttal, he argues that sexual union in the pure state of nature did not require language or settled habitation (76). Within this context, he sends the reader to note XII, in which he quotes Locke at length on the supposed naturalness of the family. The note begins: "I find in Locke's *On Civil Government* an objection that appears to me too plausible [*spécieuse*] on its face for me to be allowed to conceal it" (141). The term *spécieuse* has a visual connotation of what appears to be true, hence Rousseau's "on its face" (and does not necessarily have the negative connotation of the English word "specious"). Locke's "objection" to Rousseau is *spécieuse* in part because it is indeed what we ordinarily witness: the family. However, Rousseau argues that Locke's reasoning is based on false observations and false assumptions about natural man. Specifically, our author claims that natural man and woman would not be able to recognize one another and would have no motive to stay with one another. Locke is thus another victim of the crime of confounding natural man and civil man: "All of that philosopher's dialectic has not saved him from the error that Hobbes and the others have committed" (145). So far, then, the portrait of natural man is supported.

If we return to the main text immediately after the callout to note XII, we see Rousseau make a startling admission: language may in fact exist in the state of nature. If natural man and woman had no need of words for the business they had to conduct, mothers and children may. He admits that languages may have developed within the primitive family of mothers and children. What he denies is that these languages would have the time and opportunity to spread beyond each family and endure, thereby transforming the natural condition (76–77). Yet even beyond the fact that this admission reveals that the pure state of nature may not be as solitary as he would have us believe, given his account within the aporetic digression on the origin of languages and the faculties of reason, imagination, foresight, and the like that speech entails, Rousseau's admission concerning primitive languages implies that there is more in his account of natural man than meets the eye. Let us therefore go back and review his portrait of natural man.

Re-viewing Rousseau's Portrait of Natural Man

At the outset of this chapter I asserted that Rousseau's portrait of natural man in the pure state of nature is a kind of limit case of human nature, a condition that, whatever its historical or scientific status, can be approached so to speak asymptotically through an act of imagination guided by meditation on the human psyche. I further asserted that careful scrutiny of his account reveals that what Rousseau argues is the distinguishing characteristic of human nature, perfectibility, is already in play in natural man. His admission that the primitive family and the languages developed therein may well have existed in the state of nature is one such example. Let me transform my assertion into an argument through a brief, though I hope suggestive, review of his account.

We can begin this review with Rousseau's own summary review of his portrait, near the end of the first part of the work.

> Let us conclude that—wandering in the forests, without industry, without speech, without domicile, without war, and without contact, without any need of his fellow humans, likewise without any desire to harm them, perhaps without ever even recognizing anyone individually— savage man, subject to few passions and self-sufficient, had only the feelings and the enlightenment suited to that state, that he felt only his true needs, looked at only what he believed it was in his interest to see, and that his intelligence made no more progress than his vanity. If by chance he made some discovery, he was all the less able to communicate it as he did not recognize even his children. Art perished with the inventor. There was neither education nor progress; the generations multiplied uselessly. And since everyone always started at the same point, the centuries passed by in all the crudeness of the first ages; the species was already old, and man remained ever a child. (88)

At first sight, this summary view has the same effect of his initial portrait of natural man sitting beneath his oak or the description of him enjoying the sole sentiment of existence without any idea of the future: to enclose natural man in a timeless, static condition. We see natural man, but natural man does not see us, He does not "recognize" anyone individually, he "looked at" only what he believed it was in his interest "to see," and he does not "recognize" even his children. Upon reconsideration, however, we glimpse a less static description. Natural man "perhaps" does not recognize anyone individually; that is, he may. Natural man may "by chance" make some discovery, may practice an art. Perfectibility is thus present from the creation, despite Rousseau's apparent claims to the contrary.

If we now return to his portrait of natural man in the pure state of nature, we see similar wrinkles in the placid surface. The natural fertility of the earth exists, from natural man's perspective, in large measure because he is able to "observe and imitate" other animals, perhaps lacking any instinct of his own and instead "appropriating" those of other animals (66). Perhaps this activity can be accomplished mechanically, but it seems at minimum to foreshadow the operation of perfectibility. In this light, recall that Rousseau begins his discussion of natural man from the "metaphysical and moral side" with the example of pigeons and cats being restricted by instinct to eating one kind of food, in contrast to man, the omnivore, without instinct and without moderation (71). Other caveats concerning natural man and his natural state are buried in the details of Rousseau's account. For example, natural man is made physically vigorous by the necessities of nature, which renders strong and robust those who survive and kills the rest (66). In other words, nature is not so kind or so plentiful for those who do not learn to appropriate the instincts of other beasts. Natural man "compares his strength with the danger he runs" and has the "choice" of fight or flight, and Rousseau states as much by contrasting natural man with other animals (67). Natural man will "appropriate" the skins of beasts they overcome in cold climates (70). Perhaps most notably, as we have seen, Rousseau admits that languages may evolve in the pure state of nature in the nascent family of mother and child (76). Other examples could be cited. In short, the natural condition is not as peaceful and providential as Rousseau would have us believe, and natural man is not as stationary and simple as the image of the statue of Glaucus at the outset of the preface would suggest.[38]

As we might expect from his procedure throughout the work, Rousseau immediately turns from his concluding summary review of natural man ("Let us conclude that—wandering in the forests . . ."),to a comparison with civil man: "If I have elaborated at such length on the assumption of this primitive condition, it is because, having ancient errors and inveterate prejudices to destroy, I believed I had to dig down to the root and show in the portrayal of the genuine state of nature how far inequality—even natural inequality—is from having as much reality and influence in that state as our writers claim" (88). The reader of Rousseau's "portrayal of the genuine state of nature" will have learned to challenge what "our writers" believe to be "reality." They are thus prepared to see through the appearances regarding civil man. "Indeed, it is easy to *see* that among the differences that distinguish men, some pass for being natural that are exclusively the work of habit and the various ways of life men adopt in society," he explains. And if we compare the diversity of ways of life in the "civil state" with "the simplicity and uniformity of animal and savage life," then "it will be understood how much less the difference from man to man must be in the state of nature than in that of society, and how much natural inequality in the human species must increase through instituted inequality" (88; emphasis added).

And once again we should not be surprised to see Rousseau turn from this comparison of natural man and civil man back to natural man. Even if natural inequalities exist among humans in the state of nature, what advantage could be derived from them "in a state of things which allowed for *almost* no kind of relationship among them?" (89; emphasis added). Another hedge: "almost" no kind of relationship. The keen-sighted reader will see that there is more to natural man than first meets the eye, but the reader will also see through the appearances of civil man. Finally, then, making a transition to the second part of the work, Rousseau explains that it remains for him "to consider and to bring together the different chance events that were able to perfect human reason while causing the species to deteriorate, to make a being evil while making him sociable, and eventually to bring man and the world from so distant a beginning to the point where we now *see* them" (90; emphasis added). Rousseau's reader is prepared to see "man and the world" with new eyes.

The Eyes of the Wise Man

I have focused in this chapter on Rousseau's portrait of natural man in the first part of the *Discourse on Inequality* and the paratextual elements of the work. Many of the same techniques Rousseau uses to educate the reader with this portrait can be seen in the second part of the work in his account of human development, bringing "man and the world" from the pure state of nature to the present. I will not here undertake such an analysis, so a few examples will suffice in order to bring us to the conclusion of the work and Rousseau's statement about what the "attentive reader" will have learned from it.

As natural man begins to develop due to challenges posed by his environment—supposedly new challenges, but we might wonder whether they weren't there from the beginning—he begins to note differences in the beings surrounding him. These "perceptions" produce a "reflection of a sort" in natural man, and he comes to realize his superiority over the animals: "This is how the first glance he directed upon himself produced in him the first movement of pride" (92). The prolific use of visual language here invites us to see along with this developing being. With the advent of established families, he writes, "everything begins to change appearances" (95). The use of the present tense instead of the past tense here shifts the tableau from the static portrait of natural man to a kind of motion picture in which the reader is invited to view the changing appearances of men and women: "Each began to look at the others and to want to be looked at himself" (96). The reader now reaches the stage of the "golden mean between the indolence of the primitive state and the petulant activity of our pride," or what "must have been the happiest and most durable epoch" (97)—the stage of human development depicted in the frontispiece. And then begins the decline. Rousseau will not pause to describe the many developments that occur after the invention of property—vividly depicted at the outset of the second part with the first person who enclosed a plot of land and declared, "*This is mine*" (91)—for, he says, "it is easy to imagine the rest" (100). Instead, as in the first part, with his summary portrait ("Let us conclude that . . ."), he pauses to offer a description of mankind at this stage:

> Here, then, are all our faculties developed, memory and imagination in play, pride [*amour-propre*] involved, reason activated, and the mind having almost reached the extent of the perfection of which it is susceptible. Here are all the natural qualities set in action, the rank and fate of each man based not only on the quantity of goods and the power to help or to harm, but on the mind, beauty, strength, or skill, on merit or talents. (100)

"Here" (*Voilà*): Rousseau asks the reader to behold, to imagine along with him.

At the very end of the second part, Rousseau summarizes what the "attentive reader" should have learned from his work, and he frames the lesson in terms of a comparison of the "natural state" and the "civil state," such we have seen him do innumerable times in the course of persuading the reader:

> In thereby discovering and following the forgotten and lost routes that
> must have led man from the natural state to the civil state, in reestab-
> lishing, along with the intermediate positions I have just indicated,
> those which the pressure of time has caused me to omit or which imag-
> ination has not suggested to me, every attentive reader will not fail to
> be struck by the immense distance that separates these two states. (115)

The distance separating these two states leads the reader to sense that
"the human race of one age is not the human race of another age." This
statement captures Rousseau's argument that the distinctive characteristic of human nature is "perfectibility," or the capacity for change
on the level of the individual and the species. When he introduced this
unique faculty, we saw him do so through a comparison of civil man
and natural man. And as with a number of other instances of drawing
this comparison, he added a third figure, the Carib, that stands between
what the reader has before his eyes, civil man, and the being Rousseau
would have him imagine as even more primitive than the Carib, natural man. He does the same thing for the "attentive reader" on this occasion with two intermediary figures: "The reason Diogenes did not find
a man is that he was looking among his contemporaries for the man of
a time that no longer was," and likewise, Cato was a man out of his time
with the fall of the Roman Republic (115–16). The pairing of Diogenes
the philosopher and Cato the citizen echoes Rousseau's dual authorial
roles as a philosopher and the Citizen of Geneva. In terms of persuading his reader of the plausibility of his portrait of natural man, if he has
succeeded then his reader will accept that the human race of one age,
the reader's own age for example, is not the human race of another age,
for instance natural man. The reader will be able to imaginatively see
natural man as a possibility of human nature.

If Rousseau has succeeded, his reader will see with different eyes or
will adopt a new perspective, one that differs from what he had at the
outset of the work:

> In a word, he will explain how the soul and human passions, altering
> imperceptibly, so to speak change their nature; why our needs and our
> pleasures change objects in the long run; why, with original man grad-
> ually vanishing, society no longer offers to the eyes of the wise man
> anything but an assemblage of artificial men and fabricated passions
> that are the work of all these new relations and have no true founda-
> tion in nature. (116)

"What a spectacle the difficult and envied labors of a European minister
must be for a Carib!" he exclaims (ibid.). Once again, an intermediary

figure helps the reader to measure the distance between civil man and natural man. Now seeing through "the eyes of the wise man," the reader has learned to separate appearance from reality, to see what initially appeared to be natural as artificial, his fellow civil men, and what was artificial or imaginary as real, natural man.

Chapter 3

The Education of the Reader in *Emile*

Rousseau's treatise *Emile, or On Education* promises to be of particular interest in examining how he educates his reader. The author himself considered *Emile* to be his "greatest and best book" (*Dialogues*, *CW*, 1:23). Yet, curiously, *Emile* has received disproportionately little attention from scholars compared to his other works. Perhaps this relative inattention is due either to the content of the work or to its form, or perhaps to both. As for the content, on the one hand, the title announces a pedagogical treatise, and that is how *Emile* has often been read, often narrowly so. On the other hand, *Emile* contains far more than pedagogical advice and in fact ranges over a vast array of subjects, from moral psychology to religion to the education of females to politics, and this very complexity and variety have impeded global interpretation of *Emile* and encouraged scholars to take up in piecemeal fashion the subjects it treats. As for the form of the work, its hybrid genre as both treatise and novel, or treatise-novel, has perplexed readers and reinforced the partial approach to interpreting its contents. Over the course of this chapter and the following three, I examine how the form and content of *Emile* work together to educate the reader. In this chapter I investigate some of the narrative strategies Rousseau employs to challenge the reader to adopt a new perspective on human nature, to come to see the children before his eyes as corrupt and artificial and to see Rousseau's imaginary pupil as somehow true or real.

The title promises an educational project, and the work delivers on that promise, for it is indeed devoted to raising an imaginary pupil from before birth to adulthood in accordance with Rousseau's principle of the natural goodness of man. Yet *Emile* is nonetheless as much, if not more, an education of the reader in that same system. In fact, Rousseau himself denied that *Emile* was intended to be an educational treatise, at least not in any straightforward way. He even voiced surprise that anyone would have supposed the work was an educational manual meant to be put into practice. In reply to a correspondent who expressed skepticism about its pedagogical methods, for example, Rousseau explained: "You state quite correctly that it is impossible to make an Emile. But I cannot believe that you took the book that bears this name for a veritable treatise on education. It is a quite philosophical work on the principle put forward by the author in his other works that man is naturally good."[1] Likewise, in the *Dialogues*, the Frenchman describes *Emile* as "much read, little understood, and ill-appreciated," and he characterizes the work as "nothing but a treatise on the original goodness of man, destined to show how vice and error, foreign to his constitution, enter it from outside and imperceptibly change him" (*Dialogues*, CW, 1:213).

Rousseau cannot be entirely serious here, for certainly *Emile* is presented as a pedagogical treatise, and on one level, so it is. Indeed, one suspects that Rousseau believes that if many of the practices he preaches were put into effect, child rearing would be the better for it. Think of the moral revolution he predicts would occur if mothers once again deigned to nurse their children: "From the correction of this single abuse would soon result a general reform; nature would soon have reclaimed its rights. Let women once again become mothers, men will soon become fathers and husbands again" (*Emile*, 46).[2] Later editions of his works would testify to the fashion he inspired by featuring in the frontispiece a woman nursing her infant. Nonetheless, even if we do take *Emile* to be a pedagogical project, we still have to be persuaded of the principle of the natural goodness of man that grounds and guides its educational practices. On a more general and higher level, and regardless of its status as an educational treatise, therefore, *Emile* offers an education of the reader. As Janie Vanpée notes, "The reading of this work might constitute an education in itself. . . . By virtue of its discursive presentation and its pedagogical subject, the text confers a special status upon the reader. He is not just any reader coming to terms with any text; he is a reader cast in the role of pupil to the text's role of master."[3]

In this chapter and the following three I examine how the form of *Emile* as a treatise-novel and the rhetorical techniques Rousseau employs in it constitute an educational program for the reader. In the previous two chapters I examined the rhetorical strategies he uses to persuade and educate the reader of the two *Discourses*. The hybrid genre he adopts in *Emile* enables him to use a wider variety of literary techniques, or to use them more persistently. These techniques, such as shifting narrative voices, ironic distance, reliable and unreliable narrators, characters with various attributes, and so on, are more familiar from novels and other "literary" genres. They are therefore more at home, so to speak, in *Emile*, and they provide Rousseau with a wide range of ways of constructing narratives and of interacting with his reader. As noted in the introduction to this book, my analysis is inspired in part by the "reader response" approach in literary criticism, and in this light Iser's examination of the "implied reader" of the novel form is helpful for understanding Rousseau's strategy. Iser argues that a central purpose of the novel is to challenge the reader to examine his or her own world in light of alternative world presented in the novel, which is at once similar to the reader's world—and hence "realistic"—and yet different. To repeat: "What was presented in the novel led to a specific effect: namely, to involve the reader in the world of the novel and so help him to understand it—and ultimately his own world—more clearly," he explains. Readers are therefore "forced to take an active part in the composition of the novel's meaning, which revolves around a basic divergence from the familiar."[4] Or, as Rousseau himself writes in one of his many confrontations with the reader: "It makes very little difference to me if I have written a romance [or novel—*roman*]. A fair romance it is indeed, the romance of human nature. If it is to be found only in this writing, is that my fault? This ought to be the history of my species. You who deprave it, it is you who make a romance of my book" (416).

In the introduction I characterized Rousseau's philosophy as essentially pedagogical in form and content, and nowhere is this most evident than in *Emile*. The various rhetorical and literary devices he employs in the work are part of a strategy of engaging the reader in the educational process, not just the education of the imaginary pupil of the work but that of the reader. Harvey offers an insightful characterization of the process when she describes Rousseau's multilevel discourse in the work, sometimes attending to his pupil, sometimes to the reader: "Sometimes they occur simultaneously with the same message being directed to the would-be tutor of a would-be pupil, as well as to the reader, whose concerns extend beyond a particular pedagogical situation to the philosophical issues of pedagogy, and to philosophy ultimately as pedagogy." Rather than writing in "a simple, univocal fashion," she explains, Rousseau moves the reader to "a higher and deeper level of understanding" through silences, challenges, and other methods: "He does not tell all, explicitly, he warns us and, hence, the layering is to be seen as part of our own pedagogical puzzle."[5] In what follows, I will examine the challenges Rousseau poses over the course of his educational treatise-novel.

I begin by examining the prefatory paratextual apparatus of *Emile* and how Rousseau there commences the education of the reader. I focus in particular on his argument that others have not seen the children before their eyes properly and his claim that the fact that he does not "see as do other men," that what will be taken initially as "a visionary's dreams about education" (34), enables him to reveal the truth about human nature, hitherto hidden behind appearances. I then turn to his decision to adopt an imaginary pupil in order to avoid "getting lost in visions" (51) and therewith his choice of a hybrid treatise-novel genre for *Emile*. Here I especially attend to how he stages comparisons between "my pupil" and "your pupil" in order to educate his reader in the proper way of seeing human nature and development and to test the reader's progress. I pursue this theme of testing the reader by examining the stories Rousseau relates, some concerning Emile and some concerning other pupils, stories that challenge the reader to identify whether the lessons illustrated in these stories actually involve Emile ("my pupil") or are appropriate for him in light of principle of the natural goodness of man. I then examine a series of stories in which the question is instead whether the apologue or moral of the story Rousseau provides is apt or inapt, an issue raised in his analysis of La Fontaine's fable as being inappropriate for his pupil and as having an inapt apologue. My aim throughout these analyses is less to offer novel interpretations of these various stories and lessons than to illustrate how Rousseau challenges the reader to ask these questions in the first place and thereby to make progress in adopting Rousseau's perspective guided by the principle of the natural goodness of man.

Seeing Children Properly

In the previous chapters on the two *Discourses*, I began with the complex paratextual apparatus of the works. *Emile* has a comparatively modest paratextual apparatus, limited to a title page, frontispiece, preface, and an "Explanations of the Illustrations" for the prefatory material. There are also a fair number of footnotes added to the main text, some original and some added in a later edition. The most interesting structural features of *Emile* are instead within the text itself, especially the explicitly separate subsections imbedded in the work: the religious teaching of the "Profession of Faith of the Savoyard Vicar," the discussion of female education in "Sophie, or the Woman," and the political doctrine in "On Travel." In subsequent chapters I will examine these subsections and their role in the text. Likewise, I will devote the next chapter to the frontispiece and the other illustrations included in the work and the role they play in the education of the reader. Here I limit myself to a few remarks on the title page and preface to examine how the work is presented to the reader.

Title Page

The title page includes the title, identification of the author, and an epigraph. As already noted, the hybrid treatise-novel has a hybrid title: *Emile, or On Education*. Emile is a proper name, and as we know, Rousseau will adopt an imaginary pupil named Emile to illustrate his educational method, so the title is eponymous. "On Education" announces the subject, or putative subject, of the work. Rousseau's use of a hybrid title, and especially one with "or" separating the primary title and the secondary or alternative or supplementary title, follows a common practice of his time. Think, for example, of "Zadig, or On Destiny" (1747) and "Candide, or On Optimism" (1759), both by Voltaire. Or Rousseau's own novel *Julie, or The New Heloise*, a work to which the author referred variously as either *Julie* or *The New Heloise*. Rousseau also refers to his work alternatively as *Emile* (e.g., in the *Confessions*) or his "educational treatise" (e.g., in the *Letter to Beaumont*), although never, to the best of my knowledge, as *On Education*. The hybrid title may also evoke the traditional titles of Platonic dialogues, for example *The Symposium, or On Love* or *The Republic, or On Justice*. Rousseau himself hints at his Platonic model near the beginning of *Emile* when he writes: "Do you want to get an idea of public education? Read Plato's *Republic*. It is not at all a political work, as think those who judge books only by their titles. It is the most beautiful educational treatise ever written" (40). Our author may be warning the reader not to judge his book by the title alone.

What about his choice of name for the title and the pupil: Emile? Later in the work, when Rousseau conjures an imaginary beloved for his pupil, he at least gives a hint as to the choice of her name: "'Let us call your future beloved *Sophie*. The name Sophie augers well. If the girl whom you choose does not bear it, she will at least be worthy of bearing it'" (329).[6] Sophie is associated with wisdom (*sophia*), so perhaps she is somehow wise.[7] He offers no such explanation for Emile, simply introducing him by name: "But as for the rules which might need proofs, I have applied them all to my Emile" (51). I suggest that he chose "Emile" because of the root sense of his name: to emulate (*émuler, aemulor*). Emile himself is said to be no imitator: "But who in the world is less of an imitator than Emile?" (331). Nonetheless, Emile in some sense a model for the reader. My suggestion is based in part on the juxtaposition of the title page and frontispiece. Facing "Emile" on the title page is the frontispiece depicting Thetis dipping her son in the Styx to render him invulnerable. As I will discuss in greater detail in the next chapter in my interpretation of the engravings for *Emile*, Rousseau aims to substitute a new exemplar for the classical hero represented by Achilles.

The title page identifies the author as "Jean-Jacques Rousseau, Citizen of Geneva." One perspective from which Rousseau invites the reader to approach *Emile*, then, is that of the citizen. As we have seen, Rousseau also identifies himself as a citizen on the title pages of the two *Discourses*, and we will see him do so in the *Social Contract* as well. Yet, to anticipate, what Rousseau states about citizens at the outset of *Emile* makes this lens different from the more straightforwardly political perspective of the two *Discourses* or the *Social Contract*. In the same context, near the beginning of the work, in which he identifies Plato's *Republic* as an educational treatise and warns us not to judge books by their titles, he describes the full and genuine citizenship of such ancient polities as Rome and Sparta, only to proclaim that such citizenship is no longer possible: "Public instruction no longer exists and can no longer exist, because where there is no longer fatherland, there can no longer be citizens. These two words, *fatherland* and *citizen*, should be effaced from modern languages" (40). Rather than offering a work on public instruction, therefore, he will present a private education meant to produce a "man" instead of a "citizen." Why identify himself as a "Citizen of Geneva," then? One possibility, which I will suggest for now but explore later in the chapter on the *Social Contract*, is that the absence of true fatherlands and citizens, which requires one to turn to private education, is itself a political situation. If so, in this respect the "Citizen of Geneva" is offering a critical commentary on modern politics.

Finally, the title page includes an epigraph identified as coming from Seneca's "On Anger" (*De Ira*): "We are sick with evils that can be cured; and nature, having brought us forth sound, itself helps us if we wish to be improved" (Sanabilibus aegrotamus malis; ipsaque nos in rectum genitos natura, si emendari velimus, iuvat).[8] The reader is thereby alerted of the importance of anger for Rousseau's argument, and also of the centrality of the question of the source of the evils from which we suffer, a critical issue given his argument concerning man's natural goodness. The choice of anger is particularly apt in light of the figure across from the title page: Achilles. Once again, I will examine the frontispiece in greater detail in the following chapter, but for now it suffices to note that Rousseau is already indicating to the reader that this and other passions ascribed to the epic hero are not natural. As we shall see momentarily, anger is an important theme in Rousseau's narrative, and part of the challenge he poses to the reader in adducing examples of children's behavior is to discriminate between natural and unnatural passions.

Preface

The preface to *Emile* combines the functions we saw in the prefaces and exordiums to the two *Discourses* of announcing the subject and the author's qualifications. Unlike the two *Discourses*, *Emile* is not presented as a spoken work and is instead explicitly characterized by Rousseau as a written one, so an exordium would not be appropriate. The main thrust of the preface is to diminish expectations concerning the author and what he will have to say. "This collection of reflections and observations, disordered and almost incoherent, was begun to gratify a good mother who knows how to think," he begins. "I had at first planned only a monograph [*mémoire*] of a few pages. My subject drew me on in spite of myself, and this monograph imperceptibly became a sort of opus [*ouvrage*], too big, doubtless, for what it contains, but too small for the matter it treats" (33). Although the subtitle suggests that we are reading an educational treatise, Rousseau is oddly elusive about his "subject" and the "matter" his book treats. He will not say much about the importance of a "good education" or about how the current one is bad, for these matters are obvious; but he suggests that the "art of forming men" is both the most useful subject and one that is still fresh (33). If his book is devoted to this art, it is much more capacious and ambitious than a mere educational treatise.

Adults begin as children, but, Rousseau proclaims, "childhood is unknown." Although he frames the question of what children are capable of learning *as* children, his main point is that we mistakenly see the man in the child. In terms of his system of the natural goodness of man, this would mean that we falsely assume that the characteristics of men as they are currently formed are natural, that we mistake appearance for reality with regard to human nature. Rousseau's emphasis is therefore on making correct observations of children before they are formed and corrupted. This is the "study" to which he has devoted himself, he explains, "so that even though my entire method were chimerical and false, my *observations* could still be of profit. I may have *seen* very poorly what must be done, but I do believe I have clearly *seen* the subject on which one must work. Begin, then, by studying your pupils better. For most assuredly you do not know [or recognize—*connoissez*] them at all" (33–34; emphasis added). We must learn to see children properly.

But how to observe children before they acquire the passions and faculties by which they are corrupted, given how quickly such faults insinuate themselves? Rousseau asks his readers to see beyond the examples before their eyes, to discriminate between appearance and reality. If they do, they will see his system of the natural goodness of man. But he predicts that they will not be immediately persuaded: "As to what will be called the systematic part, which is here nothing but the march of nature, it is the point that will most put off the reader, and doubtless it is here that I will be attacked." What will "put off" or "disconcert" (*déroutera*) the reader is also what will "reroute" or "divert" him (*dé-routera*) into another path of thinking if he accepts the challenge: "It will be believed that what is being read is less an educational treatise than a visionary's dreams about education. What is to be done about it? It is on the basis not of others' ideas that I write, but on that of my own. I do not see as do other men. I have long been reproached for that" (34). Rousseau immediately commences his dialogue with the skeptical reader. His initial dampening of expectations concerning his qualifications as an author is therefore ironic in the Socratic sense of presenting himself as less worthy and less knowledgeable than he truly is.

Finally, before turning to the main text, given the visual language in the preface to which I have drawn attention—"a visionary's dreams," "I do not see as do other men," and so on—it is significant that immediately following the preface and immediately preceding the main text we encounter the Explanations of the Illustrations. The expressly visual education of the reader through these illustrations and their dialectical relationship with the text will be the subject of the following chapter; but as we turn now to the main text, we will see Rousseau continue to use visual language and imagery.

An Imaginary Pupil to Prevent Getting Lost in Visions

Rousseau admits in the preface that he sees things differently, and this admission carries with it an implicit accusation of the reader for misapprehending the world. He commences book I with a statement about the world: "Everything is good, as it leaves the hands of the Author of things, everything degenerates in the hands of man" (37). This opening statement evokes Rousseau's system of the natural goodness of man and his corruption in society. The goodness of nature is arguably evident from the order of the natural world, but the alleged goodness of human nature is not so evident, for what we currently see before our eyes is what "the hands of man" have disfigured.[9] Recall in this light Rousseau's declaration in the *Discourse on Inequality* that he has "demonstrated" that man is naturally good, a declaration that follows his account of a "famous author" drawing the conclusion that man is wicked because he was observing the corrupted civil man instead of natural man (*Inequality*, n. IX, 127). The reader of *Emile* is assumed to share the same mistaken perspective as this author, and Rousseau must persuade the reader to adopt a different perspective.

The first reader Rousseau explicitly addresses in his work is a mother, echoing his claim in the preface that he began the work to "gratify a good mother who knows how to think" (33). This overture occurs in the third paragraph of the main text after his opening claim about everything being good as it comes from the hands of the author of things and its degeneration in the hands of man and then his explanation that we cannot simply let nature take its course once we are in society because of the prejudices and social institutions in which we find ourselves submerged. "It is to you [*toi*] that I address myself, tender and foresighted mother," he writes, urging her to keep her nascent "shrub" away from "the impact of human opinions" (37–38). In order to accomplish this task, the mother must be able to recognize "human opinions" as opinions or prejudices, to discriminate what comes from nature or its author and what comes from man, to distinguish between appearance and reality. Rousseau will soon discuss how mothers are often mistaken in how they raise their children because of shortsighted maternal tenderness (46–48). Mothers have to have their vision corrected; they need to adopt the lenses through which Rousseau educates them so that they in turn can educate their children in the same way. Over the course of *Emile* Rousseau will address himself to various readers: mothers, fathers, tutors, authors, readers, and most often an unspecified "you," whether *tu* or *vous*. What is common to all of these various readers is that they, too, need to learn to see along with Rousseau.[10]

Rousseau adds a footnote, the first in the work, to the phrase in the main text where he offers a familiar address to a mother, and in this note he identifies another readership: would-be authors of treatises on education. The footnotes are one of *Emile*'s paratextual apparatuses, and rather than presenting an extended analysis of the footnotes I will limit myself to a few observations on the occasion of the first. The footnotes to *Emile* by no means have a single purpose, but perhaps most commonly they draw attention to the work as a published text and to Rousseau in his role of author. The first footnote is one such example. In the note he explains there that the first education of children incontestably belongs to mothers and he therefore offers advice to another class of readers: "Always speak [*Parlez*], then, preferably to women in your [*vos*] treatises on education" (37 n.). Other footnotes later in *Emile* provide quotations from other authors and identify the source of quotations in the text. Still others are used by Rousseau to point readers to his other works, for example the *Social Contract* (85 n. and 462 n.), the *Letter to d'Alembert* (128 n.), the *Discourse on Inequality* (258 n.), and the (posthumously published) essay *Principles of Melody* (340 n.). Perhaps most interestingly, in his role as the alleged editor of the "Profession of Faith" he adds footnotes to the document supposedly transcribed by an unknown author, much as he does in *Julie*, a subject to which I will return in chapter 5. In sum, through these various techniques, Rousseau frequently calls attention in the footnotes to the written character of the text.

To return to the main text: in our present condition the demands of nature and of society are in conflict, Rousseau explains, and therefore we are in conflict with ourselves. The current education that forms the men we have before our eyes has created beings who are evil, or at least conflicted and enervated, a type Rousseau terms the *bourgeois* (40). Rousseau seeks an education that will form a human being who is not in conflict, an education that is somehow in accordance with nature. What Rousseau means here by *nature*, an issue he directly confronts in this context, is a complicated affair and beyond the scope of the present investigation. Instead of taking the "double men" before our eyes as representing human nature, if we follow Rousseau we will see them as products of education, broadly conceived, as artificial and not natural. Doing so, we are prepared to entertain how we might produce a unified human being through a different education.

Rousseau presents the reader with two such possibilities: the "man" and the "citizen." Since we do not have these beings before our eyes, we must imagine them. As for the "citizen," Rousseau depicts this being by recounting two stories drawn from Plutarch about the virtuous Spartan male and female citizens and then warns the reader that they are now unrecognizable: "This has little relation, it seems to me, to the men we know [or recognize: *connoissons*]" (40). The examples of ancient citizens illustrate how civic education "denatures" man (and woman) by transforming him (and her) into a being whose identity is defined by citizenship. However, as already noted when discussing Rousseau's self-presentation as the "Citizen of Geneva," he immediately dismisses the possibility of creating true citizens in modern times. That leaves the "education of nature" that will produce a "man," or perhaps a "human being" (*homme*) if the term is not gender specific. The product of this education also has to be seen imaginatively. "If perchance the double object we set for ourselves," that is, of making a being who is good for himself and for others, "could be joined in a single one by removing the contradictions of man, a great obstacle to his happiness would be removed. In order to judge of this, he would have to be *seen* wholly formed: his inclinations would have to be *observed*, his progress *seen*, his development followed. In a word, it would be necessary to know [*connoitre*] natural man. I believe that one will have made a few steps in these researches when one has read this writing" (41; emphasis added). Rousseau's emphasis here is on a progression—"progress," "development," "steps"—in the process of visualization on the part of his reader through the course of reading the work.

In order to make his reader see a natural man, to make them accept his "visions" as real, Rousseau decides to illustrate his educational method by giving himself an imaginary pupil and by taking on the role of an imaginary governor. In doing so, he employs for the first time in *Emile* a pattern of rhetorical devices that we will see repeated throughout the work. Namely, he makes a programmatic statement related to his doctrine of the natural goodness of man and, immediately beforehand or afterward, stages a comparison between two examples of children's behavior, one representing the product of his natural education and the other representing the product of ordinary corrupt education. We are already familiar with a version of the device of comparing examples for a pedagogical purpose from the *Discourse on Inequality* and the repeated comparisons there between natural man and civil man.

The occasion for the first use in *Emile* of this rhetorical pattern is the subject of children crying, a substantively significant example to which we shall see him return. "A child cries at birth," he begins, and then remarks on how we react to this crying and the effects of our actions: "Either we do what pleases him, or we exact from him what pleases us. Either we submit to his whims, or we submit him to ours. . . . Thus his first ideas are those of domination and servitude." Then the programmatic statement: "It is thus that we fill up his young heart at the outset with the passions which we later impute to nature and that, after having taken efforts to make him wicked, we complain about finding him so." The child so raised has had unnatural passions instilled in him, making him a "factitious being," at once "slave and tyrant," and viewing him as natural we deplore our condition. Then the comparison of two pupils: "This is a mistake. He is the man of our whims; the man of nature is differently constituted" (48).

Since the child before our eyes whom we take to be natural is in fact artificial or "factitious," Rousseau must help us see or imagine the "man of nature." At this point in the text, therefore, he introduces the novelistic component of *Emile*. The "man of nature" needs a preceptor who understands the true "march of nature," as Rousseau phrases it in the preface when speaking of the "systematic part" of his work that will be met with disbelief (34). Who better than Rousseau himself? Acknowledging his incapacity for the role, Rousseau the author will imagine himself as "Jean-Jacques," a tutor who does possess the requisite ability (50–51). Then he gives himself an imaginary pupil. His solution to getting us to accept a reality hidden from our eyes is thoroughly paradoxical:

> I have hence chosen to give myself an imaginary pupil. . . . This method appears to me useful to prevent an author who distrusts himself from getting lost in visions; for when he deviates from ordinary practice, he has only to make a test of his own practice on his pupil. He will soon sense, or the reader will sense for him, whether he follows the progress of childhood and the movements natural to the human heart. (50–51)

In short: he will make his imaginary pupil the test case for the "vision" he has been able to see because he does not see like other men.

The paradox of Rousseau's proceeding was not lost on one of his critics, Johann Heinrich Samuel Formey, whom Rousseau took seriously enough to respond to in notes he added to a later edition of *Emile*. Commenting on this passage, Formey begins a complaint that he will echo throughout his examination of the work: "Here the chimera of the project on which this work turns becomes manifest . . . he does an act of creation rather than of invention, and one can no longer continue reading his work except based on a principle of curiosity and amusement, as one reads Utopia and other imaginary republics."[11] As it seems only fair to consider how at least one contemporary read *Emile*, I will make some further references in the notes to Formey's objections of this sort. For now it suffices to say that Formey takes *Emile* to be what it appears to be on the surface, an educational treatise, and that his protestations often concern the unrealizability or inappropriateness of the educational program. He might very well stand for the skeptical reader to whom Rousseau will often address himself in the work. At any rate, though, Formey does not consider the possibility that *Emile* is instead meant to be an education of the reader.

On this very point, and to return to his adoption of an imaginary pupil, Rousseau invites the reader to test the veracity of the methods used on his pupil independently of himself as author: ". . . or the reader will sense for him." The exercise of this prerogative is in fact one of the primary lessons in the education of the reader. Rousseau's imaginary pupil and his vision of human nature are only persuasive if we accept his teaching concerning "the movements natural to the human heart." His imaginary pupil is depicted according to this true vision of human nature, but he will be unlike the children we ordinarily have before our eyes. In order to instantiate this imaginary pupil, Rousseau fashions him out of the flesh and blood born of pen and paper: "I have been content with setting down the principles whose truth everyone should sense. But as for the rules which might need proofs, I have applied them all to my Emile or to other examples" (51). Emile and "other" examples.[12] As just remarked, Rousseau typically juxtaposes important programmatic statements concerning the fundamental principles of his thought with comparisons between "my pupil," who exists only in the mind's eye, and "your pupil," the child actually visible to the reader. The education of the reader advances as he becomes more persuaded by the "reality" of the imaginary pupil through these comparisons. Part of this education will be to learn to differentiate between those examples. The distance between Emile and other examples will grow as the work progresses:

> The result of this procedure is that at first I have spoken little of my Emile, because my first educational maxims, although contrary to those which are established, are so evident that it is difficult for any reasonable man to refuse his consent to them. But in proportion as I advance, my pupil, differently conducted than yours, is no longer an ordinary child. He requires a way of life special to him. Then he appears more frequently on the scene, and toward the last times I no longer let him out of sight for a moment. (51)

Hence *Emile* becomes more novelistic as it progresses. The rationale for this procedure is in part that his imaginary pupil becomes more and more unlike the children we have before our eyes. If he succeeds, Rousseau will have educated his reader to accept the character in his educational novel as a true depiction of human nature.

Rousseau's Choice of a Hybrid Genre for Emile

In order to highlight Rousseau's method of composition in *Emile*, it would be instructive at this point to consider the hybrid genre he chose for his work. This choice is underscored by how the final version of his work differs from the earlier version.[13] The earlier version, the so-called Favre Manuscript, covers approximately the same material as the first three books of the final version. The first version of Rousseau's educational treatise is in large measure just that: an educational treatise. The striking feature of the first version of *Emile* is what it lacks in comparison to the final version: Emile. Or almost so. Toward the end of the earlier version, Emile is suddenly introduced; he becomes the pupil through what little remains of the text of the manuscript. This point in the text of the original version is equivalent of about half way through book III of the final version.[14] It is as though Rousseau suddenly thought of the novelistic form he might give the work, ceased writing, and then began anew. Which is probably just what he did.[15]

Rousseau's decision to alter the form of his work confronts us with the question of why he did so. The closest student of the genesis and composition of *Emile*, Peter Jimack, suggests that Rousseau "seems to have been involuntarily led to identify himself with the governor and his examples," turning to the novel form to bring to life his imaginary pupil and then awkwardly inserting him into the original text. He further suggests that Rousseau himself also became confused in his own role as "I" (*je* or *moi*) in the text, with author and imaginary tutor becoming hopelessly jumbled.[16] In response to such a reading, which privileges the psychological state of the author and the process of composition over its content, Patrick Coleman correctly argues: "In the context of *Emile* as it comes to us, that is, in its hybrid form, we must ask for whose sake examples are adduced and by which 'moi,' before we can locate any possible contradiction."[17] Perhaps as much as 80 percent of the original material is incorporated into the final version, often without any change, but in the final version Rousseau interweaves this material with stories of Emile and the tutor Jean-Jacques and also of other children, examples often also supposedly involving the historic Jean-Jacques Rousseau rather than the imagined tutor. Another change he made in the final version is important for the present analysis: none of the visual language and imagery that I have highlighted in the preface and the beginning of book I exists in the original version. It would seem, therefore, that in recasting the work Rousseau shifted his focus squarely to the education of the reader through a series of rhetorical devices, often visual in nature, including foremost his imaginary pupil.

An indication of Rousseau's authorial control over what he does in the final version comes from the hints of the literary devices he would ultimately adopt that are present only in nascent form in the Favre Manuscript and how he developed these devices in the final version to both substantive and rhetorical effect. An interesting example for the present purposes comes early in the manuscript and just after recommending that we harden the physical constitution of children—"Steep them in the waters of the Styx"—which in the final version is just before Rousseau first introduces his imaginary pupil. In the earlier version, Rousseau describes the results of the usual education given by coddling women and pretentious tutors and how the product of this education—"this child, slave and tyrant"—is "cast out into the world, showing there his wretchedness, he becomes the basis for deploring that of humanity. This is a mistake. He is the man of our whims; the man of nature is differently constituted."[18] Rousseau here hints both at a philosophical position, the natural goodness of man, and at a device he will use to persuade his reader of that position, asking the reader to visualize a comparison between two children. Yet both the philosophical position and the rhetorical device are made more explicit in the final version. As for the philosophical position, in the final version Rousseau strengthens the sense of the earlier version with a more programmatic statement: "It is thus that we fill up his young heart at the outset with the passions which later we impute to nature and that, after having taken efforts to make him wicked, we complain about finding him so" (48). As for the device he uses to persuade his reader of this statement, it is slightly after this same point in the final version of the text that Rousseau introduces Emile (51). Emile thus becomes the more embodied version of the "man of nature" we are to compare to the "man of our whims." Finally, and related, it is also in this same context in both the earlier and final versions of the work that Rousseau alludes to the story of Thetis and Achilles ("Steep them in the waters of the Styx"). Whatever his intentions when he began the first draft of the work, it is this story that will serve as the frontispiece to *Emile*, and by introducing his imaginary pupil at this point in the final version, Rousseau invites us to compare Emile and Achilles. He therefore prepares another lesson in the visual education of the reader.

In sum, then, Rousseau appears to have rethought his presentation and in particular the way in which he would persuade his reader through an imaginary pupil and comparisons to other examples. This rethinking resulted in the creation of Emile himself, the most important systematic change in the final version of the work that would eventually come to bear the title *Emile*.

"My Pupil" versus "Your Pupil"

Returning to the final version of *Emile*, I have suggested that the comparisons Rousseau stages between his imaginary pupil and ordinary children, often presented with programmatic statements concerning the natural goodness of man, are part of the educational program of inducing the reader to adopt his perspective and of testing the reader's progress. I have already examined the first instance of his employment of this technique, the passage in book I concerning the crying of infants that appears right before he introduces Emile. A few more examples of how Rousseau juxtaposes examples of "my pupil" and "your pupil" from later in the work will help illustrate this repeated testing.

A subject of particular importance for the reader in learning how to read the book Rousseau has written is learning to read and write, a subject that arises in book II. After discussing how Emile will be led to learn to read by appealing to his present interest, for example his receiving invitations to parties, Rousseau turns to writing: "Shall I speak now of writing? No. I am ashamed of playing with this kind of foolishness in an educational treatise" (117). Our author approaches his work with a strong dose of irony, destabilizing the reading experience and thereby preparing a challenge to the reader: "The more I insist on my inactive method, the more I sense objections becoming stronger. If your [*vôtre*] pupil learns nothing from you, he will learn from others. If you do not forestall error by means of truth, he will learn lies. The prejudices you are afraid of giving him, he will receive from everything around him." Rousseau then invites the skeptical reader to enter into dialogue with him, only to refuse to do so: "It seems to me that I could easily answer that. But why always answers? If my method by itself answers objections, it is good. If it does not answer them, it is worthless. I shall proceed."[19] The ensuing discussion seems to be an illustration of the method and its results: "If, according to the plan I have begun to outline, you [*vous*] follow rules directly contrary to the established ones . . . you will find him capable of perception, memory, and even reasoning. This is nature's order." On the contrary, if "you" follow the opposite method, you will not achieve these ends: "If you are only a pedant, it is not worth the effort to read me" (117–18). Rousseau alternates invitations and refusals to his reader as a would-be tutor, depending on whether the reader accepts or rejects his lead.[20]

Having interacted with his reader, Rousseau now stages a comparison of the pupils produced by following these divergent paths, pupils whom he characterizes as the oafish peasant and the sagacious savage: "Learned preceptor, let us see which of our two pupils resembles the savage and which the peasant." Of course, the result is as expected.[21] Having made the comparison, Rousseau returns to his addressee: "Young teacher, I am preaching a difficult art to you, that of governing without precepts and doing everything by doing nothing" (119). Slightly afterward we get the now-expected programmatic statement: "All these practices seem difficult because one does not really consider them, but at bottom they ought not be. I have a right to assume that you possess the enlightenment necessary for exercising the vocation you have chosen. I have to assume that you know the natural development of the human heart, that you know how to study man and the individual" (121). Differently put, the reader as tutor must have been persuaded by the philosophical system of the natural goodness of man and has thereby learned to observe children (and men) correctly—precisely the substantive and methodological challenges Rousseau raises in the preface to *Emile*.

Rousseau admits the methodological hurdle to his argument near the outset of book IV, a portion of the text rich with programmatic statements about the character and limits of the natural passions, natural goodness, and so on. Previously limited to his own individuality, his pupil's awakening, adolescent-onset passions causes him to extend his relations to others and become a fully moral being. Directing these passions to prevent their corruption requires careful "observations," Rousseau explains: "These observations are difficult because in order to make them, we must reject the examples that are before our eyes and seek for those in which the successive developments take place according to the order of nature" (220). Of course, that example is his imaginary pupil.

If the reader visualizes Emile, he will be able to discern the moment in the child's development when he is capable of truly identifying and commiserating with his fellow human beings: "If this moment is not easy to notice in your children, whom do you blame for it? . . . But look at my Emile" (222). In other words, the reader must reject the examples before his eyes and "look at" the imaginative example Rousseau has portrayed. Then, after propounding "two or three" maxims for properly cultivating pity through exposure to suffering (another test of the reader, for he explicitly enumerates three maxims), Rousseau returns to the comparison of pupils: "More than one reader will doubtless reproach me for forgetting my first resolve and the constant happiness I had promised my pupil. . . . I promised to make him happy, not to appear to be. Is it my fault if you, always dupes of appearance, take it for reality?" Of course, teaching his reader to discriminate between and appearance and reality, truth and artifice, is one of Rousseau's main pedagogical goals. "Let us take two men, emerging from their first education and entering into society by two directly opposite paths," he continues. The first is thrust into society with the ordinary education: "You see him attentive, eager, curious. His initial admiration strikes you. You take him to be satisfied; but look at the condition of his soul. You believe he is enjoying himself; I believe he is suffering" (227). And somewhat later: "This is your pupil. Let us see mine" (229). Needless to say, Rousseau's pupil is happy, and having elaborated on the condition of his soul, the author returns to the comparison: "I cannot prevent myself from imagining on the face of the young man of whom I have previously spoken something impertinent, sugary, affected, which displeases, which repels plain people; and on that of my young man an interesting and simple expression that reveals satisfaction and true serenity of soul, inspires esteem and confidence" Having said enough on this matter to persuade "a reasonable reader," he concludes: "I therefore return to my method"

(230). In short, the "reasonable reader" has been persuaded by Rousseau that his imaginary pupil is somehow "true" and the children before the reader's eyes are correspondingly "false."

Later in book IV Rousseau stages one of the most aggressive confrontations with the reader. The context for this challenge is his explanation of how nascent *amour-propre*, which usually takes the corrupt form of the selfish pride the reader might assume is natural to human beings, can be healthily directed with the proper education: "Let us extend *amour-propre* to other beings, we shall transform it into a virtue, and there is no man's heart in which this virtue does not have its root." Self-love can be generalized to become the love of justice, he explains, and argues with reference to Emile: "The true principles of the just, the true models of the beautiful, all the moral relations of beings, all the ideas of order are imprinted on his understanding" (252–53). Having made these claims, he turns to his readers:

> I go forward, attracted by the force of things but without gaining credibility in the judgment of my readers. For a long while they have seen me in the land of chimeras. As for me, I always see them in the land of prejudices. . . . I know that they persist in imagining only what they see, and therefore they will take the young man whom I evoke to be an imaginary and fantastic being because he differs from those with whom they compare him. . . . This is not the man of man, it is the man of nature. Assuredly he must be very alien to their eyes.
>
> In beginning this work, I supposed nothing that everyone cannot observe just as I do, because there is a point—the birth of man—from which we all equally begin. But the more we go forward, I to cultivate nature and you to deprave it, the further we get from each other. (253)

This dialogue continues with Rousseau delivering imagined speeches of disbelief on the part of the reader, for example: "'Nothing of what you suppose exists,'" to which he replies, "I beg those judges who are so quick to censure to consider that I know what they are saying here just as well as they do, that I have probably reflected on it longer, that I have no interest in foisting anything on them." He asks the judgmental reader to examine carefully the constitution of "man," to see how powerful the effects of different educations are, and then compare "my education with the effects I attribute to it." He writes off the reader who thinks he has gone astray in his reasoning: "I shall have nothing to respond" (254).

Rousseau nonetheless does not terminate his dialogue with the more receptive reader. Instead, he develops the method of comparative observation he prescribes to those who would judge him hastily. The method he describes is useful for understanding his philosophical procedure in

Emile, and elsewhere, of investigating human nature. It is also revealing with regard to his training of the reader to see like he does. Interestingly and paradoxically, given the fact that he has given himself an imaginary pupil, he defends himself by appealing to his "observations":

> What makes me more assertive—and, I believe, more to be excused for being so—is that, instead of yielding to the systematic spirit, I grant as little as possible to reasoning and I trust only observation. I found myself not on what I have imagined, but on what I have seen. It is true that I have not restricted my experience to the compass of a city's walls or to a single class of people. But after having compared as many ranks and peoples as I could see in a life spent observing them, I have eliminated as artificial what belonged to one people and not to another, to one station and not to another, and have regarded as incontestably belonging to man only what was common to all, at whatever age, in whatever rank, and in whatever nation. (254)

Rousseau's claim makes sense if he—and his reader—has learned to observe properly, to distinguish the natural from the artificial, whether in the mind's eye of observing the imaginary pupil or in the actual eye of observing existing human beings.[22] Having outlined his method, he returns to the reader: "Now if in accordance with this method you follow a young man from childhood . . . whom do you think he will most resemble—my pupil or yours?" (254). With that said, he returns to his pupil.

Finally, still later in book IV, Rousseau provides one of his last express confrontations with the reader: "Reader, I am well aware that no matter what I do, you and I will never see my Emile with the same features. You will always picture him as similar to your young people." He then stages a dialogue between author and reader: "You will say, 'This dreamer always pursues his chimera. By giving us a pupil of his making, he not only forms him, he creates him, he pulls him out of his brain; and though he believes he is always following nature, he diverges from it at every instant.'" In reply: "I, comparing my pupil to yours, hardly find anything that they can have in common. Since they are reared so differently, it would almost be a miracle if Emile resembled yours in anything" (315). Once again, the comparison between pupils, "my pupil" versus "your pupil," is meant to educate the reader to see properly.

Cases of Mistaken Identity

The technique of staging comparisons between different children, including "my" pupil and "your" pupil, is relatively straightforward, but Rousseau also employs more complicated methods to challenge the reader. One set of related techniques involves cases of mistaken identity. These include mistakes made in the observations of children, and especially cases in which Rousseau in his persona as author relates stories about errors he himself supposedly made in his persona as the historical Jean-Jacques Rousseau.[23] They also include stories in which Rousseau in his persona as the imaginary tutor, Jean-Jacques, relates lessons he gives Emile, leaving it to the reader to judge whether the lesson was appropriate or inappropriate for the imaginary pupil educated in accordance with the system of the natural goodness of man. This tripling of himself—author, tutor, and his supposedly historical self—is paralleled by his doubling of pupils, for example Emile and Jean-Jacques, the imaginary tutor, versus an ordinary child and Jean-Jacques Rousseau.[24] By splitting himself into these various personae, Rousseau not only interacts with different children in different ways, but interacts in different ways with the reader.

In this section, I examine Rousseau's use of these related techniques through a series of stories that are thematically related to one another by the subject of anger. As noted previously, Rousseau draws our attention to the importance of anger for his work by including an epigraph from Seneca's "On Anger" on the title page. The claim there is that our "ills," including anger, do not come from nature and can be cured, or rather prevented, through proper education. We should also recall that he sets up the introduction of his imaginary pupil (and a comparison to the angry Achilles) with the example of the master-slave dialectic between a crying child and a frustrated adult, concluding: "It is thus that we fill up his young heart at the outset with the passions which we later impute to nature and that, after having taken efforts to make him wicked, we complain about finding him so" (48). Anger is therefore substantively important for Rousseau's principle of the natural goodness of man and for the education of the reader in accordance with that principle.[25]

For Crying Out Loud

The first story to be examined involves a crying infant who becomes enraged after being slapped by his nurse. Instead of Jean-Jacques the governor we have Jean-Jacques Rousseau, and instead of Emile we have an ordinary child. "I shall never forget having seen one of these difficult criers," the narration begins. The difficult crier is struck by his nurse and is immediately quiet: "I believed he was intimidated. I said to myself, 'This will be a servile soul from which one will get nothing except by severity.' I was mistaken." Rather than being servile, the struck infant was in fact angry: "A moment after came sharp screams; all the signs of the resentment, fury, and despair of his age were in his accents. . . . If I had doubted that the sentiment of the just and the unjust were innate in the heart of man, this example alone would have convinced me" (65–66).

This example is deceptively simple, and in fact deceptive. Indeed, directly after presenting it, Rousseau practically alerts us to the need to examine it more carefully: "This disposition of children to fury, spite, and anger requires extreme attentiveness" (66). Interpreting the example requires realizing that the "I" who reports witnessing this child and then draws the conclusion about the natural sentiment of justice and injustice is not necessarily the same "I"—Rousseau the author—who relates the story in his book. Or at least this may be the same "I" at two moments in time, perhaps pre– and post–illumination of Vincennes. Note that Rousseau as author states that the supposedly historical Jean-Jacques Rousseau was mistaken; if the tutor Jean-Jacques is seemingly infallible, Jean-Jacques Rousseau is fallible. The effect of relating his mistake through his historical persona is to disarm the reader, who can be excused for making the same mistake. Jean-Jacques Rousseau attributes resentment, fury, and despair to the child and allies these attributes to an innate sentiment of justice. Does Rousseau the author believe that children are naturally resentful, angry, and despairing? No. In fact, immediately after this story he counsels the reader to be wary of introducing these unnatural sentiments into the child and makes a programmatic statement about the natural goodness of man. He makes this statement against those philosophers who erringly explain children's behavior as a result of "natural vices: pride, the spirit of domination, *amour-propre*, the wickedness of man." He specifically cites Hobbes's claim that "the wicked man [is] a robust child" (67), but he might also have in mind Augustine, who interprets his crying as an infant as an incipient sign of sin.[26] Jean-Jacques Rousseau makes the same mistake as Hobbes and others in interpreting his observation of the child. In short, Rousseau the author does not agree with Jean-Jacques Rousseau as witness concerning the naturalness of anger and similar passions.

Does Rousseau as author agree with Jean-Jacques Rousseau that the child's behavior proves there is an innate sentiment of justice? This is a more complicated issue. To begin we might observe that the child's behavior is more accurately described as manifesting a sentiment of injustice, not justice, since he reacts to "the manifest intention of offending him" (66). The child's reaction is indignation, a form of anger. If anger is unnatural, then indignation is not natural. Related, such indignation requires recognizing intentionality or will, which Rousseau argues is beyond the infant's natural capacity. The angry infant has had his passions and faculties prematurely awakened, and we can anticipate that he will become the little tyrant who leads us mistakenly to infer that human nature is wicked. Even if the root of a sentiment of injustice or justice is somehow innate, it requires development of the passions and faculties not present in the child raised according to the education of nature but evidently awakened in the corrupted child in the example.[27] Jean-Jacques Rousseau as witness is therefore at best half right.

A Mistaken Lesson? Planting the Seeds of Vice

The issues of anger and injustice arise in book II in a well-known story of Emile planting beans to learn his first lesson in property. This episode also tests the reader in a different way by challenging him to ask whether the lesson is in fact appropriate for the pupil. First a few words about the context. Book II is devoted to childhood, when the child gains consciousness of himself and "the life of the individual begins" (78). The desires and faculties "in the reserve of the depth of his soul" (80) now begin to develop. In this context, then, Rousseau apostrophizes the skeptical reader: "This is, you answer me, the time to correct man's bad inclinations." To which he responds: "And how will you prove to me that these bad inclinations, of which you claim you are curing him, do not come to him from your ill-considered care far more than from nature?" (79–80). Similarly, somewhat later in the same book Rousseau argues that the usual practice of reasoning with children in order to teach them their duties actually instills vice: "With each lesson that one wants to put into their heads before its proper time, a vice is planted in the depths of their hearts. Senseless teachers think they work wonders when they make children wicked in order to teach them what goodness is. And then they solemnly tell us, 'Such is man.' Yes, such is the man you have made." Then we once again see the pattern of comparisons of children followed by a programmatic statement. "I already see the startled reader judging this child by our children. He is mistaken," he writes, and then pronounces: "Let us set down as an incontestable maxim that the first movements of nature are always right. There is no original perversity in the human heart. There is not a single vice to be found in it of which it cannot be said how and whence it entered." The pedagogical implication of his argument is that the first education ought to be "purely negative," a formulation that he states "common readers" will find paradoxical: "It consists not at all in teaching virtue or truth but in securing the heart from vice and the mind from error" (92–93). The first step in assessing the story of planting beans is to ask whether or not it is an example of such "negative education."

The story of Emile tending his garden has been examined by many interpreters, most of whom have seen in it a Lockean lesson in appropriating property through labor.[28] This is surely correct with qualification, a point to which I will return. But by focusing narrowly on the story itself, interpreters have not attended to how its immediate context calls into question the appropriateness of the lesson and also the narrative status of the story itself. The story is prepared by a warning to readers in their role as would-be tutors: "Zealous masters, be simple, discreet, restrained; never hasten to act except to prevent others from acting. . . . On this earth, out of which nature has made man's first paradise, dread exercising the tempter's function by wanting to give innocence the knowledge of good and evil" (96). We could hardly ask for a more blatant warning before a story about a garden from the philosopher of the natural goodness of man than an allusion to the Garden of Eden.

After this warning, and once again in preparation of the story of Emile and his garden, Rousseau turns to the subject of anger. He imagines "my little Emile" witnessing two neighbors arguing and saying to one of them "in a tone of commiseration": "'My good woman, you are sick. I am so sorry about it.'" This sally, he says, "will surely not remain without effect on the spectators or perhaps on the actresses" (97). A few things should be noted about this vignette. First, the remark about the "actresses" in particular indicates that it is staged, and we can anticipate that the story of planting beans is similarly staged. Second, it is unclear who the "I" is who speaks of "my little Emile." Is it Jean-Jacques the tutor or Rousseau the author? Third, there is likewise uncertainty over Emile, for he would lack the developed passions and faculties to feel commiseration, which Rousseau states in book IV only develops at adolescence according to the march of nature. The warning about zealous masters unwittingly corrupting their pupils, the subject of anger, and uncertainty concerning the identity of master and pupil all play a role in interpreting the tale of Emile and the bean sprouts. Finally, as he introduces his pupil to property rights, Rousseau warns the reader that the conventions of already-existing property are beyond the reach of children: "Readers, in this example [cet éxemple] and in a hundred thousand others, I beg you to note how we stuff children's heads with words which have no meaning within their reach and then believe we have instructed them very well" (98). "This example" appears to be the immediately following story of Emile planting beans. Is it among the hundred thousand misapplied lessons of which Rousseau warns us?

The lesson involves going back to the origin of property: "The child, living in the country, will have gotten some notion of labor in the fields." Who is "the child"? Is it Emile? The child will naturally want to imitate this gardening: "According to the principles previously established, I in no way oppose his desire." Who is "I"? The child "takes possession" of a plot by planting a bean in it and takes great joy in watching it grow. The master "I" explains that the plot belongs to the child because he has mixed his labor into it. One day they return to the plot to discover it has been torn up: "O what a sight! O pain! All the beans are rooted out, the plot is torn up, the very spot is unrecognizable. O what has become of my labor, my product, the sweet fruit of my care and my sweat? Who has stolen my goods? Who took my beans from me? This young heart is aroused. The first sentiment of injustice comes to shed its sad bitterness in it. Tears flow in streams. The grieving child fills the air with moans and cries. I partake of his pain, his indignation." After making inquiries, they discover that the gardener is responsible and imperiously summon him. But it turns out that the gardener, not the child, is the injured party, for the child has planted his "miserable beans" where the owner of the plot had planted Maltese melons—exquisite melons that, to make matters worse, he states he was going to share with the child. The child is both the unjust party and is less well-off to boot through his inconsiderate planting of beans. A dialogue ensues among "Jean-Jacques," "Robert," and "Emile." Robert protests that he has inherited, occupied, and worked the plot of land for a long time and notes that there is little fallow land left. Emile responds that he does not have a garden. Robert replies that he does not care. Jean-Jacques proposes a contract where Emile may plant beans in a corner of the plot on the condition that he will give half the produce to Robert. The gardener agrees but warns him not to touch his melons (98–99).

As noted, this story is usually taken to be a Lockean lesson in appropriating property through labor that is within children's limited reach. But is it? First, as far as the theoretical argument goes, Rousseau adds an important twist to the Lockean account: he focuses not on the original appropriation of property in a world of uncultivated land that meets the Lockean proviso that such appropriation is just so long as "there is enough, and as good, left in common to others,"[29] but on a world in which virtually all land has been appropriated. Rousseau's story takes place in a world in which there are those with gardens and those without them, a world of inequality. He makes this point emphatic shortly thereafter with a remark about the duties of the rich toward the poor stemming from the agreement to establish property (104).[30]

Second, as for the lesson, is it actually within the reach of the child or appropriate for him? Or, rather, for what child is the lesson apt? Rousseau introduced the context in which the story occurs by warning zealous masters against misapplied lessons. Even assuming that the child actually understands what it means for property to "belong" to him, the misapplication of the lesson is signaled by the role that anger and indignation play in the story. Upon discovering his beans ruined, the nameless child in the story—just before he is named "Emile" in the dialogue—cries and is indignant at the perceived injustice done toward him. We should be reminded of the story of Jean-Jacques Rousseau witnessing the anger of a child struck by his nurse. Would the child raised according to nature cry and be indignant? Has the tutor played the role of the tempter in the garden, causing the unnatural passions to sprout and planting the seeds of vice? Is this child the "true" Emile? And the tutor the "true" Jean-Jacques? The narrative status of the story is uncertain.[31]

With the story concluded, Rousseau resumes his role as author and congratulates himself on this "model" of educating the child concerning the right of the first occupant through labor. "That is clear, distinct, simple, and within the child's reach," he states, going on to brag that what "I enclose [*renferme*] here in two pages of writing" perhaps took a year to put into practice (98–99). Shifting to the authorial "I," Rousseau takes ownership of his work by enclosing the text through his own labor. By calling attention to the writtenness of his text, Rousseau may be pointing to the problems of writing raised in Plato's *Phaedrus*, a concern that is more evident in the next story I will examine. For the present, Rousseau raises question of the appropriateness of the lesson concerning property for Emile by turning next to an example of an ordinary child: "Your ill-tempered child ruins everything he touches," telling a story of an angry child who breaks the windows of his room, with the tutor proclaiming his ownership of the windows, confining the child to a windowless room, and then proposing a contract stipulating that the child will not break windows. The parallels with the story of planting beans are manifest. Is this example of an ordinary, corrupt child meant to be a contrast to the story of the "real" Emile? Or is it meant to make us ask if this is another "Emile" who, if not corrupt, has awakened passions? Rousseau follows the example of the angry, destructive child by closing the narrative circle: "Here we are in the moral world; here the door on vice opens" (100–101). And thus concludes the portion of the text that opens the warning about not playing the tempter who introduces the knowledge of good and evil.

Let me entertain an alternative interpretation of the story of Emile's garden in order to make clear my intentions in the reading of it I have offered. A number of other scholars have argued that the deliberate provocation of indignation in Emile through his initial feeling of having been wronged is defused by his discovery that he is in fact the unjust party. Emile is allowed to feel anger without the passion's deleterious effects, and he also learns a lesson concerning property. In this reading, then, the lesson is appropriate for the "real" Emile and not, as I have argued, a story involving an inappropriate lesson for an alternative pupil also (eventually) named "Emile."[32] This alternative reading is eminently plausible, and in fact the interpretation to which I myself have long subscribed. My point here is less to offer a better interpretation of this specific story, or other such stories, than to illustrate how Rousseau challenges the reader to ask whether the educational set pieces he relates, and the characters in them, accord with the principle of the natural goodness of man. Whether we agree or disagree concerning the "correct" interpretation of the story of Emile's garden, our readings of the story must be guided by the substantive argument of *Emile*, the ultimate lesson for the reader.

"Real" and "False" Emiles

Since the reader encounters characters named "Emile" and "Jean-Jacques" in the story of planting beans, it would seem at first blush that this reader has little reason to suspect that he is not reading about the "true" Emile or about a lesson that would not be appropriate for the eponymous student of the work. Lest my claim that the reader is being tested concerning the identity of the pupil in the story itself seem misapplied, later in the work Rousseau is more explicit about confounding "real" and "false" Emiles.[33] An example of this technique occurs in book III in a story in which master and tutor get lost in a forest.

The main theme of book III is teaching Emile about the physical world in which he lives, with the touchstone being utility. He explains near the outset: "It is a question not of knowing what is, but only of knowing what is useful" (166). And somewhat later: "What is that good for? This is now the sacred word, the decisive word between him and me in all the actions of our life. . . . He who is taught as his most important lesson to want to know nothing but what is useful interrogates like Socrates" (179). The reference to Socrates indicates the text with which Rousseau is in dialogue in *Emile* as a whole and book III in particular: Plato's *Phaedrus*. We have already seen his engagement with *Phaedrus* in the *Discourse on the Sciences and the Arts*, with the frontispiece depicting Prometheus bringing the gift of fire and the textual reference to the frontispiece relating it to the myth of Thoth as related in Plato's dialogue. The frontispiece to book III of *Emile* makes a parallel reference to the related myth of Hermes engraving the elements of the sciences on a column. I will return to this engraving in the following chapter.

For now, it suffices to note that the tutor teaches Emile to play the role of Thamos in the Platonic story, asking about the utility of the sciences and the arts with which he is presented. More important for the present purposes is the question of the utility of writing raised by Socrates, namely that while speech can be tailored to the character and capacity of the auditor, say a pupil, writing is indiscriminately available to any reader. Rousseau's challenge to the reader to identify "real" and "false" Emiles in book III in particular, and his alternation between different tutors and pupils in the work as a whole, is inspired by the discussion of writing and rhetoric in Plato's *Phaedrus*.

The story in question involving "real" and "false" Emiles is prepared at the beginning of book III when Rousseau illustrates the guiding pedagogical principle of utility with another story that itself involves a complicated confusion of masters and pupils. To compound the confusion, this story is imbedded in a contrast between different pupils and the apt and inapt lessons they receive, a version of the technique of staging a comparison between two pupils that we have already seen. Let us follow him step by step. First, he begins by addressing the reader in his potential role as tutor, urging "you" (*vous*) to make "your pupil" attentive to the phenomena of nature. He then accuses "you" of delivering an inappropriate lesson by teaching the pupil about geography with globes, cosmic spheres, maps, and other representations of the phenomena instead of having him observe the phenomena themselves. Second, having discussed "you" and "your pupil," he turns to himself and his pupil. "One fine evening we go for a walk in a suitable place where a broad, open horizon permits the setting sun to be fully seen," he begins, explaining how "we" note the location of its setting and then repeat the observation in the same location with the rising sun the next morning. The identity of "we" is not specified. Third, Rousseau then allows the tutor to blunder, switching the object of the narration from the first to the third person. Watching the rising sun with his pupil, "the master" wants to communicate the feelings inspired by the beauty of the spectacle to his pupil. "Pure stupidity!" comments Rousseau in his authorial voice: "It is in man's heart that the life of nature's spectacle exists. To see it, one must feel it. The child perceives the objects, but he cannot perceive the relations linking them; he cannot hear the sweet harmony of their concord" (168–69).[34] Fourth, Rousseau frames this complicated alternation from "we" to "he" by returning to the overarching narrative frame of a contrast between what "you" and "I" do with our respective pupils. He begins by addressing the reader (*vous*): "Do not make speeches to the child which he cannot understand." Then he resumes the "we" of master and pupil: "Raised in the spirit of our maxims, he"—that is, "my pupil"—"examines each new object he sees for a long time without saying anything." Finally, Rousseau turns to a proper lesson in cosmography, explaining how he gets his pupil to realize that the sun revolves around the earth, appearing in the east in the morning and setting in the west in the evening, and then suggesting how repeated observations of the location of the rising and setting sun at different times of year will transform the lesson from a Ptolemaic to Copernican one (169–70). How useful is this lesson to the pupil?

The utility of this lesson for the child is precisely what is at issue in the story of master and pupil getting lost in the forest. This story appears immediately following the passage in which he states that the pupil who asks "What is that good for?" interrogates like Socrates, thus alerting us to the problem of the appropriateness of different lessons for different recipients, a warning underscored by Rousseau when he writes just afterward, "I do not like explanations in speeches" (179–80). Rousseau sets up the story by returning to the lesson in cosmography with which he begins book III to illustrate the principle of utility with apt and inapt lessons for different pupils: "Let us suppose that while I am studying with my pupil the course of the sun and how to get one's bearings." Our immediate assumption is that "I" is the tutor Jean-Jacques and "my pupil" is Emile. But are they? Rousseau then has the tutor "I" bungle once again by delivering an inapt lesson: "What a fine speech I will make to him! . . . When I have finished, I shall have made a true pedant's display of which he will have understood not a single idea." The child, he explains, dare not interrupt the speech for fear "I" will get angry. The reference to anger should warn the reader that we may not be dealing here with the "true" Jean-Jacques or Emile. The switch of pupils becomes evident in the next paragraph when Rousseau writes that "our Emile" will not heed the elaborate explanations of the utility of the lesson by the hapless tutor (180). He then turns to the story of getting lost in the forest.

"We were observing the position of the forest north of Montmorency," he begins the story, with the child—"he"—interrupting "I" to ask about the utility of this lesson. As with the story at the outset of book III involving watching the setting sun, the identity of "we" is unspecified. The next morning "we" go for a walk before lunch and get lost in the forest: "Very hot, very tired, and very hungry, we accomplish nothing by our racing around other than to get more lost. Finally we sit down to rest and deliberate. Emile, who I am supposing has been raised like any child, does not deliberate; he cries." The child is identified as "Emile." But unlike the "real" Emile, this Emile is by supposition "raised like any child." Moreover, he cries out of frustration and perhaps anger.

A dialogue then ensues between our two heroes, "Emile" and "Jean-Jacques." In the dialogue, the tutor asks his charge: "Let me see your watch. What time is it?" It is noon. Then a dialogic lesson reminiscent of Plato's *Meno* takes place in which Emile is led by his tutor to deduce from the direction of the shadow that the town must lie to the south.[35] Off they march toward lunch, with Emile saying, "Astronomy is good for something," or, as Rousseau writes after resuming the narrative, he will at least think it, thereby calling into question the credibility of the narrative and embedded dialogue (180–81).

If the reader already has reason to suspect that he is not witnessing the "real" Jean-Jacques and the "real" Emile in this story, Rousseau reveals the trick some pages later. Returning to the principle of leading the child by utility, he states that the child will value a pastry chef over a goldsmith and will not even treat clockmaking very seriously: "The happy child enjoys time without being its slave. He profits from it and does not know its value." Then the reveal concerning the earlier story: "In assuming he has a watch as well as in making him cry, I gave myself a common [*vulgaire*] Emile, to be useful and to make myself understood; for, with respect to the true one [*le veritable*], a child so different from others would not serve as an example for anything" (187–88).[36] Now we have a "true" Emile and a "common" Emile. The contrast between them tests the reader. Would the "true" Emile cry? We were told earlier that he likely would not: "As soon as Emile has once said, 'It hurts,' very intense pains indeed will be needed to force him to cry" (77). Would the "true" Emile possess a watch?[37] The imaginary pupil has now become somehow real. Such, in fact, is Rousseau's aim: to persuade his reader to take Rousseau's "visions" for true and what he sees before his eyes as false.

Inapt Apologues

In his analysis of La Fontaine's fable "The Crow and the Fox" in book II, Rousseau complains that the morals, or apologues, maladroitly added to the fable are either unnecessary if the lesson is clear from the fable itself or inapt if the lesson drawn by the child is different (112). Or, as he protests later in the work when he returns to fables: "Nothing is so vain or so ill-conceived as the moral with which most fables end—as if this moral were not or should not be understood in the fable itself in such a way as to be palpable to the reader" (248). His analysis of how fables are read and misread is itself a lesson in reading for the reader of *Emile*. One technique he uses in his program of education is to offer inapt apologues to some of the stories he tells, challenging the reader to draw a more correct moral. These stories often also involve the confusion over pupils and tutors I have just examined.

"Tai-toi Jean-Jacques"

Just before his analysis of "The Crow and the Fox," Rousseau relates an example concerning drawing the proper lesson from a story that involves himself as the supposedly historical Jean-Jacques Rousseau and a pupil other than Emile. He prepares this example after an authorial address to the reader that can be read only ironically: "Readers, always remember that he who speaks to you is neither a scholar nor a philosopher, but a simple man, a friend of the truth, without party, without system; a solitary who, living little among men, has less occasion to contract their prejudices and more time to reflect on what strikes him when he interacts with them" (110). With this flourish, Rousseau turns witness and enters into a story of once having visited a family that trotted out their young boy in the French fashion of parading his learning before the assembled guests. The child ably relates a story from Plutarch of Alexander the Great, who downed a potion prepared by his physician Philip despite rumors that the doctor aimed to poison him. The child's governor and the other adults admire Alexander for his courage. Rousseau the witness, and bad houseguest, tells the assembled guests they are wrong: that Alexander's action was if anything foolhardy rather than courageous, and that the true lesson lies elsewhere. Before he has the opportunity to explain, a woman sitting beside him stops him and whispers, "'Keep quiet, Jean-Jacques, they won't understand you.' I looked at her; I was struck; and I kept quiet" (111).

Tai-toi Jean-Jacques.[38] A warning to the reader as well? Will readers understand? But first, what about the child? Rousseau queries the child as to what lesson he took from the story he told and is not surprised to learn that he admired Alexander for bravely downing the potion, for he himself recently had to take a bitter-tasting medicine. This is as he expects, since he knows that a child, like natural man, has no conception of death. Indeed, he later alludes in *Emile* to the story of the physician Philip when he relates a misapplied lesson "I"—the supposedly historical Jean-Jacques Rousseau—once gave to an unidentified child concerning the dangers of wine adulterated with lead, only to realize that the child did not grasp the utility of the experiment because he had no conception of death (182–83). Yet another example of Rousseau claiming to have been deceived and allowing the reader to learn from his mistake. Apparently, he has learned something by the time he encounters the young admirer of Alexander.

Thus far Rousseau has been explicit about the series of mistakes being made by the people in his story: the adults are mistaken about the moral of the story and equally mistaken about the child being capable of understanding this moral. But what is the proper moral? After being unusually taciturn, and briefly returning to the main narrative with a reference to the story of Robert the gardener and a remark about the child's difficulty in grasping abstract concepts (perhaps indicating that the garden lesson was inapt?), Rousseau returns to taunt the reader:

> Some readers, discontented with the "Keep quiet, Jean-Jacques," will, I foresee, ask what, after all, do I find so fair in Alexander's action? Unfortunate people! If you have to be told, how will you understand it? It is that Alexander believed in virtue; it is that he staked his head, his own life on that belief; it is that his great soul was made for believing in it. Oh, what a fair profession of faith was the swallowing of that medicine! No, never did a mortal make so sublime a one. If there is some modern Alexander, let him be shown to me by like deeds. (111)

The reader is no longer deceived, or at least uninformed. Or is he? The further complications raised by this story need not be pursued, but only raised. Alexander was said to have emulated Achilles, the subject of the frontispiece to *Emile*, and he also deified himself. As such, did he refuse to consider himself to be "mortal" and therefore not vulnerable to death by poisoning? If not, what is the proper lesson to be drawn from the story? Is Alexander a good model to emulate? If Rousseau's story wrapped in a story is a kind of fable with a proper moral, the key to solving the riddle lies not in being told, but in becoming the kind of reader who comes to see and feel in such a way as to grasp the meaning.

The Crow and the Fox

The challenge to draw the proper moral from the story of Alexander and the physician Philip prepares the analysis of "The Crow and the Fox" that immediately follows. Rousseau begins by stipulating that, even though all children are made to learn La Fontaine's fables, Emile will not do so because they are beyond the grasp of children. In choosing "The Crow and the Fox" for analysis to prove his contention, Rousseau draws attention to the fact that he is making a choice of one fable among others. He mistakenly states that the fable he has chosen is placed at the head of the collection of fables (in fact, it is the second) and also remarks that he considers it the author's "masterpiece" (112–13).[39] In any case, he underscores the fact that something about this particular fable would seem to be worthy of attention.

Having made his choice, Rousseau presents a line-by-line analysis of the fable intended to show how its poetic language and other elements are beyond the child's capacity and often lead him to an interpretation of the fable different than that intended by the author. At one point in the analysis, Rousseau addresses a reader of his own work, indicating that a lesson should be drawn from his analysis. The verse in question is the line that introduces the speech made by the fox to the crow: "Made to him a speech of this kind" (Lui tint à peu près ce langage). He comments: "*A speech!* [*Ce langage!*] Foxes speak, then? They speak, then, the same language as crows. Wise preceptor, be on your [*toi*] guard: weigh your response well before making it. It is more important than you think" (114). This time Rousseau does not need a prudent lady tablemate to tell him to remain silent, and he leaves it to the reader ("wise preceptor") to adduce the correct interpretation of this mysterious remark.

What is the proper response? I suggest that this story of fabular animals speaking in a garden setting (not long after the story of Emile and his garden) is a stalking horse for the biblical story of the Garden of Eden, where a demon disguised as a snake successfully communicates with Eve. After all, the apologue to La Fontaine's fable concerns the crow's being tricked by the fox into letting a piece of cheese fall from his beak by an appeal to the crow's pride, another version of the Fall. Rousseau argues that this apologue is inapt for the child, who will be corrupted by wanting to imitate the fox (115). The fable may also be a stand-in for the catechism, for, as Rousseau concludes his dismissal of fables, "In society there is needed one morality in words and one in action, and these two moralities do not resemble each other. The first is in the catechism, where it is left. The other is in La Fontaine's fables for children and in his tales for mothers. The same author suffices for everything" (116). Evidence for this interpretation can be found in *Julie*, where Julie discusses teaching her son to read by first reading La Fontaine's fables, only to realize that the child drew the wrong apologue from the fable of the crow and the fox, and then composing versions of biblical stories, only to then reveal that they do not learn their catechism (*Julie*, V.2, *CW*, 6:476–77).[40] At any rate, to return to *Emile*, despite the explicit moral Rousseau draws from his analysis of the fable and its inapt apologue, he leaves it to the reader to draw further lessons concerning his purposes in presenting it.

Jean-Jacques in the Dark

Shortly after the analysis of fables, Rousseau presents a kind of fable through a story from his childhood. The context in which the story comes is his recommendation that children become accustomed to the dark in order to overcome their natural fear of it. Mention of nurses telling stories of ghosts and goblins and making their charges superstitious indicates part of Rousseau's reasons for dwelling at such length on the subject. In the midst of his suggestions regarding "night games," then, Rousseau waxes elegiac: "There is a stage of life beyond which, in progressing, one retrogresses. . . . In getting old, I become a child again, and I recall more gladly what I did at ten than at thirty. Readers, pardon me, therefore, for sometimes drawing my examples from myself, for to do this book well I must do it with pleasure" (135).

The supposedly autobiographical story involves Jean-Jacques Rousseau when he and his cousin boarded with a minister, M. Lambercier. He emphasizes that his cousin was richer than he, and his jealousy leads him to taunt the boy for being afraid of the dark. The minister, bored by his boasting, sends Jean-Jacques one night to fetch a Bible that had been left in the church. Crossing the cemetery to reach the temple, he fearlessly reaches the church, only to get confused after entering and grow afraid. Leaving the church and unable to persuade his dog, Sultan, to accompany him, he reenters the church and once again grows fearful and runs back to the house. As he approaches the house, he hears M. Lambercier laughing, and presumes the laughter is at his expense, and then he hears Mlle. Lambercier expressing concern about him and sending someone to help: "Instantly, all my frights ceased, leaving me only the fright of being encountered in my flight. I ran—I flew—to the temple without losing my way." He fetches the Bible and runs back to the house and breathlessly presents it, "flustered by palpitating with joy at having been ahead of the help they intended for me." The moral of the story? "One might ask if I tell this story as a model to follow and as an example of the gaiety which I exact in this kind of exercise? No, but I give it as proof that nothing is more reassuring to someone frightened of shadows in the night than to hear company, assembled in a neighboring room, laughing and chatting calmly" (136).

Of course, this cannot possibly be the correct moral to this fable. Far from being reassured by laughter and chatter, the young Jean-Jacques's pride was piqued in the face of potential humiliation. The issue of pride has already been foreshadowed in the details of the story concerning his rivalry with his wealthier cousin. Moreover, his fear of the dark church suggests that he suffered from precisely the superstition that the "night games" he recommends are meant to combat. Finally, if we permit ourselves to consult some autobiographical information not available to the reader of *Emile* at the time of its publication, we can supplement this story with his account in book I of the *Confessions* of his stay with his cousin with M. and Mlle. Lambercier, incidentally with no mention of the story of the Bible in the church. What is most striking about the account is his precocious sexuality at the hands of Mlle. Lambercier—literally, for he discovered he got erotic pleasure from being spanked by her (*Confessions*, *CW*, 5:11 ff.). One strongly assumes that Rousseau is making up the story of the nocturnal raid on Scripture, as perhaps signaled by the fact that, coincidence aside, "Sultan" was the name of his dog at the time he wrote *Emile*. At any rate, the apologue he offers for it is clearly inapt. The young Jean-Jacques Rousseau is an example of a corrupt child meant to be compared to the product of a proper education.

Cake Races

Another example of a story with an inapt apologue involves a mysterious "I" narrator who once trained a proud and lazy child to run, and later in *Emile* Rousseau, in his role as the tutor Jean-Jacques, recalls the story in a way that also challenges the reader to identify the "real" Emile. So, in this complex set of stories we have potentially mistaken identities of both tutor and pupil.

The first story of running comes in book II and is introduced abruptly into Rousseau's account of how to train the senses, in this case sight. As I noted in the introduction, the training in this portion of the work of the pupil's sight should be seen as a parallel to Rousseau's education of the reader through visual techniques, for example correcting sight by introducing differences in perspective in viewing an object (say, a circular tower that initially appears square to the eye), parallels correcting the reader's perspective by comparing "my pupil" to "your pupil" and by asking the reader to identify the "true" Emile.

The story in question commences with a kind of "once upon a time" beginning: "There was an indolent and lazy child who was to be trained in running." He then provides information about the child: he was too lazy to run because, although intended for a military career, he had persuaded himself that his rank and noble birth were "going to take the place of arms and legs as well as of every kind of merit." The child is likened to an Achilles, who would require the skill of Chiron to get him to run—an allusion to the frontispiece of book II featuring Chiron and Achilles, a subject to which I will return in the next chapter. Suddenly "I" is introduced: "The difficulty was all the greater since I wanted to prescribe to him absolutely nothing. . . . Here is how I went about it—I, that is to say, the man who speaks in this example" (141). Who is "I"? Jean-Jacques Rousseau? Jean-Jacques the tutor? An unnamed other tutor?

The mysterious "I" entices his proud pupil to run by staging running races with cakes as the prize, appealing to the child's gluttony. The story is told with elaborate detail, with "I" involving other children in the races, altering the length of the course, and ensuring through various ruses that his young pupil would generally win, thus also appealing to his pride. He relates that while at first the "young knight" almost always ate his cake alone when he won, as he became accustomed to victory he displayed generosity by often sharing the prize with the vanquished. "That provided a moral observation for me," the narrator remarks, "and I learned thereby what the true principle of generosity is" (142). The reader is perhaps meant to recall the story of Jean-Jacques Rousseau having observed the infant slapped by its nurse and the indignant crying, leading him to conclude, perhaps mistakenly, that the sense of justness and unjustness is innate (65–66). Whatever the case regarding the "true principle of generosity" in this example, it is at least not clear that the narrator "I" drawing this moral lesson is Rousseau in any of his personae. The story of the running child then ends as abruptly as it began, with the narrator remarking that this training had exercised the child's sight as much as his legs: "Finally, a few months of tests and corrected errors formed the visual compass in him to such an extent that when I told him to think of a cake on some distant object, he had a glance almost as sure as a surveyor's chain" (143). Neither Rousseau nor the mysterious narrator draws an explicit moral from this fable, so the concluding remark about having successfully trained the child's "visual compass" has to stand as the purpose and moral of the lesson. But surely the chief aim of the lesson was intended not to exercise the child's sight, but to cure his pride or transform it. This proud "young knight" requires a different kind of education than Emile.

Rousseau references this story of running races within the romance of Emile and Sophie in book V. Their flirtation proceeds under the guidance of Jean-Jacques the tutor, who is likened not to Chiron but to Mentor, the tutor in Fénelon's *Telemachus*, to which I shall return in chapter 6. In the set-up to the story, Rousseau—whose narrative voice shifts between the authorial "I" and the perspective of Jean-Jacques as a character in the story itself—describes Emile: "But Emile's conduct is never devious; he does not know how to be evasive and does not want to be. He has that amiable delicacy which flatters and feeds *amour-propre* with the good witness of oneself" (435–36). Unlike the vain "young knight" of the earlier story, then, Emile's *amour-propre* has been properly developed. Sophie and Emile walk together and picnic, while Jean-Jacques and Sophie's father eat cakes and drink wine. Then abruptly: "Apropos of cakes. I speak to Emile of his former races." Emile engages in a race with a cake as the prize, and when he wins the race, "no less generous than Aeneas, he gives presents to all the vanquished." As with the earlier running story, generosity is the outcome, but unlike the earlier child, Emile does not have to learn to be generous, for his pride has been directed in a healthy manner. Sophie then challenges Emile to race, and the analogous identities are further confused when the swift Sophie is likened to Atalanta (436–37).

Perhaps the layering of one analogue upon another—Emile as Telemachus and Aeneas and possibly Achilles, Sophie as Atalanta, the tutor(s) as Chiron and Mentor—is supposed to make the reader wonder about the identity of these participants and the relationship of this running story to the earlier one. The details of the story indicate that the reader is obviously meant to recall the earlier story about racing for cakes. But the earlier story involved "an indolent and lazy child," assuredly not Emile.[41] Admittedly, this may be an instance of a Homeric nod on the part of our author, but the reaction of the "attentive" reader would nonetheless still be instructive. That reader objects, "That wasn't *really* Emile in the earlier story!" Such an objection would be evidence of Rousseau's success: he has thoroughly persuaded his reader to take Emile as somehow "real," the exemplar to which the other child, who is after all the real child or at least like a real child, must be compared.

Making a Compass: Another Inapt Lesson?

If the inapt apologue to the story of training the "young knight" to run concerned the supposed goal of training his "visual compass," the last example I want to examine is allegedly designed to make a literal compass. The story occurs in book III and relates how "I" and "my pupil" are experimenting with magnets and visit a country fair in which a magician or showman (*bateleur*) uses a magnet to draw a duck floating in a tub of water.

Just before relating the story, Rousseau addresses the reader: "Here I am once again in my lengthy and minute details. Reader, I hear your grumbling and I brave it. I do not want to sacrifice the most useful part of this book to your impatience. Make your decision about my delays, for I have made mine about your complaints" (172). This challenge should put the reader on guard. Then the story begins: "A long time ago my pupil and I had noticed that amber, glass, wax, and various other bodies when rubbed attracted straws and that others did not attract them." The identities of both tutor and pupil are uncertain. Because of their experiments, the child realizes that the magician must be using a magnet to draw his duck, and, returning home, the tutor and pupil take it into their heads to imitate the magician by constructing their own magnetized duck. The next day they return to the fair and "my little doctor, who was hardly able to contain himself," excitedly tells the magician that he, too, can do the trick. Success and applause makes "[my] proud little naturalist chatter," the narrator states, but they leave the fair with him "covered with praise." Invited by the magician to return the next day, the excited child is stunned when his trick goes awry and the duck flees rather than approaches. The magician makes the duck come and dazzles the crowd with more elaborate tricks as the humiliated child looks on and then slinks away. Finally, the following day the magician shows up at their door to complain about the child and especially the tutor taking away his paltry livelihood as a country fair magician. The next day they visit the fair one last time and approach "our magician-Socrates" with respect (172–75).

The story over, Rousseau closes the narrative circle with another address to the reader: "Every detail of this example is more important than it seems. How many lessons in one! How many mortifying consequences are attracted by the first movement of vanity! Young master, spy out the first movements with care. If you know thus how to make humiliation and disgrace arise from it, be sure that a second movement will not come for a long time. 'So much preparation!' you will say. I agree—and all for the sake of making ourselves a compass to take the place of a meridian" (172–75).

The explicit apologue to this story is that the purpose was to make a compass, but Rousseau's remarks as author in the address to the reader suggest the true motive: to humiliate vanity. As noted, the identity of tutor and pupil are never given. Is this lesson appropriate for Emile, who we suppose would not display vanity? The details of the story suggest that the tutor has in fact inflamed the child's vanity, playing the tempter who introduces him prematurely to the knowledge of good and evil. One of the challenges faced by the reader, then, is to ask whether this would be an appropriate lesson for Emile and, relatedly, whether the child in question is in fact Emile. As with the stories of running races, the reader later faces this challenge again when Rousseau states that vanity must be humiliated in "my pupil" by repeating the lesson: "The adventure with the magician would be repeated in countless ways" (245). Is "my pupil" Emile?[42]

Conclusion

I want to conclude the analyses I have presented by emphasizing what I said at the outset about my intention. Namely, I am less interested here in offering new interpretations of the various stories Rousseau tells throughout *Emile* than I am in illustrating the narrative and other techniques Rousseau employs to educate and test the reader. I fear that the readings of mistaken identity and inapt apologues I have presented may seem to verge on being too clever by half. How do we determine who the "real" Emile is, or whether the apologues Rousseau appends to his fables are inapt? In some cases, Rousseau is clearer about the fact that he is offering a test or misdirecting the reader. For example, he himself tells us that he has given us a "common" Emile as opposed to the "true" Emile in the story of getting lost in the forest, and his claim that the purpose of the elaborate story of training a boy to run in order to hone his visual compass is transparently incomplete at best. However, I suggest that the purpose is less to ask the reader to identify the "true" Emile or the proper moral than to have the reader ask the question in the first place. In doing so, the reader is applying the overarching lesson of *Emile* of learning to observe human nature correctly, a lesson that entails rejecting the examples we have before our eyes and learning to see through the perspective Rousseau offers in the work. Rousseau's challenges invite the active participation of the reader in his own education.

Chapter 4

The Illustrative
Education of *Emile*

When discussing the *Discourse on the Sciences and the Arts* and the *Discourse on Inequality*, I attended to the frontispieces to the two works as part of my analysis of the paratextual elements that initiate the education of the reader. *Emile* also includes illustrations—five of them, in fact, one for each of the five books into which the work is divided, with the frontispiece to book I doing double duty as the frontispiece to the work as a whole. The frontispieces to the two *Discourses* have received some attention from scholars, but the engravings that adorn *Emile* have earned only passing notice. As I noted in chapter 1 when discussing the frontispiece to the *Discourse on the Sciences and the Arts*, the only sustained attempts to interpret the illustrations in relation to the text in Rousseau's corpus have been for his best-selling novel, *Julie, or The New Heloise*. These analyses provide a useful interpretive approach to interpreting the engravings in all of Rousseau's works, but they are particularly apt for interpreting *Emile* because both works contain multiple illustrations and illustrations that are *explicitly* keyed to specific points in the text. To repeat what Philip Stewart argues with regard to *Julie*: "The illustration itself must be decoded and assimilated by the reader; and whether it is read before or after, it cannot be read simultaneously with or even independently of the passage to which it corresponds."[1]

In this chapter I interpret the engravings for *Emile* in relation to the text in order to understand how the dialogical interplay of the visual image and the written word educates the reader by posing an interpretive challenge designed to change the reader's perspective. Rousseau himself speaks in *Emile* of the necessity of using the language of signs when discussing how the tutor will instruct his pupil: "Let us try therefore to engrave it in his memory in such a way that it will never be effaced. One of the errors of our age is to use reason in too unadorned a form, as if men were all mind. In neglecting the language of signs that speak to the imagination, the most energetic of languages has been lost" (*Emile*, 321).² His use of the verb "engrave" here is telling. As in the previous chapters, on the two *Discourses* and the education of the reader in *Emile*, in discussing the dialogic interplay between image and text in *Emile*, I highlight Rousseau's response to the challenge posed in Plato's *Phaedrus* concerning how a written work can speak to different audiences in different ways. This interpretive path is suggested by Rousseau himself when he includes a version of the myth of Thoth in the central engraving of *Emile* of Hermes bringing the elements of the sciences and the arts to mankind.

The Design of the Engravings

Some general remarks about the engravings for *Emile* are in order before turning to their interpretation. After the title page, frontispiece, and a brief preface, Rousseau includes a page titled "Explanations of the Illustrations" (36). As noted above in chapter 1, "Explanations" (mistranslated by Bloom in the singular) translates *Explications*, the term referring to a genre included in many books of the period that presented allegorical pictures and then decoded them. Whereas the *explications* Rousseau included in *Julie* in the Subjects of the Engravings are quite elaborate, with at least a paragraph devoted to each of the twelve engravings, the Explanations of the Illustrations in *Emile* are Spartan, with a single sentence for each of the five engravings. We know that Rousseau sent detailed instructions to the designer of the engravings for *Emile*, Charles Eisen, who was earlier responsible for the frontispiece of the *Discourse on Inequality*, but the correspondence has not survived.³

The placement of the five engravings for *Emile* at the head of each of the five books into which it divided, with one important exception, suggests that Rousseau's intention was to have them serve as frontispieces. This suggestion is buttressed by his instruction to the publisher that they be placed facing the opening page of each book.⁴ The difference between *Emile* and *Julie* in this regard is instructive. There are two engravings for each of the six parts of the novel, with one near the beginning of each part and one near the end, thereby framing each part pictorially.⁵ The novel's engravings illustrate the action of the story, at least at the most obvious level. By contrast, the engravings for *Emile* do not depict the action of the work.⁶ Rather, they are allegorical devices that refer to the philosophical content of the work, and thus more akin to the frontispieces to the two *Discourses*.

Rousseau's intention to illustrate each of the five books of *Emile* with a frontispiece was frustrated by the production of the work, leading him to make a partial change in plan. The original edition of *Emile* was published in four volumes (in octavo), and he therefore had to choose how to break the five books into four volumes. At the head of the first published volume is an engraving of Thetis, which Rousseau explains in the Explanations of the Illustrations "relates to the first book and serves as frontispiece to the work," that is, to the work as a whole (36). The first volume contains the first two books of *Emile*, and so the engraving of Chiron appears partway through the first volume at the head of book II. The second volume opens with the engraving of Hermes that adorns book III. Book IV commences partway through the second volume and continues into the third, which has an engraving of Orpheus at its head. Rousseau specified the exact beginning of the third volume in a letter to his publisher: "'Thirty years ago. . . .'" This is, of course, the beginning of the dramatic introduction to the "Profession of Faith of the Savoyard Vicar," and Rousseau instructed his publisher to place the engraving of Orpheus at this point as a frontispiece to the third volume.[7] In the Explanations of the Illustrations he characterizes the engraving of Orpheus as "belonging to Book IV" (36), thereby indicating that, unlike the other engravings, it does not represent the entire book and suggesting that it is an exception that proves the rule. His decision regarding the placement of this engraving has the effect of giving each published volume a frontispiece, with the disadvantage—at least for the interpreter—of leaving book IV as a whole without an unambiguous frontispiece. Finally, the fourth published volume contains book V and is illustrated with an engraving of Circe.

If the frontispieces to the two *Discourses* ask to be read as allegories of the entire work by both their subject matter and their status as frontispieces, several features of the engravings for *Emile* indicate that Rousseau had the same intention for this work. First, and most obviously, there is the content of the illustrations themselves. Rousseau chose subjects from mythology that are already allegorical. This impression is confirmed in the first textual reference to the subject of the first engraving, where he terms the story of Achilles' mother plunging him into the Styx an "allegory" drawn from a "fable" (47). His choice of mythological subjects makes the most obvious parallel for interpretation the frontispiece to the *Discourse on the Sciences and the Arts* depicting Prometheus bringing fire to mankind, which he also therein terms an "allegory" taken from a "fable" (*Sciences*, 23 n.). The allegorical intention is underscored by the title "Explanations of the Illustrations" (36), indicating that these explanations are meant as allegorical hints, given the meaning of the term *explication* noted above.

Second, Rousseau further underscores the primary role of the engravings as allegorical frontispieces by specifying legends that refer to the subject of the image rather than to their action: Thetis, Chiron, Hermes, Orpheus, and Circe. He was adamant on this score, for in one of his instructions to his publisher he demanded that the first engraving be identified as "Thetis" instead of the engraver's initial "Thetis plunging Achilles into the river Styx."[8] Only in the Explanations of the Illustrations does he summarize the action represented in the engravings, giving us a way to begin unpacking their significance. For example, he writes that the first engraving "represents Thetis plunging her son in the Styx to make him invulnerable" (36).

Finally, unlike the two *Discourses*, where he refers in the engraving's legend to a specific point in the text and then likewise refers in the text to the frontispiece, in *Emile* he nowhere directly refers in the text to an engraving. For example, in the case cited above, where he mentions the "allegory" of Thetis plunging her son into the Styx, he does not refer to the engraving, even though it obviously represents the allegory. The engravings thus somehow at once stand alone and exist only in reference to the text: by their very nature they function as allegories. The way in which Rousseau presents the engravings as part of the text and yet separate from it creates a doubling of the allegory that requires interpreting the engraving in relation to the text and vice versa.

The reader is encouraged by Rousseau to compare text and engraving by the citations in the Explanations of the Illustrations to the page of the text where he refers to the subject of the engraving for each book. (Bloom mistakenly replaces these textual citations with references to the page numbers of the engravings themselves.) Textual references are also included on the engravings, with the page number in the top right corner of the frame surrounding the picture. The Explanations of the Illustrations, along with the references to the text on the illustrations themselves, are thus invitations to interpretation. With these preliminary considerations regarding the function of the engravings in mind, then, we can now turn to a discussion of how the engravings play a role in the education of the reader.

Thetis

The engraving that serves as a frontispiece for book I, and for *Emile* as a whole, is entitled "Thetis" and depicts the sea nymph plunging her son into the river Styx (fig. 4.1).[9] Lest there be any question that the river in question is the Styx, in the background of the engraving is a barely perceptible Charon ferrying passengers to the underworld, a detail that subtly underscores the issue of mortality. In the Explanations

4.1 Frontispiece of *Emile* and book I: Thetis

of the Illustrations Rousseau states: "The illustration, which relates to the first book and serves as frontispiece to the work, represents Thetis plunging her son in the Styx to make him invulnerable" (36). The only information provided in this explanation not obvious from looking at the engraving itself is Thetis's intention: to render her son invulnerable. (Granted, someone familiar with the story would already know that.) Note also that Rousseau's explanation does not mention Achilles by name, thus further indicating that the principal figure is Thetis. Indeed, one might have reasonably expected that a book bearing the title of its eponymous subject would have a frontispiece that allegorically represented Emile, by Achilles for example, but this is not the case. Rousseau's intention in choosing this subject and including this particular explanation as the initial hint for interpretation therefore hinges on Thetis and her intention.

In choosing to make Thetis, and not Achilles, the principal subject of the frontispiece, Rousseau puts the focus less on the recipient of education than on the educator, in the broadest possible sense of the term. In fact, all of the engravings for *Emile* depict educators. "Our first preceptor is our nurse" (42), he explains of the first steps in our education, and famously urges mothers to nurse their own children. (Oddly, while the other sea nymphs are bare-breasted, Thetis's bosom is covered.) Thetis is a mother, and Rousseau opens his work by saying that he is addressing mothers: "It is to you that I address myself, tender and foresighted mother" (37). Mothers are nonetheless not the principal addressees of *Emile*, and, in fact, despite Rousseau's initial claim and his pleas in the beginning of the work to have mothers resume their traditional role, mothers soon disappear from Emile's education.[10] As we saw in the previous chapter, Rousseau's principal addressees in *Emile* are either "governors" (or similar terms), to whom he speaks teacher to teacher once he assumes the role of his imaginary pupil's imaginary governor, or "readers" more generally. At any rate, Thetis stands as the first would-be educator or, at the most general level, the first reader. The reader is invited to put himself (or herself) in the place of Thetis and interrogate her intentions of rendering her son invulnerable through the lens provided by the text.

The passage that corresponds to the frontispiece depicting Thetis, as indicated by the page references included both in the Explanations of the Illustrations and on the engraving itself, offers what at first seems to be a straightforward interpretation of the engraving. This interpretation will nonetheless prove unsatisfactory upon further reflection. The context in which this passage occurs regards the concern for the physical vulnerability of children, especially by mothers. Whereas some mothers neglect their children, for example by not breastfeeding them, others carry their concern to excess, increasing the vulnerability of their child by preventing him from feeling his weakness and by hoping to exempt him from the laws of nature by keeping "hard blows away from him." At this point Rousseau suddenly introduces Thetis: "Thetis, to make her son invulnerable, plunged him, according to the fable, in the water of the Styx. This allegory is lovely and clear. The cruel mothers of whom I speak do otherwise: by dint of plunging their children in softness, they prepare them for suffering; they open their pores to ills of every sort to which they will not fail to be prey when grown" (47). Note that, like the Explanations of the Illustrations, this textual reference does not mention the more famous individual depicted in the engraving: Achilles. Once again, it is Thetis and her intention that are at issue.

The reader encounters the first interpretive challenge with Rousseau's claim that the allegory is "clear," for scrutiny of the passage in relation to the image soon reveals that it is not so clear after all. By contrasting Thetis with the "cruel mothers" who show excessive care for their children, he at first glance seems to approve of Thetis's intention to render her son invulnerable. In keeping with this, two paragraphs later he recommends: "Harden their bodies against the intemperance of season, climates, elements; against hunger, thirst, fatigue. Steep them in the water of the Styx" (47). This advice might make sense if the child's physical vulnerability were all that were at stake. But it is not. After first introducing Thetis, Rousseau immediately turns to the issue of psychological vulnerability, that is, the health of the soul with regard to the passions. The issues of physical and psychological vulnerability are connected through the question of human mortality, and these new concerns complicate the initial, positive interpretation of Thetis's intention to render her son invulnerable. Indeed, the reader should in fact already have realized that the initial interpretation is insufficient, for just a few pages earlier Rousseau warned: "One thinks only of preserving one's child. That is not enough. One ought to teach him to preserve himself as a man, to bear the blows of fate. . . . You may very well take precautions against his dying. He will nevertheless have to die. And though his death were not the product of your efforts, still these efforts would be ill conceived. It is less a question of keeping him from dying than of making him live" (42). This language about teaching a child to "bear the blows of fate" foreshadows the language he uses immediately before introducing Thetis as an apparently positive alternative to mothers who show excessive concern for a child by keeping "hard blows away from him" (47). Thetis's intention in making her son invulnerable is precisely to render him immune from death, or at least as immune as her hold on his foot allows.

The initial interpretation of the engraving is further complicated just a few pages later when Rousseau makes another reference to the fable depicted in the engraving in relation to the subject of medicine. In one of his characteristic diatribes against this "lying art," he warns that the effects of medicine on the body are less important than those they have on the psyche because it introduces us prematurely to the terrors of death. In order to illustrate his point, he adduces the example of Achilles: "It is the knowledge of dangers that makes us fear them; he who believed himself invulnerable would fear nothing. By dint of arming Achilles against peril, the poet takes from him the merit of valor; every other man in his place would have been an Achilles at the same price" (55). By rendering Achilles invulnerable, Thetis—or, rather, "the poet"—deprives him of the virtues appropriate for mortal human beings. Rather than instructing his reader to alter his pupil by taking hold of him by the heel and dipping him in the Styx, Rousseau counsels: "Do you, then, want him to keep his original form? Preserve it from the instant he comes into the world. As soon as he is born, *take hold of him* [*emparez-vous de lui*] and leave him no more before he is a man" (48; emphasis added). As the "poet" of his own work, as both author and tutor, Rousseau will not attempt to render Emile invulnerable. As Patrick Deneen states: "Rousseau's choice of a model here is most perplexing, given that it stands directly in contradiction to the central meaning of his lesson. Thus, his claim that the meaning of the allegory 'is clear' is wholly misleading, even deceptive."[11] In sum, the allegory of Thetis is hardly "clear" in relation to Rousseau's text.

The first mention of Achilles invites the reader to compare the epic hero with Emile. Rousseau himself seems to ask us to do so by introducing his imaginary pupil (51) in between the initial textual reference to Thetis (47) and the subsequent reference to Achilles (55). In fact, as I have noted, this comparison is already suggested by the fact that the frontispiece depicting Thetis plunging her son in the Styx is placed directly across from the title page of the work. In addition to the title and the author, the title page includes an epigraph identified as coming from Seneca's *On Anger*: "We are sick with evils that can be cured; and nature, having brought us forth sound, itself helps us if we wish to be improved" (Sanabilibus aegrotamus malis; ipsaque nos in rectum genitos natura, si emendari velimus, iuvat; 31).[12] As we saw in the previous chapter, the accounts of observing indignant infants or the stories involving angry children Rousseau challenge the reader to ask whether these children are the product of a corrupt education. To return to Achilles, it is therefore no accident that the principal characteristic of Achilles is anger, an anger that is not even satiated, much less cured. Emile is no Achilles.[13]

The epigraph Rousseau chooses for *Emile* not only reminds us of the chief characteristic of the unnamed infant depicted on the frontispiece, but also claims that the disease can be cured, or rather that it is unnatural in the first place. No more natural are the concern with glory and the knowledge of death that also characterize Achilles. These passions and this knowledge create the psychological vulnerability to which pride, anger, and despair are responses. The knowledge of death is not natural and is one of the first acquisitions we make in society, Rousseau tells us in the *Discourse on Inequality* (*Inequality*, 73). He reminds us of this argument in *Emile* immediately after mentioning Achilles: "Naturally man knows how to suffer with constancy and die in peace. It is doctors with their prescriptions, philosophers with their precepts, priests with their exhortations, who debase his heart and make him unlearn how to die" (55).[14] Likewise, in an apparent allusion to Thetis's intention as depicted in the frontispiece, Rousseau asks: "Can you conceive of some true happiness possible for any being outside of its constitution? And is not wanting to exempt man from all the ills of his species equally to make him quit his constitution?" Such a being cannot be contented, and his unfulfilled demands make him angry: "How could I conceive that a child thus dominated by anger and devoured by the most irascible passions might ever be happy?" (87). Physical vulnerability is less at issue in *Emile* than the psychological condition of a being with unnatural acquisitions that are in tension with its natural endowments. If the reader notices Rousseau's shift from physical to psychological ills with his two allusions to Achilles in the text, he will realize that Achilles is in fact an inappropriate model.

The shift in emphasis from physical invulnerability to psychological vulnerability with the references to Achilles in book I is further confirmed by a final textual reference to the subject near the end of the work as a whole, in book V. This reference comes in the context of the tutor Jean-Jacques warning Emile of his vulnerability now that he has fallen in love with Sophie: "'When you entered the age of reason, I protected you from men's opinions. When your heart became sensitive, I preserved you from the empire of the passions. If I had been able to prolong this inner calm to the end of your life, I would have secured my work, and you would always be as happy as man can be. But, dear Emile, it is in vain that I have dipped your soul in the Styx; I was not able to make it everywhere invulnerable'" (443). Note that the tutor has plunged Emile's soul, not his body, into the river Styx. Since this third reference occurs shortly after the textual reference to the subject of the engraving for book V, Circe, I will return to this issue. For now, we can say that the three references to Thetis plunging her son into the river Styx might be characterized as tests of the reader's progress in the education provided by the work.

Chiron

Psychological vulnerability in Rousseau's understanding comes most importantly from the conflict between nature and society. "Everything is good, as it leaves the hands of the Author of things; everything degenerates in the hands of man," he begins book I. He then compares a child to a shrub that grows up in the middle of the highway and asks his "tender and foresighted mother" to keep the nascent shrub away from the highway (37–38). But the human highway is here to stay. Natural man having vanished, nature cannot simply take its course; an education that manages the conflict between nature and society is required. The education Rousseau envisions demands a philosophical understanding of human nature and its development in society, an education provided to Emile and by *Emile*. The composite beast of philosopher-tutor therefore replaces the mother in the narrative. The change once again parallels the allegory Rousseau has chosen for the frontispiece, for Thetis gives the centaur Chiron charge of her son's education.[15] The principal subject of the engraving for book II remains a tutor, and once again it is the tutor's intentions with regard to his pupil that are the key to interpreting the allegory.

The subject of the engraving at the head of book II (fig. 4.2), Rousseau states in the Explanations of the Illustrations, "represents Chiron training the little Achilles in running" (36). Rousseau carries the story of Achilles through the entire first volume of the published work, both books I and II being contained in the first volume. The wise centaur Chiron has served as a representation of the educator, and Rousseau and his reader would be familiar with the fable from many sources. The specific version of the fable portrayed in the engraving is not immediately derived from Homer, where the references to the "most righteous of the centaurs" is to his skill in medicine and his teaching of that art to Asclepius and to Achilles.[16] In other classical sources Chiron acquires further credentials, and he is represented as teaching music, hunting, and other arts to Achilles and others. Such is the reputation of the semiequine educator that Xenophon begins his treatise on hunting by adducing Chiron's mastery of the art as warrant for the subject's importance.[17] Finally, the metaphorical possibilities of a teacher who

4.2 Illustration for book II of *Emile*: Chiron

is half god, half animal were not lost on authors who used Chiron for exemplary purposes. Notably, Machiavelli claims that ancient writers covertly taught princes to "use the man and the beast" through the example of Chiron teaching Achilles.[18] Rousseau also appeals to Chiron's nature as half god, half beast, but what is important in his case is the philosophic knowledge of human nature and development required for the proper education of a naturally asocial and good animal in the bosom of society. Previous thinkers and educators have failed precisely because they lacked such knowledge. They do not recognize the contradictions between "man" and "citizen" that produce a being who is good neither for himself nor for others (39–41).

While the frontispiece of book II recalls traditional depictions of Chiron and Achilles, the differences in Rousseau's version point to his philosophical departure from his predecessors. In most versions, the centaur and his young charge are depicted hunting, Achilles often astride his tutor, one or both of them with bow and arrow in hand. By contrast, in Rousseau's version Chiron and Achilles are not hunting. Further, Achilles is afoot, and we are informed in the description of the engravings that he is being trained in running (*à la Course*). In the engraving in *Emile* they are engaged in hunting of a certain sort, for Chiron is accepting a hare from Achilles, which the boy seems to have chased and caught and which appears to be still alive. In (re)turn, Achilles is receiving an apple from Chiron.[19] If this a representation of hunting, it is a decidedly bloodless one. Sword, shield, and helmet lie on the ground; Rousseau has at least partially disarmed the centaur. The mythical sources warn us of the unruly nature of centaurs, and the image of the centauromachy decorated numerous ancient artifacts, including the Parthenon, with the most famous remnants of that very scene being among the Elgin Marbles. If hunting is an appropriate pursuit for little Achilles, Rousseau's young charge pursues fruit and other sweets.

The primarily therapeutic role of the educator as represented by Chiron is clear in the textual reference in book II to the engraving, and as in the case of Thetis in book I, Rousseau's emphasis is on a psychological rather than a physical treatment. The reference to Chiron and Achilles comes in a story about getting a lazy and proud child to run, and the story involves a child other than Emile and a tutor apparently other than Jean-Jacques. This is one of the stories I examined in the previous chapter, in this case a story involving both a substitution of tutors and pupils and an inapt apologue. Since my focus here is on the visual education of the reader, let me expand now on one aspect of the story I previously mentioned only in passing. Namely, the story of training a lad to run comes in the context of Rousseau's discussion of the exercise of sight. He notes how the sense of sight can lead one to mistaken judgments because of the limitations and illusions caused by perspective. In addition to verifying what sight alone tells us by other senses, for example touch, he recommends looking at the same object from different vantage points: "What is more, the very illusions of perspective are necessary for us to come to a knowledge of extension and to compare its parts. Without false appearances we would see nothing in perspective" (140). The visual education of Emile is akin to the visual education of *Emile*, as Rousseau constantly has the reader look at the same object from different angles and to compare different objects, for example "my pupil" and "your pupil."[20]

As for the anecdote relating to the frontispiece of book II, as noted in the previous chapter, it is introduced abruptly: "There was an indolent and lazy child who was to be trained in running." Rousseau goes on to explain that this noble lad did not like to run or engage in any other exercise even though he was destined for a military career. Having said this, he makes the reference to the engraving to book II: "To make of such a gentleman a light-footed Achilles, the skill of Chiron himself would have hardly sufficed." Finally, he complicates the identity of the narrator "I" who serves as Chiron to this indolent Achilles: "Here is how I went about it—I, that is to say, the man who speaks in this example" (141). Then, through an elaborate scheme, elaborately described, the tutor gets his young charge to compete with other children, with cake for a prize. In conclusion, he offers an inapt or at least incomplete moral to the story: that the young lad had his "visual compass" trained by learning to estimate the course he would race (143). Although Rousseau began this story by suggesting the child's need for physical exercise, as we saw in the previous chapter, the details of the story of the young knight already point to the true purpose of teaching him to run: to cure his pride. Finally, as we also saw there, Rousseau returns to the topic of racing for cakes in book V in a story involving Emile, whom Jean-Jacques reminds of his supposed races as a child—"Apropos of cakes . . ." (436)—thus further complicating the identities of pupils and tutors and challenging the reader to discern what lesson is appropriate for what student.

Let us now relate this story to the engraving. First, the engraving of Chiron and Achilles seems to illustrate an episode in the book, if metaphorically, for it is a story of teaching a boy to run. The textual reference to the engraving, stating that a Chiron would be needed to teach this particular Achilles, initially seems to underscore the direct nature of the allegory. The directness of the allegory is called into question or at least complicated if the real moral of the story concerns not training in running but the taming of pride. How does the engraving of Chiron and Achilles relate to this more complicated allegory? First, we might begin by noting that the engraving itself involves the topic of exchange or substitution: an exchange or substitution of an apple for a hare. Rousseau's textual reference to the engraving therefore appropriately involves a substitution of one pupil for another and one narrator-tutor for another, as well as one moral to the story for another.

Second, the depiction of Chiron in the frontispiece may provide a clue to Rousseau's intentions. In the mythical versions of the story, Chiron teaches Achilles hunting as preparation for the epic warrior; in Rousseau's version, Chiron is disarmed and Achilles accepts an apple for his running. Rousseau plays a variation on the theme of Chiron and Achilles in a tamer key. Achilles is not at all known for his generosity or humanity, but what links the two stories of running in *Emile* is generosity. The young knight of book II shares his cakes with the vanquished through a generosity born of redirected pride. In turn, Emile in book V also apportions his pastry, but through a generosity based on a properly regulated *amour-propre* and pity. The one required a cure, and the education of the other prevented the disease in the first place. Whatever the differences in their educations, though, both the young boy and Emile are different from Achilles. An apple is an appropriate alimentary reward for a new Achilles. Recall in this light that in book II, shortly after the story where he refers to the subject of the engraving, Rousseau includes a long quotation from Plutarch on Pythagorean vegetarianism, by far the longest quotation in the entire work, which he claims is "foreign" to his work but which points to the crucial role of pity in his understanding of human nature and development (154–55). The bloodthirsty pride and anger of Achilles must be prevented, as with Emile, or cured, as with Rousseau's haughty onetime pupil.[21]

Hermes

The engraving at the head of the second volume and the beginning of book III represents Hermes engraving the elements of the sciences on a column (fig. 4.3). Once again, we have a tutor for the principal figure in the engraving, but unlike the images depicting Thetis and Chiron, Hermes does not have a specific pupil, although there are onlookers (perhaps a teacher and student?). The absence of a specific pupil turns out to be significant for interpreting the engraving in relation to the text, for Rousseau explains that Emile will not learn the sciences from books or other graven images. Nor will Emile learn the sciences from an astrolabe or the other complicated machinery scattered on the ground

4.3 Illustration for book III of *Emile*: Hermes

at Hermes' feet, a detail that parallels the sword and shield lying unused at Chiron's feet. Hermes' lessons are not appropriate for Emile, and hence no specific pupil is depicted in the engraving. Given especially that the engraving depicts engraving or writing, there is, however, an implied pupil: the reader of the book, a pupil who emphatically does require Rousseau's instruction.

While the figure depicted is clearly the winged messenger god, the mythological source of the scene does not involve the Greek god. The source is both earlier and later than classical Hellenic literature, having its roots in the Egyptian myth of Thoth and only becoming identified with Hermes (or Hermes Trismegistus) in the later hermetic tradition. As with the frontispiece to the *Discourse on the Sciences and the Arts* displaying Prometheus and the textual note referencing the story of Thoth, Rousseau is in dialogue with Plato's *Phaedrus*. The same concern with speaking to different audiences in different ways, through both text and image, that occupies Rousseau in the frontispiece of the first *Discourse* can be seen in the engraving of Hermes.

The textual reference in book III to the engraving of Hermes enunciates some of the same suspicion of the sciences and the arts as Rousseau's earlier prizewinning essay: "I hate books. They teach one to talk only about what one does not know. It is said that Hermes engraved the elements of the sciences on columns in order to shelter his discoveries from a flood. If he had left a good imprint of them in man's head, they would have been preserved by tradition. Well-prepared minds are the surest monuments on which to engrave human knowledge" (184). Emile will not learn the sciences or arts from books, but from experience. As Isabelle Michel notes: "In the case of Hermes . . . Rousseau is closer to a counter-example, despite the connection established by the teaching of the sciences."[22] Rather than constituting a contradiction, however, the misapplied example of Hermes poses a challenge to the reader.

Different lessons are appropriate for different students. The textual reference to Hermes in book III comes in between the story of the tutor Jean-Jacques and Emile lost in the forest north of Montmorency (180–81) and Rousseau's revelation of the deception that he has substituted a "common" Emile for the "true" one in order to better instruct the reader (187–88). I examined this story in the previous chapter as an example of Rousseau's challenging the reader to correctly identify pupils and the lessons appropriate for them. It is therefore no accident that immediately after the story about Montmorency, and just before the textual reference to Hermes, Rousseau regales his reader with a recollection of his own mistaken lesson given to a child. The chemistry lesson involved explaining how ink was made, and when the bored student did not see the utility of the experiment, the hapless Jean-Jacques tried another experiment showing how to test whether wine was adulterated with lead, a lesson whose utility was also lost on the child because he did not have any conception of death (182–83). With these misapplied lessons in place, Rousseau turns his declaration about his detestation of books and the reference to Hermes engraving the elements of the sciences on columns (184). The misapplied lesson and the diatribe about books are related: after all, books are printed with ink. The question therefore becomes for whom books are useful, and in what way.

Just after the textual reference to the engraving, Rousseau's pupil receives his one product of the typographer's art: *Robinson Crusoe*. Defoe's work as adapted by Rousseau depicts a condition of something analogous to a natural man with developed faculties: "This state, I agree, is not that of social man," Rousseau acknowledges; "very likely it is not going to be that of Emile. But it is on the basis of this very state that he ought to appraise all the others" (184–85). I will examine Rousseau's use of Defoe's novel in chapter 6. For now, it suffices to say that Rousseau's condemnation of books comes in a book, and his pedagogical treatise should be read in the same light.[23] The book *Emile* serves Rousseau's readers in the same way that *Robinson Crusoe* serves Emile: as the basis on which they are to appraise their own state. Rousseau's *Emile* is appropriate for the reader, but not for Emile himself.

Rousseau's condemnation in *Emile* of Hermes' gift of writing is patterned after Socrates' critique of writing in Plato's *Phaedrus*, also a written work. Several parallels between the Socratic myth and Rousseau's treatment of the sciences and the arts in book III are evident. To begin with, as noted in the previous chapter, the tutor teaches Emile to play the role of Thamos: "What is that good for? This is now the sacred word, the decisive word between him and me in all the actions of our life. . . . He who is taught as his most important lesson to want to know nothing but what is useful interrogates like Socrates" (179; see 167–68). The quest for utility inspires Emile in his imitation of Robinson Crusoe. The absence of obvious utility is also central to the cautionary tale Rousseau tells about teaching a child about ink and adulterated wine. Emile will be shown the things at their true value and not at how other people appraise them. Once again, Rousseau's education is designed to prevent vanity in Emile, or, in his other examples of less well-governed children, to cure or redirect the passion.

The "Citizen of Geneva" in the *Discourse on the Sciences and the Arts* is Prometheus bringing fire but also warning of its abuse, and so too is Rousseau Hermes in the engraving for book III of *Emile*. As tutor he engraves the elements of the sciences on Emile's mind, and as author of the very book he is writing he warns of the dangers of books. As in the *Discourse*, Rousseau addresses multiple audiences. I have already indicated one method Rousseau uses in *Emile*: including multiple students with different temperaments, therefore requiring different lessons as part of the education of the reader. The cake race related to the engraving for book II of Chiron teaching the young Achilles to run is one such example. Rousseau thereby answers Socrates' critique of writing even as he engraves his teaching into an imperishable product of the typographer's dangerous art.

Orpheus

The engraving of "Orpheus teaching men the worship of the gods," as Rousseau describes it in the Explanations of the Illustrations (36), poses certain difficulties for interpretation (fig. 4.4). As noted earlier, the placement of this engraving was at least to some degree necessitated by the practical problem of apportioning the five books of *Emile* into four published octavo volumes. The circumstantial evidence therefore suggests that the idea of illustrating book IV with Orpheus was a late decision dictated in large part by necessity.[24] "Belonging" to book IV but apparently not representing it as a whole, Orpheus seems to be less a metaphoric summary of book IV than a representation of a portion of that book, namely the "Profession of Faith of the Savoyard Vicar." At any rate, with Orpheus we have yet another tutor portrayed in the engraving, as with Hermes, an unspecified student, once again raising the question of for whom Orpheus's song—or the Savoyard Vicar's speech—is appropriate. I will devote the next chapter to a more detailed discussion of the dramatic introduction to the "Profession" and the question of audience, so for the present I will only discuss these issues as they relate to the figure of Orpheus.

The textual reference in book IV to the engraving of Orpheus comes in the introduction to the "Profession" itself with, the young Jean-Jacques Rousseau proclaiming: "The good priest had spoken with vehemence. He was moved, and so was I. I believed I was hearing the divine Orpheus singing the first hymns and teaching men the worship of the gods" (294). The emphasis in this description on the emotive effect of the Vicar's speech is central to interpreting both the engraving and the "Profession" itself. The tension between emotive effect and rational content is evident in the continuation of the passage: "Nevertheless I saw a multitude of objections to make to him. I did not make any of them, because they were less solid than disconcerting, and persuasiveness was on his side" (294). Recall that the lawgiver of the *Social Contract* (II.7)

4.4 Illustration for book IV of *Emile*: Orpheus

cannot reason with the people, so he must "persuade without convincing" by proclaiming the gods as the authors of the laws (*Contract*, 193).[25] The "divine Orpheus" sings, and so persuasively that the animals are charmed, as the engraving shows. The religious teaching of the "Profession" is at least partially directed to the emotional, to the animal, in us. The engraving therefore shows Orpheus singing to animals.

To whom is the "Profession of Faith of the Savoyard Vicar" directed, and for whom would it be an appropriate lesson? Again, I will examine these questions at greater length in the following chapter, so for now a few summary remarks will have to suffice. Rousseau frames the "Profession" with an elaborate dramatic setting that supposedly occurred some thirty years earlier and involved a young boy who encountered a kindly vicar. Although Rousseau hints that the boy is himself (264), this suggestion is itself complicated by the fact that he claims that he is transcribing what "the author of the paper" has written and offering it as a set of potentially "useful reflections" (260). At any rate, he describes the young auditor of the Vicar's profession of faith as having precociously awakened pride and sexual desire (see 261–63), and he also indicates that the "Profession" would be useful to a similarly corrupted public (see 295 and n., 313–14 n.). What about Emile? Is the "Profession" appropriate for an uncorrupted "natural man in society"? Rousseau is cagey about whether his pupil has heard anything resembling the Vicar's speech (see 313–14). He has once again engaged in a substitution of pupils, this time his supposed younger self for his imaginary pupil, who reenters the narrative just after the "Profession." Finally, to return to the engraving of Orpheus: as with Hermes, we have a teacher without a specific pupil, which would seem to indicate that Emile is not the intended recipient of Orpheus's lessons. Also, and again as with Hermes, we have a number of onlookers (or rather auditors) who might require such lessons. In this sense, then, the engraving of Orpheus that "belongs" to book IV is an apt choice not just for the "Profession," but for that book as a whole, because it represents the relationship of speaker and audience, persuasive speech and those for whom such persuasion is appropriate.

Once again, as with the engraving of Hermes, we can gain insight concerning the proper audience of the "Profession" from the Platonic source regarding the question of different lessons being appropriate for different audiences. "One of the things that makes preaching most useless is that it is done indiscriminately to everyone without distinction or selectivity," Rousseau writes just after the "Profession": "How can one think that the same sermon is suitable to so many auditors of such diverse dispositions, so different in mind, humor, age, sex, station, and opinion? There are perhaps not even two auditors for whom what one says to all is suitable" (319). The echo of *Phaedrus* is unmistakable. Just a few pages later, then, the tutor Jean-Jacques finally reveals himself to be the godlike creator of Emile (323). His description of the setting for this speech to his pupil parallels the scene chosen by the Vicar for revealing himself to the young Jean-Jacques, the scene of the rising sun seen from a hill in which "nature [was] displaying all its magnificence to our eyes in order to present them with the text for our conversation" (266). The tutor Jean-Jacques explains how he will speak "about the subject in which I want to instruct him," a coy preamble to be sure: "I shall begin by moving his imagination. I shall choose the time, the place, and the objects most favorable to the impression I want to make. I shall, so to speak, call all of nature as a witness to our conversations." Setting the scene and revealing himself to the young Emile, Rousseau comments: "It is in this way that you get a young man to listen to you and that you engrave the memory of what you say to him in the depths of his heart" (323). Another echo of Plato. But what is the elusive "subject in which I want to instruct him" here? Aside from revealing himself to Emile, Jean-Jacques turns to the subject of sex, for the time is ripe for such a discussion, given Emile's budding passions. The parallels between the dramatic setting of the "Profession" and the speech Jean-Jacques makes to Emile suggest that they are different lessons suitable for different pupils. It seems that romantic love is for Emile an appropriate substitute for the teaching presented in the "Profession."

If Jean-Jacques plays Orpheus to Emile, he sings persuasively not of the gods, but of love. No women are depicted among the auditors in the engraving of Orpheus (who in the myth dies when he is torn apart by frenzied women).[26] If sexual longing is the downfall of the Savoyard Vicar (262) and a danger to his auditor, an idealized female is introduced to complete Emile's education. Rather than stifling the imagination, the tutor will guide it: "I shall make him moderate by making him fall in love" (327). Rousseau thus introduces the imaginary figure of the object of Emile's affections, whom he calls Sophie (329). Emile and his tutor then set off in search of such a companion, who will become Emile's final preceptor. Hence the engraving of Circe and Ulysses that introduces book V.

Circe

The engraving of Circe at the head of book V appears to represent Sophie, to whose charge the tutor Jean-Jacques entrusts Emile after their marriage: "'Today I abdicate the authority you confided to me, and Sophie is your governor from now on'" (479). Like the educators depicted in the previous engravings, Circe is divine or semidivine. Romantic love of an ideal woman has sublimated or perhaps transfigured Emile's passions, preventing him from being transformed through sexual desire into an animal, like Ulysses' swinish companions. Rousseau summarizes the engraving in the Explanations of the Illustrations: it "represents Circe giving herself to Ulysses, whom she was not able to transform" (36). Emile seems to be represented by Ulysses, and the tutor's management of Emile's passions also elevates him to be someone who, if not quite divine, is heroic. Emile thus becomes an exemplar of human nature and virtue that replaces the classical exemplars represented by Achilles as well as Ulysses.[27] Nonetheless, as with the first engraving featuring Thetis, Rousseau's *explication* emphasizes not Ulysses' action or intention, but rather Circe's: giving herself to Ulysses because she was not able to transform him. Likewise, as noted above, Sophie is described in the text as Emile's final "governor," and so the key to interpreting the engraving lies in assessing Sophie's intention with regard to Emile.

The story represented in the engraving is drawn from Homer's *Odyssey*.[28] Hermes plays a role in this story, for it is the messenger god who equips Odysseus with the moly that enables him to withstand Circe's charm, and in the engraving the herb is clearly seen in Ulysses' left hand, connecting book III to book V. Rousseau too is interested in guarding his pupil against the temptations of the passions, and the moly he provides in his role as Hermes is the application of the teaching in his book regarding the natural and artificial passions. In this light, given that his aim is to persuade his reader of the natural goodness of man, it is critical to consider an alternative frame he provides for book V. Namely, he introduces the book by writing: "Now we have come to the last act in the drama of youth, but we are not yet at the dénouement. It is not good for man to be alone. Emile is a man. We have promised him a companion. She has to be given to him. That companion is Sophie" (357). Rousseau echoes the scriptural account of Adam being given a companion, but he aims to introduce Sophie without a Fall. (Although the unfinished sequel to *Emile* complicates this interpretation.) Yet if Sophie is in some sense "given" to Emile in the course of the romantic narrative, the *explication* of the engraving emphasizes that it is she who gives herself to him. Let us therefore turn to the engraving with Sophie's actions and intentions in mind.

Circe may give herself to Ulysses in part because she was unable to transform him, but Rousseau's version of the story in the engraving either expurgates or obscures one important element of the original story: the brandished sword. In the *Odyssey* Hermes counsels the hero to rush toward the sorceress with his sword as though he would kill her. He does as instructed, and the fearful Circe drops to the ground and grasps his knees in supplication.[29] As with the engraving of Chiron and Achilles, Rousseau's version is considerably tamer (fig. 4.5). Ulysses holds a sword in his right hand, but he seems to be leaning on it as though it were a cane, more an old man than a fierce warrior. Ulysses' seemingly unstable stance if anything suggests vulnerability rather than ferocity. Circe has dropped her wand and potion (another parallel to Chiron's weapons and Hermes' scientific instruments lying at their feet), and she is thus disarmed like Chiron in the engraving for book II; but she is certainly not clasping Ulysses' knees in supplication. In fact, she is slightly above the stooped Ulysses, suggesting that they are equals or even that she is his superior. Her gesture seems welcoming, and she may be beckoning him to bed, as in the story of Circe and Ulysses. How close the engraving is to Rousseau's intentions we cannot know, but the gentler representation is at any rate consistent with his other deviations from classical sources.

The textual reference in book V to Circe comes immediately after the running races that connect the action back to book II: "Apropos of cakes . . ." (436). In this same context, and just before the reference to Circe, Sophie visits Emile while he is working in a carpenter's shop. Rousseau commences this episode by stating, "This is man" (437), an echo of *Ecce homo* suggesting that Emile replaces yet another formidable traditional exemplar. Sophie's mother is piqued that Emile would not leave the shop as she requested, and Sophie upbraids her, saying that he stayed out of duty and from a true respect for her. Rousseau comments: "She did not want a lover who knew no law other than hers. She wants to reign over a man whom she has not disfigured. It is thus that Circe, having debased Ulysses' companions, disdains them and gives herself only to him whom she was unable to change" (439). Immediately after this statement, our author relates how, when Emile and Jean-Jacques are late for an evening appointment due to helping an injured man, an initially worried and angry Sophie finally gives herself to Emile as her husband, having learned that he has not been so transformed by his love for her as to forget the duties of humanity (441). And forthwith Sophie, too, becomes an exemplar: "This is woman" (442).

As noted above, it is Circe's or Sophie's actions and intentions to which Rousseau points us for interpreting the engraving for book V. Immediately prior to the textual reference to the engraving of Circe, Rousseau writes: "She has that noble pride based on merit which is conscious of itself, esteems itself, and wants to be honored as it honors itself. She would disdain a heart which did not feel the full value of her heart, which did not love her for her virtues as much as, and more

4.5 Illustration for book V of *Emile*: Circe

than, for her charms, and which did not prefer its own duty to her and her to everything else." (439). Much scholarship on Rousseau's view of the education and role of women sees Sophie as inferior or educated to be inferior, perhaps because of the threat that women or sexual desires pose to men.[30] In this vein, Patricia Parker reads Circe and Ulysses as "the classical emblem of a powerful and threatening female" who must be tamed or dominated and suggests that Sophie is likewise dominated by Emile.[31] What Rousseau states about Sophie's character and her intention in giving herself to Emile at least complicates such an interpretation. Sophie is described, at least to a certain degree, as Emile's equal and even, insofar as she is his "governor," as his superior. In an apologetic note in the *Discourse on the Sciences and the Arts*, Rousseau explains: "I am quite far from thinking this ascendancy of women is in itself an evil. . . . Men will always be what is pleasing to women. If you want them to become great and virtuous, therefore, teach women what greatness of soul and virtue are" (*Sciences*, 27 n.). If the key to interpreting the engraving of Circe lies in understanding her actions and intentions, and thus Sophie's, then it appears that Sophie gives herself to Emile because she has learned what greatness of soul and virtue are and esteems them in Emile, whom she has not been able to transform.

As for Emile, the fact that he has not been transformed by Sophie is emphasized several times, including just before this sequence of stories containing the reference to Circe: "On the days when he does not see her, he is not idle and sedentary. On those days he is Emile again. He has not been transformed at all" (435). Protected by the pedagogical moly provided by his tutor, Emile is not transformed by sexual passion. But he is still vulnerable because he is now dependent on Sophie's love. Jean-Jacques warns Emile of his dependence in a speech just after Sophie has given herself to him that commences not with the spectacle of a sunrise, but instead with a sadistic query: "'What would you do if you were informed that Sophie is dead?'" (442). Emile's reaction demonstrates that he is indeed vulnerable. In his reply to Emile, Jean-Jacques refers to the subject of the engraving for book I and for *Emile* as a whole in a passage quoted above: "But dear Emile, it is in vain that I have dipped your soul in the Styx; I was not able to make it everywhere invulnerable" (443). Rousseau thus brings us full circle.

Emile's education is designed to guard him from the psychological maladies of anger, fear of death, and other passions that might destroy his wholeness and his happiness, but perhaps the most dangerous passion is sexual. Although Emile may be unperturbed by his own mortality, having fallen in love with Sophie makes him vulnerable. Emile's passion for Sophie makes him dependent on her, and his attachment renders him vulnerable, for the soul cannot be made entirely invulnerable. Despite the apparently happy ending of the romance of Emile and Sophie, we have an intimation of our hero's Achilles' heel. Thetis, we should recall, loses her son, for he too cannot be rendered invulnerable.

Chapter 5

The Narrative Frame
of the "Profession of Faith"

As I noted in chapter 3, *Emile* has relatively sparse paratextual elements, apart from the engravings I analyzed in the previous chapter, and instead the interesting textual features of the work come inside the main text itself. Notably, *Emile* contains three stand-alone sections that are explicitly separated from the main text: the "Profession of Faith of the Savoyard Vicar" in book IV and "Sophie, or the Woman" and "On Travel" (*Des voyages*) in book V. These separate sections pose interpretive challenges both on their own terms and in relation to the main text. Why, for example, did Rousseau elect to present them as separate sections? Why, insofar as they stand alone and apart from the main text, did he include them at all?

The "Profession of Faith" is particularly difficult to assess for both structural and substantive reasons. As for the structural issues, whereas "Sophie, or the Woman" and "On Travel" are largely if not fully related to the main narrative of book V, the "Profession" is not at all related to the main narrative and in fact disrupts it. Unlike the other two stand-alone sections, the "Profession" is presented by Rousseau not as a text he himself has written, but instead as a "paper" penned by someone else. Also unlike the others, the "Profession" introduces new characters who play no role in the main narrative. In short, the "Profession" seems entirely separable from *Emile*, and evidence for this might be taken from the fact that it has been published separately, though not by Rousseau himself.[1]

As for the substantive issues, the status of the religious teaching presented by the Savoyard Vicar, in terms of its relationship both to the philosophical argument of the rest of *Emile* and to Rousseau's views on theology and religion expressed elsewhere, is extremely vexed. Is the Savoyard Vicar a "mouthpiece" for Rousseau, as many interpreters have assumed? In defending himself against the condemnation of *Emile* by the archbishop of Paris and then by his native Geneva, Rousseau maintained a distance between himself and the Vicar. He insisted that he is the "editor" of the "Profession" as opposed to its "author," consistently distinguished between the Vicar and himself, and, finally, stated that he would always consider the "Profession" as "the most useful writing in the century during which I *published* it"—that is, not the one in which he *wrote* it (*Letter to Beaumont*, *CW*, 9:17, 75, 38, 46–47; *Letters Written from the Mountain*, *CW*, 9:183; see also 159n., 168n.). Similarly, also writing in defense of *Emile*, he claimed that the Vicar's profession and Julie's profession of faith in *Julie* are "sufficiently in accord that one can explain one of them by the other, and from this agreement it can be presumed with some likelihood that if the author who published the books that contain them does not adopt both of them in their entirety, he at least favors them greatly" (*Letters Written from the Mountain*, *CW*, 9:139). In what sense he "favors" these professions he does not say, nor does he explain what parts of them he himself might adopt. Finally, in the *Reveries of the Solitary Walker*, when discussing his settling of his own religious views in the face of the doubts sown by his former friends the *philosophes*, Rousseau will only say that the result was "approximately" (*à peu près*) the same as the Savoyard Vicar's (*Reveries*, *CW*, 8:22–23). In short, Rousseau was consistently cagey about whether or in what way the views expressed by the Savoyard Vicar mirrored his own.

Despite these structural and substantive issues, however, many interpreters—and readers—have assumed that Emile must receive the religious teaching propounded in the "Profession," and probably the majority of interpreters have assumed or claimed that the theological and religious views expressed by the Vicar are Rousseau's own.[2] One advantage of my attentiveness to the rhetorical and literary aspects of Rousseau's texts is anticipated by de Man in his own reading of the "Profession," which he prefaces by complaining that the separation of the philosophical and the literary has led to misinterpretations of Rousseau's works. With respect to the "Profession," he remarks on how readers mistakenly conflate Rousseau and the Savoyard Vicar, despite his use of obvious literary devices such as authorial personae and shifts in narrative voice that a literary critic would take for granted and analyze in those terms.[3] Without speaking of taking Hamlet for Shakespeare, we all learn as schoolchildren that the narrative voice of a poem cannot be assumed to be equivalent to the poet's own voice. We should not expect otherwise with the "Profession."

In this chapter I analyze the structural and rhetorical features of the "Profession," on its own terms and in relationship to the main text, to see what role it plays in the education of the reader of *Emile*. I address the substance of the "Profession" only insofar as it relates to these structural and rhetorical features, saving an interpretation of the substance of the "Profession" for another occasion. The most important features I analyze concern the narrative frame of the "Profession," both in relation to the main text of *Emile* and in itself. This narrative frame includes a number of elements, which may be grouped into two categories: first, Rousseau's introduction to the "paper" (*papier*) supposedly written by someone else and, second, the writing itself. As for Rousseau's introduction, I consider the position of the "Profession" within the text of *Emile* in order to understand its purpose and status, and then I examine Rousseau's authorial strategy in distancing himself from the "Profession." As for the "Profession" itself, it contains a number of features: first, the introduction of the dramatis personae, the young proselyte and the Savoyard Vicar; second, the dramatic setting of the Vicar's speech; third, some dialogic elements within the "Profession" itself, including most importantly remarks made by the "author" concerning the Vicar's arguments; fourth, notes that Rousseau adds to the "Profession" in his role as the supposed editor of the work.

Although considerable scholarly attention has been paid to the substance of the "Profession," there has been very little to the narrative frame.[4] One exception is Heinrich Meier, who writes: "The framing narrative is no ornamental add-on, but the part of the writing that puts the speech about religion in perspective and determines its task. It supplies information about the circumstances in which the profession of faith takes place" and information about the characters and capacities of the young man and the Vicar.[5] As I will suggest below, given Rousseau's dialogue with Plato's *Phaedrus*, in *Emile* and elsewhere, we should expect that the character of the auditor and speaker and the dramatic setting, along with the other elements, will be important for understanding what lessons are intended, both for the auditor of the "Profession" and the reader of *Emile*.

The Context of the Text within a Text

The "Profession" poses a particular challenge to the reader of *Emile*. Rousseau himself predicts the reader's reaction as he begins his approach toward it: "I foresee how many readers will be surprised at seeing me trace the whole first age of my pupil without speaking to him of religion" (*Emile*, 257).[6] Perhaps more surprising, the expectation that Rousseau as author or Jean-Jacques as tutor—for the identity of "I" here is unclear—will now speak to his pupil about religion is immediately frustrated. Instead, Rousseau inserts a paper, supposedly written by someone else (260), that includes the Savoyard Vicar's speech, that is, the "Profession," to an unidentified young man, and not to Emile. Some eighty pages later in the Pléiade edition—or fifty pages in the Bloom edition, and a full two hundred pages in the original edition of *Emile*—the paper ends as abruptly as it began. Returning to his authorial voice, Rousseau briefly repeats his reasons for having "transcribed this writing," remains vague about what he may or may not say to Emile on the topic of religion, and returns to the project of directing his pupil's imagination in a healthy manner. Just for starters, the reader should be surprised at the sheer length of this interruption: a full third of book IV and more than a tenth of the length of *Emile* as a whole.

The Place of the "Profession" in Book IV

Rousseau undoubtedly foresees his readers' surprise at his not yet having spoken to his pupil of religion because of the centrality of religious instruction from an early age in his own times (not to speak of our own). However, if we restrict ourselves to *Emile* as it is presented to us, we might well be surprised that he is speaking—or, better, speaking of not speaking—of religion at all at this point. What we as readers are led to expect, given how Rousseau begins book IV, is a discussion of sex education, which is precisely what we get after the "Profession." Book IV marks a kind of "second birth" of the pupil as the passions are enflamed with the dawning of adolescence: "We are, so to speak, born twice: once to exist and once to live; once for our species and once for our sex" (211). Rather than stifle the passions, Rousseau explains, they must be directed so as to connect the pupil to his fellow humans, and ultimately his beloved, and to prevent the birth of corrupt, unnatural passions (esp. 212–15). The first third of book IV is devoted to making Emile sociable by directing his pity toward his fellows and educating him about human nature from afar by reading history. Perhaps significant for the placement of the "Profession," just after his discussion of studying history and just before he begins to make his approach to the "Profession," Rousseau returns to the issue of fables: "The time of mistakes is the time of fables" (248). If the censorship of the poets in book II with the critique of "The Crow and the Fox" can be seen as covert rejection of religious instruction, as I suggested in chapter 3, then perhaps the resurrection of fables in this context signals one role the "Profession" plays in taming the passions of adolescence.

Of particular importance at this point in the education of his pupil is the danger posed by the imagination. On the one hand, imagination is required for the pupil to identify with his fellows through commiseration (223, 229). On the other hand, the imagination can create new needs beyond the ability of the individual to satisfy them. Up to this point Rousseau has therefore counseled preventing the birth of imagination, but with the awakening passions its development is inevitable. He turns this inevitability to his advantage: "The adolescent fire, far from being an obstacle to education, is the means of consummating and completing it" (233). After the interruption of the "Profession" and the return to the main narrative, Rousseau focuses in particular on the imagination in relation to sexual passion. The tutor's plan is to direct Emile's imagination toward an imaginary beloved: "I shall make him moderate by making him fall in love" (327). The placement of the "Profession" in book IV therefore suggests that one intention Rousseau has for the religious teaching delivered by the Savoyard Vicar is to serve as a prophylactic: to moderate the developing passions, especially sexual passion. But for whom is this prophylactic necessary or appropriate?

Approaching the "Profession"

The "Profession" interrupts the main narrative of the text, and in fact Rousseau approaches it with a series of abrupt shifts in narrative voice and subject, as though he were intentionally destabilizing the reading experience. The disruptions commence just a few pages before he introduces the "Profession." There he steps back from his educational project to engage in an extended dialogue with his skeptical reader, a narrative technique we have seen him employ repeatedly. I examined this passage in chapter 3, so here I will address only the parts necessary for the present purpose. The substantive context in which this dialogue occurs is Rousseau's argument that *amour-propre*, which typically degenerates into vanity, can be extended to other beings and be transformed into a virtue if properly managed (252–53). Since we do not ordinarily see this healthy transformation, Rousseau anticipates incredulity on the reader's part. He therefore abruptly addresses his readers:

> I go forward, attracted by the force of things but without gaining credibility in the judgment of my readers. For a long while they have seen me in the land of chimeras. I always see them in the land of prejudices. . . . I know that they persist in imagining only what they see, and therefore they will take the young man whom I evoke to be an imaginary and fantastic being because he differs from those with whom they compare him. . . . This is not the man of man; it is the man of nature. Assuredly he must be very alien to their eyes. (253)

Having written this, he then delivers imagined speeches of disbelief on the part of the reader, for example: "'Nothing of what you suppose exists.'" Then he proposes a comparison of pupils, another technique we have seen him utilize a number of times: "Now if in accordance with this method," that is, of investigating human nature, "you follow a young man from childhood . . . whom do you think he will most resemble—my pupil or yours?" (254). Finally, he explains: "Although I want to form the man of nature, the object is not, for all that, to make him a savage and to relegate him to the depths of the woods." This natural man in society must learn to feel and think without being engulfed in the "social whirlpool" (255).

Rather than discussing how the "man of nature" can be introduced to society without becoming swept away, which is precisely what he does discuss after the "Profession," however, Rousseau suddenly embarks on a discussion of metaphysics. It is this unprepared discussion that immediately precedes the introduction to the "Profession." The discussion begins with him addressing readers in the imperative mood: "Consider also that since we are limited by our faculties to things which can be sensed, we provide almost no hold for abstract notions of philosophy and purely intellectual ideas." After stating that in order to ascend to these ideas we must "separate ourselves from the body," he turns to the divinity: "The incomprehensible Being who embraces everything, who gives motion to the world and forms the whole system of beings, is neither visible to our eyes nor palpable to our hands. He escapes all our senses. The work is revealed, but the worker is hidden." The precipitous ascent from material to immaterial substances produces either materialism or superstition, he warns, and then he offers a brief natural history of religion. Primitive humans animated the entire universe with beings whose action they believed they felt, he explains, until they began to recognize a single god by generalizing their ideas and ascending to a first cause of the universe and to the idea of a "substance." With this idea glimpsed, one can see how the notion of two substances, one material and the other immaterial, might arise. In this way, then, Rousseau explains the origin of metaphysical dualism. Nonetheless, his explanation is presented entirely either in the mode of conjectural history or with interrogatives, the passive voice, and impersonal constructions; he does not make any substantive claims in this context in his own name. Rather, he emphasizes the difficulty of conceiving of these two substances, of the divine nature, ideas of creation and annihilation, eternity, omnipotence, and so on, and the pervasive tendency of children and men to anthropomorphism (256–57). In short, the abrupt shifts in narration are compounded with uncertainty concerning the subject under discussion and its truth value.

With this propaedeutic account of the difficulties of metaphysical and theological inquiry in place, Rousseau suddenly swivels back to his reader and his pupil: "I foresee how many readers will be surprised at seeing me trace the whole first age of my pupil without speaking to him of religion" (257). As noted earlier, by anticipating the surprise of the reader Rousseau acknowledges that ordinarily religion was central to the education of children of his time. However, he argues against the common practice by stating that premature religious instruction produces erroneous ideas of the divinity and fanaticism (257–9). Rousseau gives an example through a brief story about a child he supposedly saw in Switzerland whose curiosity about the mysterious divinity turned him into a fanatic rather than a believer. He then contrasts this child to "my pupil": "But let us fear nothing of the kind for my Emile, who constantly refuses to pay attention to everything beyond his reach and listens to things he does not understand with the most profound indifference" (259). Emile's appearance in the text here will nonetheless be brief.

Given that "the faith of children and of many men is a question of geography" (258), Rousseau states that a child must be raised in his father's religion and introduced to the supposed arguments on behalf of that religion, arguments whose strength "depends absolutely on the country where they are propounded" (260). But what about Emile, who has no father? Rousseau invites the collaboration of the reader in the project by using the first-person plural:

> But we who claim to shake off the yoke of opinion in everything, we who want to grant nothing to authority, we who want to teach nothing to our Emile which he could not learn by himself in every country, in what religion shall we raise him? To what sect shall we join the man of nature? The answer is quite simple, it seems to me. We shall join him to neither this one nor that one, but we shall put him in a position to choose the one to which the best use of his reason ought to lead him. (260)

And then Rousseau abruptly drops Emile, returning to him only after a very long absence filled by the "Profession," and when he does return to Emile he once again invites the collaboration of the reader by speaking of "our pupil" (314). During the lengthy intermission the reader is left to his own devices.

Having bid adieu to Emile and the reader, Rousseau turns to brave the storm alone. He quotes Horace:

> I walk on fires
> Covered by deceitful cinders.
>
> ———
>
> [Incendo per ignes
> Suppositos cineri doloso.][7]

Rousseau changes Horace's verse to the first-person singular (*Incendo*) from the original second-person singular (*Incendis*), as noted by Bloom and by the editor of the Pléiade edition (who seems to assume it is a mistake).[8] The alteration makes sense, however, given Rousseau's having taken responsibility for what is about to happen. Or, rather, given his abdication of responsibility, for he makes another unexpected shift.

The Author of the "Profession" and the Question of Interpretive Authority

Preparing to set foot on hot coals, Rousseau addresses us: "Readers, do not fear from me precautions unworthy of a friend of the truth. I shall never forget my motto" (260). Lest the reader does not know it or has forgotten it, I will provide it: *Vitam impendere vero*—"To consecrate one's life to the truth."[9] Strangely, then, after declaring that his love of truth is consistent with distrusting his judgments as potentially mistaken, he takes another unexpected turn.

> Instead of telling you [*vous*] here what I think for my own part [*de mon chef*], I shall tell you what a man worthier than I thought. I guarantee the truth of the facts which are going to be reported. They really happened to the author of the paper I am going to transcribe. It is up to you to see if useful reflections can be drawn from it about the subject with which it deals. I am not propounding to you the sentiment of another or my own as a rule. I am offering it to you for examination. (260)

With this said, Rousseau begins to transcribe the "paper," the text in quotation marks throughout as though it were someone else's writing.

What is going on here? Few readers will likely be persuaded that someone other than Rousseau is the actual author of this paper. If he is not being truthful in this respect, his allusion to his motto, which might be characterized as gratuitously proffered, seems an affront or a deliberate provocation. Assuming he is in fact the author, why does he distance himself from the paper in introducing it? This distancing is usually taken as an attempt to evade responsibility for the unorthodox theological and religious content of the "Profession." The authorities who condemned the work certainly believed this was his intention. There are nonetheless a number of reasons for thinking it was not. First, Rousseau himself denied this was his aim, and it seems implausible that he believed he would have been successful if it were. In fact, as mentioned earlier, in the very course of denying this was his intention, he insisted on distinguishing between the "author" of the transcribed writing and himself as its "editor." Given that he had already been condemned for having published the "Profession," why not own up to his authorship? Surely continuing to maintain the fiction that he was not the author would be no more successful than it had been in the first place. Second, and more important, doing so would be inconsistent with his behavior otherwise, for he published other controversial works under his own name. Indeed, for an era of almost universally anonymous or pseudonymous works, Rousseau was unusual for *insisting* on proclaiming his authorship.[10] Such is the case with the work under examination, for in defending *Emile* he admits to the archbishop of Paris that the philosophical position he advanced in his own name was intentionally in direct contradiction with the doctrine of original sin (*Letter to Beaumont*, *CW*, 9:28–31). If he is willing to admit that in his own name, why not acknowledge that he is the author of the "Profession? In what way, then, could it be somehow true that he is not the author of this paper and that he is not taking "precautions unworthy of a friend of the truth"?

My focus on the education of the reader may provide some fresh answers. Returning to the passage quoted above, then, let us begin by noting what he says to his readers: "It is up to you to see if useful reflections can be drawn from it" and "I am offering it to you for examination." Rousseau cedes authority to the reader to examine and judge. In this light, Rousseau distances himself not so much from the content of the writing as from *judging* it in his own name.[11] A contemporary of Rousseau's, David Hume, employs a similar strategy in the set of four essays on philosophical characters—"The Epicurean," "The Stoic," "The Platonist," and "The Sceptic"—which he does not present in his own authorial voice. Like Rousseau in the "Profession," Hume even adds notes to the essays in his own voice. Although most readers see him as most sympathetic to the skeptic, he leaves it to the reader to make that judgment.[12]

Rousseau's abstention from exercising his authority as the author and instead investing the reader with this authority parallels the "Profession" itself. First, the Savoyard Vicar takes it upon himself to interrogate his religious convictions without appeal to any other authority (see especially 266–69). Second, the Vicar likewise repeatedly asks his auditor to judge the contents of his speech for himself (e.g., 266, 294–95). Like the Vicar, when Rousseau returns to the main narrative he claims that the "Profession" is meant as an example for examination, not as an authority (313–14). The line of interpretation I am suggesting is supported by Rousseau's response to the misreading of the text by an actual reader. In the *Letter to Beaumont*, Rousseau takes his critic to task for incorrectly citing a passage as coming from the "Profession" rather than the "body of the book," as he terms it, and then, having corrected the archbishop's mistake, he takes responsibility for that passage in his own name (*Letter to Beaumont*, *CW*, 9:28–31). In sum, the "Profession" appropriately stands apart from *Emile* because it is not presented as being the fruit of what Rousseau in the preface refers to as the "systematic part" of the work (34), of which he is most assuredly attempting to persuade the reader.

In this light, then, we can read Rousseau's introduction to the paper containing the "Profession" not so much as distancing himself from the text as doubling his authorial voice, much as he doubles himself to serve as Emile's tutor. If so, then he—Jean-Jacques Rousseau, author of *Emile*—both is and is not the author of this paper. A detail in the passage would seem to suggest such an interpretation, for Rousseau in the authorial "I" states that he is not propounding to "you" (*vous*) "the sentiment of *another or my own* as a rule." This formulation would make sense if he is somehow both "another" and "himself." As the author of *Emile*, Rousseau states that he guarantees the truth of the "facts": "They really happened to the author of the paper I am going to transcribe" (260). Of course, the only sure guarantee of these facts would be that the author is Rousseau himself, especially since these facts include information about the mental and emotional state of the author, as recalled thirty years later, that could be known only by the person relating them. As we shall see in the next section examining the dramatic introduction to the "Profession," Rousseau is coy about whether or not the author is indeed himself. At any rate, such an interpretation would once again be consistent with the idea that he is doubling himself as author. Finally, whereas he guarantees the truth of the "facts" to be reported, Rousseau gives no such assurances regarding the content of the "Profession." Part of the education of the readers is to examine that for themselves.

Before turning to the dramatic introduction to the "Profession," let me briefly step away from my focus on what the reader of *Emile* learns from the text itself to what Rousseau's interpreters know from his other works concerning his views on telling the truth. Recall that he refers to his motto about consecrating one's life to truth just before transcribing the "paper" containing the "Profession." Rousseau's self-declared dedication to the truth is a complicated matter, to say the least. In defense of *Emile* after it was condemned, principally because of the "Profession," Rousseau explained that he felt himself obliged to tell the truth only in matters he considered "useful," that is, useful to his readers or to the public (*Letter to Beaumont*, *CW*, 9:52). Similarly, much later in the *Reveries* he devotes the "Fourth Promenade" to an analysis of how difficult it turned out to live in accordance with his motto and explains there that what would normally be called lying is justified if the untruth is either a matter of indifference or a matter of utility, a kind of "noble lie" or what he terms a "fable" (*Reveries*, *CW*, 8:28–40). Revealingly, the subject of the "Third Promenade," which he connects to the "Fourth" by beginning the former and ending the latter with the same saying by Solon, is the skepticism he suffered by associating with the *philosophes* and the resulting establishment of his beliefs in a manner that was "approximately" like the "Profession" (*Reveries*, *CW*, 8:22–23).[13] We therefore have later, external reasons to wonder whether the contents of the "Profession" are less true than useful in some way. But what if we restrict ourselves to *Emile*? One might point to the numerous occasions on which Jean-Jacques as tutor deceives Emile or at least structures his educational environment in such a way that amounts to not revealing the truth, the whole truth, and nothing but the truth. Why should we suppose that Rousseau as author is above doing so when educating his reader?

The Dramatic Introduction to the "Profession"

"'Thirty years ago in an Italian city a young expatriate found himself reduced to utter destitution'" (260). So begins what I am calling the dramatic introduction to the "Profession." This dramatic introduction is rather lengthy—seven pages in the Pléiade edition, five in Bloom's. We must, I think, assume that Rousseau—and for simplicity's sake I will refer to him as the author—presents information to the reader that is necessary for interpreting the "Profession" and its function in the text. Much of the dramatic introduction is devoted to introducing the two characters, the young proselyte and the Savoyard Vicar. If we recall the multiple echoes of Plato's *Phaedrus* in *Emile*, and in Rousseau's writings more generally, then we should expect that these details concerning the character particularly of the auditor of the speech, the youth, are important if Rousseau is respecting the Socratic argument that speeches, as opposed to writing, can be tailored to the character and capacity of a given auditor so as to have the intended rhetorical and pedagogical effect. Indeed, just after the "Profession" Rousseau addresses the subject of rhetoric and the need to adapt speeches to suit their recipients (319–23). Later I will examine this discussion of rhetoric in relation to the dramatic setting of the "Profession."

The Young Proselyte

What do we learn about the character of the youth? Speaking of the youth in the third person, the author of this paper recounts how he left his country and found himself in an almshouse for proselytes, where he was introduced to strange doctrines and still stranger morals. The new doctrines provoke doubts he had hitherto not entertained. As for the novel morals, he had "almost became the victim" of the corrupt morals of the almshouse and was indignant at being punished for not succumbing. He asks the reader of the paper to picture the scene: "'Those who know how much the first taste of violence and injustice arouses a young heart without experience will be able to picture the condition of his own heart. Tears of rage flowed from his eyes, indignation choked him'" (260–62). This passage is strikingly similar to the story Rousseau tells in book I of having witnessed an infant struck by his nurse and exploding in tears of rage and indignation (65–66), a story I examined at length in chapter 3 as an example of his teaching the reader to distinguish corrupt from uncorrupt children. The author asks the reader to "picture" his indignation to elicit sympathy, but the reader who has encountered Rousseau's depiction of the indignant infant might also glean something about the youth's character.

While he may not have succumbed to the corrupt morals of the almshouse, the boy's passions are nonetheless already corrupt. He believes he has escaped from vice only to return to indigence, but his psychic resources are as thin as his pecuniary ones: "'Vain was the advantage of his youth; his ideas, absorbed from novels, spoiled everything.'" His romantic notions, perhaps of romantic love and heroic virtue, are poor resources for his condition. Happily, he is taken in by the Vicar, who saw that "'ill fortune had already dried up the young man's heart, that opprobrium and contempt had beaten down his courage, and that his pride [*fierté*], changed into bitter spite, took men's injustice and hardness only as proof of the viciousness of nature and the chimerical character of virtue. He had seen that religion served only as the mask of interest and sacred worship only as the safeguard of hypocrisy'" (262). Having seen through appearances, the boy thought he glimpsed the corruption hiding beneath.

The author explains of the youth that, although he was not without a noble nature, "'incredulity and poverty, stifling his nature little by little, were leading him rapidly to his destruction and heading him toward the morals of a tramp and the morality of an atheist.'" Significantly for the placement of the "Profession" in book IV, he is characterized as being sexually awakened: "'He was at that happy age when the blood is in fermentation. . . . A native shame and a timid character took the place of constraint and prolonged for him this period in which you keep your pupil with so much care'" (262–63). Note the inserted address to the reader of the paper, an unidentified "you" (*vous*)—a detail to which I will return. At any rate, at this point the boy is approximately the same age as Emile. Finally, before turning to the remedy, the author identifies the disease:

> "What was most difficult to destroy in me was a proud misanthropy, a certain bitterness against the rich and happy of the world, as though they were such at my expense and their supposed happiness had been usurped from mine. The mad vanity of youth, which revolts against humiliation, gave me only too much of an inclination to that angry humor, and the *amour-propre* my mentor tried to awaken in me, by leading me to pride, rendered men even more vile in my eyes and succeeded only in adding contempt to my hatred of them." (265)

In short, the boy is, if not beyond redemption, corrupt.

Let us first compare this description of the boy's character to Emile. To be blunt, the young proselyte is no exemplar of the natural goodness of man. His passions and faculties have been prematurely awakened and corrupted. The similarity of the boy's indignant reaction to the unjust treatment he received to the crying infant of book already suggests the contrast to Emile. There is no need to dwell on other contrasts; one example will suffice. The corrupt youth has seen through the appearances of society and his fellows, and the result is his realization concerning "'the viciousness of nature and the chimerical character of virtue'" and a "'proud misanthropy'" of jealousy, hatred, and contempt. By contrast, when Emile is taught to see through appearances through his reading of history, the result is the contrary: "Let him know that man is naturally good; let him feel it; let him judge his neighbor by himself. But let him see that society depraves and perverts man" (237). Instead of feeling jealousy, hatred, and contempt for his fellows, Emile will pity them. If we extend Rousseau's invitation to compare pupils—"my pupil" and "your pupil"—to Emile and the youth of the story, we cannot help but see the boy as a vicious product of an education not directed by the doctrine of the natural goodness of man.

Let us now compare the experience of the youth to the lessons Rousseau promotes in the education of the reader of *Emile*. As we have seen, throughout his works and in *Emile* too, one of the principal lessons Rousseau offers to his reader is learning to distinguish between appearance and reality. The main intended result of this education is to teach the reader the same lesson Emile receives in the passage quoted above: that man is naturally good but he appears to be evil owing to the corruption he suffers in society. The youth enacts the "Illumination of Vincennes" and the education of the reader of *Emile*, but with the opposite outcome: the scales having fallen from his eyes concerning the appearances of virtue and religion, he believes he sees the self-interestedness and depravity of human nature. The boy requires a stiff dose of the cure provided to the reader by the author of *Emile*.

Finally, with regard to the author's relating what happened to him thirty years ago, Rousseau suddenly breaks the fourth wall of the narrative voice by having the supposed author address the reader, or at least *a* reader: "'I am tired of speaking in the third person. And the effort is quite superfluous, for you are well aware, dear fellow citizen, that this unhappy fugitive is myself. I believe myself far enough from the disorders of my youth to dare to admit them, and the hand which drew me away from these disorders deserves, at the expense of a bit of shame, that I render at least some honor to his benefaction'" (264). Strangely, despite the break in the narrative, this address to a reader is still in quotation marks, that is, still contained in the paper Rousseau is supposedly transcribing. The only change in the narrative voice is that the author henceforth speaks of himself in the first rather than the third person. The fourth wall, it turns out, yet stands.

Most interpreters have assumed that in admitting that this unhappy fugitive is "'myself,'" Rousseau is acknowledging that the youth is himself and therefore that he is in fact the author of the paper.[14] We have some reason for rejecting this hypothesis, at least in its most straightforward version. First, if Rousseau is the author, then who is the "'dear fellow citizen'" to whom this admission is directed? If Rousseau were simply admitting his authorship, such an address would be superfluous. The most obvious candidate for the "dear fellow citizen" is the "Citizen of Geneva" himself, author of *Emile*. This would also make sense of the other brief address to the reader—"you"—noted above, where the author notes how "'you keep your pupil'" sexually innocent with so much effort, with "you" ostensibly referring to Rousseau as author or Jean-Jacques as tutor and with "your pupil" referring to Emile (263). Second, after concluding the "Profession" and returning to the main text, Rousseau still maintains the stance that he has transcribed the paper, which would be odd if he had acknowledged he was the author. Third, and similarly, if he had admitted his authorship, why would he continue to distinguish between this paper and the "body of the work" when later defending it?

If the most straightforward version of the hypothesis that Rousseau has just admitted he is the author of this paper has to be rejected, the interpretation advanced above that Rousseau is doubling his role as author does make sense of the address. As for addressing his "'dear fellow citizen,'" if Rousseau is that "'dear fellow citizen,'" then the author of the paper would be his alter ego, *a* citizen of Geneva if not *the* "Citizen of Geneva." Likewise, maintaining his authorial distance as author of *Emile* from the "Profession" and its dramatic introduction, both in the work itself and in defense of it, would make better sense. Interestingly, then, the address to the reader Rousseau makes in his own name in introducing the separate paper, abdicating his own authority and inviting the reader to examine its contents, parallels the address by the author of the paper to a reader within the dramatic introduction, paying homage to the Savoyard Vicar as a worthy man but not asserting any authority to judge. What he states about the "Profession" in defense of its condemnation buttresses this interpretation: "In transcribing the particular writing . . . I warn the reader again that he has to be wary of my judgments, that it is for him to see if he can derive some useful reflections from this writing; that I propose to him neither someone else's sentiment nor my own as a rule; that I present it to him to examine" (*Letters Written from the Mountain*, CW, 9:183).

Finally, before turning to the Savoyard Vicar, if we avail ourselves of later, external evidence then we would learn that many of the details concerning the young proselyte are in fact autobiographical. As Rousseau later related in the *Confessions*, he was an expatriate who converted to Catholicism in order to have bread, stayed at an almshouse for proselytes where he was sexually propositioned, and had absorbed ideas from novels that inflamed his imagination, among other things. He also shares a number of character traits with the youth, including indignation, pride, misanthropy, and premature sexual awakening. Finally, he relates that he met some friendly clergymen after whom he states he modeled the Savoyard Vicar (*Confessions*, CW, 5:50–58, 100).[15] He does not discuss receiving anything like the "Profession." We may conclude that Rousseau at least models the young proselyte on himself.

The Savoyard Vicar

If the young proselyte takes the place of Emile, the Savoyard Vicar substitutes for the tutor Jean-Jacques.[16] Unlike Jean-Jacques, who emerges like Athena from the head of Zeus, however, the Vicar is given a history and character. We learn biographical and other details about the Vicar both from the dramatic introduction, in the voice of the author of the paper, and from the "Profession" itself, in the voice of the Vicar. Within the dramatic introduction, the author describes the Vicar as a poor Savoyard who fell out of favor with his bishop owing to "'a youthful adventure.'" He does not know, or at least does not relate, what this misadventure was. Also like the youth, the Vicar leaves his native country to seek a living abroad, in Italy. After a turn serving as the tutor to the son of a prince's minister, he decided he preferred poverty to dependence. Thinking his character alone would recommend him, "'he cherished the illusion that he would return to his bishop's good graces and obtain some little parish in the mountains'" (262). This remark about the "illusion" the Vicar cherishes foreshadows the Vicar's own account of the disillusionment he experienced at the hands of the church authorities.

After describing how he had seen beneath the appearances of religion and virtue to the wickedness of human nature, as related above, the author notes that what he found particularly remarkable about the Vicar was that there was no gap between appearance and reality with the man: "'What struck me most was seeing in my worthy master's private life virtue without hypocrisy, humanity without weakness, speech that was always straight and simple, and conduct always in conformity with this speech.'" His "observations" of the Vicar encouraged the youth not to hide from him. We once again see a parallel to the education of the reader of *Emile* in distinguishing appearance and reality. Curiously, however, the youth soon learns that appearance and reality are not, in fact, always the same for the Vicar. If his behavior was always consistent in private and public, the opinions he expressed were not: "'But what was I to think when I heard him sometimes approve dogmas contrary to those of the Roman Church and show little esteem for all its ceremonies? I would have believed him a disguised Protestant if I had not observed him to be less faithful to these very practices by which he seemed to set little store'" (264–65). In fact, in concluding his "Profession," the Vicar urges the youth to return to the faith of his fathers, which he—a Catholic priest, no less—calls "of all the religions on earth . . . the one which has the purest morality and which is the most satisfactory to reason" (311). Yet the author relates that the Vicar was punctilious in fulfilling his priestly duties "when there were no witness as when in the public eye." He did not know how to "judge these contradictions." The Vicar's private behavior was irreproachable, he continues, with one exception, namely, "'the failing which had formerly brought on his disgrace, and of which he was not too well corrected'" (265). Now we learn that the author knows what the Vicar's failing was, though the reader does not yet.

The Vicar provides more information regarding himself, including about his failing, within the "Profession." In the brief autobiographical remarks that precede his theological ruminations, the Vicar tells how he was born poor and a peasant and how his parents decided he would earn his bread by becoming a priest. He did as he was told and took his vows. After remarking, "I know by my experience that conscience persists in following the order of nature," a remark that will be developed as a central doctrine of the "Profession," the Vicar reveals his failing: in taking an oath of celibacy he was defying nature and, out of respect for the sanctity of marriage, he limited himself to sleeping only with unmarried women (267). What the author calls the Vicar's "'failing,'" the Vicar himself calls his "resolve," a resolution he believes to be in accordance with nature and conscience. It was this resolve that led to his disgrace and exile. Similar to the youth he is addressing, his experience with what he sees as injustice leads the Vicar into disillusionment and doubt concerning the "opinions" he had received and the "principles" he had adopted: "I was in that frame of mind of uncertainty and doubt that Descartes demands for the quest for truth" (266–67). And so his examination of theological principles commences.

Toward the conclusion of the "Profession," as he wraps up his critical discussion of religious doctrines concerning miracles, revelation, Scripture, and the like, the Vicar provides further information about himself that relates to the theme of appearance and reality we have seen repeatedly arise. He relates that he remains in a state of "involuntary skepticism" concerning doctrinal and other subjects but claims that his doubts do not hinder him from the essence of devotion: "The essential worship is that of the heart." However, as a priest he has rites to perform: "I perform with all possible exactness the tasks prescribed to me. My conscience would reproach me for voluntarily failing to do so on any point." He follows all the rites, recites the Scripture, and omits not the briefest word or ceremony. While he does these things with sincerity and veneration, he also does them without believing any of it (308–9). Since the youth is the sole person to whom the Vicar has admitted this (310), his flock must assume that he believes the doctrines he preaches and the ceremonies he conducts. They take appearance to be reality, but the youth now knows that there is a gap between reality and appearance.

Is the Vicar a liar? A contemporary critic of *Emile*, a bishop (and future president of the National Assembly), posed the problem bluntly: "Here we have, not a Protestant, but a deist dressed up as a Catholic priest who performs all of his functions and who . . . does not omit a single action, a single syllable of a liturgy of which he does not believe a single word. . . . How is it not obvious that he discredits his entire doctrine by making its apostle a libertine priest, one who combines deism with the mass, and the most remarkable of hypocrites [*fourbes*]?"[17]

Insofar as he leads his flock to believe that he himself believes the doctrines he expounds and the ceremonies he performs, he is at minimum guilty of a lie of omission. If he performs these rites with a spirit of devotion, then he does not necessarily seem guilty of a lie of commission (although in the bishop's eyes he would be). Likewise, assuming we believe him, since he states only that he does not affirm the truth of the doctrines he preaches and does not affirmatively state that he believes them to be untrue, he is not guilty of a lie of commission in this case either. Put differently, he is not a hypocrite, at least not in the strict sense of the word. Whatever the gap between appearance and reality in the Vicar's behavior, he nonetheless practices what he preaches in following his conscience or the voice of nature as the guide for his conduct, at least as he interprets the voice speaking to him. However, in following nature he is sometimes led to disobey the law, as in the case of his breaking his vow of celibacy to sleep with unmarried women. In this case, outwardly he appears to follow the laws or rites of the church he serves, but inwardly he does otherwise.[18] Oddly, the Vicar's inconsistency is based on a certain consistency. We might characterize him as a sort of sincere liar.

The Vicar's attitude toward the truth turns out to be similar to what Rousseau says about himself in this regard, as mentioned above. My task here is not to examine the substance of the Vicar's arguments or their relationship to what Rousseau writes elsewhere, in his own name or otherwise, about God and religion. But a remark on the subject is perhaps appropriate here regarding what the Vicar reveals about his less-than-total frankness. Namely, even assuming that he is being fully honest in his speech to the young proselyte about his views, the fact that Rousseau puts this speech into the mouth of someone who admits he conceals his true views from others at the very least complicates any interpretation that takes them to be Rousseau's own, even "approximately" so. At any rate, Rousseau leaves it to readers of the "Profession" to judge the Vicar's arguments for themselves.

The Dramatic Setting of the "Profession"

The dramatic introduction to the "Profession" concludes with a description of the setting of the speech the Savoyard Vicar will deliver to the youth. The setting is a summer sunrise looking over the Po with the Alps crowning the landscape. The language used by the author is highly emotive:

> "The rays of the rising sun already grazed the plains and, projecting on the fields long shadows of the trees, the vineyards, and the houses, enriched with countless irregularities of light the most beautiful scene [*tableau*] which can strike the human eye. One would have said that nature displayed all its magnificence to our eyes in order to present them with the text for our conversation [*entretiens*]. It was there that after

having contemplated these objects in silence for some time, the man of peace spoke to me as follows." (266)

The passage is also highly visual: the rising sun, shadows, light, a scene or *tableau*, the human eye, "our eyes." Nature becomes a "text" to be read as a template for a speech. The questions of writing versus speech in relation to the appropriate audience should remind us again of Plato's *Phaedrus*. Just as Rousseau details the setting of the Vicar's speech, so too does Plato describe the setting of Socrates' summertime conversation with Phaedrus, a lovely spot beneath plane and willow trees by a babbling stream, with a chorus of cicadas serenading them.[19] How does the dramatic setting of the Vicar's speech relate to the content and intended effect of the "Profession," both on its auditor and on the reader?

We have encountered a sunrise scene already in book III of *Emile*, and we will also encounter a similar scene later in book IV after the "Profession" concludes; and these two scenes will help us understand the rhetorical thrust of the dramatic setting of the "Profession."[20] Before turning to them, I want to note that Rousseau writes elsewhere of how the spectacle of nature speaks differently to different individuals. In the *Letter to Beaumont*, responding to the archbishop's claim that "the great spectacle of nature" obviously proclaims the creator and governor of the world, Rousseau writes: "The order of the universe, admirable as it is, does not strike all eyes equally" (*Beaumont, CW*, 9:40). In *Julie* he illustrates the difference in responses to the spectacle of nature of the pious Julie and the atheist Wolmar: "Imagine Julie out walking with her husband; she admiring, in the rich and brilliant adornment which the earth displays, the work and gifts of the Author of the creation; he seeing nothing in all this but a fortuitous combination in which nothing is linked to anything except by blind force. . . . Alas! She says affectedly; the wonders of nature, so alive, so animate for us, are dead in the eyes of the unfortunate Wolmar, and in this great harmony of beings, where everything speaks of God in so sweet a voice, he perceives nothing but an eternal silence" (V.5; *CW*, 6:484).

The sunrise scene in book III involves a lesson in cosmography, and I analyzed it in chapter 3 as an example of the challenge Rousseau poses of discriminating the "true" and "false" versions of his pupil. As I noted there, book III is devoted to teaching the elements of the sciences, with the central lesson being that he must only be taught what is *useful*. The mantra the student learns to repeat—"What is it useful for?"—and the frontispiece depicting Hermes engraving the elements of the sciences on a column are among the features of the text that recall Plato's

Phaedrus. In order to teach his pupil about astronomy and geography, the tutor takes him one evening to observe the setting sun: "One fine evening we go for a walk in a suitable place where a broad, open horizon permits the setting sun to be fully seen." The next day they return to the same spot to witness the rising sun, but the tutor-narrator temporarily forgets the strictly utilitarian purposes of these observations and lapses into emotive prose:

> We see it announcing itself from afar by the fiery arrows it launches ahead of it. The blaze grows; the east appears to be wholly in flames. By their glow one expects the star for a long time before it reveals itself. At every instant one believes that he sees it appear. Finally one sees it. A shining point shoots out like lightning and immediately fills all of space. The veil of darkness is drawn back and falls. Man recognizes his habitat and finds it embellished. . . . The birds in chorus join together in concert to greet the father of life. . . . There is here a half-hour of enchantment which no man can resist. So great, so fair, so delicious a spectacle leaves no one cold. (168)

But then Rousseau in his role as author steps back from his impassioned tutor-narrator.

> Full of the enthusiasm he feels, the master wants to communicate it to the child. He believes he moves the child by making him attentive to the sensations by which he, the master, is himself moved. Pure stupidity! It is in man's heart that the life of nature's spectacle exists. To see it, one must feel it. The child perceives the objects, but he cannot persuade the relations linking them; he cannot hear the sweet harmony of their concord. For that is needed experience he has not acquired. (168–69)

In particular, the child does not have the emotional experience required for such associations. He does not know the "accents of love and pleasure." Nor does he know the divinity: "Finally, how can he be touched by the beauty of nature's spectacle, if he does not know the hand responsible for adorning it?" (169).[21]

The dramatic setting and poetic language used to describe this sunrise scene are strikingly similar to the dramatic setting of the "Profession." Here it is the older man, the tutor, who would communicate his enthusiasm to the youth, his pupil. The boy will not be able to feel or understand the emotions and thoughts inspired by the sunrise if, like Emile, he has been educated according to the proper "march of nature." In the case of the "Profession," it is the youth who describes the sunrise in highly emotional language. Although he is recalling the scene thirty years later, it seems from his description that even as a boy he was capable of feeling the emotions he describes. For example, unlike the youth at the beginning of book III, who would be about twelve and does not know the "accents of love and pleasure" (165, 169), the young proselyte of the "Profession" is sexually awakened. Similarly, unlike Emile, he has had religious instruction and so knows something, if confusedly or superstitiously, about the "hand responsible" for "adorning" "nature's spectacle." If the tutor's desire to communicate what he feels to his pupil is "pure stupidity," the dramatic setting of the "Profession" is precisely intended to provoke an emotional response in the auditor to aid in persuading him of the speech's content. The dramatic setting would not be appropriate for persuading Emile, but it is suitable for the young proselyte.

The other scene involving the spectacle of nature does involve Emile, and it comes after the "Profession" in book IV. Rousseau sets up the episode with a discussion of the imagination. So far he has worked to delay Emile's imagination to prevent his corruption and especially the corruption of his sexual passion, but now he will use this very imagination for the same purpose: "The true moment of nature comes at last" (316). He begins the episode with an elegiac introduction: "There are periods in human life which are made never to be forgotten. The period of the instruction of which I am speaking is such a time for Emile. . . . Let us engrave it in his memory in such a way that it will never be effaced" (321). The language of "engraving" on the memory should recall the frontispiece to book III of Hermes, and once again we are reminded of Plato's *Phaedrus*. We should not be surprised that Rousseau embarks on a discussion of rhetoric before Jean-Jacques makes his speech to Emile.

Turning to the question of rhetoric, Rousseau in his authorial voice writes: "One of the errors of our age is to use reason in too unadorned a form, as if men were all mind. In neglecting the language of signs that speak to the imagination, the most energetic of languages has been lost. . . . It is with this language that one persuades and makes others act" (321). As elsewhere, he explains the art of persuasion with a comparison of the ancients and the moderns.[22] "I observe that in the modern age men no longer have a hold on one another except by force or by self-interest; the ancients, by contrast, acted much more by persuasion and by the affections of the soul because they did not neglect the language of signs. All their covenants took place with solemnity in order to make them more inviolable. Before force was established, the gods were the magistrates of mankind," and their oaths were taken with all of nature as witness to them (321). The Savoyard Vicar acted as a good ancient would have, evoking the rising sun to serve as a witness to his speech to the young proselyte: "What the ancients accomplished with eloquence was prodigious. But that eloquence did not consist solely in fine, well-ordered speeches, and never did it have more effect that when the orator spoke least. What was said most vividly was expressed not by words but by signs." Here Rousseau gives examples of visual eloquence: Thrasybulus and Tarquin cutting off the tops of poppies, Diogenes walking before Zeno, and so on (322). Rousseau terms this discussion of rhetoric a "digression," which, "like many others, gradually carries me far from my subject, and my wanderings are too frequent to admit of being both long and tolerable. I therefore return to my subject" (323). But what if this "digression" is in fact the preparation for "my subject"?

Indeed, Jean-Jacques now applies these lessons given by Rousseau to their imaginary pupil:

> Therefore, even after the preparations of which I have spoken, I shall be very careful not to go all of a sudden to Emile's room and pompously make a long speech to him about the subject in which I want to instruct him. I shall begin by moving his imagination. I shall choose the time, the place, and the objects most favorable to the impression I want to make. I shall, so to speak, call all of nature as a witness to our conversations. I shall bring the Eternal Being, who is the Author of nature, to testify to the truth of my speech. I shall take Him as judge between Emile and me. I shall mark the place where we are—the rocks, the woods, and the mountains surrounding us shall be monuments of his promises and mine. I shall put in my eyes, my accent, and my gestures the enthusiasm and the ardor that I want to inspire in him. (323)

Jean-Jacques now proves himself to be a good ancient as well. He does not specifically describe a sunrise, although he seems to allude to something like one when he states that he will bring "the Author of nature" to testify to the truth of his speech. In any case, the language he uses echoes the "Profession." In introducing the paper containing the "Profession," Rousseau tells his readers it is up to them to draw useful reflections "about the subject with which it deals" (260), and here too he is similarly vague: "the subject in which I want to instruct him."

What is the "subject" about which Jean-Jacques wants to speak to his pupil? When Rousseau as author chastised the narrator-tutor at the beginning of book III for getting carried away by the emotions evoked by the sunrise—"Pure stupidity!"—Rousseau explained that his pupil will not experience the same sentiments because he does not know "the accents of love and pleasure" or "the hand" responsible for "adorning" "nature's spectacle." We should not be surprised, then, that the subject in which he wants to instruct Emile concerns the divinity and romantic love. First, as for the divinity, apart from the mention of the "Author of nature" he makes to the reader in setting the stage for his speech, the divinity he reveals is himself: the godlike tutor who discloses to his pupil that he is his creation (323–24). Second, it is a curious lesson in sex education. Rather than stifle pubescent boy's imagination, he will use it to direct his passion: "I shall make him moderate by making him fall in love" (327). Appealing to the boy's imagination with his speech, he conjures an imaginary lover for his imaginary pupil. He asks the reader to imagine his rhetorical powers: "Imagine whether I shall know how to get his ear when I depict for him the beloved whom I destine for him" (328). For the remainder of the work, Emile and his tutor seek and then find Sophie. If an invisible deity who watches over us is needed for corrupt beings such as the young proselyte, or perhaps the reader, Emile will worship at the foot of an ideal woman.

Let us now return to the dramatic setting of the "Profession" in light of these other sunrise stories. Given Rousseau's remarks about rhetoric in general and his particular examples of the effect or lack of effect of sunrise speeches depending on the character of the auditor, it is evident that the intended rhetorical effect on the part of the Savoyard Vicar is to move the boy's passions and imagination. As we know from the information provided about the young proselyte, information presumably also known by the Vicar, the boy's awakened passions and imagination make him susceptible to the persuasive force of the dramatic setting of the Vicar's profession and the contents of profession itself. The Vicar's success is attested to by the young man himself during an intermission after the Vicar completes his theological discourse and before the second part of the speech concerning miracles, revelation, Scripture, and so on: "The good priest had spoken with vehemence. He was moved, and so was I. I believed I was hearing the divine Orpheus sing the first hymns and teaching men the worship of the gods." This is the textual reference to the illustration of Orpheus singing of the gods that "belongs" to book IV, as we saw in the previous chapter. The Vicar's song did not, however, entirely win over his auditor: "Nevertheless I saw a multitude of objections to make to him. I did not make any of them, because they were less solid than disconcerting, and persuasiveness was on his side" (294). To resort to the language Rousseau uses in the *Social Contract* when speaking of the lawgiver: the boy may be persuaded, at least partly, but he was not convinced. At any rate, the emphasis is on persuasion, on being moved by emotional appeals, and not on rational argument.

What if we enlarge our scope to Rousseau's intention in including the "Profession" and its effect on the reader? We can get some light on this question by attending to what the Vicar states about the intended effect of his speech and what Rousseau adds in his own name as the supposed editor of the "Profession." When he agrees to deliver his profession to the young proselyte, the Vicar states that he will unburden his heart and mind in order to show him why he esteems himself happy, as against the initial incredulity on the boy's part that a poor, persecuted clergyman could possibly be happy (265–66). During the dramatic intermission between the two parts of the "Profession," the youth admits to the Vicar that, whatever his lingering doubts, in his current state he would have to "ascend rather than descend in order to adopt your opinions" (294). When he recommences his speech, the Vicar agrees: "But in your present condition you will profit from thinking as I do." To this last statement quoted, Rousseau in his role as editor adds a note: "This is, I believe, what the good vicar could say to the public at present" (295 and n.). Rousseau thereby indicates the intended audience, or at least *an* intended audience, of the "Profession": "the public," readers actual and potential writ large. Like the young proselyte, who unlike Emile has not imbibed the principles of the natural goodness of man or been educated according to these principles, ordinary readers are corrupted by society, whether or not they know it. The Vicar's profession, and the "Profession" itself, is therefore appropriate for this audience, and its persuasive force is directed at making it useful for them.[23]

Since I have just quoted one of the footnotes Rousseau adds to the "Profession" as the supposed editor, let me briefly remark on the function and effect of these notes as paratextual elements. There are eighteen such notes, nine for each of the two parts into which the "Profession" is divided, and they vary greatly in length. In general, there are two sorts of notes. First, there are notes that provide citations, quotations, and the like, that generally support the content of the text of the "Profession," as though Rousseau is providing editorial apparatus to the Vicar's otherwise unadorned speech. Second, and more important, many of the notes are critical of "modern philosophy," as Rousseau terms it at several points (279 n., 286 n.). First, he criticizes modern philosophy for being reductionist and materialist. Second, he criticizes it for the effects its skepticism and materialism have on religious belief, and therefore popular morality. This is particularly true of the last, and by far the longest, note, wherein he warns readers of the dangers posed by the "philosophic party," suggesting that, unlike religious stories of divine reward and retribution, they can offer no support for popular morality: "Philosopher, your moral laws are very fine. But I beg you to show me their sanction" (312–14 n.). If the Vicar expressly denies that he speaks as a philosopher (266), Rousseau does speak as a philosopher in the notes to the "Profession," warning both the public and philosophers themselves of the dangers of modern philosophy.

To what extent is the "Profession" merely persuasive or useful, that is as opposed to being true? This is a matter for judgment; the Vicar has urged the youth to judge for himself, and Rousseau has invited his reader to do likewise. Because it is not my purpose here to examine the substance of the theological and other arguments in the "Profession" except insofar as they relate to its structural elements, I will limit myself to one issue and will raise it as a question. If the sunrise setting of the Vicar's profession is intended to move the youth's (and the reader's) passions and imagination, how does this persuasive setting relate to its substance, that is, its arguments and their rational force? The spectacle of nature is said to be the "text" for their "conversations" and plays a decisive role in the Vicar's argument. Having established his first "article of faith," that "a will moves the universe and animates the nature," by appealing principally to the interior experience of willing (272–73), he looks out at nature to establish his second dogma, "that matter moved according to certain laws shows me an intelligence" (273–75). Notably, while making this argument he addresses the boy—"Tell me, my friend . . ."—and asks him whether he sees chaos or harmony in the universe. In other words, the boy is asked to look at the spectacle of nature that serves as the setting for his speech. Thus, the dramatic setting of the "Profession" itself provides proof for one of its central arguments. The apparently orderly and harmonious spectacle of nature also provides a kind of negative role in establishing the third and last of the Vicar's "articles of faith." Namely, turning from nature to mankind, the Vicar is struck with the disorder in the moral order, with the prosperity of the wicked and sufferings of the good. Faced with a problem of theodicy, he argues that we must have an immaterial soul (281) and that this immaterial soul exists after death as long as necessary for moral order to be reestablished (283). In short, without entering further into the question of how compelling the Vicar's arguments are, their persuasive force depends on how we interpret the spectacle of nature. This is a question the Vicar leaves to the youth and Rousseau leaves to the reader to judge.

Judging the "Profession"

When he introduces the paper containing the "Profession," Rousseau abdicates his authority to judge its contents and invests the reader with that authority: "It is up to you to see if useful reflections can be drawn from it," and "I am offering it to you for examination" (260). Likewise, the Vicar begins the "Profession" by telling his young auditor: "My child, do not expect either learned speeches or profound reasonings from me. I am not a great philosopher. . . . It is enough for me to reveal to you what I think in the simplicity of my heart. Consult yours during my speech. That is all I ask of you" (266). Finally, in concluding his "Profession," the Vicar tells the youth: "I have told you my doubts as doubts, my opinions as opinions. I have told you my reasons for doubting and for believing. Now it is for you to judge" (310). We get no explicit judgment of the Vicar's speech from either the young auditor or from Rousseau. Again, the reader is left to judge.

As mentioned above, however, in the intermission between the two parts of the "Profession" the young proselyte states that he saw "a multitude of objections" to make to the Vicar, and Rousseau thereby invites the reader to raise objections as well. Once again without analyzing the substance of the "Profession," let me point to one interesting structural element that may indicate at least one of the "multitude of objections" the youth has to the Vicar's teaching that might be intended to get the reader thinking.

In describing the dramatic setting of the Vicar's speech, the author of the paper states that the spectacle of nature would serve as the text for their conversation (*entretiens*), but there is nonetheless almost no conversation in the "Profession" itself. However, at one point there is an attempt at dialogue. Turning from the theological arguments and the "articles of faith" he has put forward to the question of how we should conduct ourselves based on these "truths," the Vicar advances his central doctrine of conscience (286). Recall that the question of conscience first arose in the dramatic introduction, when the Vicar suggested that he could break his vows of celibacy in good conscience and without remorse because he was acting in accordance with nature (267). Returning to the argument, the Vicar characterizes the conscience as the voice of the soul, as the passions are the voice of the body, and argues that when these voices are in contradiction we should follow conscience: "He who follows conscience does not fear being led astray. This point is important (continued my benefactor, seeing that I was going to interrupt him). Allow me to tarry a bit to clarify it" (286–87). The boy's attempt to interrupt is aborted.

This is the only occasion on which Rousseau inserts a dialogic element into the "Profession" itself. What was the boy going to say? At least two possibilities present themselves. First, related to the Vicar's character and actions, as revealed in the dramatic introduction as well as in the beginning of the "Profession" itself, was the boy going to ask the Vicar whether he wasn't in fact following the voice of the bodily passions in sleeping with unmarried women rather than heeding the voice of conscience? Is the Vicar's appeal to conscience a rationalization of his behavior? Or, less harshly, how do we distinguish between the voice of the body and the voice of the soul? Second, and related to the central doctrine of Rousseau's philosophy of the natural goodness of man being advanced in the main text of *Emile*, but not in the "Profession," was the boy—perhaps the future Jean-Jacques Rousseau—going to propose an alternative theory of the conflict we find within ourselves, explaining it not as a conflict between body and soul but instead as a conflict between the natural goodness of man and his corruption in society? In this case, conscience for Rousseau himself would seem to have a different basis than the dualist theory put forward by the Vicar.

Perhaps we should view this failed attempt at dialogue on the part of the auditor of the "Profession" as another invitation to the reader to compare the arguments of the "Profession" to those made in the main body of *Emile*. In this light, perhaps we should also contemplate the possibility that Rousseau presents us with another inapt apologue, or perhaps a partially apt one, when he summarizes his intention in including it in the work. Resuming his authorial role after the conclusion of the "Profession," he writes: "I have transcribed this writing not as a rule for the sentiments that one ought to follow in religious matters, but as an example of the way one can reason with one's pupil in order not to diverge from the method I have tried to establish" (313–14). Rousseau does not repeat his invitation to the reader to judge the "Profession," but perhaps that is precisely what we are asked to do.

Chapter 6

Reading with
Emile and Sophie

Since we are concerned with the education of the reader in Rousseau's works, then a fruitful field to labor is the act of reading itself as enacted in his writings. In this chapter I examine two acts of reading included in *Emile*: first a treatment of the sole book Emile reads during his youth, Defoe's *Robinson Crusoe*, and second, a more extensive examination of the role of Fénelon's *Adventures of Telemachus* in the romance of Emile and Sophie. Of course, *Emile* can easily be read without consulting the books Rousseau singles out to be read by Emile and Sophie, or even without being familiar with them, as my own experience with regard to *Telemachus* long attested. There is limited scholarly attention to the role either novel plays in *Emile*, and especially scanty work on *Telemachus*. In fact, in three of the four existing book-length studies of *Emile*, *Robinson Crusoe* is mentioned only in passing, and in two of them there is similarly only a fleeting reference to *Telemachus*.[1] Most studies that do attend to Rousseau's employment of *Robinson Crusoe* take the novel to depict a solitary man in nature and more or less leave it at that. In turn, there are very few discussions of the role of *Telemachus* in *Emile*.[2] The principal exception is Schaeffer's excellent book, in which she gives extensive attention to both novels, including to how the novels educate both the characters, Emile and Sophie, and the reader of *Emile*.[3] My analysis builds on her work.

In this chapter I examine how reading *Emile* in dialogue with the two books he assigns to his characters, and thereby indirectly to the reader of *Emile* itself, deepens our understanding of the form and content of the work with regard to the education of the reader. In doing so, I pursue two main themes. First, in the cases of both *Robinson Crusoe* and *Telemachus*, Rousseau challenges the reader to identify what lessons conveyed by these books are appropriate for the characters who read them, thus continuing his engagement with the problems of writing and rhetoric raised by Socrates in Plato's *Phaedrus*, which have remained a persistent theme throughout this book. In the case of *Robinson Crusoe*, Rousseau tests the reader by announcing that Defoe's novel must be edited to make it appropriate for Emile without entirely identifying what should be excised. I argue that it is principally the religious dimension of *Robinson Crusoe* that must be removed to make it appropriate for Emile. In the case of *Telemachus*, Rousseau further tests the reader's understanding of the effect of reading the work on different characters. He does so by varying the impact of reading the work on different characters, especially by doubling Sophie into "false" and "true" versions, with different temperaments, and by not having Emile read the work at all during his wooing of Sophie and then having him read it later with an entirely different purpose. The second theme I pursue here follows from the first with respect to *Telemachus*. Namely, I explore how Rousseau's substantive treatment of romantic love as a mixture of real and ideal is echoed in the form of the narrative of his romantic story, which vacillates between claims of being truth and fiction, for example through the personages of the true and false Sophies.

Identifying *Robinson Crusoe*'s Rigmarole

Defoe's 1719 novel was one of the most popular works of the eighteenth century, including in France, so Rousseau could count on his readers' familiarity with the work. Rousseau himself stated that he had considered writing an adaptation of the novel.[4] In his *Dialogues* he remarks (of himself in the third person) on his fondness for *Robinson Crusoe*, and he likens his metaphorical solitude to Crusoe on his island (*Dialogues*, *CW*, 1:117–18). Similarly, in the *Confessions* he alludes to the shipwrecked sailor in his account of his own brief exile on the Île St. Pierre (*Confessions*, *CW*, 5:539; see also 249).

Then as now, *Robinson Crusoe* was popularly read as a kind of adventure story of shipwreck, survival, and salvation. Rousseau's statement that he will restrict Emile's reading to the portion of the novel beginning with Robinson's shipwreck and ending with the arrival of the ship that rescues him is in keeping with the common interpretation of the work, even if he puts it to specific use in Emile's education. Eighteenth-century readers were, however, perhaps more attuned to another dimension of *Robinson Crusoe*: the narrative frame of the work concerning salvation—not of the shipwreck variety, but religious salvation. Defoe's novel is framed as a prodigal-son story, of a disobedient son who disrespects his father's wishes and comes to believe his shipwreck on a desert island is a divine punishment. During the course of his imprisonment on the island, one of Robinson's central preoccupations is this punishment and his concern for the salvation of his soul. Of course, there is much more to the novel, including, as we shall see, a strain of authorial ironic distance with regard to the religious preoccupation of the protagonist.

I suggest that the religious theme of *Robinson Crusoe*, voiced both in the narrative frame Rousseau explicitly cuts and within the portion of the narrative he retains of Crusoe on his island, is the unidentified rigmarole he hints to the reader must be cut if the work is to be appropriate for Emile. There may be other parts of the work that must be excised as well, and I will note some in passing, but the religious dimension is the important part of the novel to be removed, given its prominence in Defoe's novel and its particular inaptness for Emile. The remark about cutting rigmarole amounts to a test of the reader's progress in the education provided by Rousseau's own book.[5]

Let us begin with the context in *Emile* in which *Robinson Crusoe* is introduced. As I discussed in chapter 4, Defoe's novel is brought up at the point in book III where Rousseau alludes to the frontispiece of Hermes engraving the elements of the sciences on a column. Book III is broadly concerned with Emile's education in the natural sciences through experiential learning. The touchstone for this education is utility: "It is a question not of knowing what is but only of knowing what is useful" (166). Shortly before introducing *Robinson Crusoe*, Rousseau hints at the background role played by Plato's *Phaedrus* in his discussion: "'What is that good for?' This is now the sacred word, the decisive word between him and me in all the actions of our life. . . . He who is taught as his most important lesson to want to know nothing but what is useful interrogates like Socrates" (179). Once again, in the story told by Socrates in *Phaedrus* King Thamos asks Thoth about the utility of the sciences and the arts with which he is presented. When presented with the art of writing, which the god claims is useful for remembering, Thamos instead criticizes writing as an art that leads to forgetting. Socrates further criticizes writing as being promiscuously available to every reader, whatever that reader's capacity or character, unlike speech, which can, in principle at least, be rhetorically tailored to suit the audience.

Returning to *Emile*, Rousseau now takes up the challenge posed by Socrates: "I hate books. They only teach one to talk about what one does not know. It is said that Hermes engraved the elements of the sciences on columns in order to shelter his discoveries from a flood. If he had left a good imprint of them in man's head, they would have been preserved by tradition. Well-prepared minds are the surest monuments on which to engrave human knowledge" (184). Responding to Socrates' critique of writing (of which engraving is a form), Rousseau must have *Emile* address different audiences in different ways, and the reader's interpretation of the book Rousseau now exempts from condemnation, *Robinson Crusoe*, reveals that reader's capacity and character.

After his bibliophobic diatribe, Rousseau voices his wish that there were a book that portrayed "all man's natural needs" in such a way that a child can appreciate them, only to reveal that such a book exists, if in an unexpected place: "Ardent philosopher, I see your imagination kindling already. Do not put yourself out. This situation has been found; it has been described and, without prejudice to you, much better than you would describe it yourself—at least with more truth and simplicity." This as-yet-unidentified book will be the first Emile will read, and the only book he will possess for some time, he states, hinting to the reader that it will take the place of other books more widely possessed: "What, then is this marvelous book? Is it Aristotle? Is it Pliny? Is it Buffon? No. It is *Robinson Crusoe*" (184). Not a heavy tome of natural philosophy, but a novel.

Rousseau's seemingly gratuitous taunting of the apostrophized philosopher makes sense if we consider that he himself is writing a sort of novel to illustrate the natural needs of man, and the natural goodness of man. This suggestion is supported by an interesting fact: this is the point in the original version of his educational treatise, the so-called Favre Manuscript, in which Rousseau introduces Emile as a character. A parallel therefore exists between Emile and Robinson, *Emile* and *Robinson Crusoe*. This parallel survives in the final version of the text when Rousseau writes that Robinson Crusoe alone on his island, providing for his subsistence, preservation, and even well-being is not only agreeable to a young reader but useful as well by serving as a point of comparison: "This state, I agree, is not that of social man; very likely it is not going to be that of Emile. But it is on the basis of this very state that he ought to appraise all the others. The surest means of raising oneself above prejudices and ordering one's judgments about the true relations of things is to put oneself in the place of an isolated man and to judge everything as this man himself ought to judge of it with respect to his own utility" (184–85). One might very well say the same of *Emile* and its reader.

Emile will be a qualified imitator of the solitary Robinson:[6] "I want him to think he is Robinson himself, to see himself dressed in skins, wearing a large cap, carrying a large saber and all the rest of the character's grotesque equipment, with the exception of the parasol, which he will not need" (185). Interestingly, this portrait of Defoe's character can be seen in the frontispiece of the original edition of *Robinson Crusoe* and was the most widely reprinted image of Robinson Crusoe, and therefore an image Rousseau could count on his readers recognizing. The exception of the parasol points to the limits of Emile's imitation of the novel's protagonist, for he will examine Robinson's conduct, improve on his actions, note his failings, and so on. One example of an action taken by Robinson that might come in for negative appraisal by Emile, or any reader of *Robinson Crusoe*, is his decision to take money from the wrecked ship, despite the perils he faces in doing so and especially despite his realization of the lack of utility of doing so: "I smil'd to my self at the Sight of this Money. O Drug! Said I aloud, what art thou good for, Thou art not worth to me, no not the taking off of the Ground, one of those Knives is worth all this Heap; I have no Manner of use for thee, e'en remain where thou art, and go to the Bottom as a Creature whose Life is not worth saving. However, upon Second Thoughts, I took it away."[7] This passage indicates something of the authorial irony of *Robinson Crusoe* and Defoe's own engagement of the reader in judging its protagonist's actions.

One of Robinson's social needs is companionship. Rousseau explains that Emile will busy himself on his island for now, but the day is coming when "he will not want any longer to live there alone, and when Friday, who now hardly concerns him, will not for long be enough for him" (185).[8] That is, the pseudosolitude of Emile can last until his sexual passion awakens. On this point, it is noteworthy that Robinson's condition on his island, even after Friday's arrival, is decidedly masculine; like Rousseau's natural man in the *Discourse on Inequality*, a female does not appear to be among Robinson's natural needs, initially or indeed ever. Rousseau has chosen a resolutely nonsexual model for the preadolescent Emile, in contrast to his later introduction of *Telemachus* and its romantic dimension into the story of Emile and Sophie. A primary reason for limiting the novel to Robinson's stay on the island, then, is that the "natural state" in which he lives will give way to the "social state," which is not yet appropriate for Emile.

Limiting ourselves for the moment to the fact that Emile is meant to judge Robinson's actions according to the true needs of nature, we can initially opine, with regard to our main concern about what rigmarole should be cut from the novel, that the fact that Robinson as Defoe depicts him is a thoroughly social man with social desires and needs leads to at least two choices as to how Emile—and the reader of *Emile*—should approach the novel and the role it plays in Emile's education. First, much of Robinson's expression of his social needs and his actions to fulfill them could be retained in the expurgated work, leaving it to Emile (along with the reader) to make his own judgments about natural versus social needs.[9] Second, Rousseau could be inviting the reader to identify Robinson's social needs and cut out the parts of the narrative that would be inappropriate for Emile. Either way, by stating that Emile's role is in part to judge Robinson's actions, Rousseau poses a challenge to the reader as to whether he has been sufficiently instructed by reading *Emile* to make these judgments. What I have just sketched is basically Schaeffer's interpretation, both with regard to Emile's use of *Robinson Crusoe* to improve his judgment concerning real versus social needs and with regard to the education of the reader with the same goal.[10] I agree, and will leave the question of the utility of Defoe's novel for Emile and the reader at that, instead turning my attention to Rousseau's challenge to the reader to identify what portions of the novel would be inappropriate for Emile.

Rousseau explains that he will curtail and expurgate Defoe's novel for the pedagogical purpose he has in mind: "This novel, disencumbered of all its rigmarole, beginning with Robinson's shipwreck near his island, and ending with the arrival of the ship which comes to take him from it, will be Emile's entertainment and instruction throughout the period which is dealt with here" (185). What is this unidentified rigmarole? First, the term translated by Bloom as "rigmarole" is *fratras*, which means a hodgepodge or motley assemblage or something of that nature. The idea is that the novel has to be "cleaned up" (*débarrassé*) or the superfluous elements have to be "gotten rid of" (*débarrassé*) so that the story line of the shipwrecked Robinson is perspicuous. A number of interpreters, including the editor of the Pléiade edition of *Emile* and the editor of the edition of *Robinson Crusoe* I am using, assume that the parts of the novel before Robinson's shipwreck and after his rescue are identical with the rigmarole Rousseau has in mind.[11] This is certainly one possible reading of the sentence. However, it does not, I think, fully account for the vocabulary, for the term *fratras* suggests that something is admixed into something else and *débarrassé* suggests extracting or disentangling something rather than simply curtailing it. So, what if the rigmarole is not simply the novelistic bookends of the story of the shipwrecked hero?

Rousseau leaves it for the reader to judge, and the following argument is meant to be my own suggestion about what rigmarole of Crusoe's work must be excised to make the work appropriate for Emile. As I have already remarked, the emphatic way in which Rousseau introduces *Robinson Crusoe* as the sole book that will comprise Emile's library for some time should make the reader think about what books are being excluded. In addressing his "ardent philosopher," Rousseau mentions works of natural history: Aristotle, Pliny, and Buffon. But a more obvious candidate would be the Bible. As a portrait of man's natural state, as Rousseau characterizes Defoe's novel, *Robinson Crusoe*, with its solitary protagonist, could be thought of as a parallel to the story of Adam in Genesis. The possibility that Rousseau has this in mind might also be suggested by his remark that Friday will not long suffice for Emile as a companion, and in this light, it is revealing that he begins book V of *Emile* by alluding to scriptural verse introducing the creation of Eve: "It is not good for man to be alone" (357). Finally, the Bible is the sole book Robinson Crusoe reads while on his island, and his reading of Scripture becomes a primary preoccupation of the marooned man along with writing his diary, which itself establishes a parallel between *Robinson Crusoe* and the Bible, and thus between *Robinson Crusoe* and *Emile*.[12]

By curtailing Emile's reading of Defoe's novel to Robinson's sojourn on the island and emphasizing Emile's judgment as to whether Robinson's actions were useful for his self-preservation, Rousseau himself proffers a version of the widespread interpretation of *Robinson Crusoe* as a portrait of *Homo economicus*. This interpretation can be famously found in Marx's *Capital*, where he uses the example of Robinson Crusoe to illustrate the labor theory of value.[13] Among literary scholars, the locus classicus for this reading is the still-resilient interpretation put forward by Ian Watt in his influential *Rise of the Novel* (1957).[14] Political theorists have likewise generally emphasized the economic education provided to Emile by *Robinson Crusoe*, taking "economic" in a wide sense here, and several scholars have followed this line of interpretation in one way or another.[15] However, alongside this common interpretation of *Robinson Crusoe* (and related readings concerning colonialism, racism, and such) is a religious interpretation that locates Defoe's novel in the tradition of works such as Bunyan's *Pilgrim's Progress*.[16]

A prominent feature of *Robinson Crusoe*, from the very outset of the work and throughout, is the religious theme of a prodigal son's being punished for his sins and his concern for the salvation of his soul.[17] This religious element would be decidedly inappropriate for Emile.[18] As we saw in the previous chapter, Emile is not introduced to religion until much later in the work: "I foresee how many readers will be surprised at seeing me trace the whole first age of my pupil without speaking to him of religion. At fifteen he did not know whether he had a soul. And perhaps at eighteen it is not yet time for him to learn it; for if he learns it sooner than he ought, he runs the risk of never knowing it" (257). Let me turn to a brief discussion of *Robinson Crusoe* to reveal how central the religious theme is to the work and thereby demonstrate how inapt this theme would be for our pupil.

The reader of Defoe's novel first encounters a preface, which announces the themes of the work. It is characterized as a "Story" about a "private Man's Adventures in the World," hence the popular view of the novel as an adventure story. Lest this be the final word, however, Defoe immediately adds: "The Story is told with Modesty, with Seriousness, and with a religious Application of Events to the Uses to which wise Men always apply them (viz.) to the Instruction of others by his Example, and to justify and honour the Wisdom of Providence in all the Variety of our Circumstances, let them happen how they will."[19] Whether Defoe is attempting to justify telling tales by giving them an edifying cast or whether he is serious about the talk of providence matters little for the present purpose. The Protestant background of the novel is evident in a number of ways. One such element is the protagonist's very name. The story begins with Robinson's account of his birth in York in 1632 as the son of an immigrant from Bremen, suggesting his father was a Protestant refugee, with Robinson's original surname being Kreutznaer, a name with the root etymological sense of the noun "cross." After this start, Defoe has his narrator launch into a story of how he disobeyed his father by pursuing his desire to go to sea, the father warning him "that if I did take this foolish Step, God would not bless me," about which Robinson in retrospect remarks that his father's discourse "was truly Prophetick." A number of similar remarks are sprinkled through this framing narrative, including: "I began now seriously to reflect upon what I had done, and how justly I was overtaken by the Judgment of Heaven for my wicked leaving my Father's House, and abandoning my Duty." The fact that we are reading a parable of the prodigal son is finally made explicit: "Had I now had the Sense to have gone back to *Hull*, and have gone home, I had been happy, and my Father, an Emblem of our Blessed Savior's Parable, had even kill'd the fatted Calf for me"[20] If Rousseau wants to disencumber the mundane utility of the adventure story from its religious elements, he would have to cut much of the part of the novel preceding Robinson's shipwreck—as in fact he does.

The religious rigmarole nonetheless pervades the part of the story Rousseau retains, and so it must be surgically removed. Shortly after his shipwreck, our hero begins to think of his misfortune as "a Determination of Heaven" for his trespasses, but this also poses the problem of theodicy: "Why Providence should thus compleatly ruine its Creatures, and render them so absolutely miserable."[21] Soon thereafter he gets religion, once some grain has miraculously sprouted, granting him subsistence: "It is impossible to express the Astonishment and Confusion of my Thoughts on this Occasion; I had hitherto acted upon no religious Foundation at all, indeed I had very few Notions of Religion in my Head," but now he began to regard the miracle as one of those "pure Productions of Providence" and to heartily thank the deity.[22] This episode, and others like it, are given an ironic tone when Defoe has Robinson realize that he had accidentally scattered the grain himself but nonetheless continues to regard the event as miraculous.[23] The same interplay of religious devotion and ironizing occurs when a feverish Robinson has a dream, noting in his diary, "Pray'd to God again, but was light-headed." He nonetheless sees the dream as a message from the deity: "I never had so much one Thought of [his miserable fate] being the Hand of God, or that it was a just Punishment for my Sin, my rebellious Behaviour against my Father, or my present Sins which are great; or so much as a Punishment for the general Course of my wicked Life."[24] He then prays for the first time — "God's Justice has overtaken me . . ." — and engages in more speculation on his punishment as being providential.[25] Now Robinson is a fervent Bible reader, and Defoe suggests the parallel between Scripture and his novel by emphasizing the act of reading, Robinson of the Bible and the reader of *Robinson Crusoe*: "And I add this Part here, to hint to whoever shall read it, that whenever they come to a true Sense of things, they will find Deliverance from Sin a much greater Blessing, than Deliverance from Affliction."[26]

Numerous further examples could be adduced, but will I restrict myself to two. First, reflecting upon his condition and his account of it, Robinson considers the whole as owing to "the merciful Dispositions of Heaven" that should inform the reader of his diary of the "secret Intimations of Providence."[27] Second, just before he encounters Friday, he writes: "I have been in all my Circumstances a *Memento* to those who are touch'd with the general Plague of Mankind" that one ought to be satisfied with the station in which nature and God have placed them, "for not to look back upon my primitive Condition, and the excellent Advice of my Father, the Opposition of which, was, *as I may call it*, my ORIGINAL SIN."[28] Robinson's self-appointed mission to convert his "savage" to Christianity becomes a major theme of the novel.[29] None of this, not least the occasional ironic tone, would be appropriate for Emile.

Finally, to complete our exercise in pruning Defoe's novel, the remainder of the novel after Robinson's rescue would not be useful for Rousseau's purposes for a number of reasons. First, with the exception of Friday's late entrance, once Robinson boards the ship, and especially when he returns to civilization, he is in a social condition that is no longer a model for Emile at this stage in his education. Second, the religious theme persists; for example, Robinson thanks the captain of the ship as his deliverer: "I told him, I look upon him as a Man sent from Heaven to deliver me, and that the whole Transaction seemed to be a Chain of Wonders; that such things as these were the Testimonies we had of a secret Hand of Providence governing the World."[30] Finally, Defoe ends the novel by recurring to the theme of the novel as proof of providence: "And thus have I given the first Part of a Life of Fortune and Adventure, a Life of Providence's Checquer-Work."[31]

In sum, once we ourselves take the trouble to read the book given to Rousseau's imaginary pupil and look beyond the familiar view of the story of the solitary sailor dressed in his outlandish outfit, we see how inappropriate at least one major theme of Defoe's novel would be for Emile. The radical rewriting of *Robinson Crusoe* that Rousseau commences but leaves to the reader to complete displaces Daniel Defoe as the author, and in this regard it is interesting to note that Rousseau never mentions the author's name when discussing his creation.[32] (The novel was published anonymously, although Defoe was widely known to be its author.) In this way, then, he leaves it to the reader to rise to the challenge of identifying the rigmarole of which the novel must be disencumbered to make it appropriate for this particular audience, and thus participating in his own response to the critique of writing posed by Socrates in Plato's *Phaedrus*.

Reading *Telemachus*

Multiple audiences and partial perspectives are at issue with the other book Rousseau has his characters read. A very different work from *Robinson Crusoe*, François de Salignac de la Mothe-Fénelon's *The Adventures of Telemachus*, or simply *Telemachus* (*Télémaque*), was also an eighteenth-century best-seller—though an unintended one, for it was never Fénelon's aim to publish it. Said to have sold more copies than any other book than the Bible and ultimately outpaced only by Rousseau's *Julie*, it was originally written by the archbishop of Cambrai for an audience of one: his pupil, the *petit Dauphin*. Fénelon wrote a number of works for the education of the young prince, including fables and dialogues. He also published a brief treatise on the education of girls, to which Rousseau refers in *Emile* (369).[33] As for *Telemachus*, a manuscript was stolen and the work published anonymously in 1699. The Sun King was not amused by the none-too-thinly disguised criticism of his luxurious court or of his bellicosity. Fénelon had already just been relieved of his post as royal tutor, banished from Versailles, and exiled to his bishopric for the theological controversies in which he was involved, but the publication of *Telemachus* ensured he would not be reinstated. The book went through seventy-three editions during the following century and was translated into various languages some seventy-five times.[34] As he had with *Robinson Crusoe*, then, Rousseau could count on his readers' familiarity with the work; writes Diane Berrett Brown,

"It is safe to assume that every eighteenth-century reader of Rousseau would have already read *Télémaque*."[35] Unlike the still-popular *Robinson Crusoe*, however, readers in our own time cannot be assumed to be familiar with even the bare outlines of *Telemachus*. A brief summary of the work will therefore be helpful.

Fénelon splices his story into Homer's *Odyssey*, grafting it onto the first four books of the epic known as the *Telemacheid*. He picks up at the end of book 4, where the poet leaves the account of Telemachus's search for his father to turn in book 5 to Odysseus, whom we first encounter on Calypso's island. Fénelon begins his work with Telemachus's arrival with Mentor (Minerva in disguise) on the nymph's island, which Odysseus, referred to by the Latinized name Ulysses, has recently departed. Books 1–6 recount Telemachus's stay on Calypso's island. He relates the story of his travels in search of his father, which are largely made up of accounts of the various virtuous and vicious rulers he has encountered. Calypso begins to fall in love with Telemachus, who also begins to fall under her spell until Mentor reproves him. Instead, Telemachus falls in love with the nymph Eucharis. Mentor tears the besotted Telemachus away from the island against his will, even throwing him over a cliff into the sea, to avoid the wrath of the jealous Calypso and her allies, Venus and Cupid. Books 7–13 relate Telemachus's and Mentor's travels, with the focus once again on the virtuous and vicious princes they meet. The central story of this section involves the political education of Idomeneus, in exile from his native Crete, by Mentor. With a strong didactic streak aimed at Louis XIV's grandson, Mentor oversees the purging of the prince's luxurious city, Salente, in an obvious imitation of Plato's *Republic*. Book 14 is an interlude in which Telemachus descends into the underworld in search of his father, learning that he is still alive. Books 15–17 return to the story of Idomeneus, the defeat of his enemies with Telemachus's assistance, and the prosperous result of the reforms of the ruler's city. Telemachus falls in love with Antiope, the virtuous daughter of Idomeneus, having himself undergone a kind of purgation and explaining to Mentor that he feels a genuine love for Antiope as opposed to his infatuation for Eucharis.[36] Finally, in book 18 Telemachus and Mentor leave Salente and return to Ithaca, where they find Ulysses. This would place them in book 15 of Homer's *Odyssey*. In sum, Fénelon's *Telemachus* is in essence a work in the mirror-of-princes genre directed at the intended royal audience of the work, with an admixture of a romantic plot concerning true and false love—appropriately enough, given that the dauphin would have been about fifteen years old when his tutor wrote the book for him.

In his employment of *Telemachus* in book V of *Emile*, Rousseau essentially separates the two main themes of Fénelon's work, the love story and the education in good government, and introduces each facet to different audiences for different purposes. In fact, Rousseau reverses the priority of these two themes from the original, privileging the romantic plot over the dominant political subject.[37] Of course, whereas Telemachus sets out in search of his father, Emile seeks his beloved. This reversed priority is captured in the frontispiece to book V showing Circe giving herself to Ulysses because he alone has not been transformed into a brute. In this respect, then, Rousseau imitates Fénelon by situating his tale of Telemachus within Homer's *Odyssey*.

The romance between Emile and Sophie parallels the love stories in *Telemachus* in several ways. Most important, the different forms of erotic love experienced by Telemachus for Eucharis and Antiope is an important feature in Rousseau's treatment of love. In addition to having Emile's love for Sophie undergo something like the change experienced by Telemachus—from infatuation to a more stable version of romantic love—Rousseau presents two versions of Sophie that parallel Eucharis and Antiope: a false Sophie, who is ruined by the infatuated form of love, and a true Sophie, whose love is more tempered and who inspires such a love in Emile. Within these love stories Rousseau alludes numerous times to *Telemachus*, inviting the reader to explore the different sorts of love experienced by the characters. Second, the political education of the young prince through Telemachus's travels to various well-governed and ill-governed lands has its parallel in book V in the explicitly separate section "On Travel" (*Des voyages*), where Emile and his tutor set off to learn about different political regimes guided by the principles of political right, delivered to Emile (and the reader) as a précis of the *Social Contract*. As he is about to depart on his voyage, Emile is presented with a copy of *Telemachus*, which he has not yet read. Emile's political education might be characterized as a democratized version of Fénelon's mirror of princes, appropriately so given the different audiences of the works (the everyman Emile versus the heir to the throne) and the political principles of their authors (the democratic Rousseau versus the reformist monarchist Fénelon).[38]

Eros and Imagination

In order to see how reading *Telemachus* helps us understand the treatment of erotic love in book V, we have to go back to book IV, where Sophie is conjured as Emile's imaginary beloved. As we saw in the previous chapter in discussing the "Profession of Faith," book IV commences with the dawn of adolescence: "We are, so to speak, born twice: once to exist and once to live; once for our species and once for our sex." This second birth is a "moment of crisis" for the emerging passions threaten the happiness and virtue of the young man if they are not properly developed and directed. Interestingly for the present purposes, Rousseau at this point evokes the *Odyssey*, preparing the role Homer's epic and especially Fénelon's adaptation of it will play in book V: "If the hand of a woman placed on his makes him shiver; if he gets flustered or is intimidated near her—Ulysses, O wise Ulysses, be careful. The goatskins you closed with so much care are open. The winds are already loose. No longer leave the tiller for an instant, or all is lost" (211–12). Much of the discussion in book IV is devoted to delaying the birth of the sexual passion and the faculties that aid in its germination, principally the imagination. This birth cannot be delayed indefinitely, however, and so toward the end of book IV the tutor Jean-Jacques finally speaks to his pupil of love in order to direct his nascent imagination, in a passage I examined in the previous chapter as an example of how Rousseau argues that rhetoric must be appropriate for the character and capacity of the audience. "Do not stifle his imagination: guide it lest it engender monsters," he warns the reader (325). Interestingly, we get another reference to the *Odyssey* in this context: "'Just as Ulysses, moved by the Sirens' song and seduced by the lure of the pleasures, cried out to his crew to unchain him, so you will want to break the bonds which hinder you'" (326). The tutor's plan? "I shall make him moderate by making him fall in love" (327). Using fire to fight fire, imagination to combat imagination, the tutor conjures for his pupil an imaginary beloved: "'Your heart,' I say to the young man, 'needs a companion. Let us go seek her who suits you.'" The tutor even goes so far as to name the imaginary beloved: "Let us call your future beloved Sophie. The name Sophie augers well'" (328–29).

In this course of introducing his imaginary pupil to an imaginary beloved, Rousseau confronts the potential problems at play in the relationship between love and imagination. The first step in confronting these problems is a confident assertion from "I"—Rousseau as author, or Jean-Jacques as tutor?—about his ability to paint an appropriate beloved (328–29). He then explains:

> It is unimportant whether the object I depict for him is imaginary; it suffices that it make him disgusted with those that could tempt him; it suffices that he everywhere find comparisons which make him prefer his chimera to the real objects that strike his eye. And what is true love itself if it is not chimera, lie, and illusion? We love the image we make for ourselves far more than we love the object to which we apply it. If we saw what we love exactly as it is, there would be no more love on earth.

> When we stop loving, the person we loved remains the same as before, but we do not see her in the same way. The magic veil drops, and love disappears. But, by providing the imaginary object, I am the master of comparisons, and I easily prevent my young man from having illusions about real objects. (329).

In spite of the confident assertions about his powers that frame this passage, however, Rousseau raises a number of problems concerning love and imagination that will emerge in book V and in relation to *Telemachus*. First, what if the beloved he paints for Emile is in fact a "chimera, lie, and illusion"? That is, what if no actual object of love lives up to the image he has painted of it? This is the dilemma faced by the false Sophie, as we shall see. What if the gap between image and reality becomes apparent once the initial infatuation of erotic love begins to wane? This is the dilemma faced by the true Sophie and Emile. Returning to the passage from book IV under examination, Rousseau anticipates these problems:

> For all that, I do not want to deceive a young man by depicting for him a model of perfection which cannot exist. But I shall choose such defects in his beloved as to suit him, as to please him, and to serve to correct his own. Nor do I want to lie to him by falsely affirming that the object depicted for him exists. But if he takes pleasure in the image, he will soon hope that it has an original. (329)

And so begins the hunt.

Identifying Sophie

The search for the woman who resembles the image of Sophie and then the wooing of the flesh-and-blood Sophie is the principal subject of book V. As previously mentioned, book V begins with an evocation of Genesis and the creation of Eve: "It is not good for man to be alone. Emile is a man. We have promised him a companion. She has to be given to him. That companion is Sophie" (357). Rousseau thus assimilates his roles as author and tutor to the biblical God, and as we shall see, his powers as a creator are front and center when he commences the love story of Emile and Sophie some eighty pages later in the Pléiade edition (fifty in the Bloom edition). The interval between the beginning of book V and the commencement of the love story is encompassed by a controversial separate section of the text devoted to female education: "Sophie, or the Woman." I will not here examine the discussion of female education and will instead focus on what role it plays in the

narrative frame of the romance of Emile and Sophie and the role reading *Telemachus* plays in it.

Like the "Profession of Faith of the Savoyard Vicar" in book IV and
the section "On Travel" later in book V, this section is given a separate
subtitle and set off from the main text (357–406). Perhaps the section is
separated from the main text because it is more of an abstract treatise
and because it is not fully integrated with the narrative of the main text.
I say not fully integrated because the introduction of Sophie does come
in the last ten pages or so of the section, beginning with the statement,
"This is the spirit in which Sophie has been raised" (393). What follows
is a description of Sophie's character and history, as though she were a
character in a novel. Indeed, two characters: for we are first presented
with a fictional version of Sophie, a false Sophie whose love story turns
tragic. The romance between Emile and the true Sophie commences
only after an explicit end to this separate section (406 ff.).

Within "Sophie, or the Woman," Sophie stands as a generic representative of her sex, as indicated by the section title, and as a particularized
character (or characters) with her own history, personality, and other
attributes. Insofar as Sophie is generic, standing for "the woman," perhaps Rousseau gives an initial description of her as a more particular
member of her sex in order to direct the imagination of the reader of
"Sophie, or the Woman," much as he earlier depicted an idealized version of a beloved for his pupil. As he writes in the *Discourse on Inequality*:
"Every general idea is purely intellectual; if imagination becomes the
least involved, the idea immediately becomes particular. Try to draw for
yourself the image of a tree in general: you will never succeed in doing
so. In spite of yourself, it will have to be seen as small or large, bare or
leafy, light or dark" (*Inequality*, 79). In turn, insofar as Sophie is a particularized character at this stage, she is still not entirely defined, as
attested by the fact that Rousseau can generate two versions of her. At
any rate, running through his introduction of Sophie within the section
"Sophie, or the Woman" are the issues of truth and fiction. As we shall
see, Rousseau will play with the question of truth and fiction when he
turns to the narrative.

When he introduces Sophie in the discussion of female education,
Rousseau states that she has been raised not only in the "spirit" of the
education of women he has just discussed, but also "in accordance
with the portrait I made of her for Emile, on the basis of which he himself imagines the wife who can make him happy" (393). It would seem
that the "spirit" of her education and the "portrait" he has painted are
"in accordance" with each other because Sophie is given the specific

naturally "feminine" traits Rousseau claims the proper education of women is meant to develop. As just noted, by portraying Sophie at this point Rousseau fixes the imagination of the reader on a more determinate object. He begins his description: "Sophie is well born; she has a good nature; she has a very sensitive heart, and this extreme sensitivity sometimes makes her imagination so active that it is difficult to moderate" (393). The issue of Sophie's active imagination will turn out to be important. She is also said to love virtue (397), which will be an important feature of her attraction to Telemachus and to Emile. In accordance with his caution in book IV that he will not paint a portrait that is too perfect, lest the image not be found in reality, he emphasizes Sophie's flaws or limitations: "Sophie is not beautiful, but in her company men forget beautiful women, and beautiful women are dissatisfied with themselves. She is hardly pretty at first sight, but the more one sees her, the better she looks" (393). Likewise, she is said to be overly fastidious in her concern with cleanliness (395).

Sophie is given a history with well-born parents who have lost much of their fortune and moved to the countryside. Her parents have left to her the choice of husband, a decision that Rousseau presents to us as a speech by her father: "If that character is such as I imagine it, why would her father not speak to her pretty much as follows" (399). After finishing the speech, Rousseau addresses a challenge to his readers: "Readers, I do not know what effect a similar speech would have on girls raised in your way. As for Sophie, it is possible she will not respond with words" (401–2). As with the frequent comparisons between "my pupil" and "your pupil" I examined in chapter 3, now we are asked to compare Sophie to girls raised "in your way." What character and actions are appropriate for Sophie? Rousseau presents a test to the reader by first introducing a false Sophie, whom we are meant to compare to the true Sophie of the main narrative to follow. Importantly, however, the reader does not know at this point that we are being presented with a false Sophie.[39] In fact, a number of interpreters have not distinguished between the false and true Sophies.[40] Part of the test Rousseau gives the reader apparently involves being aware that there is a test in the first place.

"Let us take the worst case and give her an ardent temperament which makes a long wait painful for her," Rousseau begins, inviting the reader to participate in his novelistic enterprise. The liberty she has been given to choose her mate gives her "a new elevation of soul and [makes] it harder to please in the choice of her master," and her love of decency and virtue makes her love what appears to baser souls as "chimerical" (402). This provisional Sophie is presented by Rousseau as an example for such souls—such readers—that do not believe in virtue. But isn't she a fiction?

> If I said to them that Sophie is not an imaginary being, that her name alone is of my invention, that her education, her morals, her character, and even her looks have really existed, and that her memory still brings tears to every member of a decent family, they undoubtedly would believe nothing of it. Nonetheless, what would I risk in straightforwardly completing the history [*histoire*] of a girl so similar to Sophie that her story [*histoire*] could be Sophie's without occasioning any surprise? Whether it is believed to be true or not, it makes little difference. I shall, if you please, have told fictions, but I shall still have explicated my method, and I shall still be pursing my ends.
>
> The young person with the temperament I have just given to Sophie also resembled her in all the ways which could make her merit the name, and I shall continue to call her by it. (402)

Is Sophie real or not? Is she based on a real individual or not? Does she merit the name "Sophie" the tutor Jean-Jacques has given to Emile's imaginary beloved because she lives up to her? Is this a real story (or "history") or not? Once again, the relationship between truth and fiction, the ideal and the real is in question, both with regard to the passion of love and the status of Sophie, and Rousseau as author-narrator thereby makes the substantive issue one of form as well.

Sophie's parents decided to send her to the city to stay with an aunt in order to find an eligible mate. After she returned home she was distracted, sad, and dreamy and hid herself to cry. Her parents believed she was in love. Unable to learn the cause of her troubles, her mother learns that the poor girl was unable to find the man after her heart: "'How unhappy I am!' she said to her mother. 'I need to love, and I see nothing pleasing to me. . . . Ah, that is not the man for your Sophie! The charming model of the man for her is imprinted too deeply on her soul. She can love only him.'" Her mother was struck with this "singular discourse" and viewed her daughter's delicacy as "extravagant"; the stuff of novels, which in fact it was. Where did this "model of the lovable man with which she was so enchanted" come from? Pressed to answer, Sophie leaves the room and returns with a book in her hand: "'Pity your unhappy daughter. Her sadness is without remedy. Her tears will never dry up. You want to know the cause. Well, here it is,' she said, throwing the book on the table. The mother took the book and opened it. It was *The Adventures of Telemachus*. At first, she understood nothing of this enigma. But by dint of questions and obscure answers, she finally saw, with a surprise that is easy to conceive, that her daughter was the rival of Eucharis" (404).

Our author anticipates and even encourages the surprise the reader must feel at this strange episode, and I have quoted rather more of it than I otherwise would in order to convey a sense of the strangeness of the episode and Rousseau's presentation of it. Let me follow Rousseau by finishing the story before discussing it. Sophie was in love with Telemachus and could not be cured of it. Her father and mother at first laughed at her "mania." They tried reasoning with her, but Sophie had her own reasons which could not easily be gainsaid: "'Is it my fault if I love what does not exist? I am not a visionary. I do not want a prince. I do not seek Telemachus. I know that he is only a fiction. I seek someone who resembles him. And why cannot this someone exist, since I exist—I who feel within myself a heart so similar to his?'" After quoting (if that is the right word) Sophie's pathetic speech, Rousseau once again dances on the tightrope between truth and fiction. "Shall I bring this sad narrative to its catastrophic end? Shall I tell of the long disputes which preceded the catastrophe? Shall I portray an exasperated mother exchanging her earlier caresses for harshness?," and so on, he writes, with Sophie finally on the verge of death: "No, I put aside these dreadful objects. I need not go so far as to show by what seems to me a sufficiently striking example that, in spite of the prejudices born of the morals of our age, enthusiasm for the decent and the fine is no more foreign to women than to men, and that there is nothing that cannot be obtained under nature's direction from women as well as from men" (405). After this apologue and some further remarks, to which I will return, Rousseau transitions to the story of the true Sophie and Emile.

Let me begin by focusing on the role Fénelon's *Telemachus* plays in the story of the false Sophie. The reason for Sophie's unhappiness is that no actual man lives up to the model she has imaginatively encountered through reading *Telemachus*. So we now have precisely the tension between the real or actual, on the one hand, and the ideal or imaginary or fictional, on the other, that Rousseau emphasized in book IV when discussing the nature of erotic love and portraying an imaginary beloved for Emile. This first Sophie would seem to represent the problem he warned about there, of portraying a beloved that is too ideal. After being told the source of the girl's misery, Sophie's mother sees that her daughter considers herself the rival of Eucharis, that is, of the nymph with whom Telemachus is infatuated—a love that we might say paints the beloved with the hues of the ideal. Yet, if she is the rival of Eucharis, she would be Calypso, a seductive goddess—an even more idealized beloved. Sophie's parents therefore find her infatuation with Telemachus to be ridiculous and try to reason with her, presumably by insisting to her that Telemachus is not real. But Rousseau states that Sophie "had her own reason" in this dispute. What could this mean? If love is a "chimera, lie, and illusion," as Rousseau stated in book IV, then her "reason" must be that she is aware of the illusory character of love and her beloved. This conjecture is supported by Sophie's response: "I know that he is only a fiction. I seek someone who resembles him. And why cannot this someone exist, since I exist." Ironically, then, it is a fictional character (and a "false" one to boot), Sophie, who protests that she exists and who recognizes that Telemachus is only a fiction. Or does she exist? Recall that, in introducing this Sophie, Rousseau confronts the reader with the possibility that Sophie is real or at least based on a real individual, that the story may be true or a fiction. When he concludes the story before it reaches its tragic denouement, Rousseau calls it a "narrative," a term that could be applied to fact or fiction. The form of his narrative therefore tracks its subject, erotic love.

What does Rousseau desire as a response, or responses, from his readers to this episode? A difficult and dangerous question to answer, but perhaps the apologue gives us a clue. Having decided not to follow the story through to its catastrophic conclusion, Rousseau characterizes it as a "sufficiently striking example" that, contrary to "the prejudices born of the morals of our age," women and men alike can experience "enthusiasm for the decent and the fine" (405). This explanation echoes what he said when introducing the story: "It does not belong to everyone to feel what a source of energy the love of decent things can give the soul and what strength one can find within oneself when one wants to be sincerely virtuous. There are people to whom everything great appears chimerical, and who in their base and vile reasoning will never know what effect even a mania for virtue can have upon the human passions. To these people one must speak only with examples." (402). The false Sophie is an example of the potential power of a "mania for virtue," an example meant to challenge what the "base and vile reasoning" and the "prejudices born of the morals of our age" consider possible. In chapter 3 I examined a number of stories in which the apologue Rousseau provides is inapt, thereby testing the reader, and here the apologue seems at best partially apt. The more obvious lesson from this story appears to me to be that the false Sophie's love for the fictional Telemachus is the source of her unhappiness, and that such a love for an ideal is unsuited to the real. Yet perhaps this interpretation is consistent with the one Rousseau provides. In book IV Rousseau himself characterized love as a "chimera," and here he states that there are people who find anything great, here the love of virtue, to be "chimerical." Because the false Sophie is sincere in her love of virtue, she is sincere in her love of Telemachus—even though she acknowledges that he is a fiction and even though she perhaps also recognizes that the virtue she so admires is not fully attainable and is to that extent chimerical.

To return to the question of what response or responses Rousseau is trying to evoke from his readers, let me suggest two possibilities, both of which turn on the issue of the relationship between the ideal and the real he has persistently invoked in how he tells this story. Some readers will view both the "mania for virtue" and Sophie's love for Telemachus as fictions, chimeras, because their imagination of what is possible has been stunted by the morals of the age; they take what they consider to be real to preclude the ideal. Alternatively, other readers will see Sophie's love of virtue and of Telemachus as noble, if tragic, pursuits of the ideal with the (at least partial) recognition that the real will fall short. In other words, the story of the false Sophie is meant to test what kind of reader you are.

Support for this interpretation comes from *Julie*, where Rousseau plays similar authorial games with the reader concerning whether the epistolary story is real or a fiction. Especially helpful in this regard is the second preface that he added to the second edition of the work, entitled "Conversation about Novels." After "N" returns the manuscript of the work, "R" asks for his judgment:

N. My judgment depends on the answer you are going to give me. Is this correspondence real, or is it a fiction?

R. I don't see that it matters. To say whether a book is good or bad, how does it matter how it came to be written?

N. It matters a great deal for this one. A portrait always has some value provided it is a good likeness, however strange the original. But in a tableau based on imagination, each human figure must possess features common to mankind, or else the tableau is worthless. Even if we allow that both are good, there remains a difference, which is that the portrait is of interest to few people; the tableau alone can please the public. (*Julie*, *CW*, 6:7)

R asks N to suppose that the letters are a fiction, so his interlocutor pronounces them worthless because "the characters are people from the other world" (ibid., 7); in other words, they are not accurate representations of the human beings we know.

The distinction here between a portrait as an accurate representation of a person and a tableau as a depiction of events that may or may not seem possible concerns what is possible for human nature. If the letters are a portrait, if they are real, then N is willing to accept them as unfamiliar but potentially instructive depictions of human nature. On the other hand, if the letters are a tableau, a fiction, then N rejects them as not being in accordance with our experience of the human beings we know. The conversation continues on that theme with R explaining that readers in cities like Paris will consider *Julie* to be a tableau, as lacking verisimilitude—a judgment that reveals more about their prejudices than about the truth of the portrayal. In turn, readers in the provinces will recognize the characters in the work as portraits. Rousseau's hope is that the novel will be useful insofar as it converts some readers who initially take the work to be a tableau to come to see it as a portrait, thus leading them to reconsider their conception of human nature and its possibilities (see *Julie*, *CW*, 6:16–17).[41]

To return to the false Sophie: after stating that he will not pursue her story any further, Rousseau imagines a reader asking precisely the question about human nature at issue in the question of the different ways in which he anticipates we might respond to *Julie*: "Here someone will stop me and ask whether it is nature that prescribes our expending so much effort for the repression of immoderate desires. My answer is no, but it also is not nature that gives us so many immoderate desires." In other words, the false Sophie's immoderate desires are a product of her education, of her reaction to reading *Telemachus*. Rousseau therefore changes course, in company with the reader of *Emile*: "Let us render his Sophie to our Emile. Let us resuscitate this lovable girl to give her a less lively imagination and a happier destiny. I wanted to depict [*peindre*] an ordinary woman, and by dint of elevating her soul I have disturbed her reason. I myself went astray. Let us retrace our steps. Sophie has only a good nature in a common soul. Every advantage she has over other women is the effect of her education" (405–6).[42]

Revising Sophie

When he returns to the main narrative after the section "Sophie, or the Woman," Rousseau first pauses to muse over his role as author of *Emile*, indeed as the creator of his characters.

> I proposed to say in this book all that can be done and leave it to the reader the choice—among the good things I may have said—of those that are within his reach. I had thought at the beginning that I would form Emile's companion at the outset and raise them for and with each other. But on reflection I found that all the arrangements were too premature and ill-conceived, and that it was absurd to destine two children to be united before being able to know whether this union was in the

order of nature and whether they had between them the compatibili-
ties suitable for forming it. (406)

But wait: isn't Rousseau the self-proclaimed "master of comparisons"
(329) who can invest his characters with whatever personality traits he
wishes? Isn't that precisely what he has just done with the false Sophie?
He makes it appear that Emile and Sophie are independent of his control as author, all the while saying in a stage whisper to the reader that
his pupil's search for his beloved is "feigned," for the tutor already
knows where Sophie resides (407). After some reflections on the considerations relevant to choosing a suitable mate, during which he challenges his readers twice—"I expect that many readers . . . will accuse
me of a contradiction"; "Readers, I leave it to you: answer in good faith"
(408–9)—Rousseau turns to the true Sophie. As with similar challenges
when he compares "my pupil" to "your pupil," or, more to the point
here, when he leaves it to the reader to identify the true Emile, Rousseau
addresses the skeptical reader as he describes the true Sophie: "Such
are the reflections which have determined me on the choice of Sophie"
(410). Once again he straddles the line between truth and fiction.

The first thing we learn about our resuscitated and revised heroine
after a few brief remarks about her initial appearance of ordinariness—
"She does not enchant at first glance, but she pleases more each day"—is
about her reading: "She has read no other books than Barrême, and
Telemachus, which fell into her hands by chance" (410). Of course, in
terms of Rousseau's authorship, this is no more chance than the chance
meeting of Emile and Sophie. If the only book Emile reads, *Robinson
Crusoe*, is read with an eye to utility, then the only book Sophie is given is
even more practical: a handbook on double-entry accounting. Whereas
Emile's reading is appropriate for a sort of natural man, a solitary of a
kind, Sophie's reading is for someone destined for a more social role.
The reader will thank me for not examining Sophie's reading of Barrême, which at any rate we have only through hearsay.[43] How will the true
Sophie respond to Fénelon's dangerous novel? "But does a girl capable
of becoming impassioned about Telemachus have a heart without sentiment and a mind without delicacy?" (410). In other words, the true
Sophie is impassioned with Telemachus, but not to the same degree as
her more ardent double. "Let us work to bring them together," Rousseau
declares, inviting the reader to join him (410).

"We are sad and dreamy as we leave Paris," Rousseau writes as
narrator-tutor in embarking on his story. Pedagogue and pupil travel,
exploring the world around them, whenever possible on foot: "To travel
on foot is to travel like Thales, Plato, and Pythagoras" (412; see *Discourse*

on Inequality, n. X). Without yet evoking Telemachus in relation to Emile, Rousseau establishes a parallel: they are both travelers. But they travel with different activities and aims. Whereas Telemachus learns about political rule and seeks his father, Emile pursues the lessons of *Robinson Crusoe* by exploring the natural world, and he seeks his beloved.

The hungry travelers encounter a kindly peasant who invites them to share his humble repast but recommends them to some good people over the mountain. They make their way to the home in the rain, ask for hospitality, and are welcomed. Hints of the heroic age are made explicit when Emile remarks, "'I believe I am living in Homer's time.'" The groundwork is laid for the introduction of *Telemachus*. The master of the house presents his wife to the travelers, and they enter the dining room. A girl enters and modestly seats herself without speaking, Emile hardly noticing her: "'Sir,' the master of the house says to [Emile], 'you appear to me to be a likable and wise young man, and that makes me think that you and your governor have arrived tired and wet like Telemachus and Mentor on Calypso's island.'" To which Emile replies: "'It is true . . . that we find here the hospitality of Calypso.' His mentor adds, 'And the charms of Eucharis.'" The narrator explains: "But although Emile knows the *Odyssey*, he has not read *Telemachus*. He does not know who Eucharis is. As for the girl, I see her blush up to her eyes, lower them toward her plate, and not dare to murmur" (413–14).

By having the narrator depict and explain how the characters react to the allusions to *Telemachus*, Rousseau creates an ironic distance for the readers of *Emile* with regard to the readers of Fénelon's book and their reactions to it (that is, predicated on the reader of *Emile* having read *Telemachus*). As Berrett Brown states: "*Les Aventures de Télémaque* functions as a marker that identifies readers and nonreaders, those who recognize intertextual reference and those who do not."[44] Everyone in the story except Emile appears to have read *Telemachus*, and the reader of *Emile* who has not read the book would share Emile's ignorance. Let us assume the reader has read it. The father likens Emile and his tutor to Telemachus and Mentor as we encounter them at the outset of Fénelon's novel, arriving on Calypso's isle. The shipwrecked pair are welcomed by the nymph, invited to bathe, and are clothed and fed. To this extent, then, the hospitable welcome Emile and his tutor have received is analogous. There is a nonetheless a darker thread of the story in *Telemachus*, and the father's reference to Calypso is therefore potentially ominous: the reader of *Telemachus* is made aware of Calypso's concealed motives, creating an ironic distance for the reader with regard to the protagonist, for she mourns the recent departure of Ulysses and sees a potential replacement in the son, lying to him about his father's fate to encourage him to stay. After they eat, she encourages Telemachus to tell her and the assembled nymphs about his adventures.[45] At the outset of book 4, Mentor warns his charge that the pleasure of telling his story has "seduced your heart; you have charmed the goddess . . . by this have you more and more inflamed her passion, and prepared for yourself a more dangerous captivity."[46] Warned not to succumb, Telemachus continues the narrative of his adventures, further inflaming Calypso's desire, until the beginning of book 6, when she offers him the nymph Eucharis, with whom he becomes infatuated. In short, the father's allusion raises the potentially treacherous nature of erotic love.

How do the different characters respond? Not having read *Telemachus*, Emile is oblivious to the father's allusion. In fact, he takes him to be referring to the story of Calypso in Homer's *Odyssey*. His mistake is compounded by the fact that his own reference to the *Odyssey* is decidedly inapt. Whatever initial hospitality Calypso may have shown toward Ulysses, when we encounter the two of them in book 5 of the *Odyssey*, after the account of Telemachus's search for his father and precisely at the point where Fénelon splices in his story, the nymph has kept Odysseus hostage as her lover for seven years and allows him to leave only when ordered to do so by Zeus. It seems that Emile unwittingly reveals precisely the same problematic aspects of erotic love in his misapplied allusion to the *Odyssey* as was contained in the father's reference to *Telemachus*.[47] As for Jean-Jacques, he picks up on the father's reference and presses it further by alluding to the object of Telemachus besotted love: Eucharis. This allusion has an ominous undercurrent similar to the father's reference to Calypso.[48] Finally, as for the girl, we already know she has read *Telemachus*, and she blushes at the tutor's reference to Eucharis. Whereas the false Sophie is described as considering herself the rival of Eucharis for Telemachus's affections, however, the as-yet-unnamed girl is identified with Eucharis. At first blush, this seems odd: Telemachus's love for Eucharis is an infatuated love, one that idealizes the beloved, much as the false Sophie overidealized Telemachus to the point where she could not find anyone who resembled him. However, this makes sense if the love Emile feels for Sophie is initially idealized, and even more so if Sophie is aware of this. As Berrett Brown remarks: "Indeed, the final chapter of *Emile* spirals around reading, misreading, ownership, and transmission of *Les Aventures de Télémaque*."[49] Let us return to the story with this in mind.

The father recounts the misfortunes that led him to this rural retreat and the consolation offered by his loving wife. Emile is moved, and all are touched by Emile's good heart. As for the girl, she "believes she sees Telemachus affected by Philoctetes' misfortunes. She furtively turns her eyes toward him in order to examine his face better. She finds nothing there that denies the comparison."[50] The mother perceives the girl's agitation and sends her on an errand, and when she returns her mother addresses her by name: "Sophie." We finally learn her name: "At the name Sophie, you would have seen Emile shiver. Struck by so dear a name, he is wakened with a start and casts an avid glance at the girl who dares to bear it. 'Sophie, O Sophie! Is it you whom my heart seeks? Is it you whom my heart loves?'" The young man now observes the girl more carefully: "He does not see exactly the face he had depicted to himself. He does not know whether the one he sees is better or worse." Confused, Emile looks at his tutor for affirmation that she is indeed Sophie. "Sophie's mother smiles at the success of our projects," Jean-Jacques writes, letting the reader in on the plot. We do not know whether the mother has read *Telemachus*, but she too is a perceptive reader. "She reads the hearts of the two young people. She sees that it is time to captivate the heart of the new Telemachus," a phrasing that leaves it ambiguous as to whether the mother sees Emile as a new Telemachus or the narrator is speaking to the reader of *Emile*. She gets her daughter to speak: "At the first sound of this voice Emile surrenders. It is Sophie. He no longer doubts it" (414–15).

What, again, are the reactions of the characters? Sophie begins to see Emile's resemblance to the fictional character with whom she was said to be impassioned. She sees something of the ideal Telemachus in the real Emile. This is in contrast to the false Sophie, who fails to see anyone who resembles her idealized beloved. As for Emile, when he learns the girl's name he examines her to see whether the real Sophie resembles the ideal his tutor has portrayed for him. Whereas Sophie seems initially persuaded of her own accord that she may be facing her Telemachus, Emile is less sure and seeks his mentor's affirmation.[51] If so, then it seems that Sophie is more aware of the problem of overideal-izing the beloved than is Emile, as is indicated by the fact that she sees Emile as only "resembling" Telemachus. The reader of *Emile* who has not read *Telemachus* would be less aware of the problematic relationship between imagination and eros, the ideal and the real, than the reader who catches the allusions.

With act 1 of his drama complete, Rousseau reassumes his role as author to reflect on the scene: "If I enter into the perhaps too naïve and too simple history [*histoire*] of their innocent love, these details will be regarded as a frivolous game, but this would be incorrect." He explains that the first liaison of love has a powerful formative effect on an individual and complains that we are given "treatises on education" that talk nonsense about the "chimerical duties of children" but say nothing about "the most important and difficult part of the whole of education—the crisis that serves as a passage from childhood to man's estate." "If I have been able to make these essays useful in some respect, it is especially by having expounded at great length on this essential part," he explains: "It makes very little difference to me if I have written a romance [*roman*]. A fair romance it is indeed, the romance of human nature. It is to be found only in this writing, is that my fault? This ought to be the history [*histoire*] of my species" (416).

What is the genre in which Rousseau is working? I have focused on how Rousseau blurs the lines between ideal and real, truth and fiction, in his depiction of romantic love: "a chimera, lie, and illusion." Now, speaking in his role as the author of *Emile*, presumably to the reader, he confounds and problematizes the genre of his work. Is it a "treatise on education," though one superior to others? Is it a set of useful "essays," a term he does not use anywhere else to describe the work (although I think he uses the term here less to identify a genre than, in the root sense of *essayer*, to describe what he is doing as "attempts")? Or a *roman*, a novel or romance of human nature? Or an *histoire*, a history or story of his species? He also terms it a "writing" (*écrit*), and perhaps this is a clue as to how to read this passage if we once again recall his constant engagement with Plato's *Phaedrus*. In short, different readers will have different responses. For some readers the story of Emile and Sophie will be a fiction, a novel or romance to which they expect to have an aesthetic response based in part on how they judge its verisimilitude, much as Rousseau discussed in the second preface to *Julie*. For others it will be a treatise, and they will judge it true or false based not on aesthetic criteria but on its truth value. The other option we are given here is that the work is an *histoire*. This term that can refer either to a history, and thus what is real or factual, or to a story, and thus what may or may not be imagined or fictional. Many eighteenth-century novels traded on this ambiguity in their titles, notably one of the books that served as a model for Rousseau's *Julie*: Richardson's *Clarissa, or, The History of a Young Lady*, translated into French by the Abbé Prévost with the same title using the word *histoire*.[52] Recall that Rousseau gave himself an imaginary pupil in his treatise so that he would not get lost in visions. Throughout *Emile* he asks his readers to compare his imaginary pupil to the ones they know. Having brought into question the genre of his work, then, he speaks to precisely this issue. What strengthens his determination in pursuing the love story, he explains, is that he is not dealing with an ordinary pupil, "a young man given over from childhood" to the corrupt passions born of "common educations," but instead with his pupil, raised in accordance with nature and thus innocent in his first love (415–16). The romance of Emile and Sophie will appear truthful to the reader persuaded of the truth of Rousseau's imaginary pupil and fanciful to the unpersuaded.

Telemachus *as a Democratized Mirror of Princes*

Emile has not read *Telemachus* before or during his courtship of Sophie, and his ignorance of the work renders him unaware of the dangers of the real and the ideal in romantic love. This awareness is shared at least by the author of *Emile* and his reader, if that reader has read *Telemachus*, and perhaps the other characters as well, most important among them Sophie herself. Emile's limited understanding of love is the occasion for his eventual introduction to Fénelon's novel, though its purpose in his education turns out to be very different from the romantic element of the work Rousseau has privileged thus far.

Emile successfully woos Sophie by proving his dedication to virtue over love, showing Sophie, who is said to love virtue above all else, that, like Ulysses, he has not been bewitched by Circe's charms (439). This is perhaps similar to Telemachus, who ultimately learns to follow his duty as his infatuated love for Eucharis wanes and his more sober love for Antiope waxes. Nonetheless, whereas Sophie is earlier analogized to Eucharis, there is no mention of her transformation into Antiope in Telemachus's eyes. Has Emile perhaps been bewitched? The tutor tests his pupil one morning, entering his room and asking: "'What would you do if you were informed that Sophie is dead?'" Emile is distraught and—significantly, given the importance in *Emile* of anger as an unnatural passion, a subject I discussed in chapter 3—enraged. His anger might remind one of the hero depicted in the frontispiece to *Emile*: Achilles. The tutor makes just that comparison when he tells Emile: "'But, dear Emile, it is in vain that I have dipped your soul in the Styx; I was not able to make it everywhere invulnerable. A new enemy is arising which you have not learned to conquer and from which I can no longer save you. This enemy is yourself'" (442–43). Emile's love for Sophie has rendered him dependent on her. The tutor makes a recommendation: "'Do you want, then, to live happily and wisely? Attach your heart only to imperishable beauty'" (446). Emile must somehow reconcile the ideal and the real, Sophie and his love for her both as an ideal that informs and inspires his love and as the flesh and blood, and thus perishable, woman he loves. The course of instruction? "'What must be done?' he asks me, almost trembling and without daring to raise his eyes. 'That which must be done!' I answer in a firm tone: 'You must leave Sophie'" (447). Interestingly, his leaving his beloved has its parallel in *Telemachus*, for Mentor counsels the young prince to leave Antiope temporarily in order to return to Ithaca and tend to the suitors.

Emile's two-year separation from his beloved serves two purposes. First, it allows him to educate his eros. "'You want to marry Sophie,'" the tutor says to him, "'and yet you have known her for less than five months! You want to marry her not because she suits you but because she pleases you—as though love were never mistaken about what is suitable'" (447). Second, if they are to marry they must settle somewhere and, importantly, possess property and thus be subject to the laws of their country. Emile must learn about politics to choose his abode (448). Emile and his tutor will travel to accomplish these two goals. This, then, is the context in which Emile is finally given *Telemachus*: "'Sophie,' I say to her one day, 'make an exchange of books with Emile. Give him your *Telemachus* in order that he learn to resemble him, and let Emile give you *The Spectator*, which you like to read. Study in it the duties of decent women, and recall that in two years these duties will be yours'" (450). I will not discuss *The Spectator* (whether Addison and Steele, or Marivaux's adaptation) for the completion of Sophie's education, in part because I do not understand the choice of book, which at any rate we do not see her read. The role of *Telemachus* in the first goal of educating Emile's eros is apparent here in the tutor's remark that reading the book will enable Emile to "learn to resemble him," suggesting that the initial resemblance Sophie saw to Telemachus is not yet complete.[53] The need for such an education is also suggested by the fact that in introducing this scene the narrator compares Sophie's tearful leave-taking of her beloved to "the regrets of Eucharis and really believes she is in her place" (450). Perhaps Sophie needs further instruction in eros as well. The second goal of educating Emile about politics is the focus of the separate section that follows this scene: "On Travel."

Emile and his tutor take a two-year voyage with the aim of learning about politics. After some didactic discussion of how to travel properly, as opposed to how the young ordinarily travel, Rousseau pauses before presenting a discussion of "the science of political right" to address his readers: "I do not know whether all my readers will perceive where this proposed research is going to lead us. But I do know that if Emile, at the conclusion of his travels, begun and continued with this intention, does not come back versed in all matter of government, in public morals, and in maxims of every kind, either he or I must be quite poorly endowed—he with intelligence and I with judgment" (458). Since the ensuing précis of the *Social Contract* is addressed to the reader of *Emile*, though in part as a description of the course of education "we" will pursue, Rousseau's remark here must be read as yet another challenge. At the conclusion of the précis, Jean-Jacques turns to his pupil: "I would not be surprised if my young man, who has good sense, were to interrupt me in the middle of all our reasoning and say, 'Someone might say that we are building our edifice with wood and not with men, so exactly do we align each piece with the ruler!' 'It is true, my friend, but keep in mind that right is not bent by men's passions, and that our first concern was to establish the true principles of political right. Now that our foundations are laid, come and examine what men have built on them, and you will see some fine things!'" (467). Perhaps a reader of *Emile* is the "someone" who would object that the principles are too ideal (to keep to the language I have been using), but Rousseau's response is that, even so, the real must be examined in light of the ideal. I will take up this subject in the next chapter.

Enter Fénelon's novel: "Then I make him read *Telemachus* while proceeding on his journey." Like Telemachus and Mentor, they will see virtuous and vicious princes, well-governed and ill-governed lands. Rousseau mentions several of the princes and lands visited by the fictional pair, and especially "happy Salente and the good Idomeneus, made wise by dint of misfortune." Rather than continuing the narrative, however, Rousseau explains: "But let us leave the readers to imagine our travels—or to make them in our stead with *Telemachus* in hand; and let us not suggest to them invidious comparisons that the author himself dismisses or makes in spite of himself" (467). Rousseau alludes here to the "invidious comparisons" Fénelon made in his novel to the corrupt court of Louis XIV in an effort to educate his princely pupil. The suggestion to the reader of *Emile* would appear to be that, with *Telemachus* in hand and the principles of political right in mind, very few if any political regimes will be found to be legitimate. Unlike the presumably monarchical principles of Fénelon, or at least of his pupil, Rousseau's principles of political right are democratic. He thereby transforms Fénelon's mirror of princes into a democratic document: "Besides, since Emile is not a king and I am not a god, we do not fret about not being able to imitate Telemachus and Mentor in the good that they did for men. . . . We know that Telemachus and Mentor are chimeras. Emile does not travel as an idle man, and he does more good than if he were a prince" (467).

What lessons does Emile take from his travels in the company of Fénelon's novel? Upon completing their two-year journey, Jean-Jacques asks him what he has learned. Switching to the authorial "I," Rousseau states that, unless he is mistaken, Emile will answer that he will remain in place and make himself and his family as independent as possible within the constraints imposed by society, and he gives Emile a speech that says as much. A dialogue ensues between master and student that is restricted to the social or political dimension of Emile's decision, with the exception of his admission that his passions—especially his love for Sophie, one presumes—make reconciling himself with his duties necessary (471–75). After this dialogue, Rousseau resumes his authorial voice: "Why am I not permitted to paint Emile's return to Sophie and the conclusion of their love or rather the beginning of the conjugal love which united them. . . . No; I also feel that my pen is weary. I am too weak for works requiring so much endurance and would abandon this one if it were less advanced. In order not to leave it imperfect, it is time for me to finish" (475). Rousseau concludes the narrative by depicting the young couple's wedding and first days of marriage and finishes with Emile's announcement that he is to become a father. The main emphasis in this narrative is Jean-Jacques's advice to the couple on how to remain lovers while being married, that is, how to keep alive their romantic or erotic love in the face of the all-too-human reality of conjugal union. The tension between the ideal and the real in romantic love with which Rousseau began his story by depicting for Emile an imaginary beloved and which continued through the false and true stories and into the narrative of the romance of Emile and Sophie remains. Whether or not it can be resolved is another question.

Chapter 7

Reading the *Social Contract*

So far in examining how Rousseau educates his readers, I have been able to take cues from his direct addresses to the reader, among other features of the works. In the *Discourse on the Sciences and the Arts*, for example, he speaks to his judges — "Gentlemen" — as part of the putatively spoken "discourse" and separately addresses the readers of the published *Discourse*. In the *Discourse on Inequality* he addresses several audiences, including his fellow citizens in the dedication, his true judges, the philosophers, in the "discourse" itself, and "attentive readers" of his published *Discourse*. And, of course, *Emile* is filled with exhortations and accusations directed at various categories of readers. Finally, in examining these apostrophes of various readers, I have emphasized how Rousseau takes up the challenge posed by Socrates' critique in Plato's *Phaedrus* of written works being indiscriminately available to all readers and therefore how one might write a work that matched its rhetoric to different types of readers in order to educate or persuade them appropriately.

In this light, then, *On the Social Contract* poses a challenge. Only twice in the treatise does Rousseau address the reader directly, and only one other time does he speak to a specified audience. Moreover, the treatise is emphatically a written work, and lacks any clear indication of the different types of audiences Rousseau might have in mind. The first time he addresses the reader directly is in a note (II.4 n.) in which he addresses "attentive readers" who may have noticed an inconsistency in his terminology, a problem he blames on the poverty of language. The second time is similar and comes at the beginning of his discussion of government in book III: "I warn the reader that this chapter should be read with due care, and that I do not know the art of being clear for those who are not willing to be attentive" (III.1).[1] In both cases, the emphasis is on the comparatively bloodless issue of terminology and not on the intended rhetorical or educative effect on readers. Apart from discriminating between attentive and inattentive readers, Rousseau gives no indication of the intended audience or audiences of his work and his relationship as author to his readers.[2] The one time he does speak to a specific audience is accusatory: "As for you, modern peoples, you do not have slaves, but you yourselves are slaves" (III.15). The contrast to how Rousseau proceeded in his projected *Political Institutions*, from which the *Social Contract* was drawn, is instructive. "I am going to state the truth, and I shall do so in the manner appropriate to it," he begins, and then addresses various classes of readers: "Faint-hearted readers, who are disgusted by its simplicity and revolted by its frankness, close my book; it is not written for you. Satirical readers, who love only that part of the truth that can nourish the malignity of your souls, close my book and throw it away; you will not find in it what you are seeking, and you would soon see in it all the horror its author feels for you. . . . If this work falls into the hands of an honest man who cherishes virtue. . . . My heart is going to speak to his" (Political Fragments, *CW*, 4:16).[3] None of this survives in the *Social Contract*. Indeed, in a letter to his publisher (apparently in a mood of self-sabotage), he explained that his political treatise contained "difficult material, fit for few readers." His contemporaries often agreed with this assessment.[4] Compared to the other works examined so far, then, the *Social Contract* seems almost like an orphan left by its creator to its own devices.[5]

In this chapter I examine less the relationship between the author and the reader of the *Social Contract* than the different readings of the work Rousseau makes available. I suggest that he invites two principal readings: first, as a treatise that articulates the principles of political right, and second, as a work that describes the conditions necessary for instituting and maintaining an actual or imagined political association in accordance with those principles.

These two readings map onto the leading interpretations the work has received, and I therefore hope that my interpretation will add to and clarify scholarly debates on the *Social Contract* and Rousseau's political theory in general. On the one hand, many interpreters have read the *Social Contract* as a treatise in which Rousseau presents the principles of political right, especially democratic sovereignty. They tend to do so in abstraction from the parts of the work in which Rousseau discusses what he sees as the conditions necessary for such a regime, for example the need for a godlike lawgiver and the requirements of civil religion. These interpreters often find these parts of the work unnecessary or embarrassing, relics of Rousseau's mistaken anthropology or patriotic nostalgia.[6] Other interpreters insist on the portions of the work discussing the conditions for creating an actual regime based on the principles of political right. They offer such an interpretation for different reasons: from a principle of interpretive generosity or comprehensiveness, or from a desire to bring into existence such a regime, or with the design to condemn the author and his work as illiberal or even totalitarian.

The readings I am suggesting also correspond in interesting ways to interpretations by scholars who have investigated Rousseau's political theory, including through examining the structure the *Social Contract* and what it suggests about his aims. Notably, through an analysis of the draft version of the treatise, known as the Geneva Manuscript, and the *Social Contract* itself, Masters argues that there are two main aspects of Rousseau's political theory: the enunciation of the principles of political right, on the one hand, and attention to the "science of the legislator" and the "maxims of politics," on the other.[7] His reading is representative of what I termed just above as issuing from a principle of interpretive generosity or comprehensiveness. My analysis parallels and builds on Masters in certain respects. An analogous reading from a very different interpretive tradition also corresponds in interesting ways with my reading. Notably, de Man comes to the text through a deconstructive approach that argues for the instability and self-deconstructive nature of the sign (e.g., text) in relation to the referent (e.g., the real-world object to which the sign is alleged to refer), examining a number of Rousseau's works from this perspective. As for the *Social Contract*, he argues that the relationship between the principles of political right and any attempt to particularize them in a specific law, regime, or other system reveals a similar unstable and self-deconstructive character.[8]

In order to see how Rousseau indicates and prepares these two principal readings of his political treatise, I begin with the précis of the *Social Contract* in *Emile*. The précis suggests these two readings by including one and excluding the other. Namely, the summary is limited to articulating the principles of political right by which all political associations must be judged, or the first reading of the work I am suggesting, without any attention to the conditions for creating or maintaining a legitimate state, or the second reading. I then turn to the *Social Contract*, first examining the paratextual apparatus of the work with an eye to these two readings, then analyzing the structure of the work and suggesting three alternative structures of the treatise that underscore the two principal readings of the work. Finally, I sketch the two principal readings of the work.

From *Emile* to the *Social Contract*

Rousseau's educational treatise and his political treatise were published a month apart, with the *Social Contract* appearing in April 1762 and *Emile* in May. The official reaction was swift and violent, with the twin works by the Citizen of Geneva censured as threatening both throne and altar. In Paris *Emile* was condemned by both governmental and religious authorities. The focus of his critics was on the unorthodox religious sentiments expressed in the work, especially in the "Profession of Faith." These authorities and other critics also saw the work as an assault on the ancien régime, given the close connection between religious and political authority. Of course, his educational treatise also contains a summary of his political treatise, enough to horrify the powers that be. In Geneva both *Emile* and the *Social Contract* were condemned for both their religious and their political content, although the specifics were different from those that obtained in Paris. Other cities and states followed suit. In any case, many of Rousseau's contemporaries viewed *Emile* and the *Social Contract* as somehow conjoined.[9] As for Rousseau himself, in addition to signaling a close relationship between the two works by including a précis of his political treatise in his educational treatise, in a letter to his publisher he explained that the *Social Contract* "should be considered as a sort of appendix" to *Emile* and stated that "the two of them together make a complete whole."[10]

In what sense is the *Social Contract* an appendix to *Emile*? Or, more broadly, how did Rousseau conceive of the relationship between the two works? This question has been widely debated by scholars. In general, while viewing both works as in some sense sketching constructive answers to the question "what is to be done?" left by the wrecking ball of the *Discourse on Inequality*, views on the relationship between *Emile* and the *Social Contract* tend to emphasize either disjunctive aims or a continuous purpose. On the one hand, as for the disjunctive view, taking their cue in part from Rousseau's statement at the outset of *Emile* that we no longer have either "fatherlands" or "citizens" properly speaking (*Emile*, 40), scholars argue that the purpose of his educational treatise is to raise a "man," an individual independent of any strong political ties, while the purpose of his political treatise is by contrast to create a "citizen." Even if these two beings, man and citizen, share certain traits such as "wholeness," they are two very different beings.[11] On the other hand, another group of readers sees *Emile* as educating an individual who is meant, at least under the right circumstances, to be the citizen of the regime envisioned in the *Social Contract*.[12] My interpretation of the *Social Contract* will largely place me in the disjunctive camp. Nonetheless, my primary purpose here is not to adjudicate this dispute. Rather, I want to see how Rousseau's presentation of the précis of the *Social Contract* within *Emile* helps us to understand the principal readings of the political treatise he makes available.

As we saw in the previous chapter, the précis is included in a separate section of *Emile*, "On Travel," in which Emile and his tutor set out, *Telemachus* in hand, to learn about politics so that Emile can decide where he and his family will reside. The précis of the *Social Contract* is included in this context as an examination by tutor and pupil of the principles of political right, although its source is not identified at the outset. Instead, Rousseau introduces this examination as follows: "Before observing, one must make some rules for one's observations. One must construct a standard to which measurements one makes can be related. Our principles of political right are that standard. Our measurements are the political laws of each country." As we shall see, he will return to the language of standards and measurements after outlining the principles. "Our elements are clear, simple, and taken immediately from the nature of things," he writes in introducing the questions they will address in their examination (*Emile*, 458). His language indicates that the principles of political right are universal: they are derived from the "nature of things," that is, from the nature of the political association per se, everywhere and always. To anticipate, he will restrict himself to the principles of political right in the précis.

The examination of the principles of political right in *Emile* tracks the *Social Contract* fairly closely, with some changes in emphasis, some notable omissions, and one revealing addition. It is not my intention here to examine this subject in any detail, but let me summarize these aspects to see how they suggest the two principal readings of the *Social Contract* I am proposing.[13]

As for the change in emphasis, Rousseau tends to underscore his point that the sovereign (the people acting in its legislative capacity) must be distinguished from the government (the subordinate body charged with executing the laws). This emphasis is indicated by the fact that it is at the outset of his treatment of government that Rousseau finally, and in a note, identifies the précis *as* a précis: "Most of these questions and propositions are extracts from the treatise *The Social Contract*, itself an extract from a larger work that was undertaken without consulting my strength and that has long since been abandoned. The little treatise I have detached from it—of which this is the summary—will be published separately" (*Emile*, 462 n.). His language in this note is almost exactly the same as in the "Notice" at the head of the *Social Contract*. We can anticipate that a central lesson Emile, and the reader,

will learn from the examination of existing regimes in light of the principles of political right will be that the sovereign and government are
not clearly distinguished in those regimes, and that the government
has usually usurped the sovereign power, a state of affairs signaled by
the fact that monarchs call themselves "sovereigns."

As for the omissions, the beginning of the note stating that "most"
of the questions and propositions summarized here come from the
Social Contract hints that "some" issues discussed in the political treatise are absent. There are two notable omissions. First, the entire discussion of the lawgiver is missing—not just the chapter titled "On the
Lawgiver" (II.7), but the remainder of book II on the people and the
extralegal measures taken by the legislator (II.8–12). Second, also missing is almost the entirety of the work following the initial discussion of
government in general and its various forms (III.1–3). Since his summary of this initial discussion might be said effectively to incorporate
the more detailed treatment of these forms and related concerns in the
subsequent chapters of the *Social Contract* (III.4–9), we might characterize what is omitted as the discussion in the remainder of book III
of the tendency of governments to degenerate and the measures that
can be taken to slow this decay (III.10–18). As for book IV, with one odd
exception, the entirety is missing, including, most notably, any mention whatsoever of the longest chapter of the *Social Contract*, "On Civil
Religion" (IV.8). The exception is the disproportionate attention to the
final chapter of the work, "Conclusion" (IV.9), where Rousseau states
that what remains to be discussed are federations, foreign relations,
and so on, subjects he explains are beyond the scope of his "little treatise." In a strange way, then, this concluding chapter is also absent from
the summary because its purpose in the *Social Contract* is to say what
is missing, and so filling in its contents to even a limited extent makes
something entirely different of it. To summarize, then, what remains
from the *Social Contract* is: book I, entire; book II, chapters 1–6; and
book III, chapters 1–9.[14] As we shall see when I turn to the *Social Contract*, what is retained in and omitted from this summary maps on to
the structure of the political treatise.

Finally, as for the revealing addition, after his summary of the initial
discussion in the *Social Contract* of government and its various forms,
Rousseau adds a brief paragraph that has no analogue in the political
treatise: "By following the thread of these researches, we shall come to
know what the duties and the rights of citizens are, and whether the
former can be separated from the latter. We shall also learn what the
fatherland is, precisely what it consists in, and how each person can
know whether or not he has a fatherland" (*Emile*, 466). These questions

are particularly germane for Emile—and for the reader of *Emile*—for his travels will reveal to Emile that no existing state is fully legitimate. To take these questions in reverse order, then, he will learn that he does not have a fatherland, properly speaking. After the return to the main narrative, Jean-Jacques speaks to Emile of what they have learned: "'If I were speaking to you of the duties of the citizen, you would perhaps ask me where the fatherland is, and you would believe you had confounded me. But you would be mistaken, dear Emile, for he who does not have a fatherland [*patrie*] at least has a country [*pays*]'" (*Emile*, 473). As for the first question, of whether the duties and rights of citizens can be separated, the implication is that, unlike in the legitimate political association, where they are reciprocal, there is a more contingent relationship between duties and rights in an illegitimate regime. Emile will exercise his duties as a citizen to the extent possible consistent with his natural right, in accordance with the "eternal laws of nature and order" engraved on his heart but at best imperfectly reflected in the laws of any existing state (*Emile*, 473).

After completing the examination of the principles of political right, Rousseau stages an imagined dialogue between tutor and pupil that indicates the purpose of that examination and adumbrates the answers to the questions I just discussed.

> I would not be surprised if my young man, who has good sense, were to interrupt me in the middle of all our reasoning and say, "Someone might say that we are building our edifice with wood and not with men, so exactly do we align each piece with the ruler!" "It is true, my friend, but keep in mind that right is not bent by men's passions, and that our first concern was to establish the true principles of political right. Now that our foundations are laid, come and examine what men have built on them; and you will see some fine things!" (467)

In short, their examination was restricted to "the true principles of political right," the "foundations" of any political association. They will utilize those principles to assay existing political associations—"what men have built on them"—not to build an edifice themselves. As I noted at the outset of this section, this interpretation places me in the camp of those who view the aims of *Emile* and the *Social Contract* as disjunctive.[15]

What, then, does the précis of the *Social Contract* in *Emile* indicate about Rousseau's intentions in his political treatise, and how it should be read? I suggest that the emphases, omissions, and additions in the précis relative to the *Social Contract*, especially in light of this concluding dialogue about the purpose of the examination at hand, point to the two principal readings of the *Social Contract* I have suggested, one by commission and the other by omission. The reading by commission is a treatise on the principles of political right, in order to understand the nature of the political association and to examine existing regimes in light of these principles. The reading by omission is what is absent from the summary but present in the *Social Contract* itself: the question of how to establish and maintain a legitimate state.

The Prefatory Paratext to the *Social Contract*

With the works I have previously examined, I began by exploring paratextual elements such as frontispieces, title pages, prefaces, exordiums, notes, and so on in order to see how they condition the reading of the main text, suggest various audiences for the work, and prepare the reader for the lessons Rousseau wishes to impart. The *Social Contract* has a comparatively spare paratextual apparatus, perhaps in part because there are almost no direct addresses to the reader. My examination of these prefatory paratextual elements will therefore be brief.

Title Page

The title page contains the title, identifies the author, includes an epigraph, and also presents an illustration. The work has no separate frontispiece.

The title of the work, like that of *Emile*, is compound: *On the Social Contract, or Principles of Political Right*. Such compound titles for treatises and other works were quite common in Rousseau's time. We know from draft versions of his political treatise that he entertained various subtitles, suggesting that he chose the final version with due deliberation. Those subtitles included "Essay on the Constitution of the State," "Essay on the Formation of the Body Politic," "Essay on the Formation of the State," and "Essay on the Form of the Republic," this last version being the subtitle of the fullest draft version we possess, the so-called Geneva Manuscript.[16] To return to the final version of the title, then, dropping any mention of an "essay" turns the subtitle into a potential alternative title as opposed to a supplementary title: the work is potentially *either* "On the Social Contract" *or* "[On the] Principles of Political Right." Such a potentially disjunctive reading of the title would then allow two alternative purposes or readings of the work.[17] Indeed, these two titles might be said to suggest the two principal readings of the work I am suggesting Rousseau makes available: first, as a treatise on the principles of political right; and second, as a work on the conditions necessary for an actual or imagined political association in accordance with those principles, with the "social contract" being an event and not just a concept. Further evidence for positing such a relationship between the twofold title of the work and its twofold intention can be gleaned from the fact that the preliminary versions of the subtitle seem to vacillate between these two readings, with "Form" and "Constitution" indicating the proper form according to the principles of political right and "Formation" indicating the coming into being of the regime. In any case, the potentially disjunctive reading of the final title he did choose for the work would then allow two alternative purposes or readings. Nonetheless, I do not think the two readings of the work I am proposing are obvious from the title alone, and are therefore not yet available to the uninitiated reader. What the reader can glean at this point is that the work is devoted to explicating the principles of political right within the social contract tradition.

The author of the work is identified as "J.-J. Rousseau, Citizen of Geneva." As with the *Discourse on the Sciences and the Arts*, the *Discourse on Inequality*, *Emile*, and certain other works, then, Rousseau indicates that one perspective from which the work should be written is that of a citizen. He will emphasize his citizenship, indeed his Genevan citizenship, in the proemium to book I.

The epigraph is identified as coming from the *Aeneid*, book 11: "In an equitable pact / We will make laws" (foederis aequas / Dicamis leges).[18] As Masters explains, the appearance from the epigraph that laws result from an "equitable pact" is ironic given the context of Virgil's poem from which it is drawn. By identifying the passage as coming from book 11 of the *Aeneid*, Rousseau could count on many readers recognizing at least the general context of the quotation. It is part of a speech by the king of Latium, whose people has just been defeated by the Trojans. He suggests making a pact or treaty with the enemy, but the people instead demand a man-to-man combat between their heroic warrior, Turnus, and the Trojan leader, Aeneas. The deliberations are interrupted by a Trojan attack, and eventually Turnus is killed and the Latins routed. Rousseau will soon argue that the "right of the stronger" is not a source of legitimate political power (I.3), but his choice of epigraph implies that many or perhaps all existing political communities are in fact founded through force or fraud. Rousseau's aim is not to examine the historical foundations of states, but rather to ask how our "chains" can be legitimated.[19]

Finally, the title page includes an illustration, which to the best of my knowledge nobody has attempted to interpret (fig. 7.1). This illustration is a version of the image on the title page of the *Discourse on Inequality*. Both show Liberty as a woman dressed in the Roman style and holding aloft a Phrygian cap, the symbol of manumission in ancient Rome, with

PRINCIPES

D U

DROIT POLITIQUE.

Par J. J. ROUSSEAU,
CITOYEN DE GENEVE.

Dicamus leges. —— *fœderis æquas*

Æneid. XI.

A AMSTERDAM,
Chez MARC MICHEL REY.
MDCCLXII.

7.1 Illustration on the title page of the *Social Contract*

a cat beside her and a birdcage behind her. As I discussed with regard to the version included in the *Discourse on Inequality*, these elements are all symbols of freedom and delivery from slavery, a point underscored in the *Discourse* version by the birds flying out of the open cage and especially by the broken shackles lying at the woman's feet. For all these similarities, however, there are important differences between the two versions. First, in the *Discourse* Liberty holds the Phrygian cap aloft with a cane or something like a cane, whereas in the *Social Contract* she holds the cap in her right hand and what appears to be a sword in the other hand. If so, then in the political treatise's version she holds symbols of both liberty and authority. Second, the birdcage appears to be closed, with the birds inside. Third, there are no broken shackles at her feet. (The cat is also standing rather than lying at her feet, whatever that means.) Fourth, whereas the setting in the version in the *Discourse on Inequality* is natural, with Liberty sitting on a sort of hill with foliage framing her figure, in the *Social Contract* she is indoors, seated on a chair, with a natural setting glimpsed beyond through the columns of the building (temple?) enclosing her. In short, Liberty is enclosed within the walls of political society. What could be more telling for a work whose most famous phrase is "Man is born free, and everywhere he is in chains" (I.1)? The project of the *Social Contract* is not to release us from our chains, but to render those chains legitimate, to reconcile liberty and authority.

Notice

After the title page, the reader is presented with a Notice (*Avertissement*) from the author, which I quote in full:

> This short treatise is extracted from a more extensive work, undertaken years ago without having considered my strength and long since abandoned. Of the various portions that could be taken from what had been completed, this is the most considerable and appeared to me to be the least unworthy of being offered to the public. The rest no longer exists. (155)

Let us begin with a few of the more obvious aspects of this Notice. First, Rousseau identifies the genre: it is a "treatise," and a short one at that. As opposed to a "discourse," such as his two works by that title, or an "essay," which is what he considered calling this work in the various subtitles he tried out, a treatise is a formal treatment or account of a subject, by Rousseau's time one in a written form. The *Social Contract* will not disappoint in that regard. Second, he identifies an audience: the public.

What about his remarks on the more extensive work he abandoned, which as an autobiographical matter refers to his projected *Political Institutions* (see *Confessions, CW*, 5:339–40, 432)? Why draw attention at the outset to this more extensive but abandoned work, and thus to the less extensive and incomplete nature of the *Social Contract*? In fact, he frames his political treatise by calling attention to its incompleteness, repeating the point in the concluding chapter of the work (IV.9).[20] Ironically, then, the opening and closing of the treatise both indicate something that comes before and after, but that is no longer present. One answer to this question is suggested by the first chapter of the Geneva Manuscript version of the treatise, titled "Subject of This Work." Explaining that many famous authors have discussed the "maxims of government" and "rules of civil right," Rousseau nonetheless opines that the more fundamental question of the "nature" of the social body is not sufficiently understood: "This is what I have tried to do in this work. It is, therefore, not a question here of the administration of the body, but of its constitution. I make it live, not act. I describe its mechanisms and parts, and set them in place. I put the machine in running order. Wiser men will regulate the movements" (Geneva Manuscript I.1, *CW*, 4:76). This explanation also makes sense for the *Social Contract*, I think, even if he does not explain the incompleteness of his treatise in exactly the same way. In any case, this explanation also raises another issue related to the two principal readings of the *Social Contract* I have suggested: namely, he draws a distinction between the "nature" of the social body, that is, the principles of political right, and its coming into existence by making it "live" and then "act."[21] Even if he does not make the state act in the *Social Contract*, he will make it live.

Table of the Books and the Chapters

The "Table of the Books and the Chapters," or the table of contents, as I will refer to it, is not included in the vast majority of editions of the *Social Contract* and has therefore received no attention from scholars. Nonetheless, Rousseau was scrupulous about including it.[22] Why? The table of contents does provide a handy summary of the contents and page references to each chapter, thus fulfilling its usual function. But it also contains information for the reader not provided elsewhere in the treatise, namely Rousseau's descriptions of the contents of each book:

Book I: Investigating how man passes from the state of nature to the civil state and what the essential conditions of the compact are.
Book II: Discussing legislation.

Book III: Discussing political laws, that is, the form of the government.
Book IV: While continuing the discussion of political laws, the means for
strengthening the constitution of the state are explained.

The principal piece of new information to be gathered here is, I suggest,
the purpose of book IV and the fact that it is intended as a kind of continuation of book III. Many readers have viewed book IV, especially its
lengthy discussion of Rome and the chapter "On Civil Religion" (IV.9),
as being tacked on or not integrated into the treatise.[23] The table of
contents reveals that book IV continues the discussion of political laws
begun in book III and the means of strengthening the constitution of
the state. Since the subject matter of book IV does not specifically relate
to the government and the various forms it can take (III.1–9), it seems
that book IV continues the treatment begun in III.10 of the abuse of
government, the impending death of the body politic, and then especially the means for maintaining the sovereign authority in the face of
the government's tendency to usurp it. As much is suggested by Rousseau's characterization in the table of contents of book IV as explaining
the means for strengthening the constitution of the state. Recall from
my discussion of the précis of the *Social Contract* in *Emile* that one of
the two major omissions is precisely this content, from III.10 onward—
the material that relates to the maintenance of an actual or imagined
political association.

The Structure of the *Social Contract*

Because the table of contents details the contents of the *Social Contract*, and because I have dropped several hints that the structure of his
political treatise is related to the two principal readings of the work I
am suggesting Rousseau makes available to the reader, let us examine
the complex structure of the work. To be clear from the outset, I am
not arguing that the structure reveals any "hidden" meaning. Nor do I
maintain that the principal readings of the work derive from examining
its structure or are evident only through scrutiny of its structure. After
all, as I noted at the outset of this chapter, a number of scholars have
centered in one way or another on these two principal readings of the
Social Contract, quite independently of examining the structure. Rather,
I am suggesting that the complex structure of the work underlies and
underscores the different ways of reading it.

As a preliminary matter, it will be helpful to outline the structure of
the draft version, the Geneva Manuscript, in comparison to the final
version in order to make more manifest the choices Rousseau decided

upon in structuring the final version. Since the manuscript is not complete, this is necessarily a tentative venture. Moreover, because the comparisons I want to make are broad, this sketch does not account for details in content and structure.

Let us now take note of the most important changes in structure.

Book I of the Geneva Manuscript largely resembles book I of the final version, although the contents are arranged differently. The main changes were to move the discussions in the earlier version of the necessity of laws (I.4) and of sovereignty (I.6 and I.7) to book II of the final version.

Book II of the Geneva Manuscript corresponds generically to book II of the *Social Contract*, both of them being concerned with legislation, but the actual contents are no more than partly the same. Namely, with the exception of a discussion of the nature of laws (II.4), which became part of II.6 of the *Social Contract*, the contents of book II of the Geneva Manuscript map onto the last half of book II of the *Social Contract* (II.7–12), that is, the discussion of the lawgiver and his activity in adapting the laws to the people. Overall, then, book II of the Geneva Manuscript might be characterized as dealing with the "*Establishment* of Laws," to emphasize part of its title—that is, the coming into being of an actual or imagined state. In turn, Rousseau distributes the contents of book II of the *Social Contract* into two halves. The first half discusses sovereignty and laws in general or in accordance with the principles of political right (II.1–6), incorporating the parts in books I and II of the Geneva Manuscript dealing with the subject. The second half attends to the conditions for birth of an actual or imagined state that could act in accordance with those principles (II.7–12). He so to speak postpones the birth of the state in the final version.

As for book III, both the earlier version and the final one are concerned with the institution and form of government—that is the executive power—but the fragmentary nature of the Geneva Manuscript in this regard makes any further comparison impossible. Finally, although we have a draft of the chapter "On Civil Religion," which became IV.8 in the *Social Contract*, we do not know whether Rousseau intended the Geneva Manuscript to have three or four books or what their contents might have been.

In sum, then, the principal change Rousseau made from the Geneva Manuscript to the *Social Contract* was to distribute the discussion of legislation in book II and to do so in two parts, the first dealing with the topic in principle (II.1–6) and the second with the topic in practice, so to speak (II.7–12). I suggest that this distribution of the contents of book II of the final version according to principle and practice

Table 7.1 Comparison of contents of the Geneva Manuscript and the *Social Contract*

Geneva Manuscript		Analogue in *On the Social Contract*
Book/chapter no.	Book/chapter title	
Book I	*Preliminary Concepts of the Social Body*	
I.1	*Subject of This Work*	I. Proemium (but very different)
I.2	*On the General Society of the Human Race*	
I.3	*On the Fundamental Compact*	I.1 Subject of This First Book I.6 On the Social Compact I.7 On the Sovereign I.8 On the Civil State I.9 On Real Property
I.4	*What Sovereignty Consists Of and What Makes It Inalienable*	II.1 That Sovereignty Is Inalienable
I.5	*False Conceptions of the Social Bond*	I.2 On the First Societies I.3 On the Right of the Stronger I.4 On Slavery
I.6	*On the Respective Rights of the Sovereign and the Citizen*	II.4 On the Limits of the Sovereign Power
I.7	*Necessity for Positive Laws*	II.6 On Law (concluding paragraphs)
Book II	*Establishment of the Laws*	
II.1	*End of Legislation*	II.6 On Law (first paragraph)
II.2	*On the Lawgiver*	II.7 On the Lawgiver
II.3	*On the People to Be Founded*	II.8 On the People II.9 Continued II.10 Continued
II.4	*On the Nature of Laws and the Principle of Civil Justice*	II.6 On Law (beginning paragraphs)
II.5	*Classification of Laws*	II.12 Classification of Laws
II.6	*On the Various Systems of Legislation*	II.11 On the Various Systems of Legislation
Book III	*On Political Laws, or On the Institution of Government*	
	Proemium	III. Proemium
III.1	*What the Government of a State Is*	On Government in General (beginning)
	[On Civil Religion—draft]	IV.8 On Civil Religion

Table 7.2 Three ways of distributing the contents of the *Social Contract*

Distribution into books		Principle vs. practice		Life of the state	
I.1–9	Social contract	I.1–9 + II.1–6 + III.1–9	Principle	I.9–II.7	Foundation (gestation)
II.1–12	Legislation				
III.1–18	Government	II.7–12 + III.10–18 + IV.1–9	Practice	II.8– III.11	Life (birth to death)
IV.1–9	Maintenance of constitution			III.12– IV.9	Maintenance (extending life)

suggests an alternative way of envisioning the structure of the *Social Contract*.

Let me now suggest three different ways of thinking of the structure of the *Social Contract* that I believe are revealing for thinking about its contents and therefore the readings of the work Rousseau makes available. I will present them first in summary tabular form (table 7.2).

First, the most obvious way to think of the structure of the *Social Contract* is the organization Rousseau himself gave the work: the distribution of the contents into four books. The forty-eight total chapters of the treatise are divided unevenly across books I (9), II (12), III (18), and IV (9).

Second, the structure of the *Social Contract* might also be approached from the two main aspects of the work, or what we might call principle and practice. The principles are the principles of political right, whereas the practical aspect concerns the founding and maintenance of an actual or imagined political association. Several points discussed so far have suggested this alternative structure. First, I have remarked that these two main aspects, and therefore the two principal readings of the *Social Contract*, are potentially signaled in the title of the work. Second, the distribution by principle and practice is also suggested by the précis of his political treatise in *Emile*, which, as we saw, was limited to an examination of the principles of political right, without any attention to the establishment of a legitimate political association. In summarizing what is retained in and omitted from this précis, I concluded that the parts of the *Social Contract* included in table 7.2 under "principle" were retained and those included under "practice" were omitted. Third, the comparison of the structure of the Geneva Manuscript and the *Social Contract* revealed how Rousseau split his discussion of legislation in book II of the final version into two equal halves, the first dealing with sovereignty and law in light of the principles of political right (II.1–6) and the second dealing with the founding of the legitimate regime (II.7–12). Similarly, my analysis of the précis in *Emile* indicates that he likewise split book III into two equal halves, the first treating govern-ment in general (III.1–9) and the second dealing with the degeneration of government and how to prevent it (III.10–18). The division of books II and III into two halves then permits a relatively neat redistribution of its contents according to the two aspects of the work. In short, if we arrange the structure of the *Social Contract* according to its two main aspects, principle and practice, we find that the forty-eight chapters are distributed into two equal parts of twenty-four chapters each.[24]

Third, the *Social Contract* can also be divided into three equal parts corresponding to the foundation, existence, and maintenance of the legitimate state, or, if we pursue Rousseau's metaphor, the gestation, life, and the life support of the body politic. The textual anomaly that drew my attention to this restructuring is the groups of three chapters each in both books II and III, with the first chapter in the group bear-ing a title and the two following chapters simply titled "Continued." In book II this group begins with the chapter "On the People" (II.8), and the group in book III begins with the chapter "How Sovereignty Is Main-tained" (III.12). Why divide what could easily be one chapter into three? There are certainly chapters in the *Social Contract* that are as long as or longer than the three chapters together, especially in the case of the triple chapters in book III, which are only a few pages total. Dividing up the chapters in this way allows the potential restructuring of the *Social Contract* I suggested above and the restructuring I am now proposing, and in such a way that divides up the contents evenly.

As for this third potential restructuring, then, what I noticed was that these groups of three chapters mark the birth of the state in book II and the death of the state in book III. What precedes the life of the state from birth to death is the principles of political right, or what Rousseau terms the "foundations" of the political association (I.1–II.7). As for the birth of the state, the group of three chapters "On the People" (II.8–10) initiates the second portion of the restructured work dedicated to the life of the state and follows the chapter on what might be called the act of conception performed by the lawgiver (II.7). The actual birth of the state comes in II.8, although instead of using a bodily analogy Rousseau begins with an architectural analogy of the "founder" erecting a build-ing by first examining the foundation, here the character of the people. This second or middle portion of the restructured text runs through the chapter in which Rousseau proclaims the inevitable demise of the state, "On the Death of the Body Politic" (III.11)—from II.9 to III.11. As for the death of the state, the group of three chapters titled "How Sovereignty Is Maintained" (III.12–14) initiates a final portion of the work dedicated to prolonging the life of the state. This last portion of the restructured text runs through the end of the *Social Contract* (III.12–IV.9). In short, this structure distributes forty-eight chapters of the work into three groups of sixteen chapters each, making the work as a whole a kind of triptych.[25]

To repeat, I am not claiming that these alternative restructurings of the *Social Contract* allow us to glimpse esoteric readings not otherwise available, but I do suggest that these restructurings underscore the two main issues of principle and practice he takes up in his treatise and therefore the two principal readings of the work that I suggest he makes available. Let me now turn to those readings.

Two Principal Readings of the *Social Contract*

My aim in the chapter is not to present a comprehensive interpretation of the *Social Contract*, in part because there are already many fine analyses, but instead to sketch the two principal readings of the treatise that I have suggested Rousseau makes available. I have already shown how these readings are indicated by considerations drawn from beyond the work itself, namely in the précis of the work included in *Emile*, and by features of the structure of the *Social Contract* itself. In examining the substance of the work, then, I begin with Rousseau's introduction to the *Social Contract* in the Proemium to book I in order to show how he initiates these readings. I will then sketch them.

The Proemium

The *Social Contract* does not include a separate preface, which we might have expected, or exordium, which we should not expect given that this is not a spoken genre. Instead, Rousseau begins with a proemium to book I, that is, a separate address to the reader concerning the treatise as a whole after the heading "book I" and before the first chapter of book I: "Subject of This First Book" (I.1). Why he adopts this structure is not clear.[26] At any rate, the proemium serves the traditional functions of a preface and exordium by defining his subject matter, as in a preface, and by speaking to his qualifications to address it, as in an exordium.

Let me begin with his qualifications. First, as some interpreters have noted, the very first word of the treatise (putting aside the heading "Notice") is "I" (*Je*): "I want to inquire" (I. Proemium). This first-person perspective is echoed by the very last word of the work, "myself" (*moi*): "I should have always set my sights closer to myself [*plus près de moi*]" (IV.9).[27] This is strikingly personal for a work that is so impersonal. Second, the authorial "I" of the proemium is underscored by Rousseau's explaining why he chooses to write the treatise: "I begin my discussion [*entre en matière*] without proving the importance of my subject. I will be asked whether I am a prince or a lawgiver, given that I am writing about politics. I reply that I am not, and that it is for this very reason that I write about politics. If I were a prince or a lawgiver, I would not waste my time saying what needs to be done; I would do it, or I would remain silent" (I. Proemium). Rousseau presents himself here emphatically as an author of a written work. His qualifications for writing it are, so to speak, negative: he is not a prince or a lawgiver. Princes and lawgivers attend to practice, whereas we can infer that authors of political treatises attend to principle. As we saw above, Rousseau was explicit about this division of labor in the parallel introductory passage in the Geneva Manuscript, restricting himself to discussing the "nature" and "constitution" of the body politic and leaving it to others to make it "act" (Geneva Manuscript, I.1, *CW*, 4:76). We therefore have another indication of a division of the subject of the *Social Contract* into principle and practice. If he were a prince or lawgiver, he would either do what needs to be done or remain silent. Rousseau himself is not silent, however, so his writing would seem to be a type of political activity.

Rousseau's qualifications to write about politics are signaled in an interesting way in the next paragraph: "Born a citizen of a free state, and a member of the sovereign, the right to vote there is enough to impose on me the duty to learn about public affairs." The "Citizen of Geneva" underscores his citizenship: "How happy I am, every time I meditate about governments, always to find in my research new reasons to love that of my country [*pays*]" (I. Proemium). This sentence is reminiscent of the Dedication to the Republic of Geneva in the *Discourse on Inequality*. Unlike in 1755, when he wrote this dedication, when the self-proclaimed "Citizen of Geneva" had not yet in fact regained his citizenship, by the time he published the *Social Contract* in 1762 he was a citizen. Yet, as we know, the "Citizen of Geneva" was not an active member of his fatherland—or, as he specifies in the proemium, of his country (*pays*), suggesting that he, like Emile, has a *pays* but not a *patrie*. His treatise is an investigation of politics that takes place outside of an actual political association, even his own, a stance that permits him a critical perspective. His criticism was not lost on the political leaders of his country, who banned and burned the *Social Contract*. Rousseau soon thereafter renounced his citizenship. At any rate, the implication of this paragraph is that his qualifications for writing the *Social Contract* are his being a "citizen of a free state" in the abstract rather than in the concrete. If he were a citizen of a truly free or legitimate state, one presumes he would act rather than write. Instead, again like Emile, whose allegiance is to the principles of political right, he is a citizen through his activity of writing about politics: he is the "Citizen of Geneva."

Turning to the subject matter of his treatise, Rousseau specifies the question he is addressing at the very outset of the proemium:

> I want to inquire whether there can be any legitimate and reliable rule of administration in the civil order, taking men as they are and laws as they can be. In this inquiry I will always try to join what right permits with what interest prescribes, so that justice and utility are not always at odds. (I. Proemium)

Two of Rousseau's tools—one might even say tics—as a writer are to structure his terms, conceptual and written, in binary form (natural versus civilized, force versus right, etc.) and, relatedly, to destabilize or complicate these binary terms through chiasmus, a rhetorical figure in which terms are reversed from their anticipated order (e.g., "the rich and the poor, the weak and the strong"). The use of chiasmus structures this first paragraph in a revealing way. Schematically:

Legitimate : Reliable :: *Men (as they are)* : *Laws (as they can be)* ::
Right : Interest :: Justice : Utility

The first and second terms in each of the binary pairs are parallel, with the exception of the second pair, that is, men and laws. Thus, on the one hand we have legitimate—right—justice, and then, on the other, reliable—interest—utility. One might expect laws to be in parallel with legitimate—right—justice, and men to be in parallel with reliable—interest—utility, but Rousseau frustrates that expectation by reversing them. Further, one might wonder why it is men "as they are" and laws "as they can be," rather than the opposite. After all, in the *Social Contract* Rousseau insists that laws are what they are by definition and can be nothing else and still be laws. Likewise, he argues in the chapter "On the Lawgiver" (II.7) that men can self-legislate only if the lawgiver makes them into what they "can be," rather than leaving them as they currently "are." In other words, only after men are as they can be will they make laws that are what they are by their very nature. Only then will there be a legitimate and reliable rule where right and interest, justice and utility are not at odds. In other words, the chiasmus in the opening paragraph signals the problem with which Rousseau is concerned in his political treatise and also the solution. Or perhaps, rather than the solution, the perennial problem. For as Rousseau wrote five years after the publication of the *Social Contract*: "Here, according to my old ideas, is the great problem of politics, which I compare to that of squaring the circle in geometry, and to that of longitudes in astronomy: *To find a form of government that places the law above man.*"²⁸

Finally, the opening statement of the proemium concerning the subject of his work points to the two principal readings of the *Social Contract* I am suggesting. We can see this by redescribing what I have just characterized as the problem and the solution contained in the chiasmus. First, insofar as men cannot be refashioned into what they need to be ("can be") in order to act within a legitimate political association, actual or imagined, Rousseau's political treatise is an examination of the principles of political right regardless of whether or to what extent they can be put into practice. Second, if men "can be" what they need to be to self-legislate, for example through the activity of the lawgiver, then his political treatise can be read as discussing the conditions necessary for forming an actual or imagined political association in accordance with the principles of political right.

Reading 1: A Treatise on the Principles of Political Right

One tempting and common reading of the *Social Contract* is to view the principles of political right as functioning something like an architectural blueprint for constructing a legitimate political association, either as an actuality to be realized or as an ideal to be approached. As for the latter possibility, old-fashioned readers have characterized the *Social Contract* as belonging in one way or another to the genre of utopia. More contemporary analytically inclined theorists term it an "ideal theory," perhaps never realizable given nonideal conditions. Interestingly, in making the now-familiar distinction between ideal and nonideal theories, John Rawls appealed to precisely Rousseau's claim to take "men as they are and laws as they can be" as an inspiration.²⁹

Rousseau himself expressly rejected the utopian or ideal-theory reading of his work. In the *Letters Written from the Mountain* he explains: "Sir, if I had only made a system, you can be sure that they would have said nothing. They would have been content to relegate the *Social Contract* along with the *Republic* of Plato, *Utopia*, and *Severambes* into the land of chimeras. But I depicting an existing object, and they wanted to change that object's face." Now, in the context from which this statement is drawn, Rousseau claims that the "existing object" his treatise depicts is Geneva: "What do you think, Sir, upon reading this short and faithful analysis of my book? I guess it. You are saying to yourself, there is the history of the government of Geneva" (*CW*, 9:233–34). And a critical analysis at that, in fact, for it turns out that Geneva illustrates not so much an exemplar of a legitimate state in accordance with the principles of political right, although Rousseau generously attributes democratic sovereignty to its original constitution, as a cautionary example of the usurpation of sovereign authority by an oligarchic government. In any case, I suggest that the "existing object" depicted in the *Social Contract* should more generally be characterized as *any* political association, actual or potential.

To explain: Rousseau's treatise outlines the principles of political right upon which *all* political associations are based by their very nature as political associations. Put differently, the principles of political right are, properly speaking, *immanent* or *inherent* in political associations as such. To return to the common reading of the work as a blueprint for constructing an actual or ideal state, then, I am suggesting that the *Social Contract* not only should not be envisioned as a portrait of a utopia or an unrealizable ideal, but also that it should not be characterized as a novel blueprint for constructing a state in accordance with the principles of political right. If his political treatise is a blueprint, it contains the plans for all actual or potential associations. Let me establish what I have just put forward.

In the first chapter of the *Social Contract*, Rousseau suggests that his project is not to rid men of their chains, but to make those chains legitimate: "Man is born free, and everywhere he is in chains." The foundational claim concerning natural freedom puts Rousseau squarely in the social contract tradition, as the title of his work suggests. He goes on to argue that political authority or right does not come from nature but must instead be founded on "conventions" (I.1). The nature of those conventions is determined by their purpose. After eliminating the arguments commonly advanced for the natural origins of political right based on the family (I.2), the right of the stronger (I.3), and slavery (I.4), Rousseau returns to the point from which he began: "That It Is Always Necessary to Go Back to a First Convention" (I.5). He explains that the so-called natural foundations of the state and even the pseudo-contract of slavery may produce a "multitude" or "aggregation," but it does not create a "people" or "association" or "body politic," *properly speaking* (I.5). That is, the aggregation does not meet the definition of a true political association.

From this perspective, then, Rousseau's political theory might be said to be quasi-teleological. Think in this light of Aristotle's remark that the "hand" on a statue of a human being is not a hand properly speaking; it is only a hand in a manner of speaking. He notoriously uses the same logic to argue that a natural slave is in a sense not a complete human being because the slave lacks the full capacity that makes a human being a human being: speech or reason (*logos*). Aristotle's teleology is of course a natural teleology: beings, including human beings, are naturally directed toward their proper end (*telos*). And he famously argues that man is by nature a political animal and that the *polis* is therefore by nature the condition for the completion of human nature.[30] To return to Rousseau, he emphatically rejects any theory of natural teleology, including the claim that humans are political animals by nature and that the political association is natural. The principles of political right for Rousseau do have a natural basis insofar as they are grounded in natural right ("man is born free"), but the political community itself is the product of an act of will, a conventional body created for certain purposes. Rousseau's political theory can be said to be quasi-teleological only in a voluntarist or constructivist sense: the principles of political right are such by definition.

The most important passage in the *Social Contract* for grasping how Rousseau conceives of the principles of political right as immanent or inherent in every political community is, naturally enough, in the chapter "On the Social Compact" (I.6). After stating that he assumes men have reached a point where the obstacles to their self-preservation in the state of nature have become too great to overcome, he argues that they must form an association. The "difficulty" they face is expressed by Rousseau as finding a way in which naturally free individuals can form an association in which they obey only themselves and remain as free as before. The solution is found in the social contract. Now the important passage: "The clauses of this contract are so completely determined by the nature of the act that the slightest modification would render them null and void. As a result, *although they may never have been formally enunciated, they are everywhere the same, everywhere tacitly acknowledged and recognized*" (I.6; emphasis added). As this passage reveals, the social contract is not an act in the sense of an action that actually took place, although it could have, but is instead what I might call a "principle" related to the very nature of the political association as such, always and everywhere.

Now, of course, the very language of social contract theory in Rousseau, as in Hobbes, Locke, and others, evokes a temporal event, whether it is intended as such or not. Later in this same chapter, therefore, Rousseau articulates the social contract as though it were an actual event: "If, then, everything that is not of the essence of the social contract is set aside, it will be found that it comes down to the following terms. *Each of us puts his person and all his power in common under the supreme direction of the general will; and as a body we received each member as an indivisible part of the whole*" (I.6; emphasis in original). This quasi speech turns out to be a performative utterance: "Instantly, in place of the particular person of each contracting party, this act of association produces a moral and collective body made up of as many members as there are voices in the assembly, which receives from this same act its unity, its common *self* [*moi*], its life, and its will" (I.6). We thus witness the birth of the state. But I suggest that at this point it is a birth in thought alone, not in time and space. Rousseau tries to rid the act of its apparent diachronic character by making it instantaneous: "Instantly. . . ." The change is in how the participants in the social contract view their status, from private individuals to members of an association. The perspective of the participants in the act can be generalized, including to any reader of the *Social Contract* considering his or her relationship to an actual or imagined political association.

The definitional character of the principles of political right is exhibited in the passage that follows the conceptual birth of the political association.

> This public person thus formed by the union of all the others formerly took the name *city*, and now takes that of *republic* or of *body politic*, which is called *state* by its members when it is passive, *sovereign* when it is active, *power* when comparing it to similar bodies. With regard to the associates, they collectively take the name *people*, and individually they are called *citizens* as participants in the sovereign authority, and *subjects* as subjects to the law of the state. (I.6)

Many of Rousseau's terms amount to putting new wine in old bottles. He reveals as much when he writes: "But these terms are often confused and are mistaken for one another. It is enough to know how to distinguish them when they are used with complete precision" (I.6). Recall that the two explicit addresses to the reader in the *Social Contract* concern using terms in their precise signification.

What might be called the geometric nature of Rousseau's principles of political right, as being based on axiomatic terms, helps elucidate certain of his claims that are otherwise surprising or even alarming. For example, in the chapter "On the Sovereign" (I.7), he explains that the sovereign cannot impose a law on itself because doing so would be "contrary to the nature of the body politic." By "nature" he cannot mean that the body politic is a natural being; rather, he means that by definition it cannot bind itself since the sovereign is, also by definition, the source of the law itself. Later in the same chapter he writes: "The sovereign, by the very fact of what it is, is always all that it ought to be" (I.7). This perhaps disquieting claim should be understood as definitional, even tautological. The passage precedes the infamous claim that whoever refuses to obey the general will must be "forced to be free," but I will not attempt here to disarm that passage.

The definitional conceptual project continues in book II with his further explanation of sovereignty as "inalienable" (II.1) and "indivisible" (II.2), again by its very nature. He explains: "For the general will is either general or it is not; it is either the will of the body of the people or only of a part. In the first case, this will when declared is an act of sovereignty and constitutes law. In the second case, it is merely a particular will, or an act of magistracy; it is at most a decree" (II.2). In other words, what might appear at first to be a general will and a law may not upon examination fit the precise definitions of the terms, and therefore is not actually a general will or a law. The same is true for sovereignty if it is alienated: since it cannot be alienated, the supposed sovereign who receives the power is not truly a "sovereign." Compare this again to Aristotle. Aristotle argues that, despite his having classified tyranny as a form of regime, tyranny may in fact not be a regime, properly speaking, because it does not meet the definition, in his terms the "end" or *telos*, of a *politeia* or a *polis*.[31] So too for Rousseau, but in a voluntarist version. Another famously disconcerting passage that makes better sense when viewed as conceptual-definitional is Rousseau's opening claim in the chapter "Whether the General Will Can Err" (II.3): "From the preceding it follows that the general will is always right [*droit*] and always tends toward the public utility. But it does not follow that the people's deliberations always have the same rectitude." For Rousseau, the will as such is directed toward what the individual believes is good, and is always rightly directed—*droit*—in this sense, even though the individual may be mistaken about what is in fact good. The will is always "right" in this tautological sense: as a will, then, the general will is likewise always right. In this sense the claim is admittedly not very substantively interesting. However, the claim that the general will is always right does not eliminate the problems Rousseau admits in the second sentence quoted concerning that point that public deliberations do not always have the same rectitude. For example, he goes on in the same chapter to distinguish the general will from the "will of all" (*volonté de tous*), which is the sum of the particular wills of the members individually. The will of all does not meet the definition of the general will, which consists in them all exercising their general will as citizens (II.3). The distinction is at bottom a definitional one, although the act of willing in actual time and place carries with it a host of problems. Similarly, the problem of deliberations by people who are not adequately informed, for example about what is truly good for them, is an issue Rousseau raises at several points. He does so most sharply when he wonders how "a blind multitude, which often does not know what it wants because it rarely knows what is good for it," can make laws for itself, a problem whose solution is found by appealing to the lawgiver (II.6).

The requirement of using the terminology of the principles of political right comes to the fore in book III with Rousseau's discussion of government. Like book I, book III begins with a proemium, in this case a very brief one:[32] "Before discussing the various forms of government, let us try [*tâchons*] to determine the precise meaning of this word, which has not yet been especially well explained" (III. Proemium). Who is "us" or "we" in this statement? Throughout his treatise Rousseau generally moves between the first-person singular "I" and what might be called a generic first-person plural "we." This is very unlike *Emile* in particular, where "we" often explicitly includes the reader. Yet this is now the occasion for one of the two direct addresses in the work to the reader, so perhaps "we" here includes the reader: "I warn the reader that this chapter should be read with due care, and that I do not know the art of being clear for those who are not willing to be attentive" (III.1). In any case, the task is to determine the "precise meaning" of the word *government*, which has not yet been explained precisely, whether by Rousseau in his political treatise or by those who have previously written on the subject. Indeed, his insistence on distinguishing the sovereign from the government is one of his major conceptual innovations.[33]

Rousseau's call for precision with regard to the meaning of *government* goes back to his insistence on a precise meaning of *sovereignty*. In the chapter "That Sovereignty is Indivisible" (II.2) he explains that the error of believing that sovereignty can be divided "comes from not having established precise notions of sovereign authority, and for having mistaken for parts of this authority what are only its manifestations. Thus, for example, the act of declaring war and that of making peace have been regarded as acts of sovereignty, which they are not, because neither of these acts is a law but merely an application of the law, a particular act which decides the case at issue, as will clearly be seen once the idea attached to the word *law* is established" (II.2). That is, laws, precisely speaking, are acts of the sovereign people and are necessarily general in form and application, like the general will that produced them. Particular acts do not meet the definition of laws and therefore cannot be the act of the sovereign; instead, they are acts of the government. To return to his discussion of government, then, he explains near the outset of the chapter "On Government in General" (III.1), the chapter he warns must be read with due care: "We have seen that the legislative power belongs to the people and can belong only to it. On the contrary, it is easy to see, by the principles established above, that the executive power cannot belong to the general public in its legislative or sovereign capacity, because this power consists solely in particular acts which are not within the province of the law nor, consequently, within that of the sovereign, all of whose acts can be nothing but laws." As is evident here, Rousseau admits that the sovereign and the government are frequently confused or confounded—*confondre* having both meanings. And that is precisely the problem. As he reveals after his discussion of government in principle in the first half of book III, and when he turns to the second half concerning the problems of government in practice, the tendency for government to be abused by the magistrates, and especially their usurpation of the sovereign power, is the main cause of the disease and death of the body politic. This issue leads us to the second principal reading of the *Social Contract*.

Reading 2: A Treatise on the Creation and Maintenance of a Legitimate Political Association

The second principal reading of the *Social Contract* I am suggesting Rousseau makes available regards the creation and maintenance of an actual or imagined political association in accordance with the principles of political right. Before sketching this reading, let me make two general comments.

First, this reading related to political practice is not an alternative to the first reading concerning political principle, but rather a supplement to it. That is, whereas the first reading of the work as a treatise restricted to elaborating the principles of political right can stand on its own, the second reading presupposes the principles of political right of a legitimate political association.

Second, thus far I have been using without explanation the phrase "actual or imagined" political association when referring to this second reading. My phrasing suggests two possible subreadings of the *Social Contract*. First, Rousseau can be seen as discussing the requirements for the creation and maintenance of an actual political association. In this sense the principles of political right can be seen as something of a blueprint. When I rejected the reading of the *Social Contract* as a blueprint for an actual or imagined political association, I contested only the view that it is a novel blueprint for a novel political association. Instead, I argued that Rousseau sees himself as elaborating the principles that underlie any political association as such, of anything in principle worthy of being called a political association in the first place. Thus, although Rousseau's articulation of those principles may be novel, the principles themselves are not. Insofar as the *Social Contract* is meant to inspire the creation of an actual political association, or perhaps to reform an actual state, the issue would be the degree to which the conditions for its creation and maintenance exist in a given place and time. This leads to the second subreading. By stating that the second principal reading of the *Social Contract* concerns the creation and maintenance of an imagined political association, I am suggesting that he sketches the necessary conditions for such an enterprise, without, however, believing that such an enterprise is possible or perhaps even desirable, at least under existing conditions. Rousseau would thereby be asking the reader to imagine along with him what would be required to realize the principles of political right. Such an interpretation of the *Social Contract* would be analogous to interpretations of Plato's *Republic* that see Socrates' "city in speech" as meant to reveal what would be necessary to achieve perfect justice, regardless of possibility or cost. After all, even though Rousseau is a notorious champion of Sparta, he cites Montaigne, apparently without objection, in calling Lycurgus's legislation "in truth monstrously perfect" (*Sciences*, 30 n.). Indeed, I would suggest that all of the readings of Rousseau's *Social Contract* I have outlined are analogous to various readings of Plato's *Republic*, and perhaps this is not accidental. Let me now sketch the second principal reading, or readings, that Rousseau makes available.

As I noted when discussing the structure of the *Social Contract*, the turn from principle to practice occurs with Rousseau's move from the chapter "On Law" (II.6) to the chapter "On the Lawgiver" (II.7). "On Law" is the culmination of his discussion of sovereignty in the first half of book II. The law itself is a matter of definition: it is the expression of the general will of the people, legislating in its capacity of sovereign. The actual act of legislating, however, raises all the problems of the citizens' exercising their general will as citizens instead of their particular wills as individuals, the people being adequately informed, and so on. Hence, as we saw above, the chapter "On Law" ends with his saying that the "blind multitude" requires a lawgiver to make it capable of properly enacting laws as a "people."

The chapter "On the Lawgiver" (II.7) discusses the godlike creative power of the lawgiver. To appeal to the chiasmus in the proemium to book I, the task of the lawgiver is to transform men from what they are to what they can be. "What men are" could mean at least two things. First, what they are by nature, for example as described by Rousseau in the *Discourse on Inequality*: as naturally asocial or naturally individuals in the strong sense. But, in addition, what men are by nature is capable of development, owing to the uniquely human attribute of perfectibility.

Second, therefore, men as they are could refer what they are now, as they have developed in society. Rousseau also describes that development in the *Discourse on Inequality*, namely how natural asocial self-love (*amour de soi*) is transformed in society to pride (*amour-propre*). In either case, men as they are, then as now, are not suited for citizenship.

To return to the lawgiver's mission: "He who dares to undertake to establish a people's institutions must feel that he is capable of changing, so to speak, human nature; of transforming each individual, who by himself is a complete and solitary whole, into a part of a greater whole from which this individual receives as it were his life and his being" (II.7). In short, the lawgiver must make "men" into "citizens" by redirecting their natural self-love toward love of the political association, which is artificial. There are various complications in doing so, Rousseau admits, for the lawgiver cannot use either force or reasoning to accomplish this goal. He cannot use force because to do so would violate the principle that the people must freely make laws, and he cannot use reasoning because he is faced with a "blind multitude," as Rousseau states in the previous chapter. As such, "he must of necessity have recourse to an authority of a different order which might be able to motivate without violence and persuade without convincing" (II.7). In other words, the lawgiver must persuade the people that his laws come from the gods. In discussing the lawgiver, then, Rousseau appeals to such familiar figures as Lycurgus and Numa, Moses and Mohammed, and also Calvin. To what extent does Rousseau believe that this transformation of human nature is fully possible, especially in modern times? This is a difficult question, the answer to which would be one criterion for determining whether the *Social Contract* should be read according to the principal subreadings I discussed above, namely as proposing the creation of an *actual* political association or as portraying an *imagined* political association by articulating what would be necessary in principle for creating it without the intention of doing so.

The chapters that follow "On the Lawgiver" witness the birth of the people midwifed by the lawgiver, who must attend to particular circumstances to ensure that the laws suit a given people. The next three chapters are therefore those "On the People" (II.8–10), which I discussed above when sketching the alternative restructurings of the political treatise. Finally, the last two chapters of book II concern "legislation," abstractly outlining various types of legislation in general and their aim. Of particular note is a type of legislation Rousseau states is unknown to "our politicians," namely the lawgiver's attention to "morals, customs, and especially opinion," or what he terms the "keystone" of the arch of the building he constructs (II.12).

The second turn from principle to practice occurs in book III when Rousseau moves from his treatment in the first half of book III of government in principle (III.1–9) to a discussion in the second half of the tendency of government in practice to degenerate and how to attend to this degeneration in order to forestall the inevitable death of the body politic (III.10–18). Book IV continues this discussion with particular attention to republican Rome as an example and to civil religion as among the principal elements necessary for unifying the state, a discussion that circles back to the lawgiver.

As I noted at the outset of this chapter, aside from the two occasions on which Rousseau directly addresses the reader as a reader, there is one other place in the work where he speaks to an audience: in the portion devoted to the maintenance of the body politic in order to forestall its death. Specifically, this speech comes in the chapter "On Deputies or Representatives" (III.15). The chapter begins with the principal psychological cause of the decline of the political association, namely the resurgence of natural self-love. "As soon as public service ceases to be the principal business of citizens, as soon as they prefer to serve with their pocketbooks rather than with their persons," he begins the chapter, "the state is already close to its ruin." The cooling enthusiasm for the fatherland and the warming of self-interest has led to the measure of using deputies or representatives to attend to the people's business. Rousseau asserts that representative government is a modern invention. Given this, he addresses modern peoples: "Your harsher climates give you more needs, six months of the year the public place is unbearable, your muted languages cannot be heard in the open, you give more thought to your gain than to your freedom, and you fear slavery much less than poverty." So far, this address to "you" could be seen as a generic use of the second-person plural. But Rousseau now makes a more direct and specific harangue. Noting that the freedom of the ancient peoples was maintained only through having slaves, he turns to moderns: "As for you, modern peoples, you do not have slaves, but you yourselves are slaves. You pay for their freedom with your own. Boast as you may of this choice; I find in it more cowardice than humanity" (III.15).

This passage is difficult to interpret. Rousseau avers in the immediate sequel that he is not proposing reintroducing slavery, for he has already proved that slavery is illegitimate. He is therefore not praising the ancients for having slaves, but rather pointing out the trade-offs of civilized life. He is certainly criticizing "modern peoples" for their hollow self-congratulation with regard to freeing slaves and their self-deceit with regard to their own slavery. Is he arguing that civic freedom, the fruit of the principles of political right, is impossible to realize in modern times? In his *Letters Written from the Mountain* Rousseau hurls a similar accusation at his fellow Genevans: "Ancient peoples are no longer models for modern ones; they are too alien to them in every respect. . . . You are neither Romans, nor Spartans; you are not even Athenians. Leave aside these great names that do not suit you. You are merchants, artisans, bourgeois, always occupied with their private interests, with their work, with their trafficking, with their gain; people for whom even liberty is only a means for acquiring without obstacle and for possessing in safety" (*CW*, 9:292–93). Returning to the *Social Contract*, seemingly speaking of modern states but potentially speaking of any political association, Rousseau states: "Since law is nothing but the declaration of the general will, it is clear that the people cannot be represented in its legislative power. . . . This makes it clear that, on proper examination, very few nations would be found to have laws" (III.15). This, of course, is what Emile learns by measuring existing political associations with the ruler of the principles of political right. In short, Rousseau does not seem optimistic that a fully legitimate state, or even one not so fully legitimate, is possible in his own time.

To return to his discussion of how modern peoples turn to deputies or representatives to do the public business, interestingly, it is also in this context that he proposes what might be a solution to part of the problem of reconciling the small republics necessary to achieve civic freedom internally with the need to defend them against external threats from large modern states. This potential solution is federation. "I will show below* how the external power of a great people can be combined with ease of administration and the proper ordering of a small state," he writes, then explaining in the note: "This is what I proposed to do in the sequel to this work, when, in dealing with foreign relations, I would have come to federations. This subject is entirely new and its principles have yet to be established" (III.15 and n.). Why include the passage and note when simple editing would have removed the reference to this aborted discussion? If federations are among the potential solutions for "modern peoples" to form a legitimate and sustainable political association, wouldn't Rousseau want to discuss them? It seems that he leaves intentionally unresolved the question raised in the harangue to "modern peoples" as to whether the principles of political right can be realized in modern times.

Conclusion

Who is the intended reader of the *Social Contract*? Apart from twice cautioning the reader to be attentive to his technical vocabulary, the only clue we get from Rousseau is paradoxical: "modern peoples" who seem incapable of realizing the principles of political right or perhaps even comprehending them. Insofar as he wrote his political treatise with Geneva in mind, as he claims in the *Letters Written from the Mountain* in defending the work after his compatriots condemned it, the issues of incapacity and incomprehension are merely compounded. If we assume that Rousseau believes that a fully legitimate political association is highly unlikely in modern times, or perhaps ever, then we are left with a treatise on the principles of political right by which to assess existing regimes and perhaps bring them into closer alignment with those principles. If, as I have argued, Rousseau's claim is that these principles are immanent or inherent in any political association worthy of being called such, true everywhere and always, then the intended audience of the *Social Contract* is any reader.

Conclusion

If I have been successful in my examination of the rhetorical and literary strategies Rousseau employs in his philosophical works to persuade and educate his reader, then I hope that I have also succeeded in persuading my own reader of the fruitfulness of my interpretive approach concerning the author-reader dialogue as staged within the text. In conclusion, then, I would like to return to the methodological manifesto with which I began in the introduction and to illustrate it through a brief application to another classic work in the history of political philosophy: Hobbes's *Leviathan*.

The relationship between philosophy and rhetoric in Hobbes's thought, including *Leviathan*, has been a lively subject of scholarly debate. Interpreters of Hobbes have been often struck by the fact that, on the one hand, he strongly criticizes rhetoric and urges the use of clear and precise definitions in philosophy on the model of geometry, and, on the other, he himself freely and forcefully employs rhetorical devices in his writing. One particularly impish instance on Hobbes's part comes in his discussion of the defects plaguing the intellectual virtues. In the "rigorous search of truth," he explains, metaphors "are in this case utterly excluded. For seeing they openly profess deceit; to admit them into counsel, or reasoning, were manifest folly." Then, just two paragraphs later, he explains that the secret thoughts of man run over things holy and profane without shame or blame but then suggests that it would be foolish to write these extravagant things, illustrating his point with a metaphor: "As if a man, from being tumbled into the dirt, should come and present himself before good company" (*Leviathan*, 46–47). Indeed, the very title of *Leviathan* contains the arch-metaphor of the great sea creature found in Job. And the famous frontispiece displaying the sovereign composed of his subjects, wielding sword and crozier as he looms over his peaceful and prosperous realm, positioned above the symbols of terrestrial and spiritual power, is nothing if not a complex metaphor meant to illustrate the fruits of the civil science contained in the book. In my own view, the question of the relationship between philosophy and rhetoric in Hobbes is largely a false debate based in large measure on a misunderstanding of both of the terms of the debate.[1] Philosophy and rhetoric are not antithetical for Hobbes, and like Rousseau he sees the need to persuade and educate his reader.

Much of *Leviathan* is indeed concerned with defining terms and reasoning from them in an almost geometric manner, but the work also contains a number of interesting and revealing interactions between Hobbes as author and the reader he evokes in his text. As for the author, once we look for his presence within the text, it is striking how often Hobbes uses the first person. Many of these instances of "I" are the author simply explaining what he is doing. For example, in chapter 5 he writes: "I have said before, (in the second chapter,) that a man did excel all other animals in this faculty, that when he conceived any thing whatsoever, he was apt to inquire the consequences of it, and what effects he could do with it. And now I add this other degree of the same excellence" (*Leviathan*, 29–30). Similarly, he sometimes inserts himself in the text when offering definitions, for example: "By *Consequence*, or TRAIN of thoughts, I understand that succession of one thought to another" (*Leviathan*, 15). Or, more famously, he draws consequences from his own train of reasoning: "So that in the first place, I put for a general inclination of all mankind, a perpetual and restless desire of power after power, that ceaseth only in death" (*Leviathan*, 66). Likewise, he clarifies his subject, for example in his chapter on civil laws, where he states: "But that is not it [i.e., the Roman civil law] I intend to speak of here, my design being not to show what is law here, and there, but what law is; as Plato, Aristotle, Cicero and divers others have done" (*Leviathan*, 175). Many such instances could be adduced.

Yet other cases of Hobbes's overt presence in the text are more revealing, and such is his very first use of the first-person pronoun. In the introduction to the work, after explaining that the commonwealth is an artificial man produced by man in an act that he likens to "the *let us make man*, pronounced by God in the creation," Hobbes states: "To describe the nature of this artificial man, I will consider [,] First, the *matter* thereof, and the *artificer*, both of which is *Man*" (*Leviathan*, 7). What "I" will consider in order to describe this artificial man seems innocuous enough, with the philosopher methodically explaining the construction of the book that contains a scientific explanation of the construction of the commonwealth. And yet this statement follows a breathtakingly bold pronouncement of Promethean ambition of imitating God. Nay, once we have read chapter 13 on the natural condition of mankind, of remedying the divine creation by an act of human will with Hobbes's urging and guidance, we realize: Let *us* make Leviathan.

The tension between Hobbes as civil scientist propounding universal truths about the commonwealth and Hobbes as innovator and even creator glimpsed in this first use of the first-person pronouns can be seen at a number of junctures where he steps forward in his role as author. One amusingly demure example comes when he argues that a principal duty of the sovereign is to instruct the people in the main tenets of civil science: "It is therefore manifest, that the instruction of the people, dependeth wholly, on the right teaching of youth in the universities. But are not (may some man say) the universities of England learned enough already to do that? or is it you, will undertake to teach the universities. Hard questions." Hobbes then answers his imaginary interlocutor, responding to the first question that the universities have been the seat of seditious learning that have led to civil conflict: "But to the latter question, it is not fit, nor needful for me to say either aye, or no: for any man that sees what I am doing, may easily perceive what I think" (*Leviathan*, 228). If the sovereign by virtue of being authorized through the covenant that creates the great Leviathan has the authority to examine opinions and dictate that certain tenets should be taught, what is Hobbes's authority as author of *Leviathan*? If the civil science of *Leviathan* is true, universally and demonstrably, as Hobbes claims, then doesn't the truth of the doctrine itself authorize it? Not according to the doctrine of *Leviathan* itself.

The same tension comes out in the last chapter of the work. Explaining the workings of the Kingdom of Darkness, which reigns through the introduction of erroneous doctrines that redound to the benefit of priestcraft, he writes: "With the introduction of false, we may join also the suppression of true philosophy, by such men, as neither by lawful authority, nor sufficient study, are competent judges of the truth." Alluding to the condemnation of Galileo by the Catholic Church, he asks: "But what reason is there for it? Is it because such opinions are contrary to true religion? That cannot be, if they be true. Let therefore the truth be first examined by competent judges, or confuted by them that pretend to know the contrary" (*Leviathan*, 456). But what if the astronomer had been silenced by a proper political authority, a Hobbesian sovereign? Would such condemnation be any the less legitimate on Hobbesian grounds for not being examined by "competent judges"? No. At the very end of this chapter, then, Hobbes concludes: "And this is all I had a design to say, concerning the doctrine of the POLITICS. Which when I have reviewed, I shall willingly expose to the censure of my country"

(*Leviathan*, 465). Whatever the authority his work may have by being true, on the very basis of the doctrines propounded by the work itself, he must expose it to the judgment of the authorities.

Hobbes as author of *Leviathan* needs someone to complete his task, and so he must persuade and educate the reader. The first address to the reader comes at the end of the same introduction in which Hobbes first uses the first-person pronoun as author. After having counseled the reader to "read thyself" in order to learn "that for the similitude of the thoughts, and passions of one man, to the thoughts, and passions of another," he will be able to read the thoughts and passions of other men, Hobbes concludes: "And yet, when I shall have set down my own reading orderly, and perspicuously, the pains left another, will be only to consider, if he also find not the same in himself. For this kind of doctrine admitteth no other demonstration" (*Leviathan*, 8). The choice of the term *reading* here is interesting, for it could refer to Hobbes's own reading of himself—"read myself"—which he sets down in writing, or the reader's reading of himself—"read thyself"—having followed Hobbes's counsel, or, finally, the reader's reading of *Leviathan*. Ultimately, Hobbes requires a correspondence in the reader's experience as the "demonstration" of his reading. At several points in the text, therefore, Hobbes introduces the skeptical reader, as we saw above. Perhaps most famously, within his account of the natural condition of mankind as "a war, as of every man against every man," Hobbes pauses: "It may seem strange to some man, that has not well weighed these things; that nature should thus dissociate, and render men apt to invade, and destroy one another: and he may therefore, not trusting to this inference, made from the passions, desire perhaps to have the same confirmed by experience. Let him therefore consider with himself" (*Leviathan*, 84).

Finally, then, Hobbes hopes for a very specific reader of *Leviathan*. At the end of the second part of the work, "Of Commonwealth," Hobbes concludes:

> And thus far concerning the constitution, nature, and rights of sovereigns; and concerning the duties of subjects, derived from the principles of natural reason. And now, considering how different this doctrine is, from the practice of the greatest part of the world, especially of these western parts, that have received their moral learning from Rome, and Athens; and how much depth of moral philosophy is required, in them that have the administration of the sovereign power; I am at the point of believing this my labour, as useless, as the commonwealth of Plato. . . . But when I consider again, that the science of natural justice is the only science necessary for sovereigns. . . . I recover some hope,

that one time or other, this writing of mine, may fall into the hands of a sovereign, who will consider it himself, (for it is short, and I think clear), without the help of any interested, or envious interpreter; and by the exercise of entire sovereignty, in protecting the public teaching of it, convert this truth of speculation, into the utility of practice. (*Leviathan*, 244–45)

Here we have all of the elements of the author-reader interaction in *Leviathan* I have sketched so far. Hobbes at once proclaims the universality of his civil philosophy as derived from the "principles of natural reason" and concedes the novelty of his teaching. He proclaims his authorship of "this writing of mine," but needs a reader, a sovereign reader, to complete the reading, so to speak, and to convert the truth into practice. *Leviathan* is a book that must persuade and instruct.

Acknowledgments

I had the great good fortune to study with two of the best Rousseau scholars. Roger Masters first introduced me to Rousseau and taught me the demands and pleasures of close reading. Allan Bloom made me alive to the more rhetorical and literary elements of Rousseau's works, and especially *Emile*. I have also benefited over the years from the friendship and encouragement of another great scholar, Christopher Kelly. Among the generous people from whom I have learned, and who gave me advice on this project, are Tom Keymer, Ourida Mostefai, Michael O'Dea, and Julia Simon. I developed many of the themes of this book in my graduate seminars over the years, and I thank my students for what should perhaps be called their collaboration on this project. John Warner read the entire draft with care and offered useful suggestions. Amanda Dorney compiled the index. John Tryneski's enthusiasm for this project and his sound advice were crucial, and Chuck Myers continued with his support.

Versions of some of the chapters in this book appeared previously. A portion of chapter 1 was published in somewhat different form and coauthored with Sally Howard Campbell as "The Politic Argument of Rousseau's *Discourse on the Sciences and the Arts*," *American Journal of Political Science* 49 (2005): 819–29 (copyright Midwest Political Science Association; reprinted with permission). Chapter 3 is a much-revised and expanded version of "Do You See What I See? The Education of the Reader in Rousseau's *Emile*," *Review of Politics* 74 (2012): 443–63 (copyright Cambridge University Press; reprinted with permission). Finally, chapter 4 is a revised version of "The Illustrative Education of Rousseau's *Emile*," *American Political Science Review* 108 (2014): 533–46 (copyright Cambridge University Press; reprinted with permission).

Notes

Introduction

1 Rousseau does not explicitly list the *Social Contract* as among these principal works, but since he characterized the work as "a sort of appendix" to *Emile*, with the two works together making a "complete whole," I have included it. For his remark about *Emile* and the *Social Contract*, see Rousseau to Nicolas-Bonaventure Duchesne, 23 May 1762, *CC*, 10:281.

2 Rousseau to Marc-Michel Rey, 8 July 1758, *CC*, 5:111.

3 Velkley, *Being after Rousseau*, 33. Velkley compares Rousseau's thought and writing to Plato's (ibid., 37–38). See also Launay, "Rousseau écrivain," 214–19, on Rousseau as a dialogic and dialectical writer. Other scholars have emphasized the importance of Plato for Rousseau, though in very different ways. See, e.g., Cooper, "Human Nature and the Love of Wisdom"; Hendel, *Jean-Jacques Rousseau: Moralist*; Williams, *Rousseau's Platonic Enlightenment*.

4 Plutarch, "On the Glory of the Athenians," *Moralia* 347A.

5 Quintilian, *Institutio Oratoria*, quoted in Johnston, *Rhetoric of "Leviathan,"* 19–20.

6 E.g., Aricò, *Rousseau's Art of Persuasion in the "Nouvelle Héloïse,"* on the art of persuasion in *Julie*; and Beaudry, *Role of the Reader in Rousseau's "Confessions."*

7 Quoted by Yamashita, *Jean-Jacques Rousseau face au public*, 63–64, from the 1 December 1758 edition of the *Correspondence littéraire, philosophique, et critique*.

8 Russell, *History of Western Philosophy*, 623.

9 E.g., Cohen, *Rousseau: A Free Community of Equals*; Gauthier, *Rousseau: The Sentiment of Existence*; Neuhouser, *Rousseau's Critique of Inequality* and *Rousseau's Theodicy of Self-Love*.

10 Shklar, *Men and Citizens*, 1.

11 Melzer, *Natural Goodness of Man*, 2.

12 Rawls, *Lectures on the History of Political Philosophy*, 192.

13 Plato, *Gorgias* 462b–66a.

14 Plato, *Phaedrus* 274c–75b.

15 See, e.g., Dorter, "Plato's Use of the Dialogue Form"; Griswold, *Platonic Readings, Platonic Writings*, chaps 6–9. Not surprisingly, Russell, *History of Western Philosophy*, chaps. 14–18, does not attend to the form of Plato's works beyond calling them "dialogues" and treats Plato as a doctrinal philosopher.

16 For a discussion of the protreptic tradition in philosophy, see Collins, *Exhortations to Philosophy*.

17 On Hobbes's *Leviathan* and other writings, see Evrigenis, *Images of Anarchy*, and Johnston, *Rhetoric of "Leviathan."* On Smith's *Theory of Moral Sentiments* as a protreptic work, see Griswold, *Adam Smith and the Virtues of Enlightenment*. On Kant's *Groundwork*, see Satkunanandan, *Extraordinary Responsibility*, chap. 5.

18 Schlanger, *Trop dire ou trop peu*, esp. 79–92.

19 For a discussion of Rousseau's self-understanding as a philosopher and his criticisms of philosophy, see Kelly, *Rousseau as Author*, postscript.

20 Plato, *Phaedrus* 264b–c.

21 Quoted in Booth, *Rhetoric of Irony*, 88.

22 De Man, *Allegories of Reading*, 135.

23 Hirsch, *Validity in Interpretation*, esp. 16–17, 76, 173–98. The concept of the "hermeneutic circle" was developed largely in nineteenth- and twentieth-century German thought from Schleiermacher to Gadamer, but the basic idea is implicit in the concept of "logographic necessity" put forward by Socrates in Plato's *Phaedrus*.

24 Booth, *Rhetoric of Irony*, 13, 14–21.

25 Booth, *Rhetoric of Fiction*, 138.

26 See Beaudry, *Role of the Reader in Rousseau's "Confessions,"* 27; Yamashita, *Jean-Jacques Rousseau face au public*, 79–80.

27 Booth, *Rhetoric of Fiction*, 303–4.

28 Booth, *Rhetoric of Fiction*, 397–98. Swenson makes a similar argument and applies it to Rousseau: "Each text can be show to stage within its narrative the action of readers by the sort of *mise-en-abîme* so dear to literary criticism of the last thirty years, and thereby to provide a script or at least a model for its own reception" (*On Jean-Jacques Rousseau*, 25–26).

29 Booth, *Rhetoric of Irony*, 28, 40, 119, 204–6.

30 Booth, *Rhetoric of Irony*, 126.

31 Iser, *Implied Reader*, xi–xii.

32 Fish, *Surprised by Sin*, 1.

33 Iser, *Act of Reading*, 21, 27–29, 34.

34 Booth, *Rhetoric of Fiction*, 122–5.

35 Mall wrestles with the question of judging *Emile* by aesthetic versus philosophical criteria, a problem generated in part by Rousseau's choice of the hybrid treatise-novel for the work (*Emile, ou les figures de la fiction*, 1–11).

36 Textual exegesis: e.g., among book-length treatments, Cassirer, *Question of Jean-Jacques Rousseau*; Cooper, *Rousseau, Nature, and the Problem of the Good Life*; Goldschmidt, *Anthropologie et politique*; Masters, *Political Philosophy of*

Rousseau; Melzer, *Natural Goodness of Man*; Philonenko, *Jean-Jacques Rousseau et la pensée du malheur*; Strauss, *Natural Right and History* and "On the Intention of Rousseau." Analytic philosophy: see, e.g., Cohen, *Rousseau: A Free Community of Equals*; Dent, *Rousseau*; Neuhouser, *Rousseau's Critique of Inequality* and *Rousseau's Theodicy of Self-Love*.

37 Starobinski, *Jean-Jacques Rousseau: Transparency and Obstruction*. Of course, this assumption is a tempting one for his autobiographical writings in particular. In this case, one might instead view Rousseau's remarks about his forthright honesty and desire for transparency as intentionally adopting an authorial pose. We might entertain the possibility that Rousseau as author is the first knowingly to tempt the reader to put Jean-Jacques on the therapist's couch. For a study of the author-reader relationship in the *Confessions*, see Beaudry, *Role of the Reader in Rousseau's "Confessions."*

38 Shklar, *Men and Citizens*, 1. For other interpretations that emphasize sincerity or authenticity as Rousseau's aim, see Babbitt, *Rousseau and Romanticism*; Berman, *Politics of Authenticity*; Ferrara, *Modernity and Authenticity*.

39 For those who have grappled with this issue see, among others, Taylor interprets Rousseau as being concerned with authenticity (*Ethics of Authenticity*, chap. 3, and *Sources of the Self*, 362–63). Maguire argues that, at least outside his specifically philosophic works, Rousseau sought to convert his readers' imaginations to a "eudaemonic" conception of truth rather than a correspondence theory of truth (*Conversion of Imagination*, chaps. 3–4, esp. 204–6). Neidleman presents Rousseau as a specific type of truth seeker (*Rousseau's Ethics of Truth*, esp. chap. 3). For a different account of Rousseau on truthfulness in relation to his responsibility as an author, see Kelly, *Rousseau as Author*.

40 Starobinski, "Rousseau et l'éloquence," 195.

41 While this is generally true of Starobinski's landmark *Transparency and Obstruction*, his later writings on Rousseau do attend to his use of various rhetorical and literary devices.

42 Ellrich, *Rousseau and His Reader*, 17–24. Ellrich does not use the term *ideal reader* in the sense used in literary criticism.

43 Ellrich, *Rousseau and His Reader*, 55.

44 Strong, *Jean-Jacques Rousseau: The Politics of the Ordinary*, 8–9, 17–18.

45 Launay, "Rousseau écrivain," 211, 219; emphasis supplied.

46 Grimsley, "Rousseau and His Reader," 227, 233.

47 Goodman, *Criticism in Action*, 107. By contrast, she considers Diderot to be a "dialogic" author who invites the reader to participate in his critical enterprise (ibid., esp. chap. 6, beginning).

48 DeJean, *Literary Fortifications*, chap. 4.

49 Melzer, *Natural Goodness of Man*, 7–8.

50 Harvey, *Labyrinths of Exemplarity*, 121.

51 Collins, *Exhortations to Philosophy*, 17–18.

52 Maguire, *Conversion of Imagination*, 99, 104–5.

53 See Masters, *Political Philosophy of Rousseau*, chap. 5; Strauss, "On the Intention of Rousseau." For Rousseau as a writer in the esoteric tradition in philosophy, see Melzer, *Philosophy between the Lines*, 141, 274–75.

54 Launay, "Rousseau écrivain."

55 Anderson, "Starobinski on Rousseau," 121–24.

56 Starobinski, "Rousseau et l'éloquence," 188–89.

57 Baker, "Le route contraire," 133.

58 Schlanger, *Trop dire ou trop peu*, 8, 63–65.

59 Mall, *Emile, ou les figures de la fiction*. Like Mall, I have also been influenced in this regard by de Man, *Allegories of Fiction*.

60 Schaeffer, *Rousseau on Education, Judgment, and Freedom*.

61 Trousson, *Jean-Jacques Rousseau jugé par ses contemporains*. Perhaps the best-known such study is Robert Darnton's account of literary sensation sparked by *Julie* (*Great Cat Massacre*, chap. 6). Drawing on the flood of fan mail Rousseau received, especially from women, Darnton documents how readers expressed their identification with both the characters of *Julie* and its author and asked Rousseau to confirm the reality of the tale of the lovers or to confess that he was the model for St. Preux. Rousseau himself both encourages and thwarts these expectations in his readers through refusing to confirm whether he is the author rather than the editor of the letters and whether the characters are real or not. However, Darnton does not attend to the author-reader relationship as a literary device, although he seems to assume something like Starobinski's interpretation of Rousseau trying to establish a "transparent" relationship with his readers. This assumption has been questioned by Paige precisely through a reevaluation of the correspondence Darnton used in his study based on a different understanding of the more sophisticated expectations Rousseau and his readers would have based on the novelistic conventions of the time ("Rousseau's Readers Revisited").

Chapter One

1 Among those accepting Rousseau's claims that the *Discourse* is based on the same principle as his later works, see Black, *Rousseau's Critique of Science*; Campbell and Scott, "Politic Argument of Rousseau's *Discourse on the Sciences and the Arts*"; Goldschmidt, *Anthropologie et politique*; Gourevitch, "Rousseau on the Arts and Sciences"; Masters, *Political Philosophy of Rousseau*; Strauss, "On the Intention of Rousseau." Among those who argue that the *Discourse* is not philosophically mature, see Hope Mason, "Reading Rousseau's *First Discourse*"; Rosenblatt, *Rousseau and Geneva*, chap. 2; Starobinski, "Le premier *Discours* à l'occasion de deux cent cinquantième anniversaire de sa publication"; Wokler, "*Discours sur les sciences et les arts* and Its Offspring."

2 Academies usually first appointed members to read the submissions and select a number of finalists whose essays were read aloud. See Caradonna, *Enlightenment in Practice*, 57–65.

3   Henceforth in this chapter all references in the text are to the *Discourse on the Sciences and the Arts* (*Sciences*) unless otherwise noted.

4   See Caradonna, *Enlightenment in Practice*, 45.

5   For a treatment of academic prize competitions in France in the seventeenth and eighteenth centuries, see Caradonna, *Enlightenment in Practice*.

6   See Caradonna, *Enlightenment in Practice*, 121.

7   See Darnton, *Literary Underground of the Old Regime*.

8   See Caradonna, *Enlightenment in Practice*, 125–28.

9   See Black for a discussion of the various proposals made by scholars concerning the added passages (*Rousseau's Critique of Science*, Appendix 1).

10 This does not include the "Notice" preceding the work that Rousseau wrote in 1763 for a collected edition of his work (*Sciences*, 5). In his edition of the *Discourse*, Allard uses the same procedure of distinguishing between the text of the original discourse and the paratextual matter Rousseau added for the published version in order to try to identify the two passages Rousseau added to the main text. See Allard, *Rousseau sur les sciences et les arts*, as summarized in Black, *Rousseau's Critique of Science*, Appendix 1.

11 Genette, *Paratexts*. The only scholar of whom I am aware to discuss the paratextual elements of the *Discourse on the Sciences and the Arts* in Genette's terms is Yamashita, *Jean-Jacques Rousseau face au public*, 39–44.

12 This is the reason given in the records of the Academy of Dijon, but Caradonna suggests that the academicians ceased reading Rousseau's entry when they recognized its author, not wanting to repeat the controversy sparked by the first *Discourse* (*Enlightenment in Practice*, 140–41). See also Tisserand, *Les concurrents de J.-J. Rousseau à l'académie de Dijon pour le prix de 1754*, 28–29.

13 E.g., Aristotle, *Rhetoric* 1358a–59a.

14 Descartes, *Discours sur la méthode, in Œuvres et lettres*, 125, 127.

15 Rousseau's emphasis on the spoken character of the *Discourse* would appear to be unusual. Of the eleven extant entries for the 1754 competition, which do not include Rousseau's lost submission, only two (numbers 1 and 10) even address the audience as *Messieurs* (number 1 several times, number 10 only once at the outset), much less speak of the "judges," "tribunal," etc., as does Rousseau. See Tisserand's collection of these entries in *Les concurrents de J.-J. Rousseau à l'académie de Dijon pour le prix de 1754*.

16 See Caradonna, *Enlightenment in Practice*, 123–27.

17 See esp. Black, *Rousseau's Critique of Science*, 25–27; Masters, *Political Philosophy of Rousseau*, 205–8.

18 Ovid, *Tristia* 5.10.37.

19 As previous scholars have noted, Rousseau characterizes Ovid in the text of the *Discourse* as one of the "obscene authors" of corrupted Rome (15), and he thereby raises an interpretive issue concerning his apparent condemnation of the arts in the work by paradoxically associating himself with a poet, and even an "obscene" one. See esp. Masters, *Political Philosophy of Rousseau*, 208.

20 Ovid, *Tristia* 1.1: "Parue—nec inuideo—sine me, liber, ibis in urbemi."

21 Horace, *Ars poetica* 5.25.

22 See esp. Black, *Rousseau's Critique of Science*, chap. 6; Kavanagh, *Writing the Truth*, 125–29; Masters, *Political Philosophy of Rousseau*, 225–26.

23 Bredekamp, "Thomas Hobbes' Visual Strategies"; Skinner, *Hobbes and Republican Liberty*, 182–98; Strong, "How to Write Scripture."

24 Maloney, "Hobbes, Savagery, and International Anarchy"; Skinner, *Hobbes and Republican Liberty*, 98–103.

25 Skinner, *Hobbes and Republican Liberty*, 7–10.

26 Discussing the cost of executing engravings in mid-eighteenth-century Scotland, Sher reports that the cost of a single engraving for a certain book accounted for 40 percent of the book's total production cost (*Enlightenment and the Book*, 167).

27 Rousseau to Sophie d'Houdetot, 26 December 1757 (*CC*, 4:408). Translation by Black, *Rousseau's Critique of Science*, 165 n. 6.

28 See Rousseau to Sophie d'Houdetot, 26 December 1757 (*CC*, 4:408).

29 Stewart, "*Julie* et ses légends," 19. See also Labrosse, *Lire au XVIIIe siècle*, chap. 5; Marshall, *Frame of Art*, chap. 4; Ramon, "Autour des sujets d'estampes de *La nouvelle Héloïse*"; Stewart, *Engraven Desire*, 19–24.

30 In fact, one of his critics notes how Rousseau alters the Prometheus myth (*Refutation by an Academician* [Lecat], in *CW*, 2:156).

31 Plato, *Phaedrus* 274c–75b.

32 See Yamashita on Rousseau addressing the problem of writing as articulated in *Phaedrus* in general and on the frontispiece in particular (*Jean-Jacques Rousseau face au public*, 13–14, 42–44). Meier argues that the frontispiece satisfies the conditions of Platonic rhetoric as seen in *Phaedrus* (*On the Happiness of the Philosophic Life*, 6–8).

33 Black, *Rousseau's Critique of Science*; Goldschmidt, *Anthropologie et politique*; Gourevitch, "Rousseau on the Arts and Sciences"; Masters, *Political Philosophy of Rousseau*; Strauss, "On the Intention of Rousseau."

34 Horace, *Ars poetica* 5.25.

35 See Black, *Rousseau's Critique of Science*, 27–29.

36 See Cicero, *De Inventione* 1.18; [pseudo-] Cicero, *Ad C. Herennium de ratione dicendi* 1.2 ff. For a discussion of the purpose of an exordium in contemporary texts, see Goldschmidt, *Anthropologie et politique*, 23–24.

37 At the end of the *Discourse*, Rousseau also adduces an interior authority of judging when he urges "vulgar men" such as himself "to return into oneself and to listen to the voice of one's conscience in the silence of the passions" (35–36).

38 See *Reply* [by the king of Poland], in *CW*, 2:29; *Refutation of the Observations* [Lecat], *CW*, 2:56–57; *Refutation by an Academician* [Lecat], *CW*, 2:134, 171–2.

39 In an early essay predating the *Discourse*, "Idée de la méthode dans la composition d'un livre," Rousseau states that one should begin one's argument by appearing to agree with accepted opinion (1959–95, 2:1242–44). See Goldschmidt for a reading of the *Discourse* that takes this early essay for its guide

(*Anthropologie et politique*, 21 ff.). See also Yamashita, *Jean-Jacques Rousseau face au public*, 39–40.

40 Rousseau is more explicit about his opposition to this school of thought in the *Preface to Narcissus*: "Writers all regard as the masterpiece of the politics of our century the sciences, arts, luxury, commerce, laws, and the other ties which, by tightening among men the ties of society from personal interest, put them all in mutual dependence, give them reciprocal needs, and common interests, and oblige each of them to cooperate for the happiness of the others in order to be able to attain his own" (*CW*, 2:193). See Keohane, "'Masterpiece of Policy in Our Century'"; Mendham, "Enlightened Gentleness as Soft Indifference"; Rosenblatt, *Rousseau and Geneva*, chap. 2.

41 In the *Preface to Narcissus*, Rousseau emphasizes the difference between reality and appearance even more strongly. The sciences and the arts, he explains, "destroy virtue, but leave its public simulacrum, which is always a fine thing," here adding a note: "This simulacrum is a certain softness of morals that sometimes replaces their purity, a certain appearance of order that prevents horrible confusion, a certain admiration of beautiful things that keeps the good ones from falling completely into obscurity. It is a vice that takes the mask of virtue, not as hypocrisy in order to deceive and betray, but under this loveable and sacred effigy to escape from the horror that it has of itself when it sees itself uncovered" (*CW*, 2:196 and n.).

42 Williams relates the distinction between appearances and reality in this passage to the allegory of the cave in Plato's *Republic* (*Rousseau's Platonic Enlightenment*, 137–39).

43 See Black, *Rousseau's Critique of Science*, Appendix 1.

44 In the *Dialogues* Rousseau wrote of his early writings, including the *Discourse on the Sciences and the Arts*, that he tried "to destroy that magical illusion which gives us a stupid admiration for the instruments of our misfortunes and to correct that deceptive assessment that makes us honor pernicious talents and scorn useful virtues" (*CW*, 1: 213).

45 On this point, see also Black (*Rousseau's Critique of Science*, 120) and Goldschmidt (*Anthropologie et politique*, 56).

46 The following two sections borrow in part, but with a different emphasis, from Campbell and Scott, "Politic Argument of Rousseau's *Discourse on the Sciences and the Arts*."

47 As he later explained: "I made my proposition general: I assigned this first of the decadence of morals to the first moment of the cultivation of Letters in all the countries of the world, and I found the progress of these two things was always in proportion" (*Letter to Raynal*, *CW*, 2:25; see also *Observations*, *CW*, 2:48; *Preface to Narcissus*, *CW*, 2:190).

48 See Masters, *Political Philosophy of Rousseau*; Strauss, "On the Intention of Rousseau." Black does analyze the metaphor (*Rousseau's Critique of Science*, 75–76), and in this regard he is in part following the article by Campbell and Scott, "Politic Argument of Rousseau's *Discourse on the Sciences and the Arts*."

49 Plutarch, "How to Profit by One's Enemies," *Moralia*, 2:7–9. The subject of Plutarch's essay is also relevant for the *Discourse* for his theme is how to find remedies within what is harmful, which for Rousseau would mean finding beneficial effects of the sciences and the arts which are otherwise harmful.

50 See Black, *Rousseau's Critique of Science*, 146–50; Kavanagh, *Writing the Truth*, 125–29; Masters, *Political Philosophy of Rousseau*, 225–26.

51 See Kelly, "Rousseau and the Case for (and against) Censorship," 1239.

52 In the *Final Reply* he explains: "The vanity and idleness that have engendered our sciences have also engendered luxury. The taste for luxury always accompanies that of letters, and the taste for letters often accompanies that for luxury. All these things are rather faithful companions, because they are all the work of the same vices" (*CW*, 2, 112). See also *Observations*, *CW*, 2:48–51.

53 In the *Observations*, he explains: "I had not said either that luxury was born from the sciences, but that they were born together and that one scarcely went without the other. This is how I would arrange the genealogy. The first source of evil is inequality. From inequality came wealth, for those words poor and rich are relative, and everywhere that men are equal, there are neither rich nor poor. From wealth are born luxury and idleness. From luxury come the fine arts and from idleness the sciences" (*CW*, 2:48).

54 In the *Preface to Narcissus*, Rousseau explains that the taste for letters "cannot be born in this way in a whole nation except from two bad sources which study maintains and increases in turn, namely idleness and the desire to distinguish oneself" (*CW*, 2:191).

55 Trousson, *Socrate devant Voltaire, Diderot et Rousseau*, 112–15.

56 See Masters, *Political Philosophy of Rousseau*, 239–41; Orwin, "Rousseau's Socratism," 177–79; Trousson, *Socrate devant Voltaire, Diderot et Rousseau*, 112–15. For the most extensive examination of the changes Rousseau makes, see Black, *Rousseau's Critique of Science*, 106–14 and Appendix 2.

57 The following interpretation is indebted in part to Orwin, "Rousseau's Socratism," 179–82.

58 Plato, *Apology of Socrates* 22e; see 21d.

59 See Black, *Rousseau's Critique of Science*, 114–19.

60 On the irony, see Masters, *Political Philosophy of Rousseau*, 230–33. On the passage being a potential addition, see Black, *Rousseau's Critique of Science*, Appendix 1.

61 For d'Alembert's response to Rousseau, see "Preliminary Discourse" to the *Encyclopedia*, 103–4. For a study of the "Preliminary Discourse" as a whole as a response to Rousseau, see Goldschmidt, *Études de philosophie moderne*, 81–128. Finally, for an examination of Rousseau's reference to d'Alembert's criticism in his *Observations*, see Tully and Scott, "Rousseau's *Observations* on Inequality and the Causes of Moral Corruption."

62 In the *Preface to Narcissus* Rousseau writes: "I admit that there are some sublime geniuses who know how to pierce through the veils in which the truth is enveloped, some privileged souls, capable of resisting the stupid-

ity of vanity, base jealously, and other passions that engender the taste for letters. . . . It is fitting for them alone to exert themselves in study for the benefit of everyone, and this exception even confirms the rule; for if all men were Socrates, science would not be harmful to them, they would have no need of it" (*CW*, 2:195).

Chapter Two

1   Henceforth in this chapter all references in the text are to the *Discourse on Inequality* (*Inequality*) unless otherwise noted.

2   See esp. Masters, *Political Philosophy of Rousseau*, 118. See also Cooper, *Rousseau, Nature, and the Problem of the Good Life*, 17–18, 39; Plattner, *Rousseau's State of Nature*.

3   Gourevitch makes a similar argument that the "putative pure state of nature is a thought-experiment, a systematic 'bracketing' of all artifice and of all moral needs and relations. . . . It is to extrapolate to the limits or conditions of humanity" ("Rousseau's Pure State of Nature," 37).

4   Similar interpretations can be found in Gourevitch, "Rousseau's Pure State of Nature"; Marks, *Perfection and Disharmony*; and Velkley, *Being after Rousseau*, chap. 2.

5   Rousseau, *Confessions*, *CW*, 5:326: "It had been written to compete for the prize, thus I sent it, but I was certain in advance that it would not get it, knowing well that the prizes of Academies are not established for pieces of this stuff."

6   It has also been claimed that they ceased reading it when they realized it was by Rousseau, given in part the controversy stirred up by the first *Discourse*. See Tisserand, *Les concurrents de J.-J. Rousseau à l'académie de Dijon pour le prix de 1754*; Caradonna, *Enlightenment in Practice*, 140–41.

7   Almost all of the extant submissions for the prize essay competition were divided into two parts, perhaps in part because the question asked by the Academy of Dijon was in two parts: the origin of inequality and whether it is authorized by natural law. See the other entries compiled in Tisserand, *Les concurrents de J.-J. Rousseau à l'académie de Dijon pour le prix de 1754*.

8   See Kelly, *Rousseau as Author*.

9   See Klausen, *Fugitive Rousseau*, 78–79 and n. 10, quoting Launay quoting the iconographical dictionary. Klausen suggests the cap represents a liberty cap, but not a specifically Phrygian one.

10   See Zaretsky and Scott, *Philosophers' Quarrel*, 36.

11   See Aristotle, *Politics* 1.5.1254a. The source is misidentified on the original edition as coming from *Politics* 1.2.

12   See esp. Masters, *Political Philosophy of Rousseau*, 112–13.

13   That is, p. 147 being the relevant page of the edition I am using. Furthermore, also following this edition and the Pléiade edition, I use roman numerals (I, II, III, etc.) for the notes. As I will discuss below, Rousseau originally used a different system of notes combining numbers and letters. In the original edition, the note to which he refers the reader on the frontispiece is n. 13.

14 Interestingly, the story of the North American chief assessing the utility of the products of the arts that relates to the frontispiece of the *Discourse on Inequality* parallels the myth from Plato's *Phaedrus* of King Thamos judging the utility of the arts presented by Thoth, including writing, which relates to the frontispiece of the *Discourse on the Sciences and the Arts*.

15 The passage in the original Rousseau is quoting (as he specifies, from Kolben and drawn from the collection *Histoire des voyages*), also uses the word "discourse" (*discours*) here. Since Rousseau made some changes in the quoted passage, his decision to retain this word should be seen as intentional.

16 In the *Confessions* he later explained: "Before my departure from Paris, I had sketched out the dedication of my *Discourse on Inequality*. I finished it at Chambéry and dated it from the same place, judging that it was better not to date it either from France or from Geneva in order to avoid all quibbling" (*CW*, 5:329).

17 See Masters, *Political Philosophy of Rousseau*, 192–94. In a letter to M. Perdiau dated 28 November 1754, Rousseau admits that his praise of Geneva is a calculated exaggeration (*CC*, 3:55–60). For the controversy over the *Social Contract* and Geneva, see Rousseau's *Letters Written from the Mountain*. See also Rosenblatt, *Rousseau and Geneva*, 178–85.

18 A point also made by Strong, *Jean-Jacques Rousseau: The Politics of the Ordinary*, 35.

19 Compare Masters, who argues that the notes to the *Discourse on Inequality* have the primary purpose of providing potential scientific evidence for Rousseau's inquiry into human nature, for example as found in the leading natural scientist of his time, Buffon (*Political Philosophy of Rousseau*, 123–24).

20 Masters, *Political Philosophy of Rousseau*, 113–15.

21 In discussing the statue of Glaucus, Velkley writes: "Rousseau seems to follow some aspects of the Platonic account of knowing: knowing must proceed through images. It begins with unreflective assent to the image, following by seeing the image as mere image. . . . The Glaucus analogy is a prime example of Rousseau's mastery of the Platonic art of educating through images, which he employs in every writing as part of his philosophic rhetoric" (*Being after Rousseau*, 37–38).

22 See Velkley, *Being after Rousseau*, chap. 1.

23 For a kindred argument, see Marks, *Perfection and Disharmony*, chap. 1.

24 Persius, *Satires* 3.71–73. Rousseau may have taken the quotation from Montaigne's "On the Education of Children" (*Complete Essays*, II.26, 116–17). If so, the context is interesting, for Montaigne has just written: "This great world . . . is the mirror in which we must look at ourselves to recognize [or know—*connaitre*] ourselves from the proper angle. In short, I want it to be the book of my student. . . . To these examples [from the world], may properly be fitted all the most profitable lessons of philosophy, by which human actions must be measured as their rule. He will be told . . . ," and here Mon-

taigne quotes the passage from Persius from which Rousseau draws his epigraph.

25 In fact, a pirated version of the *Discourse on Inequality*, also published in 1755, moved the Notice to the very outset of the work.

26 The actual wording of the announcement for the prize had the word *source* where Rousseau has *origin*.

27 See Rousseau, *CC*, 2:Appendice 98. My thanks to Michael O'Dea for this reference.

28 On Rousseau's substitution of judges, see Masters, *Political Philosophy of Rousseau*, 107.

29 See Masters, *Political Philosophy of Rousseau*, 111–18.

30 Velkley also notes Rousseau's use of visual imagery and argues that his account of the pure state of nature is an "imaginative construction" (*Being after Rousseau*, 41). Goldschmidt characterizes the image as a "proposition" that begins the "rhetorical processes" of Rousseau's argument (*Anthropologie et politique*, 223).

31 For a discussion of the production of the 1792 edition, see Birn, *Forging Rousseau*.

32 Meier, *Jean-Jacques Rousseau, Diskurs über die Ungleichheit*.

33 Goodman makes a similar argument concerning the narrative pacing of the two parts of the *Discourse*, including with regard to the distribution of notes (*Criticism in Action*, chap. 5, esp. 144).

34 On Rousseau's supposed primitivism, see Lovejoy, "Supposed Primitivism of Rousseau's *Discourse on Inequality*."

35 Masters, *Political Philosophy of Rousseau*, 115–17.

36 See Velkley, *Being after Rousseau*, chap. 2, and esp. n. 14. See also Gourevitch, who writes: "Human life may always, everywhere, necessarily, be a mixture of the natural and the artificial or conventional, and it may be perfectly 'natural' that this be so" ("Rousseau's Pure State of Nature," 34).

37 Goldschmidt makes a similar point about the timelessness of Rousseau's account of natural man in the main text and how the notes disrupt this (*Anthropologie et politique*, 238, 246–47).

38 For an analysis of Rousseau's apparent-versus-true argument concerning pity, see Schwarze and Scott, "Mutual Sympathy and the Moral Economy." We argue that that Rousseau calculatedly overstates the role pity plays in natural man, among other reasons in order to make the state of nature seem more peaceful than it truly is, and this is seen in his polemic against Hobbes. Although we do not explicitly focus on the visual imagery Rousseau uses in his discussion of pity, it is pervasive and important, as should not be surprising given that pity requires seeing another being as similar to oneself, as a *semblable*. Two examples of his use of visual imagery will suffice. First, he adduces various observations of animal behavior as supposed proof of the naturalness of pity—for example, horses not trampling on a living being or cattle lowing as they enter a slaughterhouse—as supposed proof of the naturalness of pity (83). Yet, apart from the fact that these are

examples of animal and not human behavior, one might reasonably interpret these behaviors as stemming from self-love and not pity (see also Boyd,
"Pity's Pathologies Portrayed," 529; Cooper, *Rousseau, Nature, and the Problem of the Good Life*, 96–97; Masters, *Political Philosophy of Rousseau*, 140).
Second, he cites Mandeville's description of a prisoner (*Fable of the Bees*,
1:155-56) witnessing a child being dismembered by a wild beast outside his
prison cell as an example of the naturalness of pity. While the reader is thus
invited to identify with the prisoner observing this spectacle, this example
is at best an instance of the activity of pity in developed human beings, not
in natural man, and one might conjecture that the prisoner would avert his
eyes if he could to avoid the pangs of pity (83–85). His entire account of pity
might be characterized as a challenge to the reader's ability to discriminate
an apparent versus true argument.

Chapter Three

1 Rousseau to Philibert Cramer, 13 October 1764, *CC*, 21:248.
2 Henceforth in this chapter all references in the text are to *Emile* (*Emile*)
   unless otherwise noted.
3 Vanpée, "Rousseau's *Emile ou de l'éducation*," 158–59. She continues: "The
   text conveys its pedagogical mission in at least two modes: as a story describing the process by which an orphaned child will be educated . . . and thus
   become the ideal pedagogue of his own offspring; and as a performative
   discourse enacting the very process it describes and implicating the reader
   as the agent by whose means its transmission proceeds" (ibid., 159). See
   also Harvey, *Labyrinths of Exemplarity*, 121; Yamashita, *Jean-Jacques Rousseau
   face au public*, 100.
4 Iser, *Implied Reader*, xi–xii.
5 Harvey, *Labyrinths of Exemplarity*, 132.
6 Jimack suggests that Rousseau chose the name "Sophie" because he was
   still infatuated with Sophie d'Houdetot and therefore sees Sophie as an
   extension of Julie from *Julie, or The New Heloise* (*La genèse et la rédaction de
   l'"Emile,"* 200).
7 Other interpretations of the choice of name are of course possible, including the possibility that Rousseau is echoing and revising Plato's *Symposium*,
   with Sophie being the object of Emile's *eros* instead of philosophic wisdom
   (*sophia*) in Plato.
8 Seneca, *De Ira* 2.13.
9 In the "Profession of Faith of the Savoyard Vicar," the Vicar will adduce the
   goodness of the author of nature from the order of the universe (272–75) and
   will confront the evident disorder in the human realm by putting forward
   the consoling teaching that we must have an immaterial soul that enables
   God to restore the moral order in the afterlife (278–83).
10 Harvey argues that Rousseau's addresses to readers, including both invitations and challenges, are essentially pedagogical in purpose (*Labyrinths
   of Exemplarity*, 132).

11   Formey, *Anti-Emile*, 35. Similarly: "The example of Emile proves nothing; it is a fiction" (ibid., 77). Ellrich also uses Formey as an example of an actual contemporary reader of *Emile* to analyze the education of Rousseau's imaginary pupil (*Rousseau and His Reader*, 51–55). Trousson notes that most contemporary reactions to *Emile* focused on the supposedly chimerical character of the educational method (*Jean-Jacques Rousseau jugé par ses contemporains*, 272–73).

12   For another interpretation of *Emile* that notes the device of comparing examples of other children to the exemplary case of Emile, see Mall, *Emile, ou les figures de la fiction*, 75 ff.

13   For a general discussion of the "Favre version" of *Emile*, see Rousseau, *OC*, 4:xlii–lxxxvii.

14   Specifically, Emile is introduced at p. 110 in *Collected Writings* edition of the "Favre Manuscript" (*CW*, 13: 110), which is equivalent to p. 180 in the Bloom edition of *Emile*.

15   Since writing this book, I have learned from Jimmy Swenson that the Pléiade edition of the Favre Manuscript is incomplete, and that the editors chose to reproduce a portion of the original manuscript, which continues past the point I have noted. Swenson is now editing a full version of the manuscript.

16   Jimack, *La genèse et la rédaction de l'"Emile,"* 195.

17   Coleman, "Characterizing Rousseau's *Emile*," 767. See also Mall (*Emile, ou les figures de la fiction*, 3): "The fiction—hypothetical or novelistic—does not come to be added to the treatise, is not an ornament or adjunct, is not a weakness of the work, but on the contrary constitutes the sole condition of the possibility of the text, and can alone establish its authority." See ibid., 20–21, for a more general argument against Jimack.

18   Rousseau, *Favre Manuscript of "Emile,"* CW, 13:14–16. For other instances in the original version of comparing pupils or other similar devices, all of them rather incidental, see ibid., 37–38, 57, 94, 101.

19   Formey comments with unwitting accuracy: "M. R. confounds his Emile with his Emile. Emile succeeds as so desired: so the method that forms him is excellent. But who is Emile? Let him be shown, him or his like!" (*Anti-Emile*, 86).

20   As Grimsley explains: "Rousseau knows that he and his reader hold opposite points of view and he soon emphasizes their different attitudes by changing the 'nous' into 'vous' and 'moi.' It is his reader, not Jean-Jacques, who goes against nature. . . . Through his method of confrontation Rousseau seeks to challenge his reader's perspective" ("Rousseau and His Reader," 229–30).

21   Once again, Formey is unintentionally perceptive: "All that follows is merely *petitio principii*, into which the author perpetually falls. All young men raised by the ordinary method are flighty and fatuous. Emile on the contrary is perfection itself; he becomes such by the method of his governor, and with this method one can make as many Emiles as one likes" (*Anti-Emile*, 133).

22   Formey comments on the passage where Rousseau states that he founds himself on what he has seen rather than what he has imagined: "It is pre-

cisely entirely the contrary. Emile is a purely imaginary being, and he will never be seen except in the work for which he serves as title and subject" (*Anti-Emile*, 147).

23 DeJean complains that Rousseau's autobiographical intrusions damage the consistency of the narrative (*Literary Fortifications*, 140).

24 Schaeffer uses the language of "doubling" in her analysis of the same rhetorical technique (*Rousseau on Education, Judgment, and Freedom*, 12). In turn, Jimack suggests that these doublings of pupils, shifts from the authorial to the narrative and the tutorial "I," and other similar devices are due to the fact that, after deciding to give *Emile* a novelistic aspect by giving himself an imaginary pupil, Rousseau did not fully edit the final version of the work and therefore left contradictions and mistakes (*La genèse et la rédaction de l'"Emile*," chap. 8).

25 See Nichols on the importance of anger for Rousseau's project ("Rousseau's Novel Education in the *Emile*," 536–41).

26 See Hobbes, *On the Citizen*, Preface to the Readers, 11. See also *Discourse on Inequality*, 81–82, for Rousseau's argument against Hobbes on this point. For Augustine, see *Confessions* 1.7.

27 Kelly examines the naturalness of the sentiment of injustice by analyzing by apparently contradictory evidence in Rousseau concerning its naturalness or unnaturalness. He cites the example of the crying child as evidence on the side of the naturalness of the sentiment, not noting the fallibility of the witness. Kelly does however come to a similar conclusion about the unnaturalness of the sentiment of injustice and its (natural) emergence in the course of development ("On the Naturalness of the Sentiment of Injustice").

28 E.g., Strong, *Jean-Jacques Rousseau: The Politics of the Ordinary*, 117–18.

29 Locke, *Second Treatise of Government*, para. 33.

30 See Vargas for a similar emphasis on the problematic character of property in this story, especially in relation to the *Discourse on Inequality* (*Introduction à l'"Emile" de Rousseau*, 50–55).

31 Mall also questions the identity of the tutor and child, and of the latter she writes: "Emile is here only an example, and not an exemplary pupil" (*Emile, ou les figures de la fiction*, 105). In turn, Cherpack complains of this episode: "If it seems obvious that the heterogeneity of linguistic levels and the complexity of narration distract one from the ideas of his work and make the fictional sections seems both hallucinatory and inadequate as examples, it also seems clear that Rousseau, by blurring the identities of his major characters, was at pains to avoid drawing up a tight fictional contract that would permit the readers' surrender to illusion while reading these fictional sections" ("Narration and Meaning in Rousseau's *Emile*," 22).

32 E.g., Nichols, "Rousseau's Novel Education in the *Emile*," 538–40.

33 Scholars who have noticed how Rousseau doubles Emile (and Sophie, as we shall see in chap. 6) include Mall (*Emile, ou les figures de la fiction*, 97 ff.),

Schaeffer (*Rousseau on Education, Judgment, and Freedom*, 12), and Yamashita (*Jean-Jacques Rousseau face au public*, 102).

34 I will return to this passage in chap. 5 when discussing the "Profession of Faith of the Savoyard Vicar," which also involves the spectacle of the rising sun.

35 Earlier in book II, Rousseau writes: "As for me, I do not intend to teach geometry to Emile; it is he who will teach it to me; I will seek the relations, and he will find them, for I will seek them in a way as to make him find them" (145).

36 Mall also notes the difference here between "true" and "false" Emiles, and disputes Jimack's suggestion that Rousseau was confused (*Emile, ou les figures de la fiction*, 106–7).

37 Curiously, Rousseau will later write of Emile: "He loves his sister as he loves his watch, and his friend as his dog" (219). Of course, Emile has neither a sister nor a watch, and perhaps neither a friend nor a dog.

38 Formey uses the quotation as an epigraph to his *Anti-Emile*.

39 In a copy of *Emile*, Rousseau added a note for the 1765 edition admitting that his critic, Formey, is correct in pointing out that "The Crow and the Fox" is the second fable in the collection (*OC*, 4:352 n. (*a*)). He does not, however, correct the mistake in this case. He does correct the error, if it was one, when he returns to fables in book IV by adding a note (ibid., 542 n. (*a*).)

40 Similarly, an important source for *Emile*, Fénelon's *Traité de l'éducation des filles*, pairs fables and Bible stories as appropriate reading for young children and states that they are superior to the catechism, which is beyond children's grasp (chap. 6). Rousseau refers to this work at p. 369.

41 Jimack adduces this example as an instance where Rousseau simply forgot what he had earlier written (*La genèse et la rédaction de l' "Emile,"* 185 n.). Cherpack argues Rousseau's narrative in this story and others is inconsistent ("Narration and Meaning in Rousseau's *Emile*," 22–23). Nichols ("Rousseau's Novel Education in the *Emile*," 540) and Vargas (*Introduction à l' "Emile" de Rousseau*, 61, 76) both assume the earlier running story involved Emile.

42 Formey complains about the length of what he sees as the digression containing this story and also about its plausibility (*vraisemblance*) (*Anti-Emile*, 103–4). In a note to the 1765 edition at the point where the story begins, Rousseau writes: "I haven't been able to stop myself from laughing at reading a fine criticism by M. de Formey of this little story. . . . The spiritual M. de Formey hasn't been able to consider that this little scene was arranged and that the magician was coached in the role he was to play; for, indeed, I had not said this. But how many times, in turn, have I declared that I have not written for people who must be told everything?" (*OC*, 4:437 n. (*a*)). See also ibid., 450 n. (*a*). Ellrich is sympathetic to Formey, stating that there is no indication on Rousseau's part that this story was staged and, further, reporting that he asked thirty people whether they detected any such staging with the result that no one had (*Rousseau and His Reader*, 53). Likewise,

DeJean argues that this story is an example of Rousseau's lack of narrative control (*Literary Fortifications*, 152–59).

Chapter Four

1 Stewart, "*Julie* et ses legends," 19.
2 Henceforth in this chapter all references in the text are to *Emile, or On Education* (*Emile*) unless otherwise noted.
3 Eisen also designed a sixth engraving for the version of *Emile* published in the 1764 collected edition of Rousseau's works. The additional engraving serves as a frontispiece for the work as a whole and depicts a woman breast-feeding her child, testament to the influence of Rousseau's advice on that subject in the work. This subsequent engraving was not done under the author's direction, and so is beyond the present analysis.
4 See Rousseau to Nicolas-Bonaventure Duchesne, 29 April 1762, *CC*, 10: 222–23.
5 See Labrosse, *Lire au XVIIIe siècle*. See also Lewis for a treatment of how the original and especially later engravings included in *Julie* emphasized different aspects of the narrative (*Sensibility, Reading, and Illustration*, chap. 4).
6 Interestingly, however, later editions of the work beyond the author's control were illustrated in just that manner thus emphasizing the novelistic aspect of the Janus-faced treatise-novel (see Michel, "Les illustrations de l'*Emile* au XVIIIe siècle").
7 See Rousseau to Nicolas-Bonaventure Duchesne, 8 November 1761, *CC*, 9:223.
8 See Rousseau to Nicolas-Bonaventure Duchesne, 12 March 1762, *CC*, 10: 150–51.
9 The action of the engraving might also be read as evoking baptism, in which case it would allude to Rousseau's denial of original sin, which is implicit in the very first line of book I: "Everything is good, as it leaves the hands of the Author of things" (37). For his explicit denial of original sin, see *Letter to Beaumont*, *CW*, 9:31.
10 See Zerilli, *Signifying Woman*, 40.
11 Deneen, *Odyssey of Political Theory*, 135. See also Mall, *Emile, ou les figures de la fiction*, 18; Michel, "Les illustrations de l'*Emile* au XVIIIe siècle," 529, 539.
12 Seneca, *De Ira* 2.13.
13 See Deneen, *Odyssey of Political Theory*, 200.
14 Rousseau's phraseology about learning to die also recalls Socrates (Plato, *Phaedrus* 64a) and Montaigne (esp. "That to Philosophize Is to Learn to Die," *Complete Essays* I.20).
15 One possible source for Thetis and Chiron is Statius's unfinished *Achilleid*, a major theme of which is the disagreement between the Thetis and Chiron over Achilles' education. If Rousseau has this account in mind, then the suggestion would seem to be that mothers must be replaced by philosophers, or at least educated by them. My thanks to Jeff Black for pointing out this possible source to me.

16 See Homer, *Iliad* 4.219, 11.832.

17 Xenophon, *Cynegeticus* 1.

18 Machiavelli, *The Prince*, chap. 18.

19 If the frontispiece to book I and to *Emile* as a whole depicting Thetis dipping her son into a river also recalls baptism, perhaps the offering of an apple to the innocent child also references the scriptural account. This possibility is further underscored by the fact that the story in book II, where the reference to the engraving of Chiron and Achilles occurs, involves pride.

20 For the importance of sight in the education of the reader and in relation to the story involving running, see Schaeffer, *Rousseau on Education, Judgment, and Freedom*, 43–50.

21 Curiously, however, the tutor will later use hunting to divert Emile by putting him off the scent of his nascent passions: "Diana has been presented as the enemy of love, and the allegory is quite accurate. . . . I do not want Emile's whole youth to be spent in killing animals, and I do not even pretend to justify in every respect this ferocious passion. It is enough for me that it serves to suspend a more dangerous passion" (320–21).

22 Michel, "Les illustrations de l'*Emile* au XVIIIe siècle," 529.

23 See Schaeffer, "Utility of Ink."

24 Did Rousseau originally have in mind another subject for an engraving to represent book IV as a whole? Ulysses would have been a logical choice. Consider a reference to Ulysses near the beginning of book IV within a warning about the child's budding sexuality: "Ulysses, O wise Ulysses, be careful. The goatskins you closed with so much care are open. The winds are already loose. No longer leave the tiller for an instant, or all is lost" (212). Similarly, toward the end of book IV the tutor warns Emile: "Just as Ulysses, moved by the Sirens' song and seduced by the lure of the pleasures, cried out to his crew to unchain him, so you will want to break the bonds which hinder you" (316). Ulysses would be an appropriate subject for book IV both for novelistic reasons, since the story of Emile's wandering begins there and continues into book V, and for theoretical reasons, because the taming of Ulysses' wily pride and his return to domesticity would parallel Rousseau's reinterpretation of the story of Achilles in the engravings for the first two books. Finally, the choice of Ulysses as a subject for book IV would have given symmetry to *Emile* as a whole, with the first two books relating the story of Achilles and the last two that of Ulysses.

25 For discussions of the relationship between musical language and politics, especially founding, see Kelly, "'To Persuade without Convincing,'" and Scott, "Rousseau and the Melodious Language of Freedom."

26 Women are a central feature of the Orpheus story as related in Ovid's *Metamorphoses*, which, based on various details of the engraving of Orpheus, seems to be Rousseau's principal source. Most notably, the first and principal story in Ovid's telling is of Orpheus's failed attempt to bring back Eurydice from the underworld, after which he swears off women and then

sings of the gods (*Metamorphoses* 10.1–142), and then of love, generally ill-fated; the last story is of Orpheus's death by being torn apart by Maenads (ibid., 11.1–66).

27 See Deneen, *Odyssey of Political Theory*.

28 See Homer, *Odyssey* 10.281 ff. Rousseau frames the narrative of book V not in relation to the *Odyssey*, but to Fénelon's *Telemachus*. I discuss this framing in chap. 6.

29 See Homer, *Odyssey* 10.293–301, 321–24.

30 See, e.g., Okin, *Women in Western Political Thought*; Weiss, *Gendered Community*; Zerilli, *Signifying Woman*.

31 Parker, *Literary Fat Ladies*, 207–8.

Chapter Five

1 Rousseau did, however, make at least one separate manuscript copy of the "Profession," which he presented to his friend Moultou (see Rousseau, *Oeuvres complètes (Edition thématique du tricentenaire)*, 8:760 ed. n. 1). One of the first to publish part of the "Profession" separately was, curiously enough, Voltaire. Specifically, Voltaire published the second part of the "Profession," the part containing a critique of miracles and Scripture and a defense of toleration, in his *Recueil nécessaire* (1765). See Scott, "Between Religious Fanaticism and Philosophical Fanaticism."

2 E.g., MacLean, *The Free Animal*, chap. 3; Douglass, *Hobbes and Rousseau*, 12–13; Masson, *La religion de J.-J. Rousseau*; Cranston, *Noble Savage*, 192 ff.; O'Hagan, *Rousseau*, 237 ff.; Williams, *Rousseau's Platonic Enlightenment*, chap. 3. For examples of scholars who distinguish between Rousseau's own views and those of the Savoyard Vicar, see Emberley, "Rousseau versus the Savoyard Vicar"; Masters, *Political Philosophy of Rousseau*, chap. 2; Plattner, *Rousseau's State of Nature*, 43.

3 De Man, *Allegories of Reading*, 226.

4 Many scholars do discuss the "Profession," but they give at best passing attention to the narrative frame, mainly to remark on the change of tutor from Jean-Jacques to the Vicar and of pupil from Emile to the young proselyte, whom they almost always presume to be the young Jean-Jacques Rousseau. See de Man, *Allegories of Reading*; Dent, *Rousseau*; Hendel, *Jean-Jacques Rousseau: Moralist*; Masson, *La religion de J.-J. Rousseau*; Masters, *Political Philosophy of Rousseau*; Nichols, "Rousseau's Novel Education in the *Emile*"; O'Hagan, *Rousseau*; Schaeffer, *Rousseau on Education, Judgment, and Freedom*; Vargas, *Introduction à l'"Emile" de Rousseau*; Williams, *Rousseau's Platonic Enlightenment*.

5 Meier, *On the Happiness of the Philosophic Life*, 229; see also 237. Meier presents perhaps the lengthiest existing analysis of the narrative frame (ibid., 229–37). He notes many of the same things I do concerning the characters and capacities of the youth and the Vicar, but he does not relate them to the problems of rhetoric and writing raised by Rousseau's dialogue with Plato's *Phaedrus*.

6   Henceforth in this chapter all references in the text are to *Emile* (*Emile*) unless otherwise noted.

7   Horace, *Odes* 2.1.7–8. Horace is addressing Asinius Pollio concerning his writing a history of the civil wars. Pollio took part in the wars either as an opponent of Octavian or having remained neutral, so his writing a history of the civil wars in 23 BCE, soon after Octavian had become effective sole ruler as Augustus, the topic was a potentially hot one.

8   Meier also notes the change and how doing so Rousseau applies the quotation to himself (*On the Happiness of the Philosophic Life*, 218 and n. 11).

9   Juvenal, *Satires* 4.91. Rousseau first uses this motto, and so translates it, in his *Letter to d'Alembert* (*CW*, 10:348 n.). The context of the line in Juvenal may be revealing. The dictate to dedicate life to telling the truth is ironically said of Quintus Crispus, a bottle companion of the emperors who is said by Juvenal to have been capable of giving good advice but instead remained quiet out of caution. Perhaps truth telling for Rousseau is consistent with sometimes remaining quiet.

10 See Kelly, *Rousseau as Author*.

11 Schaeffer also emphasizes the role of judgment in assessing the "Profession" on the reader's part (*Rousseau on Education, Judgment, and Freedom*, esp. 129).

12 Hume, *Essays Moral, Political, and Literary* I.15–18. The first two editions of the *Essays* (1741 and 1742) were published anonymously, and the essays on philosophical characters were published in the second edition. Later editions were published under Hume's name.

13 For an analysis of Rousseau's discussion of lying in relation to the structure of the *Reveries*, see Butterworth, "Interpretative Essay," 181–89. See also Gourevitch, "Rousseau on Lying."

14 E.g., Ellrich (*Rousseau and His Reader*, 58–60); Nichols ("Rousseau's Novel Education in the *Emile*," 545); Strong (*Jean-Jacques Rousseau: The Politics of the Ordinary*, 125), who states: "The narrator of the story drops the third person and tells the reader that the young man is actually the same *I* as the *I* of the tutor"; and Schaeffer (*Rousseau on Education, Judgment, and Freedom*, 108), although she notes the "narrative slippage."

15 Ellrich assumes that the story of the young proselyte is straightforwardly autobiographical and notes the discrepancies between the accounts in the "Profession" and the *Confessions*, which he takes to be the "true" version of events. He concludes that the (inaccurate) fictionalization of the story in the "Profession" provoked a bout of "uneasy conscience" in Rousseau, especially given that he had appealed to his motto in introducing the story, leading Rousseau to increasing doubts as he progressed in *Emile* (and his career as a writer) concerning whether he could satisfy his supposed desire to communicate transparently with his reader (*Rousseau and His Reader*, 58–60).

16 Mall makes the interesting observation that vicars themselves act as temporary replacements for clergy with permanent posts, so the Vicar appro-

priately acts as a temporary replacement for Jean-Jacques. In addition, she points to the root sense of the term *vicaire*, which is also the source of the word *vicarious*, noting that the experience of the reader of the "Profession" is vicarious (*Emile, ou les figures de la fiction*, chap. 9).

17 Jean-Georges Lefranc de Pompignan, *Instruction pastorale* (1763), quoted in Trousson, *Jean-Jacques Rousseau jugé par ses contemporains*, 259.

18 Since the Vicar begins his theological inquiry by stating that he is "in that frame of mind of uncertainty and doubt that Descartes demands for the quest for truth" (267), perhaps we are authorized to characterize his approach to morality and law as something like Descartes's "provisional morality" in part 3 of the *Discourse on the Method*: that he will always *outwardly* adhere to established morality and law. See Descartes, *Discours sur la méthode*, in *Oeuvres et lettres*.

19 Plato, *Phaedrus* 230b–c.

20 Schaeffer compares these other sunrise stories to the setting of the "Profession" in terms of the aporia Rousseau raises in arguing that we have to experience erotic longing, for love and wisdom, in order to raise ourselves to the divinity but also seem to have to have notions of the divinity before such longing (*Rousseau on Education, Judgment, and Freedom*, 110–11).

21 In *Julie*, Rousseau has St. Preux write to Julie: "O Julie! O dear and precious half of my soul, let us hasten to add to these springtime ornaments the presence of two faithful lovers; let us bring the sentiment of pleasure to those places which offer its vain image; let us go animate all of nature; it is dead without the flames of love" (I.28, *CW*, 6:65–66).

22 See esp. Rousseau, *Essay on the Origin of Languages*, chap. 1: "Open ancient history; you will find it full of those ways of presenting arguments to the eyes. . . . The object, presented before speaking, stirs the imagination, arouses curiosity, holds the mind in suspense and anticipation of what is going to be said" (*CW*, 7:290–91).

23 Rousseau emphasizes the utility of the "Profession" in defense of the work by describing what its effects would be if it were put into practice (*Letter to Beaumont, CW*, 9:66–67). For his argument that religions must be examined for both their truth and their utility, and his caution that truth and utility do not necessarily go together in any given religion, see ibid., 54–55.

Chapter Six

1 Jimack does not even discuss *Robinson Crusoe* (*La genèse et la rédaction de l' "Emile"*), and Mall (*Emile, ou les figures de la fiction*, 33) and Vargas (*Introduction à l' "Emile" de Rousseau*, 109) mention it only in passing. As for Telemachus, Jimack remarks on Rousseau's use of the novel as part of his brief discussion of Fénelon's influence on his educational thought but does not otherwise analyze it (*La genèse et la rédaction de l' "Emile*," 357–59), and Vargas very briefly discusses it (*Introduction à l' "Emile" de Rousseau*, 222–23). Mall (*Emile, ou les figures de la fiction*, chap. 8) devotes a chapter to the role of Telemachus in Emile. There is one other book-length analysis of Emile

by Ellis (*Rousseau's Socratic-Aemelian Myths*), which I do not discuss here because the reading is eccentric.

2   As for *Robinson Crusoe*, see Rousselière ("Rousseau on Freedom in Commercial Society") and Wolf ("Economic Education of Emile"). For *Telemachus*, see Deneen (*Odyssey of Political Theory*, chap. 3) and Mall (*Emile, ou les figures de la fiction*, chap. 8).

3   Schaeffer, *Rousseau on Education, Judgment, and Freedom*, chaps. 3 and 6.

4   Jacques-François-Daniel Burand to Rousseau, 18 March 1763, *CC*, 15:289–92. See also J. H. Füssili to L. Usteri, c. 28 June 1763, *C.C.*, 16:354–56. Interestingly, during the French Revolution someone published a version of *Robinson Crusoe* that claimed to follow Rousseau's intentions in editing the work: *Histoire corrigée de Robinson Crusoé, dans son isle déserte. Ouvrage rendu propre à l'instruction de la jeunesse, sur l'avis et le plan de Jean-Jacques Rousseau* (Rousseau, *Oeuvres complètes* (*Edition thématique du tricentenaire*), 7:548 ed. n. 1).

5   Schaeffer also discusses Rousseau's remarks about cutting the "rigmarole" as part of the education of the reader in judgment, and characterizes Rousseau as "inviting" the reader to think about what should be cut (*Rousseau on Education, Judgment, and Freedom*, 74–81).

6   DeJean does not notice that Emile does not simply imitate Robinson, but critically judges him as well. This fact alone would call into her psychoanalytically infused argument that Rousseau (the individual) identified with Robinson Crusoe so strongly that, in his role as the governor Jean-Jacques, he makes Emile identify with Defoe's hero to such an extent that all individuality of the pupil is absorbed into tutor and therefore author, erasing individuality and exercising complete control over his creation (*Literary Fortifications*, 149–52). For similar readings, see Berrett Brown, "Constraints of Liberty at the Scene of Instruction," 165; Harari, *Scenarios of the Imaginary*, chap. 4.

7   Defoe, *Robinson Crusoe*, 50.

8   As I will briefly note below, much of Robinson's imperious treatment of Friday as his master, if not his "master" in the sense of a master of slaves, raises a series of further questions about what might need to be cut from Defoe's novel. See Flanders, "Rousseau's Adventure with Robinson Crusoe," 321–25.

9   See Schaeffer, *Rousseau on Education, Judgment, and Freedom*, esp. 72 ff. See also Flanders, "Rousseau's Adventure with Robinson Crusoe," 321–25.

10 See esp. Schaeffer, *Rousseau on Education, Judgment, and Freedom*, 72–82; Schaeffer, "Utility of Ink." See also Kelly, *Rousseau as Author*, 93–94.

11 Charles Wirz, *OC*, 4:1430 (ed. n. 1 to p. 455); see also Keymer's introduction to Defoe, *Robinson Crusoe*, viii. Harari (*Scenarios of the Imaginary*, 120) and Vargas (*Introduction à l'"Emile" de Rousseau*, 109 and n.) make the same assumption.

12 Flanders also notes the parallels and Rousseau's suppression of Scripture ("Rousseau's Adventure with Robinson Crusoe," 325).

13 Marx, *Capital*, book I, part 1, chap. 1 end.

14 Watt, *Rise of the Novel*, chap. 3. Watt argues that Rousseau saw in *Robinson Crusoe* a model of autarchy, social and economic (ibid., 86).

15 E.g., Bellhouse, "On Understanding Rousseau's Praise of Robinson Crusoe"; Rousselière, "Rousseau on Freedom in Commercial Society"; Wolf, "Economic Education of Emile."

16 See esp. Hunter, *Reluctant Pilgrim*.

17 See Hunter, *Reluctant Pilgrim*, chap. 6.

18 See Flanders, "Rousseau's Adventure with Robinson Crusoe." Flanders hints at the argument I am making without developing it when he writes: "Only by reading Defoe could the reader of *Emile* become aware of those elements Rousseau suppressed. Only by reading Defoe might the attentive reader discover that, in drawing attention to those very elements by his silence, Rousseau appears to be engaging an enemy" (ibid., 331–32).

19 Defoe, *Robinson Crusoe*, 3.

20 Defoe, *Robinson Crusoe*, 5, 7, 9, 14. Flanders also notes the importance of the prodigal son narrative as an element Rousseau would have to eliminate ("Rousseau's Adventure with Robinson Crusoe," 322).

21 Defoe, *Robinson Crusoe*, 54.

22 Defoe, *Robinson Crusoe*, 67–68.

23 Hunter seems deaf to any irony on Defoe's part (*Reluctant Pilgrim*, 155 ff.).

24 Defoe, *Robinson Crusoe*, 75–76.

25 Defoe, *Robinson Crusoe*, 78–79.

26 Defoe, *Robinson Crusoe*, 83.

27 Defoe, *Robinson Crusoe*, 148.

28 Defoe, *Robinson Crusoe*, 164.

29 Like Adam before him, Robinson also takes it upon himself to name him or rather, ironically, to misname him, because in his delirium Robinson lost count of a day, meaning that Friday should be named Saturday (see Defoe, *Robinson Crusoe*, 174 and ed. n.). Indeed, one wonders whether much of the text concerning Friday wouldn't have to be excised as well given Robinson's imperious treatment of his servant and the racist and colonial themes of the story, including Robinson's former occupation as a slave plantation owner.

30 Defoe, *Robinson Crusoe*, 230.

31 Defoe, *Robinson Crusoe*, 256.

32 Flanders notes that Rousseau does not mention Defoe ("Rousseau's Adventure with Robinson Crusoe," 331).

33 For Fénelon's influence on Rousseau in general, see Gouhier, "Rousseau et Fénelon"; Hanley, "Rousseau and Fénelon."

34 See Berrett Brown, "Emile's Missing Text," 54; Mall, *Emile, ou les figures de la fiction*, 262n.

35 Berrett Brown, "Emile's Missing Text," 54.

36 Fénelon, *Telemachus*, 302.

37 Mall also notes this reversal of priority and, I think rightly, remarks on how

bizarre it is to read *Telemachus* as a love story in the first place (*Emile, ou les figures de la fiction*, 259).

38 While Rousseau's political principles can be confidently characterized as democratic and egalitarian, with certain qualifications, Fénelon's ultimate political leanings are more debatable, with scholarly views ranging from him being an absolutist with reformist views to a republican.

39 I follow a number of interpreters in referring to the character as the "false" Sophie. See Mall, *Emile, ou les figures de la fiction*, 257; Schaeffer, *Rousseau on Education, Judgment, and Freedom*, 145–46. Wingrove (*Rousseau's Republican Romance*, 77 ff.) generally refers to the character as the "original" Sophie, but she does refer to what I am terming the "true" Sophie as the "real" Sophie.

40 E.g., Deneen, *Odyssey of Political Theory*, 144–45.

41 Rousseau's anticipation of the reaction of different kinds of readers to the novel is more dramatically expressed when he states that virtuous readers will throw it in the fire, whereas corrupted readers will read it precisely because they are corrupt (*Julie, CW*, 6:3, 19).

42 Crosthwaite argues that Rousseau abandons the first Sophie because "she has too much a mind of her own. . . . Her function is to be a pleasing companion to her husband." Hence he creates a more docile Sophie ("Sophie and *Les aventures de Télémaque*," esp. 191).

43 And my reader may be interested to learn of a curious parallel in *Robinson Crusoe*: shortly after his shipwreck, our *Homo economicus* reckons up the evil and good in his situation in the form of double-entry accounting (Defoe, *Robinson Crusoe*, 57–58).

44 Berrett Brown, "Emile's Missing Text," 60.

45 Fénelon, *Telemachus*, 3–8.

46 Fénelon, *Telemachus*, 45.

47 Deneen also notes Emile's mistake regarding Calypso but does not pursue the point (*Odyssey of Political Theory*, 143). Mall also remarks that although Emile has not read *Telemachus* and so does not understand the interchange, the reader of *Emile* has read it and therefore sees his mistake (*Emile, ou les figures de la fiction*, 261).

48 Berrett Brown similarly notes: "Emile, constrained by his own ignorance, is blissfully unaware of the sexually charged nature of the scene." She also remarks on the "jarring" reference to Eucharis, suggesting that by doing so "the tutor allows himself to play the same role as Mentor does in *Les aventures de Télémaque*. Were he to align Sophie with Antiope, he would, in essence articulate his own obsolescence" ("Constraints of Liberty at the Scene of Instruction," 167). In an earlier article, Berrett Brown argues that associating Sophie with Eucharis rather than Antiope marks her "as an object of sexual desire" ("Emile's Missing Text," 63). Similarly, Crosthwaite argues that associating Sophie with Eucharis rather than Antiope emphasizes "her sexual power," which Rousseau views as defining women ("Sophie and *Les aventures de Télémaque*").

49 Berrett Brown, "Emile's Missing Text," 57.

50   Note that by having the father recount his story to Emile and the tutor
     as the parallel to Telemachus telling his story to Calypso and the other
     nymphs, Rousseau de-eroticizes this aspect of his application of *Telema-
     chus*. Instead, he substitutes a later story from the work of Telemachus
     encountering Philoctetes, Ulysses' resentful rival, and sympathizing with
     his woes (*Telemachus*, book 12).
51   Schaeffer argues that Sophie's ability to judge according to her own criteria
     makes her a better judge at this point than Emile (*Rousseau on Education,
     Judgment, and Freedom*, 139).
52   On the blurring between reality and fiction as a type of "aesthetic experi-
     ence" in eighteenth-century novels, including *Julie*, see Marshall, *Frame
     of Art*.
53   Contrast Berrett Brown, who argues: "The book changes hands, from Sophie
     to Emile, because it has served its purpose" ("Constraints of Liberty at the
     Scene of Instruction," 168).

Chapter Seven

1   There are also a number of cases in the work where Rousseau addresses
     what might be termed an "assumed" reader. For example, in the same chap-
     ter that contains the first direct address to the reader in the note, after stat-
     ing that when the Athenian people acted by particular decrees they were no
     longer properly speaking acting as sovereign, he writes: "This will appear
     to be contrary to commonly held ideas, but I must be allowed the time to
     present my own" (II.4). That is, the point will not be clear until he defines
     "government," which is the occasion for his second direct address to the
     reader (III.1).
2   See Yamashita, *Jean-Jacques Rousseau face au public*, 88.
3   Rousseau to Marc-Michel Rey, 4 April 1762 (*CC*, 10:180).
4   See Trousson for numerous examples of readers finding the work difficult,
     dry, abstruse (*Jean-Jacques Rousseau jugé par ses contemporains*, chap. 7).
5   Among those who have also noted the near absence in the *Social Contract* of
     identification of readers and author-reader interactions are de Man (*Allego-
     ries of Reading*, 268), Ellrich (*Rousseau and His Reader*, 37), Masters (*Political
     Philosophy of Rousseau*, 309), and Yamashita (*Jean-Jacques Rousseau face au
     public*, 88).
6   E.g., Stilz discusses but ultimately rejects what she terms Rousseau's "cul-
     tural model" in favor of a "freedom model" (*Liberal Loyalty*, chap. 5), and
     Cohen simply puts aside what he terms Rousseau's "political sociology" to
     focus exclusively on the principles of political right (*Rousseau: A Free Com-
     munity of Equals*). From a very different direction, most theorists of direct
     or participatory democracy inspired by Rousseau also tend to ignore his
     discussion of the lawgiver, mores, civil religion, etc. See, e.g., Barber, *Strong
     Democracy*; Pateman, *Participation and Democratic Theory*.
7   Masters, *Political Philosophy of Rousseau*, esp. 301–6.
8   De Man, *Allegories of Reading*, chap. 11. The two readings I am suggesting

also parallel to a certain degree Althusser's structuralist analysis of the "discrepancies" (*décalages*) within Rousseau's text, and especially the third and fourth "discrepancies," which he argues underlie the first two and that concern the relationship between the theory of the social contract and its confrontation with actuality (*Politics and History*, 153).

9 See Trousson for a discussion of the reception of the *Social Contract*, including in relation to *Emile* (*Jean-Jacques Rousseau jugé par ses contemporains*, chap. 7).

10 Rousseau to Nicolas-Bonaventure Duchesne, 23 May 1762, *CC*, 10:281.

11 E.g., Melzer, *Natural Goodness of Man*; Scott, "Theodicy of the Second Discourse"; Shklar, *Men and Citizens*; Todorov, *Frail Happiness*.

12 E.g., Bloom, introduction; Gomes, "Emile the Citizen?"; Neuhouser, *Rousseau's Theodicy of Self-Love*.

13 For a detailed examination of the precis contained in *Emile* to the *Social Contract*, see Scott, "*Emile* et les principes du droit politique."

14 Rousseau includes another brief summary of the *Social Contract* in the *Letters Written from the Mountain* (*CW*, 9:231–33). Most of the summary is devoted to an outline of the basic elements of the principles of political right, but he does very briefly remark on the discussion of the degeneration of the government and ways to slow down the process and on the discussion of Rome and of civil religion. He does not mention the lawgiver and related material.

15 Mara offers a similar reading with regard to the difference between *Emile* and the *Social Contract* as regards Rousseau's views of the applicability or lack thereof of the principles of political right in different political contexts ("Rousseau's Two Models of Political Obligation").

16 See Rousseau, "Manuscrit de Genève," *OC*, 3:1410 n. (*a*) to p. 279.

17 See Masters for a similar reading of the titles (*Political Philosophy of Rousseau*, 259–60, 301–2).

18 Virgil, *Aeneid* 11.321–22.

19 Masters, *Political Philosophy of Rousseau*, 302–3.

20 He also calls attention to its incompleteness in a note to a passage that concerning how to overcome the problems of small states, presumably through federations, in a passage that begins: "I will show below . . . ," with a callout to a note that explains that this material is in fact not discussed "below" and is part of the abandoned project (III.15 and n.). I will discuss that passage below.

21 Kamuf presents a deconstructive analysis of the beginning and ending of the *Social Contract* that emphasizes the indeterminacy and lack of closure of the text (*Signature Pieces*, chap. 2).

22 See Rousseau to Marc-Michel Rey, 28 February 1762, *CC*, 10:122. The only editions of which I am aware that do include the table are the tricentenary edition of the *Oeuvres complètes* (5:615–16), the *Collected Writings* edition (*CW*, 4:129–30), and my own edition (*Major Political Writings*, 157–59).

23 Strikingly, among the scholars who effectively dismiss book IV, apart from

the chapter "On Civil Religion" (IV.8), are the editors of the two most important French editions of the work (until recently): Vaughn, in the first critical edition of Rousseau's political writings, and Derathé, the editor of the
Pléiade edition. See Masters, *Political Philosophy of Rousseau*, 305 n. 21. In
his helpful commentary on the *Social Contract*, Bertram (*Rousseau and the
"Social Contract"*) skips book IV with the exception of the discussion of civil
religion.

24   Interestingly, and I think encouragingly for my argument, although Masters does not attend to the structure of the *Social Contract*, he ends up following precisely the division into two parts I am suggesting by presenting
his commentary according to the two principal aspects of principle and
practice (*Political Philosophy of Rousseau*, chaps. 6 and 7). I only discovered
the parallel with my structural analysis after rereading his book. Likewise,
although they follow the organization of the *Social Contract* with a chapter-
by-chapter analysis, both Gildin (*Rousseau's "Social Contract,"* chaps. 2–5)
and Williams (*Rousseau's "Social Contract,"* see 64 and 107) present their
commentaries on the work by dividing each book II and III into the two
halves I have suggested.

25   Goldschmidt similarly suggests that the *Social Contract* is structured according to the birth and death of the state, but he argues that the birth takes
place in II.6 and continues for the remainder of the treatise, thereby dividing it into two (very unequal) parts of I.1–II.5, devoted to the principles of
political right, and II.6–IV.8, devoted to practical matters and especially
the activity of the lawgiver. He also notes (ibid., 139) that book III is divided
into two equal halves, he but does not take account of this in his argument
concerning the structure of the book as a whole (*Études de philosophie moderne*, 136–44).

26   E.g., by contrast, in the "Geneva Manuscript" he includes an introduction
in the very first chapter, "Subject of this Work" (I.1).

27   See Kamuf, *Signature Pieces*, chap. 2.

28   Rousseau to Victor Riqueti, Marquis de Mirabeau, 26 July 1767, *CC*, 33:
239–40.

29   See Rawls, *Law of Peoples*. Rawls elsewhere characterizes Rousseau's theory
as a "realistic utopia" (*Lectures on the History of Political Philosophy*, 191–250).
For a different reading of Rousseau's political theory as being concerned
with "ideals," see Simpson, *Rousseau's Theory of Freedom*. For an example
of an intelligent utopian reading, see Shklar, *Men and Citizens*.

30   See Aristotle, *Politics* 1.2.1253a for the remark on the "hand" and 1.4.6.1253b–
55b for his argument about slavery.

31   See Aristotle, *Politics* 4.2.1289b, 4.10.1295a.

32   The parallel of books I and III having a proemium suggests yet another structuring of the *Social Contract* into two halves of books I–II and books III–IV.
The grouping of books III and IV is also suggested by Rousseau's summary
in the table of contents of book IV as continuing the discussion begun in
book III.

33 In his *Sleeping Sovereign*, Tuck traces back the distinction to Bodin and
    Hobbes as predecessors to Rousseau, but in my view he underestimates
    Rousseau's innovation.

Conclusion

1 Two valuable studies of the relationship between philosophy and rhetoric
   in Hobbes are Johnston, *Rhetoric of "Leviathan,"* and Evrigenis, *Images of
   Anarchy*.

Bibliography

Rousseau's Works

Rousseau, Jean-Jacques. *Oeuvres complètes.* 5 vols. Paris: Gallimard, Bibliothèque de la Pléiade, 1959–95.

Rousseau, Jean-Jacques. *Correspondence complète.* Edited by Ralph A. Leigh. 50 vols. Oxford: Voltaire Foundation, 1965–91.

Rousseau, Jean-Jacques. *Emile, or On Education.* Translated by Allan Bloom. New York: Basic Books, 1979.

Rousseau, Jean-Jacques. *The Collected Writings of Rousseau.* Edited by Roger D. Masters and Christopher Kelly. 13 vols. Hanover, NH: University Press of New England, 1990–2010.

Rousseau, Jean-Jacques. *The Major Political Writings of Jean-Jacques Rousseau: The Two Discourses and the "Social Contract."* Edited and translated by John T. Scott. Chicago: University of Chicago Press, 2012.

Rousseau, Jean-Jacques. *Oeuvres complètes: Édition thématique du tricentenaire.* Edited by Raymond Trousson and Frédéric S. Eigeldinger. 17 vols. Geneva: Éditions Slatkine. Paris: Éditions Champion, 2012.

Secondary Literature

Allard, Gérard. *Rousseau sur les sciences et les arts.* 2nd ed. Sainte-Foy, Quebec: Griffon d'argile, 2003.

Althusser, Louis. *Politics and History: Montesquieu, Rousseau, Marx.* Translated by Ben Brewster. London: Verso, 1972.

Anderson, Wilda. "Starobinski on Rousseau, or the Heuristic Power of Opacity." *Modern Language Notes* 128 (2013): 820–27.

Aricò, Santo L. *Rousseau's Art of Persuasion in the "Nouvelle Héloïse."* Lanham, MD: University of American Press, 1994.

Aristotle. *The Politics.* Translated by Carnes Lord. Chicago: University of Chicago Press, 1984.

Babbitt, Irving. *Rousseau and Romanticism.* Boston: Houghton Mifflin, 1919.

Baker, Felicity. "Le route contraire." In *Reappraisals of Rousseau*, ed. Simon Harvey, Marian Hobson, David Kelley, and Samuel S. B. Taylor, 132–62. Manchester: Manchester University Press, 1980.

Barber, Benjamin R. *Strong Democracy: Participatory Politics for a New Age.* Berkeley and Los Angeles: University of California Press, 1984.

Beaudry, Catherine A. *The Role of the Reader in Rousseau's "Confessions."* New York: Peter Lang, 1991.

Bellhouse, Mary L. "On Understanding Rousseau's Praise of Robinson Crusoe." *Canadian Journal of Social and Political Theory* 6 (1982): 120–37.

Berman, Marshall. *The Politics of Authenticity: Radical Individualism and the Emergence of Modern Society.* New York: Atheneum, 1970.

Berrett Brown, Diane. "Emile's Missing Text: *Les aventures de Télémaque.*" *Symposium* 63 (2019): 51–71.

Berrett Brown, Diane. "The Constraints of Liberty at the Scene of Instruction." In *Rousseau and Liberty*, ed. Christine McDonald and Stanley Hoffmann, 159–73. Cambridge: Cambridge University Press, 2010.

Bertram, Christopher. *Rousseau and the "Social Contract."* London: Routledge, 2004.

Birn, Raymond. *Forging Rousseau: Print, Commerce and Cultural Manipulation in the Late Enlightenment.* Oxford: Voltaire Foundation, 2001.

Black, Jeffrey J. S. *Rousseau's Critique of Science: A Commentary on the "Discourse on the Sciences and the Arts."* Lanham, MD: Lexington Books, 2009.

Bloom, Allan. Introduction to Jean-Jacques Rousseau, *Emile, or On Education.* Edited and translated by Allan Bloom. New York: Basic Books, 1979.

Booth, Wayne C. *A Rhetoric of Irony.* Chicago: University of Chicago Press, 1974.

Booth, Wayne C. *The Rhetoric of Fiction.* 2nd ed. Chicago: University of Chicago Press, 1983.

Boyd, Richard. "Pity's Pathologies Portrayed: Rousseau and the Limits of Democratic Compassion." *Political Theory* 32 (2004): 519–46.

Bredekamp, Horst. "Thomas Hobbes' Visual Strategies." In *The Cambridge Companion to Hobbes' "Leviathan,"* ed. Patricia Springborg, 29–60. Cambridge: Cambridge University Press, 2007.

Butterworth, Charles E. "Interpretative Essay." In Jean-Jacques Rousseau, *Reveries of the Solitary Walker*, trans. Charles E. Butterworth, 145–239. New York: New York University Press, 1979.

Campbell, Sally H., and Scott, John T. "The Politic Argument of Rousseau's *Discourse on the Sciences and the Arts.*" *American Journal of Political Science* 49 (2005): 819–29.

Caradonna, Jeremy L. *The Enlightenment in Practice: Academic Prize Contests and Intellectual Culture in France, 1670–1794.* Ithaca, NY: Cornell University Press, 2012.

Cassirer, Ernst. *The Question of Jean-Jacques Rousseau.* 2nd ed. Edited and translated by Peter Gay. New Haven, CT: Yale University Press, 1989 [1932].

Cherpack, Clifton. "Narration and Meaning in Rousseau's *Emile.*" *French Forum* 13 (1988): 17–30.

Cohen, Joshua. *Rousseau: A Free Community of Equals*. Oxford: Oxford University Press, 2010.

Coleman, Patrick. "Characterizing Rousseau's *Emile*." *Modern Language Notes* 92 (1977): 761–78.

Collins, James Henderson, II. *Exhortations to Philosophy: The Protreptics of Plato, Isocrates, and Aristotle*. Oxford: Oxford University Press, 2015.

Cooper, Laurence D. "Human Nature and the Love of Wisdom: Rousseau's Hidden (and Modified) Platonism." *Journal of Politics* 64 (2002): 108–25.

Cooper, Laurence D. *Rousseau, Nature, and the Problem of the Good Life*. University Park, PA: Penn State University Press, 1999.

Cranston, Maurice. *The Noble Savage: Jean-Jacques Rousseau, 1712–1762*. Chicago: University of Chicago Press, 1991.

Crosthwaite, Jan. "Sophie and *Les aventures de Télémaque*: Amorous Nymphs and Virtuous Wives in Rousseau's *Emile*." *British Journal for Eighteenth-Century Studies* 15 (1992): 189–201.

d'Alembert, Jean le Rond. *Preliminary Discourse to the Encyclopedia of Diderot*. Translated by Richard N. Schwab. Indianapolis: Bobbs-Merrill, 1963 [1751].

Darnton, Robert. *The Great Cat Massacre and Other Episodes in French Cultural History*. New York: Basic Books, 1984.

Darnton, Robert. *The Literary Underground of the Old Regime*. Cambridge, MA: Harvard University Press, 1982.

Defoe, Daniel. *Robinson Crusoe*. Edited by Thomas Keymer. Oxford: Oxford University Press, 2007 [1719].

DeJean, Joan. *Literary Fortifications: Rousseau, Laclos, Sade*. Princeton, NJ: Princeton University Press, 1984.

de Man, Paul. *Allegories of Reading: Figural Language in Rousseau, Nietzsche, Rilke, and Proust*. New Haven, CT: Yale University Press, 1979.

Deneen, Patrick. J. *The Odyssey of Political Theory: The Politics of Departure and Return*. Lanham, MD: Rowman & Littlefield, 2000.

Dent, N. J. H. *Rousseau*. London: Basil Blackwell, 1988.

Descartes, René. *Oeuvres et lettres*. Paris: Gallimard, 1953.

Dorter, Kenneth. "Plato's Use of the Dialogue Form: Skepticism and Insemination." In *Literary Form, Philosophical Content: Historical Studies of Philosophical Genres*, ed. Jonathan Lavery and Louis Groarke, 41–52. Madison, WI: Farleigh Dickinson University Press, 2010.

Douglass, Robin. *Hobbes and Rousseau: Nature, Free Will, and Passions*. Oxford: Oxford University Press, 2015.

Ellis, Madeleine B. *Rousseau's Socratic-Aemelian Myths: A Literary Collation of "Emile" and the "Social Contract."* Columbus: Ohio State University Press, 1977.

Ellrich, Richard J. *Rousseau and His Reader: The Rhetorical Situation of the Major Works*. Chapel Hill: University of North Carolina Press, 1969.

Emberley, Peter. "Rousseau versus the Savoyard Vicar: The Profession of Faith Considered." *Interpretation* 14 (1986): 299–330.

Evrigenis, Ioannis D. *Images of Anarchy: The Rhetoric and Science in Hobbes's State of Nature*. Cambridge: Cambridge University Press, 2014.

Fénelon, François de Salignac de la Mothe-. *Telemachus*. Edited and translated by Patrick Riley. Cambridge: Cambridge University Press, 1994 [1699].

Fénelon, François de Salignac de la Mothe-. *Traité de l'éducation des filles*. Paris: Pierre Aubouin, Pierre Emery, et Charles Clousier, 1687.

Ferrara, Alessandro. *Modernity and Authenticity: A Study of the Social and Ethical Thought of Jean-Jacques Rousseau*. Albany, NY: SUNY Press, 1993.

Fish, Stanley Eugene. *Surprised by Sin: The Reader in "Paradise Lost."* London: Macmillan, 1967.

Flanders, Todd R. "Rousseau's Adventure with Robinson Crusoe." *Interpretation* 24 (1997): 319–37.

Formey, Johann Heinrich Samuel. *Anti-Emile*. Berlin: Joachim Pauli, 1763.

Gauthier, David. *Rousseau: The Sentiment of Existence*. Cambridge: Cambridge University Press, 2006.

Genette, Gérard. *Paratexts: Thresholds of Interpretation*. Translated by Jane E. Lewin. Cambridge: Cambridge University Press, 1997. Original ed.: *Seuils* (Paris: Éditions du Seuil, 1987).

Gildin, Hilail. *Rousseau's "Social Contract": The Design of the Argument*. Chicago: University of Chicago Press, 1983.

Goldschmidt, Victor. *Anthropologie et politique: Les principes du système de Rousseau*. Paris: Vrin, 1974.

Goldschmidt, Victor. *Études de philosophie moderne*. Vol. 2. Paris: Vrin, 1984.

Gomes, Bjorn. "Emile the Citizen? A Reassessment of the Relationship between Private Education and Citizenship in Rousseau's Political Thought." *European Journal of Political Theory* 17 (2018): 194–213.

Goodman, Dena. *Criticism in Action: Enlightenment Experiments in Political Writing*. Ithaca, NY: Cornell University Press, 1989.

Gouhier, Henri. "Rousseau et Fénelon." In *Reappraisals of Rousseau: Studies in Honor of R .A. Leigh*, ed. Simon Harvey, 279–89. Manchester: Manchester University Press, 1980.

Gourevitch, Victor. "Rousseau on Lying: A Provisional Reading of the Fourth *Rêverie*." *Berkshire Review* 15 (1980): 93–107.

Gourevitch, Victor. "Rousseau on the Arts and Sciences." *Journal of Philosophy* 69: 20 (9 November 1972): 737–54.

Gourevitch, Victor. "Rousseau's Pure State of Nature." *Interpretation* 16 (1988): 23–60.

Grimsley, Ronald. "Rousseau and His Reader: The Technique of Persuasion in *Emile*." In *Rousseau after Two Hundred Years*, ed. R. A. Leigh, 225–38. Cambridge: Cambridge University Press, 1982.

Griswold, Charles L., Jr. *Adam Smith and the Virtues of Enlightenment*. Cambridge: Cambridge University Press, 1999.

Griswold, Charles L., Jr., ed. *Platonic Readings, Platonic Writings*. London: Routledge, 1988.

Hanley, Ryan Patrick. "Rousseau and Fénelon." In *The Rousseauian Mind*, ed. Christopher Kelly and Eve Grace, 87–97. London: Routledge, 2019.

Harari, Josué V. *Scenarios of the Imaginary: Theorizing the French Enlightenment*. Ithaca, NY: Cornell University Press, 1987.

Harvey, Irene E. *Labyrinths of Exemplarity: At the Limits of Deconstruction*. Albany: State University of New York Press, 2002.

Hendel, Charles W. *Jean-Jacques Rousseau: Moralist*. 2 vols. Indianapolis: Bobbs-Merrill, 1934.

Hirsch, E. D., Jr. *Validity in Interpretation*. New Haven, CT: Yale University Press, 1967.

Hobbes, Thomas. *Leviathan*. Edited by John Gaskin. Oxford: Oxford University Press, 1996.

Hobbes, Thomas. *On the Citizen*. Edited by Richard Tuck and Michael Silverthorne. Cambridge: Cambridge University Press, 1998.

Hope Mason, John. "Reading Rousseau's *First Discourse*." *Studies in Voltaire and the Eighteenth Century* 249 (1987): 251–66.

Hume, David. *Essays Moral, Political, and Literary*. Edited by Eugene F. Miller. Indianapolis, IN: Liberty Fund, 1987.

Hunter, J. Paul. *The Reluctant Pilgrim: Defoe's Emblematic Method and the Quest for Form in "Robinson Crusoe."* Baltimore, MD: Johns Hopkins University Press, 1966.

Iser, Wolfgang. *The Implied Reader: Patterns of Communication in Prose Fiction from Bunyun to Beckett*. Baltimore, MD: Johns Hopkins University Press, 1974.

Iser, Wolfgang. *The Act of Reading: A Theory of Aesthetic Response*. Baltimore, MD: Johns Hopkins University Press, 1978.

Jimack, Peter D. *La genèse et la rédaction de l'"Emile" de Jean-Jacques Rousseau*. Genève: Voltaire Foundation, 1960.

Johnston, David. *The Rhetoric of "Leviathan": Thomas Hobbes and the Politics of Cultural Transformation*. Princeton, NJ: Princeton University Press, 1987.

Kamuf, Peggy. *Signature Pieces: On the Institution of Authorship*. Ithaca, NY: Cornell University Press, 1988.

Kavanagh, Thomas. *Writing the Truth: Authority and Desire in Rousseau*. Berkeley and Los Angeles: University of California Press, 1987.

Kelly, Christopher. "On the Naturalness of the Sentiment of Injustice." *Esprit créateur* 52 (2012): 68–80.

Kelly, Christopher. "Rousseau and the Case For (and Against) Censorship." *Journal of Politics* 59 (1997): 1232–51.

Kelly, Christopher. *Rousseau as Author: Consecrating One's Life to the Truth*. Chicago: University of Chicago Press, 2003.

Kelly, Christopher. "'To Persuade without Convincing': The Language of Rousseau's Legislator. *American Journal of Political Science* 31 (1987): 321–35.

Keohane, Nannerl O. "'The Masterpiece of Policy in Our Century': Rousseau on the Morality of Enlightenment." *Political Theory* 6 (1978): 457–84.

Klausen, Jimmy Casas. *Fugitive Rousseau: Slavery, Primitivism, and Political Freedom*. New York: Fordham University Press, 2014.

Labrosse, Claude. *Lire au XVIIIe siècle: "La nouvelle Héloïse" et ses lecteurs*. Lyon: Presses Universitaires de Lyon and CNRS, 1985.

Launay, Michel. "Rousseau écrivain." In *Rousseau after Two Hundred Years*, ed. R. A. Leigh, 207–21. Cambridge: Cambridge University Press, 1982.

Lewis, Ann. *Sensibility, Reading, and Illustration: Spectacles and Signs in Graffigny, Marivaux and Rousseau*. London: Legenda, Modern Humanities Research Association and Maney Publishing, 2009.

Locke, John. *Two Treatises of Government*. Edited by Peter Laslett. Cambridge: Cambridge University Press, 1994.

Lovejoy, Arthur O. "The Supposed Primitivism of Rousseau's *Discourse on Inequality*." *Modern Philology* 21 (1923): 165–86.

Machiavelli, Niccolò. *The Prince*. Translated by Harvey C. Mansfield. 2nd ed. Chicago: University of Chicago Press, 1998.

MacLean, Lee. *The Free Animal: Rousseau on Free Will and Human Nature*. Toronto: University of Toronto Press, 2013.

Maguire, Matthew. *The Conversion of Imagination: From Pascal through Rousseau to Tocqueville*. Cambridge, MA: Harvard University Press, 2006.

Mall, Laurence. *Emile, ou les figures de la fiction*. Oxford: Voltaire Foundation, 2002.

Maloney, Pat. "Hobbes, Savagery, and International Anarchy." *American Political Science Review* 105 (2011): 189–204.

Mandeville, Bernard. *The Fable of the Bees*. 2 vols. Indianapolis: Liberty Fund, 1988.

Mara, Gerald M. "Rousseau's Two Models of Political Obligation." *Western Political Quarterly* 33 (1980): 536–49.

Marks, Jonathan. *Perfection and Disharmony in the Thought of Jean-Jacques Rousseau*. Cambridge: Cambridge University Press, 2005.

Marks, Jonathan. "Rousseau's Discriminating Defense of Compassion." *American Political Science Review* 101 (2007): 727–39.

Marshall, David. *The Frame of Art: Fictions of Aesthetic Experience, 1750–1815*. Baltimore, MD: Johns Hopkins University Press, 2005.

Marx, Karl. *Capital*. Translated by Ben Fowkes. 3 vols. Harmondsworth: Penguin, 1976.

Masson, Pierre Maurice. *La religion de J.-J. Rousseau*. Paris: Hachette, 1916.

Masters, Roger D. *The Political Philosophy of Rousseau*. Princeton, NJ: Princeton University Press, 1968.

Meier, Heinrich., ed. *Jean-Jacques Rousseau, Diskurs über die Ungleichheit*. 1st ed. Munich: Schöningh, 1984.

Meier, Heinrich. *On the Happiness of the Philosophic Life: Reflections on Rousseau's "Rêveries" in Two Books*. Translated by Robert Berman. Chicago: University of Chicago Press, 2016.

Melzer, Arthur M. *Philosophy Between the Lines: The Lost History of Esoteric Writing*. Chicago: University of Chicago Press, 2014.

Melzer, Arthur M. *The Natural Goodness of Man: On the System of Rousseau's Thought*. Chicago: University of Chicago Press, 1990.

Mendham, Matthew D. "Enlightened Gentleness as Soft Indifference: Rousseau's Critique of Cultural Modernization." *History of Political Thought* 31 (2010): 605–37.

Michel, Isabelle. "Les illustrations de l'*Emile* au XVIIIe siècle: questions d'iconographie." In *Annales de la société Jean-Jacques Rousseau*, 529–65. Geneva: Droz, 2003.

Montaigne, Michel de. *Complete Essays*. Translated by Donald M. Frame. Palo Alto, CA: Stanford University Press, 1965.

Neidleman, Jason. *Rousseau's Ethics of Truth: A Sublime Science of Simple Souls*. London: Routledge, 2017.

Neuhouser, Frederick. *Rousseau's Critique of Inequality: Reconstructing the Second Discourse*. Cambridge: Cambridge University Press, 2014.

Neuhouser, Frederick. *Rousseau's Theodicy of Self-Love*. Oxford: Oxford University Press, 2008.

Nichols, Mary P. "Rousseau's Novel Education in the *Emile*." *Political Theory* 13 (1985): 535–58.

O'Hagan, Timothy. *Rousseau*. London: Routledge, 1999.

Okin, Susan Moller. *Women in Western Political Thought*. Princeton, NJ: Princeton University Press, 1979.

Orwin, Clifford. "Rousseau's Socratism." *Journal of Politics* 60 (1998): 174–87.

Paige, Nicholas. "Rousseau's Readers Revisited: The Aesthetics of the *Nouvelle Héloïse*." *Eighteenth-Century Studies* 42 (2008): 131–54.

Parker, Patricia. *Literary Fat Ladies: Rhetoric, Gender, Property*. London: Methuen, 1987.

Pateman, Carole. *Participation and Democratic Theory*. Cambridge: Cambridge University Press, 1970.

Philonenko, Alexis. *Jean-Jacques Rousseau et la pensée du malheur*. 3 vols. Paris: Vrin, 1984.

Plato. *Apology of Socrates*. In *Four Texts on Socrates*, trans. Thomas G. West and Grace Starry West. Ithaca, NY: Cornell University Press, 1984.

Plato. *Gorgias*. Translated by James H. Nichols. Ithaca, NY: Cornell University Press, 1998.

Plato. *Phaedrus*. Translated by James H. Nichols. Ithaca, NY: Cornell University Press, 1998.

Plattner, Marc F. *Rousseau's State of Nature: An Interpretation of the "Discourse on Inequality."* De Kalb: Northern Illinois University Press, 1979.

Plutarch. "How to Profit by One's Enemies." In *Moralia*, vol. 2. Loeb Classical Library. Cambridge, MA: Harvard University Press, 1928.

Plutarch. "On the Glory of the Athenians." In *Moralia*, vol. 4. Loeb Classical Library. Cambridge, MA: Harvard University Press, 1936.

Ramon, Catherine. "Autour des sujets d'estampes de *La nouvelle Héloïse*: Estampes dramatiques et tableaux romanesques." In *Annales de la société Jean-Jacques Rousseau*, 511–28. Geneva: Droz, 2003.

Rawls, John. *The Law of Peoples*. Cambridge, MA: Harvard University Press, 1999.

Rawls, John. *Lectures on the History of Political Philosophy*. Cambridge, MA: Harvard University Press, 2007.

Rosenblatt, Helena. *Rousseau and Geneva: From the "First Discourse" to the "Social Contract," 1749–1762*. Cambridge: Cambridge University Press, 1997.

Rousselière, Geneviève. "Rousseau on Freedom in Commercial Society." *American Journal of Political Science* 60 (2016): 352–63.

Russell, Bertrand. *History of Western Philosophy*. London: George Allen & Unwin, 1946.

Satkunanandan, Shalini. *Extraordinary Responsibility: Politics Beyond the Moral Calculus*. Cambridge: Cambridge University Press, 2015.

Schaeffer, Denise. "The Utility of Ink: Rousseau and Robinson Crusoe." *Review of Politics* 64 (2002): 121–48.

Schaeffer, Denise. *Rousseau on Education, Judgment, and Freedom*. University Park, PA: Penn State University Press, 2014.

Schlanger, Judith. *Trop dire ou trop peu: La densité littéraire*. Paris: Éditions Hermann, 2016.

Schwarze, Michelle A., and Scott, John T. "Mutual Sympathy and the Moral Economy: Adam Smith Reviews Rousseau." *Journal of Politics* 81 (2019): 66–80.

Scott, John T. "Between Religious Fanaticism and Philosophical Fanaticism: Rousseau's 'Profession of Faith of the Savoyard Vicar.'" In *Enlightenment and Secularism*, ed. Christopher Nadon, 189–98. Lanham, MD: Lexington Books, 2013.

Scott, John T. "Do You See What I See? The Education of the Reader in Rousseau's *Emile*." *Review of Politics* 74 (2012): 443–63.

Scott, John T. "*Emile* et les principes du droit politique: Le précis partiel du *Contrat social* et la double visée de la théorie politique de Rousseau." In *Jean-Jacques Rousseau en 2012: Puisqu'enfin mon nom doit vivre*, ed. Michael O'Dea, 140–61. Oxford Studies in the Enlightenment 2012:01. Liverpool: Liverpool University Press, 2012.

Scott, John T. "The Illustrative Education of Rousseau's *Emile*." *American Political Science Review* 108 (2014): 533–46.

Scott, John T. "Rousseau and the Melodious Language of Freedom." *Journal of Politics* 59 (1997): 803–29.

Scott, John T. "The Theodicy of the *Second Discourse*: The 'Pure State of Nature' and Rousseau's Political Thought." *American Political Science Review* 86 (1992): 686–711.

Sher, Richard B. *The Enlightenment and the Book: Scottish Authors and Their Publishers in Eighteenth-Century Britain, Ireland, and America*. Chicago: University of Chicago Press, 2006.

Shklar, Judith N. *Men and Citizens: A Study of Rousseau's Social Theory*. Cambridge: Cambridge University Press, 1969.

Simpson, Matthew. *Rousseau's Theory of Freedom*. London: Continuum, 2006.

Skinner, Quentin. *Hobbes and Republican Liberty*. Cambridge: Cambridge University Press, 2007.

Starobinski, Jean. *Jean-Jacques Rousseau: Transparency and Obstruction*. Translated by Arthur Goldhammer. Chicago: University of Chicago Press, 1988. Originally published in French in 1957.

Starobinski, Jean. "Le premier *Discours* à l'occasion de deux cent cinquantième anniversaire de sa publication." In *Annales de la société Jean-Jacques Rousseau*, 9–40. Geneva: Droz, 2001.

Starobinski, Jean. "Rousseau et l'éloquence." In *Rousseau after Two Hundred Years*, ed. R. A. Leigh, 185–200. Cambridge: Cambridge University Press, 1982.

Stewart, Philip. *Engraven Desire: Eros, Image, and Text in the French Eighteenth Century*. Durham, NC: Duke University Press, 1992

Stewart, Philip. "*Julie* et ses legends." *Studies on Voltaire and the Eighteenth Century* 260 (1989): 257–78.

Stilz, Anna. *Liberal Loyalty: Freedom, Obligation, and the State*. Princeton, NJ: Princeton University Press, 2009.

Strauss, Leo. "On the Intention of Rousseau." *Social Research* 14 (1947): 455–87.

Strauss, Leo. *Natural Right and History*. Chicago: University of Chicago Press, 1953.

Strong, Tracy B. "How to Write Scripture: Words, Authority, and Politics in Hobbes." *Critical Inquiry* 20 (1993): 128–59.

Strong, Tracy B. *Jean-Jacques Rousseau: The Politics of the Ordinary*. Thousand Oaks, CA: Sage, 1994.

Swenson, James. *On Jean-Jacques Rousseau Considered as One of the First Authors of the Revolution*. Palo Alto, CA: Stanford University Press, 2000.

Taylor, Charles. *Sources of the Self: The Making of Modern Identity*. Cambridge, MA: Harvard University Press, 1989.

Taylor, Charles. *The Ethics of Authenticity*. Cambridge, MA: Harvard University Press, 1991.

Tisserand, Roger. *Les concurrents de J.-J. Rousseau à l'académie de Dijon pour le prix de 1754*. Paris: Boivin & companie, 1936.

Todorov, Tzvetan. *Frail Happiness: An Essay on Rousseau*. Edited and translated by John T. Scott and Robert Zaretsky. University Park, PA: Penn State University Press, 2001. Originally published in French in 1985.

Trousson, Raymond. *Jean-Jacques Rousseau jugé par ses contemporains: Du "Discours sur les sciences et les arts" aux "Confessions."* Paris: Honoré Champion, 2000.

Trousson, Raymond. *Socrate devant Voltaire, Diderot et Rousseau: La conscience en face du mythe*. Paris: Minard, Lettres modernes, 1967.

Tuck, Richard. *The Sleeping Sovereign: The Invention of Modern Democracy*. Cambridge: Cambridge University Press, 2016.

Tully, Kendra A., and Scott, John T. "Rousseau's *Observations* on Inequality and the Causes of Moral Corruption." Unpublished paper. N.d.

Vanpée, Janie. "Rousseau's *Emile ou de l'éducation*: A Resistance to Reading." *Yale French Studies* 77 (1990): 156–76.

Vargas, Yves. *Introduction à l'"Emile" de Rousseau*. Paris: Presses universitaires de France, 1995.

Velkley, Richard L. *Being after Rousseau: Philosophy and Culture in Question*. Chicago: University of Chicago Press, 2002.

Watt, Ian. *The Rise of the Novel*. Berkeley and Los Angeles: University of California Press, 1957.

Weiss, Penny A. *Gendered Community: Rousseau, Sex, and Politics*. New York: New York University Press, 1993.

Williams, David Lay. *Rousseau's Platonic Enlightenment*. State College, PA: Penn State University Press, 2007.

Williams, David Lay. *Rousseau's "Social Contract": An Introduction*. Cambridge: Cambridge University Press, 2014.

Wingrove, Elizabeth Rose. *Rousseau's Republican Romance*. Princeton, NJ: Princeton University Press, 2000.

Wokler, Robert. "The *Discours sur les sciences et les arts* and Its Offspring: Rousseau in Reply to His Critics." In *Reappraisals of Rousseau: Studies in Honor of R. A. Leigh*, 250–78. Manchester: Manchester University Press, 1980.

Wolf, Brianne. "The Economic Education of Emile: Reinterpreting Rousseau's Use of *Robinson Crusoe*." *History of Political Thought* 39 (2018): 662–89.

Yamashita, Masano. *Jean-Jacques Rousseau face au public: Problèmes d'identité*. Oxford: Voltaire Foundation, 2017.

Zaretsky, Robert, and Scott, John T. *The Philosophers' Quarrel: Rousseau, Hume, and the Limits of Human Understanding*. New Haven, CT: Yale University Press, 2009.

Zerilli, Linda M. G. *Signifying Woman: Culture and Chaos in Rousseau, Burke, and Mill*. Ithaca, NY: Cornell University Press, 1994.

Index

Machiavelli, Niccolò, 175
Maguire, Matthew, 19
Mall, Laurence, 21
Marx, Karl, 223
Masters, Roger, 19, 94, 105, 116, 249, 255
Meier, Heinrich, 114, 192
Melzer, Arthur, 6, 18
Meno (Plato), 154
metaphysics/metaphysical, 95, 108, 121, 195
Michel, Isabelle, 179
Mohammed, 275
Montaigne, Michel de, 57, 60, 68, 274
Montesquieu, Charles-Louis de Secondat, Baron de, 36, 49
Moses, 275

natural goodness of man, 1, 2, 8, 27, 66, 75, 115, 126, 132, 133, 136, 140–42, 146, 202
natural law, 92, 96, 97, 100
natural right, 96, 97, 103, 253, 269
New Criticism, 10
Newton, Sir Isaac, 55, 64, 70–73
Nietzsche, Friedrich, 4
Numa, 275

Observations (Rousseau), 71
Omar, Caliph, 61
Orpheus, 181–84, 212
Otanes, 90, 115
Ovid, 35, 59

Parker, Patricia, 188
perfectibility, 75, 77, 95, 108–11, 120, 121, 124, 274
Phaedrus (Plato), 7, 9, 23, 25, 26, 28, 41, 44, 45, 49, 59, 60, 79, 99, 150–52, 165, 179, 180, 184, 192, 200, 208–10, 218, 219, 226, 242, 247
Pierre, Jean-Baptiste-Marie, 38
pity, 97, 142, 177, 193
Plato, 4, 6, 7, 9, 18, 23, 25, 26, 28, 41, 42, 44, 45, 47, 57, 59, 60, 65–69, 94, 95, 99, 102, 130, 131, 150–54, 165, 179, 180, 184,
192, 200, 208–10, 218, 219, 226, 227, 242, 247, 267, 274
Plutarch, 5, 59, 135, 155, 156, 177
pride, 24, 58, 59, 63, 73, 110, 143, 157–61, 172, 176, 177, 274, 275
Prometheus, 23, 28, 38, 40, 41, 45, 46, 58–60, 71, 73, 83, 151, 166, 179
property, 123, 147, 148–51
providence, 224–26
psyche, 58, 76, 120, 171
psychology/psychological, 111, 112, 172, 173, 175, 188, 276

Quintilian, 5

Rawls, John, 6, 267
reader response theory, 10, 12, 13
Republic (Plato), 94, 130, 131, 227, 267, 274
republican, 47, 80
Reveries of the Solitary Walker (Rousseau), 16, 17, 73, 191, 199, 200
Rey, Marc-Michel, 30
Richardson, Samuel, 242
Robinson Crusoe (Defoe), 25, 180, 217, 218–26, 237, 238, 239
Rome, 51, 56, 62, 67, 80, 89, 131, 255, 259, 276
Rousseau, Isaac, 91
Russell, Bertrand, 6

Schaeffer, Denise, 21, 217, 222
Schlanger, Judith, 8, 20
self-consciousness, 15, 117
self-love (*amour de soi*), 143, 275–76
Seneca, 131, 145, 171
sentiment of existence, 121
Shklar, Judith, 6, 15
Skinner, Quentin, 37
Smerdis, 90
sociability, 49, 97
Socrates, 4, 7, 9, 18, 23, 28, 41, 42, 44, 45, 47, 57, 59, 65–70, 72, 73, 92–95, 151–53, 180, 208–10, 218, 219, 226, 247, 267, 274
Sparta, 57, 65, 73, 74, 131, 274

.